Contemporary Indian Cases In Marketing

CONTEMPORARY INDIAN CASES IN MARKETING

Dr Mukesh Pandey
Associate Professor of Marketing
FORE School of Management, New Delhi

Published by:

biztantra
Management for the Flat World!

An Imprint of dreamtech PRESS

19-A, Ansari Road, Darya Ganj, New Delhi - 110 002
Website: www.biztantra.in

Edition : 2008

Printed at : HARDEV PRINTERS, MAYA PURI, NEW DELHI

Dedicated to
my MBA students
and
working managers
who attended my MDPs

PREFACE

As a Corporate Manager with MNCs and Indian companies and later on as teacher of Marketing over several years, I have always felt the need of Indian case studies—be it for classroom discussions or for Executive development programs. The cases and examples from the Indian milieu "ring a bell" in the minds of students and working managers as they find a familiar context to relate to. There is ready involvement from the participants as they "put on their thinking caps" for ferreting out the solutions of the cases with a closer-home feel to them, and thus imbibe the tenets of marketing, in the process developing a problem-solving orientation.

While reading Western literature on the subject, we as teachers are able to impart to our students an excellent analytical framework for designing appropriate marketing strategies but there is a flip side too. There is a feeling of incompleteness of the subject matter, which appears pronounced when we realize the vast difference between the Western and Indian context in terms of marketing. This is where the present collection of Indian case studies written by me will surely come in handy to marketers in India—both practicing as well as those in the making.

These case studies have taken into cognizance the unchaining of Indian economy post-1990s, globalization of culture, competition posed by foreign companies and brands, choking up of distribution channels, and aggressive marketing strategies of extremely customer focused and market-research savvy new entrants.

The book begins with the "What" and "Why" of Case Method building on the virtues of learning through real-life case studies followed by the "Finance of Marketing" elucidating the fundamental concepts in quantitative analysis of a case from a marketing professional's point of view.

Divided into 20 Sections, the book touches upon all facets of the marketing discipline with the Conceptual Framework (recapitulating key concepts applicable in each Section to provide a quick refresher) at the beginning of each Section being followed by the pertinent case/s along with space for taking notes.

All cases (32 in no.) included in the book are lively, contemporary and relate to the current issues and companies in news in India. Each case begins with purpose of the case and ends with questions requiring students and executives to exercise their faculties of reasoning, problem solving and lateral thinking. The selection of the cases is based on utility in terms of teaching Marketing Management as an integral part of various business administration courses conducted by management institutes and universities all over India.

The book is meant to reflect the multi-faceted dynamics of a country frenetically emerging from the shadows after economic liberalization of the early 1990s. The focus is on honing the powers of observation, fostering insightful analysis of marketing situations, and raising one's comfort level with the Internet- induced information explosion beginning to change the contours of marketing, as we knew.

These case studies are based on my research, consultancy and interaction with corporate managers during various MDPs as also on published data and articles/cases published in various business magazines/ journals and newspapers/information available on various websites about Indian companies or MNCs working in India.

I hope the management students and practicing managers will find the book immensely useful. Constructive feedback and suggestions are most welcome from the readers and would be duly incorporated in the future editions of the book

— Dr Mukesh Pandey
Associate Professor of Marketing
FORE School of Management,
New Delhi

ACKNOWLEDGEMENTS

I thankfully acknowledge the quality time spent by senior managers of various Indian organisations and MNCs with me like Apollo Tyres, McKinsey Knowledge Centre, Ranbaxy, Nokia, Rockwell Automation, ORG-MARG, NCAER, Mahindra & Mahindra, Eureka Forbes, Pidilite Industries, Eveready Industries, McDonalds, ITC, Asian Paints, Polar Fans, Naukri.com, HLL and Pepsi, etc. These discussions, at times animated, really helped in crystallizing business issues and understanding of marketing problems that the company is facing vis-a-vis opportunities and challenges. I appreciate the time spent by these gentlemen in constantly improving on my analytical framework and giving me a good feel of the real challenges at ground level faced by the marketing teams of companies.

I thank my PGDM students and participants of various MDPs who would assertively yet analytically articulate their viewpoints on various facets of marketing and in the process refined my own ideas of marketing discipline.

I thank all my faculty colleagues and our Director, Dr Seema Sanghi, at FORE for always encouraging us to research and also for creating an extremely conducive environment for publications.

The book would not have been possible without the efforts of the young and dynamic publisher of Biztantra, Rahul Gupta and their extremely professional, learned and meticulous Editor Pradeep Kapoor and Anuranjan too for being so forthcoming with ideas. I also express my sincerest thanks to Nagendra Kumar Pandey of Biztantra, for his very competent work of data processing and illustrating the book with suitable photographs.

I offer this book with a prayer in my heart, heartfelt regards for my parents and parents-in-law, deep sense of gratitude to my wife Dr Deepali and brother Dr Siddhesh. Well, how do I express the joy the young kids (Paritosh and Siddhant) bring to my otherwise rigorous and regimented life……….all I can say, God is kind……….very kind indeed.

— Dr Mukesh Pandey

ABOUT THE AUTHOR

Dr. Mukesh Pandey is an "Associate Professor of Marketing" at FORE School of Management, New Delhi. He is a PGDBM from IIM-Calcutta and a B.Tech in Mechanical Engineering from College of Technology, G.B. Pant University of Agriculture & Technology, Pantnagar, Uttaranchal. Prior to a career in academia, *inter alia* he handled Branding, Sales and Distribution functions in leading MNC's and Indian companies. He has conducted training programs at IIT-Delhi, IIT-Roorkee, CABM-Pantnagar as well as conducted several MDPs widely attended by managers of Maruti-Suzuki, GlaxoSmithKline, Sundaram Mutual, Godrej, SRF, Schiller Healthcare, Indraprastha Gas, Nippo Batteries, Linc Pens, SIEL, JK Cement, Zee Turner Ltd, GCMMF, Airtel, etc.

Contents

PREFACE vii

ACKNOWLEDGEMENTS viii

BACKGROUND NOTES

What and Why of "Case Method" of Teaching 1-3

The "Finance" of Marketing 5-9

SECTIONS

SECTION - ONE

A PRELUDE TO MARKETING

Conceptual Framework 11-12

CASE 1 TIC : A Haven of Fun & Frolic 13-17

SECTION - TWO

MARKETING ENVIRONMENT

Conceptual Framework 19-20

CASE 2 Strategic BPO Location Analysis : Identifying Global Locations 21-36

CASE 3 Apollo Tyres : Learning from Environmental Scanning 37-44

SECTION - THREE

CONSUMER BEHAVIOR

Conceptual Framework 45-46

CASE 4 AVAL : Marketing to the 'Indian' Consumer 47-59

CASE 5 The Changing Face of Youth in India 61-68

SECTION - FOUR

SEGMENTATION, TARGETING AND POSITIONING

Conceptual Framework 71-72

CASE 6 Zee Telefilms Ltd. : Breaking the Jinx 73-80

SECTION - FIVE

MARKETING RESEARCH

Conceptual Framework 83-85

CASE 7 Rockwell Automations : Researching Customer Perceptions 87-91

SECTION - SIX

PRODUCT

Conceptual Framework 93-95

CASE 8 Scorpio from Mahindra – Geared up for Success 97-108

CASE 9 Amul : Milk Turns to Gold 111-118

SECTION - SEVEN
BRAND MANAGEMENT
Conceptual Framework 121-122
CASE 10 Eureka Forbes Ltd. : Turning a Friend for Life 123-127
CASE 11 Pidilite Industries Ltd. : Brand Bigger than the Company? 129-135

SECTION - EIGHT
SALES MANAGEMENT
Conceptual Framework 137-138
CASE 12 Polar Electrical Appliances Ltd. : Dilemma over Sales Contest 139-140
CASE 13 Assam Farm Fresh Tea : Handling Sales Pressures 143-146

SECTION - NINE
DISTRIBUTION
Conceptual Framework 147-148
CASE 14 Eveready : Building a Strong Network 149-156
CASE 15 Wardha Soap Company : Taking on Price Undercutting 157-160
CASE 16 Pacific Pneumatic India Ltd. : Dwindling Distributors' Margins 161-163

SECTION - TEN
MARKET STRATEGY
Conceptual Framework 165-167
CASE 17 Kadilla Soaps Ltd. : Reacting to Competitor's Gameplan 169-174
CASE 18 Formulating LeasePlan's Car Remarketing Strategy 175-182

SECTION - ELEVEN
PRICE
Conceptual Framework 183-184
CASE 19 Low Cost Aviation in India – Changing Realities 185-196
CASE 20 Easy Charge – Great Potential or a Myth? 197-207

SECTION - TWELVE
PROMOTION
Conceptual Framework 209-210
CASE 21 Cadbury's Dairy Milk Chocolate – Evolving "Positioning" over Time 211-216
CASE 22 Celebrity Endorsement – Is it Worth it? 217-227

SECTION - THIRTEEN
SERVICES MARKETING
Conceptual Framework 229-231
CASE 23 Medical Tourism : 'First World Treatment' at 'Third World Prices' 233-247

SECTION - FOURTEEN
INTERNATIONAL MARKETING
Conceptual Framework 249-250
CASE 24 Ranbaxy Laboratories Ltd. : A True Indian MNC 251-257
CASE 25 Growth Strategies of Nokia in China 259-265

SECTION - FIFTEEN
ADVERTISING & COMMUNICATION
Conceptual Framework 267-268
CASE 26 Asian Paints : Going Where the Consumer is 269-278
CASE 27 Launching a Cigarette under Banned Promotional Environment 279-288

SECTION - SIXTEEN
B2B MARKETING
Conceptual Framework 291-292
CASE 28 Centaur India : Better Business through Better Customer Satisfaction 293-299

SECTION - SEVENTEEN
INTERNET MARKETING
Conceptual Framework 301-302
CASE 29 Naukri.com : Challenges and Opportunities 303-313

SECTION - EIGHTEEN
SUPPLY CHAIN MANAGEMENT
Conceptual Framework 315-316
CASE 30 McDonald's & Domino's – Supply Chain to Enhance Customer Value 317-325

SECTION - NINETEEN
RURAL MARKETING
Conceptual Framework 327-328
CASE 31 CavinKare Ltd. : Challenges in Rural India 329-335

SECTION - TWENTY
RETAILING
Conceptual Framework 337-338
CASE 32 Large Format Rural Retail Stores : *Mera Gaon, Mera Desh* 339-345

What and Why of "Case Method" of Teaching

A. What is a "Case Discussion Method"?

Case discussion = "Case" + "discussion"

Obviously, there are two components here:

(i) A "Case" is a description of a real life business problem that a businessman has faced at some point of time and as such needed his attention, analysis and decision.

(ii) "Discussion" means resource-pooling of analytical minds, cerebral insights and experience of various group members to arrive at better solutions through cooperative and creative thinking.

B. Why do top-B schools use Case method for teaching Marketing?

Till their graduation, majority of PGDM students, whether graduates in Engineering or Commerce or Science or Math (Honours) or Economics (Honours), acquire so-called knowledge by the route of the textbook-oriented-lectures thus acquiring wisdom and ideas passively. The case method, according to leading marketing practitioners, leads to *"real management education"* as it develops skills to tackle a problem, break it down, sort out the facts, see what must be done, and then get it done.

Case study method equips the student not just with bookish learning but also with power to deal with situations, particularly power to deal with new and unfamiliar situations. Case study method of teaching ensures students acquire managerial skills by rigorous personal effort, by questioning and debating all possible situations and finding workable solutions. It is the process of drawing out the student's mind, not of pouring in the instructor's ideas.

The lecture method of teaching is based on an extremely questionable assumption namely, the assumption that it is possible to tell wisdom. This is a great delusion because for the learning process to be effective, the learner must eventually acquire skills, which must help him take certain actions. It is important to understand that managerial insights and prudent judgmental abilities will not develop in a student until and unless he is put under conditions of responsibility as is simulated in a case method.

The case method is different from other methods of teaching, and it requires that students take an active rather than a passive one. The case method places the student in a simulated business environment and substitutes the student in the place of the business manager as the person required to make a set of decisions.

In the process of learning through case studies, the learner's active, analytical cooperation is ensured. The instructor does not tell a student; he expects the student to study the case and tell him. Then, he cross-questions, at times playing a devil's advocate, to see whether the student can logically justify the position which he takes. Case-method of teaching, thus, shifts much of the responsibility to the student and a great deal of time is required on the part of the student.

C. Group dynamics under "Case Method" of Teaching

Unlike lecture method, in a case method, all members of the class viz. teacher and students, are in possession of the same study material; everyone has to put forth his analysis based on identical opportunities available. Since, everyone is at par yet everyone is in competition, the valuable art of exchanging ideas is cultivated. Such an exchange stimulates thought, provides a lesson in how to learn from others, and also gives experience in effective transmission of one's own ideas.

In case study method, a student, to start with, often discovers that despite how hard he prepared the case yet it's the other students who bring out all sorts of interpretation and arguments. By the end of 2 trimesters, despite growing competition for high academic standing, students start acquiring the art of mutual giving and taking of assistance; they accept the common cause and thereby learning the pleasure of group pooling of intellectual efforts. Finally, by the time they are about to enter their last 2 trimesters of PGDM, students appreciate and realise that the instructors do not always or necessarily know the "best" answers and, even when they do seem to know them, each students is free to present and hold to his own views.

Flow Chart – Steps in Case Discussion

Step I
- Identify the key problem areas.
- Are they 'problems' on which action is required or mere 'symptoms'.

↓

Step II
- Generate alternative courses of action.
- Are you substantiating it by analysis?
- Have you marshalled evidence?

↓

Step III
- Evaluate each course of action individually.
- Debate pros and cons/cost-benefit analysis of alternative courses of action.

↓

Step IV
- Make suitable assumptions.
- Think of what can go wrong 'if we proceed with each course of action'?
- What macro-environment conditions will be favorable/unfavorable?

↓

Step V
- Taking decisions either as stand alone or a combination of alternatives debated in Step III.

↓

Step VI
- Debate the short-term and long-term implications of the 'decision taken'.

Studying under the case method results in the development of skills in critical thinking and cogent reasoning. Students also learn to defend their analysis and plan of action against the criticism of others in the class. An outstanding effect of the case systems, in other words, is to put upon students the burden of independent thinking.

D. How to Analyze and Prepare a Case

There is no standard "one coat size fits all" formula for the analysis of cases; as each case highlights a unique business problem. The approach that appears to be appropriate for one case is more than likely quite inappropriate for another. There are, however, certain general procedures that can be followed in the preparation of cases.

A vital first step in preparing for a class based on case-method is to read and reread carefully making mental note of major issues.

After that a student should assimilate the facts and list down major issues to start with. Identifying the problem(s) correctly and accurately and at the same time understanding the difference between problem and symptoms is half the job done. At times, the issues may be very obscure. Often there will be a number of sub-issues involved and it will be necessary to break the problem down into component parts. This stage in the handling of a case is analogous to a doctor attempting to diagnose his patient's illness. A patient may suffer from fever (symptom), which can be due to any of the problems like Malaria, jaundice, typhoid, UTI, etc. An incompetent doctor would try and solve the symptom without attempting to reach the root cause of the problem. However, it is important to note that, skill in diagnosis seldom comes from reading textbooks; it comes from repeated observation of actual cases.

Having diagnosed the crux of the problem and its likely causes, the student must creatively and logically generate several alternative courses of action, which can help solve the business issue in hand, The idea is to do a brainstorming and make a complete listing of all the conceivable courses of action.

The next stage then is to consider each possible course of action individually, The goal for the student is to integrate all his ideas, relate them to the goals of the company, the strengths and weaknesses of the company and its competition, the way consumers buy, and the resources available. It is important to cogently weigh the pros and cons of these alternatives and then eliminate the unworthy from further consideration. It is at this stage of the analysis that the student is required to marshal and analyze all the facts for each alternative program. The assumptions the student is required to make are very important here and the student must apply all the analytical skills possible, including both qualitative and quantitative.

At last, this procedure will possibly reduce the short-listed alternatives to just two or three evenly balanced feasible ones. Often there will not be sufficient information at this point to cross-examine each and every alternative left which may prove frustrating. However, the student should realize that vast majority of real life business decisions are made on the basis of incomplete information. What is required in those situations is the making of reasonable assumptions and learning to make decisions under uncertainty. There is often a strong reluctance on the part of the student to do this, but the ability to make decisions based on well-reasoned assumptions is a skill that must be developed for a manager to be truly effective. Businessmen often do not have the necessary facts at any point of time so they do make informed guesses. In attempting to make do with limited information the student will be experiencing some of the very real difficulties that face businessmen every day.

References

1. Prof M. N. Vora's (IIM-Ahmedabad) note on Case-study method
2. David S.R. Leighton and Donald, H. Thain, Canadian Problems in Marketing (Toronto; McGraw-Hill Company of Canada Limited, 1965) p.11
3. Brown, England and Matthews, Problems in Marketing (McGraw-Hill Book Company, Inc., 1961) p. 18
4. Malcolm P. McNair and Anita C. Hersum, (Eds.), The case method at the Harvard Business School (New York: McGraw-Hill Book Company, 1954), pp. 6-14
5. Malcolm P. McNair and Anita C. Hersum (Eds.). The Case Method at the Harvard Business School (New York: McGraw-Hill Book Company, 1954) p.-83
6. Marketing Definitions, (Chicago: American Marketing Association, 1960)
7. Melvin T. Copeland, Mark an Era: The Story of the Harvard Business School.

Notes

The "Finance" of Marketing

"Money makes the mare go"........this adage can't be truer when it comes to business. The ultimate goal of all marketing activities is how much money the company eventually makes in short term and long term. Since, most companies normally have a particular "Return on Investment" and "growth rate" in mind; it is imperative that proposed marketing activities aimed to achieve them are regularly evaluated for their financial implications, so that corrective and timely actions can be taken. Can you imagine asking your boss for Rs.10 crore for a new showroom or an advertising campaign without having to present the financial implications of such a request? A student of marketing must understand that presenting marketing ideas without projecting their financial attractiveness would hardly endear them to their bosses. It does not happen in the real marketing world, nor should it happen in a good case analysis.

It should clearly be understood that financial considerations are only one aspect in the evaluation of marketing alternatives. Marketing alternatives just cannot be reduced to a set of numbers, as qualitative aspects derived from the situation analysis are also relevant. The task of the student, as such, is to formulate both types of arguments - quantitative as well as qualitative while analysing case studies, so that a suitably argued solution to marketing issue on hand can be found.

Some concepts, which may be of use in marketing decision-making, are presented here:

CONTRIBUTION

Contribution per unit is defined as the difference between the "selling price" of an item and the "variable costs" of producing and selling that item. It is in essence the amount of money per unit available to the marketer to cover fixed production costs and corporate overhead, and, having done that, to yield a profit. So, if a manufacturer sells a pen for Rs.15.00, and the variable costs are Rs.10.00, then

Contribution per unit	=	Selling price – Variable costs
	=	Rs.15.00 – Rs. 10.00
	=	Rs 5.00

Each unit of the product that this company sells gives it Rs. 5.00 to cover fixed costs.

Total contribution is the contribution per unit times the number of units sold. So, if this firm sold 1,00,000 units:

Total contribution = Contribution per unit × Units sold
= Rs.5.00 × 1, 00,000
= Rs.5, 00,000

If the total relevant fixed costs of this product were Rs.1, 50,000 the profit earned by this product would be:

Profit = Total contribution – Fixed costs
= Rs.5, 00,000 – Rs. 1, 50,000
= Rs.3, 50,000

COSTS

Costs are of two types: Variable cost and fixed cost.

a. Variable costs are those costs that are fixed per unit and, therefore, vary in their total amount depending upon the number of units produced and sold. That is, it takes a certain amount of raw materials and labor to produce a unit of product. The more we produce, the more total variable costs are. Thus, labour, raw materials, packaging, and salespersons' commissions would be variable costs.
b. Fixed costs are those costs that remain constant in total amount despite changes in the volume of production or sales. These costs would thus vary per unit depending upon the number of units produced or sold.

BREAK EVEN POINT

The break-even point is defined as the point where "sales revenues" equal "expenses". There is no profit made or loss incurred at the break-even point. This figure is important for a manager who manages the business since the break-even point is the lower limit of profit when setting prices and determining margins. Obviously the break-even point becomes very important when calculating a strategy for net profit.

We define

1. $$\text{Break-even point in units} = \frac{\text{Total Fixed costs}}{\text{Contribution per unit}}$$
2. $$\text{Break-even point in rupees} = \frac{\text{Total Fixed costs}}{1-\dfrac{\text{Variable cost per unit}}{\text{Selling price per unit}}}$$

or

= Break-even point in units × Selling price per unit

Let's carry the same pen example forward. Suppose that for the pen manufactured and marketed

1. Direct labor cost is Rs.4.00 per unit,
2. Raw materials costs is Rs.6.00 per unit,
3. Selling price is Rs.15.00 per unit,
4. Advertising and sales force costs are Rs.4,00, 000, and
5. Other relevant fixed costs are Rs.100,000.

Contribution per unit = Selling price – Variable costs
= Rs.15.00–(Rs.4.00+Rs.6.00)
= Rs.15.00–Rs.10.00
= Rs.5.00

$$\text{Break-even point in units} = \frac{\text{Total Fixed costs}}{\text{Contribution per unit}}$$

$$= \frac{\text{Rs. }4{,}00{,}000 + 1{,}00{,}000}{\text{Rs. }5.00}$$

= 1,00,000 units

$$\text{Break-even point in rupees} = \frac{\text{Rs. }5\ 00{,}000}{1-\dfrac{\text{Rs. }10.00}{\text{Rs.}15.00}}$$

or

= Break-even point in units × Selling price per unit

Break-even point in rupees
= 100,000 units × Rs.15.00 per unit
= Rs.15, 00,000

PROFIT TARGETS

Breaking even is not the reason why companies do business, although it is the first hurdle to cross, while trying to achieve great profits and profitability. Thus, companies want to incorporate a profit target level into their calculations.

A marketing manager continuously attempts to answer the question as to what volume he must sell to earn Rs. X profits? Covering a profit target is just like covering a fixed cost. So in the previous example, if the organisation has set Rs.6,00,000 as their profit target, they would have to sell an additional number of units equal to:

$$\text{Units to cover profit target} = \frac{\text{Profit Target}}{\text{Contribution per unit}}$$

$$= \frac{\text{Rs. }6{,}00{,}000}{\text{Rs. }5.00} = 1{,}20{,}000 \text{ units}$$

Total units to reach this target is

1,00,000 + 1,20,000 = 2,20,000 units

or

$$\frac{\text{Total fixed costs} + \text{Profit target}}{\text{Contribution per unit}}$$

$$= \frac{5,00,000 + 6,00,000}{\text{Rs. } 5.00} = 2,20,000 \text{ units}$$

Break- even analysis is a useful tool for comparing alternative marketing programs. It tells us how many units must be sold, but does not help us with the critical question of how many units will actually be sold.

MARKET SHARE

Market share refers to a brand's share of the total sales of all products within the product category in which the brand competes. Market share is determined by dividing a company's sales level (or the brand's sales volume) by the total market (category) sales volume.

$$\text{Market share} = \frac{\text{Company sales level}}{\text{Total market sales}}$$

This calculation adds perspective to proposed action plans. Extending the above example, suppose that the total market sales are 50,00,000 units and company's sales level needed to break even is 1,00,000 units, then, the required market share to break even is:

$$\frac{1,00,000}{50,00,000} = 2.0\%$$

The question then to ask is whether this market share of 2% can be obtained with the proposed marketing program, or a modified aggressive program needs to be formulated.

CAPITAL EXPENDITURE

Often, a particular marketing program requires expenditures to be undertaken by the company towards purchase of capital equipment. This means, there would be fixed costs associated with the proposed program. Typically, they should not all be charged to the relevant fixed cost for that year. For example, suppose that Rs.5 crore are to be spent for equipment that will last 20 years. If we charge all this to the break-even calculation in year one, it will be very high. Further, for all subsequent years after first year when equipment is bought, the break-even point will fall substantially. It makes better sense to allocate this Rs.5 crore equally over all the 20 years. Thus, Rs.25,00,000 would be a relevant fixed cost in each year associated with the equipment. What a marketer needs to do is to consult specialists and make approximate yet well-informed assumption about the useful life of capital assets, and divide the total cost over useful life time of the asset.

RELEVANT COSTS

The issue often arises as to what fixed costs are relevant to a particular proposal. The rule to use is: A fixed cost is relevant if the expenditure varies due to the acceptance of that proposal. Thus, new equipment, new research and development, and so on, are relevant. Last year's advertising, or previous research and development costs, for example, do not vary with the current decision, and thus are not a relevant cost of the proposed program. Past expenditures are referred to as sunk costs. They should not enter into current decisions as decisions by their very nature are "future-oriented".

Corporate overhead presents a special problem. Generally, it does not vary with a particular decision. We don't fire the Director in selecting between marketing programs. However, in some instances, some overhead may be directly attributable to a particular decision and as such would be a relevant cost. We should recognize that, to stay in business, a firm must cover all its costs in the long run.

MARGINS

Often a case-study will present a student with a retail selling price and he will be required to know the manufacturer's selling price. To be able to work back and calculate the manufacturer's selling price, he must understand how channel margins work.

When firms buy a product at a particular price and attempt to sell it at a higher price, the difference between the cost price and the selling price is called margin or markup or mark-on. Thus,

Selling price = Cost price + Margin
An example could be:

Rs.100 = Rs.80 + Rs.20

So a company has bought a product for Rs.80, added on Rs.20 margin, and is charging Rs.100 for the product.

Margins are usually expressed as percentages. This raises the question as to the base on which the margin percentage should be expressed. Should it be expressed with cost price or the selling price as base? Here, if the Rs.20 margin is expressed as a percentage of selling price, the margin is

Rs.20/Rs.100 = 20 per cent.

The most common practice in marketing especially among distributors, dealers and retailers is to express margins as a percentage of selling price as margins expressed in this fashion are easier to work with especially in a multilevel channel situation. Unless explicitly stated otherwise, a student may assume that all margins in the cases in this book use selling price as the relevant base.

A number of different types of margin-related problems arise. They include:

1. **Determining the selling price, given you know the cost price and the percentage margin on selling price.** Suppose that a retailer buys a pen for Rs.15 and wants to obtain a margin on selling price of 40 percent. What selling price must be charged? In case , you get an answer as Rs.21, please realise it is not correct because this margin (Rs.6 = Rs.15 x0.4) would be on cost price. To answer this question, we must remember one fundamental relationship:

Selling price = Cost price + Margin

Here we are taking selling price as the base equal to 100 percent, we can write

100% = Rs.15 + 40%

That is, the cost price plus the margin must add to 100 percent. Clearly, the Rs.15 must then be 60 percent of the desired selling price. Thus,

Derived selling price = Rs.15/60%
= Rs.25

The rupee margin is then Rs.10, which is Rs.10/Rs.25 = 40 per cent of selling price.

The general rule then is to divide 1 minus the percentage margin expressed as a decimal on selling price into the cost price. For example, if cost price is Rs.110.00 and the margin on selling price is 25.0 per cent, then the desired selling price is

Rs.110 / (1 – 0.25) = Rs.110/0.75 = Rs.146.70

2. **Conversion of margin bases. Sometimes a margin is given on a cost price, and we wish to convert it to a selling-price base, or vice versa.** How do we make the conversion? Suppose that a pen costs Rs.7.50 and retailer sells for Rs.10.00. The margin is Rs.2.50. On a selling- price basis, the margin is Rs.2.50/Rs.10.00 = 25 percent. On a cost-price basis, the margin is Rs.2.50/Rs.7.50 = 33.33 percent. The conversion from one percentage margin to the other is easy if we remember that selling price is composed of two parts: margin and cost.

For selling- price base:

Selling price = Margin + Cost
Rs.10.00 = Rs.2.50 + Rs.7.50
or more importantly
100% = 25% + 75%

For cost-price base:

Selling price = Margin + Cost
Rs.10.00 = Rs.2.50 + Rs.7.50

but here the cost is the 100-per cent base, so

Rs.10.00 = Rs.2.50 + 100%
or
133.33% = 33.33% + 100%

That is, the selling price should be thought of as 133.33 per cent of the cost price.

Conversion from selling-price to cost-price base:

A simple formula for making this conversion is: Percentage margin on cost price

$$= \frac{\text{Percentage margin on selling price}}{100\% - \text{Percentage margin on selling price}}$$

In our example, this is

$$\frac{25\%}{100\% - 25\%} = \frac{25\%}{75\%} = 33.33\%$$

Note, that the only information that we need to make this conversion is the margin percentage on selling price.

Conversions from cost-price to selling-price base:

A simple formula for making this conversion is

Percentage margin on selling price

$$= \frac{\text{Percentage margin on cost price}}{100\% + \text{Percentage margin on cost price}}$$

In our example, this is:

$$\frac{33.33\%}{100\% + 33.33\%} = \frac{33.33\%}{133.33\%} = 25\%$$

Note that the only piece of information that we need to make this conversion is the margin percentage on cost price.

MARGINS UNDER MULTI-LEVEL CHANNEL NETWORK

Let's say the same pen manufacturer gives a Maximum retail price (MRP) and suggested retail and wholesale margins. For example, the Maximum retail price is fixed at Rs.15.00, with a retail margin of 20 percent and a wholesale margin of 15 percent. Let's determine the manufacturer's selling price in this situation, we simply take the appropriate margins off one at a time. Thus,

Maximum Retail price	Rs.15.00
Less retail margin (20% of Rs.15.00)	–3.00
Equals retail cost price or wholesale selling price	Rs.12.00
Less wholesale margin (15% of Rs.12.00)	–1.80
Equals wholesale cost price or manufacturer's selling price	Rs.10.20

No matter how many levels there are in the channel, the approach to arrive at manufacturer's realisation will remain the same. The student should simply take the margins off one at a time.

It is important to note that the student cannot just add up the margins and subtract this amount. Here 20% + 15% = 35% and 35% of Rs.15.00 is Rs.5.25, making the manufacturer's selling price Rs.15.00 – Rs.5.25 = Rs.9.75. This is obviously not correct.

This chapter has outlined some financial concepts that will add to the student's abilities to make sound marketing decisions. These concepts should be applied wherever needed in the cases in this book.

Notes

A Prelude to Marketing

Section - One

CONCEPTUAL FRAMEWORK

To facilitate a better debate on the case in this section, a quick exploratory review of the marketing function as a whole along with areas that need discussion are recapitulated briefly as follows:

- **Marketing** offers many exciting career opportunities. When you take up jobs in marketing after you complete your MBA, you may be involved in marketing a good, a service or an idea for an organization (or as an entrepreneur, if you strike out on your own). The essence of marketing is to **develop satisfying exchanges** from which both customers and marketers benefit. It is a process of creating, distributing, promoting, and pricing goods, services, and ideas in a dynamic environment.
- The marketer must try to understand the target market's needs, wants and demands. **Needs** are basic human requirements. Needs become **wants** when they are directed to specific objects that might satisfy the need. **Demands** are wants for specific products backed by an ability to pay.
- Customers are the focal point of all marketing activities. An organization generally focuses its marketing efforts on a specific group of customers, or **target market**.
- Companies address needs by putting forth a **value proposition**, a set of functional and emotional benefits, which they offer to customers to satisfy their needs.
- Marketing is **not merely selling**. It does much more than that, and creates and sustains needs and wants that may not have existed before. Marketing personnel encourage consumers to spend more money than they would have normally spent on goods and services to satisfy their growing number of wants. Marketing activities are performed in both business and non-profit organizations. The patronage for a product or a service is sustained, or the acceptance is more "deeply entrenched" among the consumers' psyches. Make them expect more from you and fulfill their expectations; you may have those customers for a lifetime!
- Marketing involves developing and managing a product that will satisfy customer needs, making the product available in the right place and at a price acceptable to customers, and communicating information that helps customers determine if the product will satisfy their needs. These activities - **product, distribution, promotion,** and **pricing** - are known as the **marketing mix** because marketing managers decide what type of each element to use and in what amounts.

- Marketing managers strive to develop a marketing mix that matches the needs of customers in the target market. Before marketers can develop a marketing mix, they must collect in-depth, up-to-date information about customer needs. The **product variable** of the marketing mix deals with researching customer's needs and wants and designing a product that satisfies them. In dealing with the **distribution variable,** a marketing manager tries to make products available in the quantities desired to as many customers as possible. The **promotion variable** relates to activities used to inform individuals or groups about the organization and its products. The **price variable** relates to decisions and actions associated with establishing pricing policies and determining product prices.
- The **marketing environment,** which includes competitive, economic, political, legal and regulatory, technological, and socio-cultural forces, surrounds the customer and the marketing mix. These forces can create threats to marketers, but they also generate opportunities for new products and new methods of reaching customers. These forces can fluctuate quickly and dramatically.
- Relationship marketing involves establishing long-term mutually satisfying buyer-seller relationships. **Customer relationship management (CRM)** focuses on using information about customers to create marketing strategies that develop and sustain desirable customer relationships. Managing customer relationships requires identifying patterns of buying behavior and using that information to focus on the most promising and profitable customers.
- **Value** is a customer's subjective assessment of benefits relative to costs in determining the worth of a product. Benefits include anything a buyer receives in an exchange, while **costs** include anything a buyer must give up to obtain the benefits the product provides. The marketing mix should be so designed and delivered that overall 'perceived value of offering' is higher than or at least equal to the costs incurred.
- **Marketing management** is the process of planning, organizing, implementing, and controlling marketing activities to facilitate effective and efficient exchanges between seller and buyers.
- Planning ensures systematic assessment of opportunities and resources, determining marketing objectives, developing a marketing strategy, and preparing for implementation and control. Organizing marketing activities involves developing the marketing unit's internal structure. Proper implementation of marketing plans depends on coordinating marketing activities, motivating marketing personnel, and communicating effectively within the unit. The marketing control process consists of establishing performance standards, comparing actual performance with established standards, and reducing the difference between desired and actual performance.
- Globalization, rapid advances in technology, and deregulation are three major challenges and opportunities facing businesses today.
- There is a shift from making everything inside the company to buying more goods and services from outside if they are cheaper and better **(Outsourcing)**. More companies are preferring to own brands rather than physical assets. The stress is on being marketing organizations rather than production-oriented ones.

TIC - A Haven of Fun & Frolic

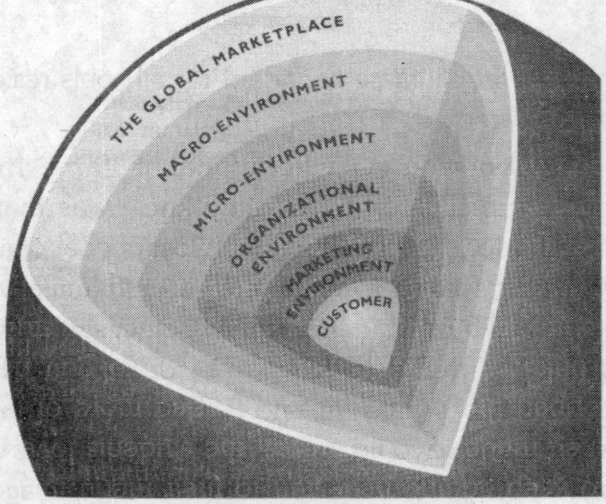

A Prelude to Marketing Case - 1

Purpose of the Case

The idea is to assimilate the relevant concepts at work and analyse along the following lines:

- To discuss what led to the fast growth and evolution of TIC from a mere tea shanty to an eating joint providing a variety of foods
- To focus on the importance of building your product range/services around customer needs, his growing expectations in a subtle and unobtrusive manner
- To debate how the principles of marketing are in operation at TIC, in a most elementary way

Thakur was very happy, ecstatic in fact, choked with emotions, he flashed the bank draft of Rs. 5,000 he was holding in his right hand and told all young students sitting on concrete slabs strewn all around TIC and enjoying their CNN (twin pleasures of caffeine and nicotine), "Do you know Pant? That *lamboo* got confirmed posting in Pune in TELCO...*Arrey yaar,* the same tall, lanky fellow who strummed the guitar...*Arrey yaar*, the one always trying to impress that Lucknow BT girl from CBSH...*Arrey yaar*, all those *Angrezi gaaney wala*, what you call them...yes, yes...*arrey yaar*...Dhillon songs." Thakur had cultivated this habit of saying '*arrey yaar*' before every sentence he spoke and well, students had by now deciphered the Morse code...Thakur wanted to convey... 'Dylan' not 'Dhillon' songs. Most Engineering students knew which Biotechnology ma'am of College of Basic Sciences and Humanities was being referred to.

It was a routine affair at TIC; the young students knew what exactly Thakur meant...their Mechanical Engineer super-senior Manish Pant, the one who loved to strum Bob Dylan songs had probably cleared his *khaata* (balance money to be paid) with Thakur. Thakur knew they would always pay even when they left campus...often substantially more than they owed him. Their existed an unwritten rule between Thakur and his beneficiaries, of course within tacitly agreed boundaries: for final year students, if your campus interviews were on, you could practically have endless *udhaar*; for others you were supposed to pay upfront the moment you got your draft or your parents transferred money in your ATM at start of the month. And well, well, well !! Pant Sir had formally proposed to Alpana ma'am of Biotechnology department and she had smiled. Of all the people in the world, these youngsters knew Thàkur was the one to be told first, he was the ultimate confidant for all souls residing in the campus.

Nobody knew where Thakur came from, nobody really cared…all they knew was that he meant a lot. He was a friend, philosopher and guide to almost every student there. The *junta* (*junta* was a term used by all students for every other student who studied in the hallowed portals of the G.B. Pant University of Agriculture and Technology, Pantnagar) knew how he would console first year students who suffered from various demons in Ist semester: ragging to top it all, pressure of studies, cut-throat competition to excel and worst was the sultry weather and those power cuts.

Lots of students had faced this question during ragging: What does TIC stand for? It was pet question asked with we-know-it-all arrogance and certitude by seniors while they sipped tea and circulated fags amongst themselves. Not knowing thatTIC stood for 'Thakur Inter Continental' would be further extending your ordeal of getting on your haunches to become a *murga*. Students, especially the freshers, often wondered why such a modest establishment with thatched roof, open air kitchen, eggs and maggi packets hanging from the rafters in makeshift hangers, a bluish white display stand where Wills and Gold Flake King-size cigarettes would temptingly be placed, a running tap in the corner where an omnipresent *chhotu* would be washing utensils,in full public view, over a concrete slab strategically placed below the tap was called TIC. Well, the answer lay in knowing the fact that in 1981, Thakur had accompanied a Professor of Computer Engineering for 15 days to AIT, Bangkok; it was summer vacations time and an unmarried Prof. Singh had asked him to come along, probably to cook Indian food for him there. Well, when Thakur returned, he once began to cook fish and possibly declared its Thai curry, and from that very moment onwards, students rechristened Thakur dhaba as TIC.

Today everybody, actually everybody, be it faculty, staff, housewives, schoolgoing kids, shopkeepers, students for whom TIC is the *raison d'etre;* everyone knows TIC like they know their own home. In fact, for all the 2-lakh inhabitants of Pantnagar, the intersection of road leading from Machine shop and hostel road connecting Tagore hostel (Ist year hostel) to Badi market is TIC…a prominent landmark - a permanent fixture of

Pantnagar, more often than not used by the residents to give directions to visitors.

This university was no exception and all students were exposed to quintessential 'hostel food'…especially harsh for a teenager who would join the University after being dog-pampered by mother at homes for years…the staple diet of watery dal and rotis that would decapitate a pig if thrown at the correct angle and the cafeteria version of veggies…that glob of sticky stuff that went by the generic term '*Subzi*' . It was a different matter though that every day a daily menu was put up on the door of the mess that gave The Glob a different and pretty creative name to compensate for the lack of taste. One day the *subzi* appeared as *Alu-Gobhi* next day it would appear as *Gobhi-Alu*. On those days when the amount of red chillies was too much for an average student to handle, the menu would term it as *Shahi Gobhi*. On Saturdays, the mess served 'non-veg' dinner; unless the guys put an alarm of starting time of mess i.e., 8.30 pm and then acted like a cross between Carl Lewis and Ben Johnson sprinting towards the mess, they would have to deal with long queues and only 'chicken flavoured curry'.

Pantnagar University was opened in1960s under collaboration with few leading US universities and students had heard how the great Prime minister Nehru and lots of *phirang* scientists had initially joined the University as Vice-Chancellor and Professors. Thakur knew each and every detail and regaled students with the anecdotes liberally enlivened with his imagination; he was the unofficial 'Encyclopedia Britannica' of Pantnagar University, a University geographically spread across 12 kilometres or more.

He told them how every senior position in this country, in any large employment sector of India had a Pantnagarian on top... One could barely argue with him. Otherwise he would parrot out names, he appeared to remember them all...their designations, even their hostel room numbers when they studied here.

It seemed Pantnagar was some kind of *kaala-paani*, as only two kinds of people constituted the population here which was very systematically organised as township: either you were a student or you were working to improve the intellectual lot either as a Professor or lab assistant or else you worked in support departments like electricity, gardening, water section. Pantnagar University was self-contained with its own cinema hall, international-quality stadium, swimming pools and gymnasiums. The library was a tourist attraction not only because of its 4-storied magnificent building and great collection of journals, periodicals and books but also because invariably every student would take his parents or relatives there on a sight seeing trip and then in return expect a compliment like 'Did you see what a great place our son studies in!'. The University was lush green...vegetation and gardens all around. Wasn't it a historical fact that the University was the harbinger of green revolution in this country? Didn't it bring pride to all of us when we could face the world and see straight in their eyes? Thakur knew all these stories; he even knew how Shastriji, our late Prime Minister felt crassly humiliated when he went to USA asking for foodgrains when there was an acute drought in India and how we (as he passionately thumped his chest) toiled day and night to fulfill his promise of "Jai Jawan, Jai kisan".

Pantnagar University had 6 professional colleges viz.,Technology, Biotechnology and Basic Sciences, Veterinary, Fisheries, Agriculture and Forestry. About 4,000 students would be studying here at any point of time and living in over 12 hostels (design of girl's hostels was inspired by Roman fortress, seniors always told juniors!). However the place was absolutely isolated in terms of its geography and distance from anything that could be called a city - it was a world cocooned in itself - every inhabitant had resigned himself or herself to the monotony of life there and over a period of time cultivated his or her own world of fun, pleasure, hopes, insecurities, love , hate, pride and win all around the campus; this was a place where everybody knew everyone, didn't you bump across the same faces wherever you went - to the college or library or Badi Market (a shopping centre of some 50-odd shops was called so). Incidentally, Badi Market also had a few coffee houses and ice-cream parlours which facilitated breeding of nascent friendships and burgeoning romances in Pantnagar.

How Thakur landed in Pantnagar is an apocryphal story but most students believed it for whatever it was worth. However Thakur seems fiercely protective about it and never discussed the same. It is said Thakur's father, a poor peasant in some village of Bihar, came with some relative in search of a job as farm labourer in Pantnagar in early 1960s. His two kids apparently died of some unknown disease in Pantnagar and he found his mental state and income too unsporting, when he pleaded before the Vice-Chancellor to give him a permanent job in 1967. The VC, who was a very humane and emotional gentleman, instead offered him a small plot of land at a nominal rent near Engineering college hostels; probably he too was fed up of students' complaints about food, but one is not too sure if he thought of the *dhaba* beyond tea and some occasional snacks at that time.

Mahatam Singh, better known as Thakur today, was a mere young 7 years old kid then. The rest they say is history, at least for the students.

Thakur took *de facto* charge of the *dhaba* pretty young; his father did not maintain good health and left for his native place in Bihar leaving the whole business in the hands of an 18 years old boy. Well, he did go back off and on for few days but he went for a relatively longer stretch of 15 days in 1985 and got married. His wife turned out to be even more enterprising…the couple would stay up late till well past 10 pm everyday, 7 days a week, making tea and serving fags for nightbirds of hostels. By 6 am, the couple were up again making tea, coffee and *tilk* (an indigenous preparation of tea made in milk was called *tilk in junta's jargon*). Didi (as Thakur's wife was lovingly called by students) encouraged him to keep adding new stuff to their menu. One day they made some *samosas*, the students loved and lapped them all…they demanded more of it. But Thakur was a very strict quality control guy, he was fanatic about cleanliness and crispiness of stuff that he served. Once when it was Ramnavami, they decided to try and make some *jalebis*…The hot *samosas* and *jalebis* were like ambrosia to the gourmet starved students and were devoured in no time at all. The eternally hungry and ever-appreciative students kept encouraging Didi to try something new.

Since students had limited influence over the mess food, they concentrated on getting Thakur to extend the menu beyond *samosas* and *jalebis* which by now along with *sambhar vada*, *idli* and *dosa* were being perfected by Didi. Students, when they came back from vacations vouched that one got better South Indian food at TIC than at leading restaurants in Delhi and, obviously, at highly affordable prices. Somewhere in late 1980s, someone had picked up quick noodles on a trip to Delhi. Thakur was not sure whether they would be able to dish it out, they tried it a couple of times but Thakur was not in favour of serving it to students till he could make it as good as you get in Delhi. Didi was very persuasive and took a few cooking lessons from some Mrs. Mehta, a newly married Professor's wife who apparently had studied from some leading convent school in Dehradun and had also done her F&B training in Taj during her Hotel Management. Students relished it this time and Thakur was lifted in arms amid loud cheers, due accolades were also given to Didi for her culinary expertise…and why not, she had become a surrogate mother to all the students in this God-forsaken isolated place, where all one had to do was slog …and slog more to relax.

No matter what TIC made, it was a huge improvement over the mess food but more important than that TIC was a place for students to hang out at, just to get away from the maddening medley of pontificating professors, hourlies, quizzes, lab tests and taxing syllabi, it was a place to relax and listen to Thakur play the mouth organ. TIC was witness to innumerable heated discussions, arguments and confessions…Bill Gates to Brian Lara to Brazilian soccer to Reservations to English August to Tom Hanks to Bryan Adams to American-Iran imbroglio—they were all animatedly debated, shredded to pieces and put together again into packages of optimum solution- if only the people concerned would heed these young turks

Thakur very soon realised that if he has to get more business, he cannot go on with TIC being an all-boys joint all his life. He had noticed that boys would spend more when there was a girl along; the entrepreneur in him started thinking of innovative ideas. He realised that the ultimate mark of customer confidence would be demonstrated when couples start making TIC their preferred stopover rather than those ice cream parlours at Badi Market. Some guys suggested Thakur why he did not constructively utilize a shallow but around 3 feet wide canal and two huge peepal trees that were just there at the backyard of TIC. This area was virtually littered with leaves and other dead plantation. In summers of 1989, Thakur got the place cleaned up, grew green soft grass, cultivated a hedge along the boundaries and put lots of plastic chairs. The canal was also cleaned up and in turn gave TIC a chilled, cool, fun look. A bevy of girls also started joining the refreshing and relaxed environment of TIC, Thakur cashed in on the popularity by extending the range of cuisine - from just *samosas* , *jalebis* , *idli, dosa, sambar-vada* to chowmein, burgers, finger fries, momos , *chikkan* (Chicken as spelt on TIC's handwritten menu cards) and mutton tikkas to vegetable and chicken fried rice - to keep evolving with changing food preferences. Slowly the students started going there for lots of activities - and they all knew what it meant. Going to TIC was not all about food ; it was an experience to share, the enjoyment of thrill, fun, freedom and camaraderie, few minutes of breathing space from never-ending grind of routine, academic life.

Soon, Thakur opened a PCO also in TIC as he noticed students shouting to each other to rush up as they would exhort each other to go to Badi Market, which was 4 kilometres away, just to make a phone call. Thakur also noticed that in every paper in every semester, students wrote 3 hourlies (sessional exam of 1 hour) and 1 lab practical before they wrote their final exams. During these days, most students would burn the midnight oil. Sensing an opportunity Thakur opened TIC till 2 am serving tea, coffee, Haldirams and Lays kurkure and peanuts, maggi and of course 'nicotine sticks'.

The astute observer in Thakur also noticed that during chilly winter nights, students wanted to remain in their cosy rooms, moreover some students found it stylish to get aluminium foil wrapped food in their rooms, a starting of 'home delivery' within university campus. Getting food 'room-delivered' when pariahs would go to the well to drink, was a conspicous symbolism to flaunt your 'first-among-equal' status. Thakur had a couple of times sent wrapped *alu-paranthas* to hostel whenever someone was not well. Thakur would personally go and meet the student who was not well, offer him a lift to the University hospital in his old Yamaha motorcycle...it never looked he was doing this with a business motive; he seemed a very caring, sensitive soul who felt from his heart and that it was his pre-ordained duty to help these youngsters who lived away from their families- a self appointed foster father. But even foster fathers have expenses, hence Thakur started charging one rupee extra over and above the bill for room services and it became a major hit with some students, the *ghotu* (your typical 'nerds' in junta's parlance) the types who thought leaving their book for even a second, will diminish their 'fundas'.

Very soon, Thakur started keeping basic medicines like Paracetamol, Combiflam and ORS solutions at TIC. Soon the range of products at TIC widened to include chocolates, Reynolds pens and rough notebooks. It also ensured increase in business per student because any student who came to buy a notebook would more often than not end up drinking tea and feasting on a bread *pakora* at least. In summers of 2000, Thakur installed 2 major equipments at TIC which most students found revolutionary: one was a freezer to store Amul ice-creams and those 5-rupee bottle cold drinks of Coke and Pepsi and second was an OTG (Oven-Toaster-Griller) to start serving hot patties too...

These were the days of alumni meet in 2005 in Pantnagar, we all friends, around 20 of us from Delhi decided we will be there in September. We all attended a formal function, listened to lots of speeches about the progress the institution has made...increasing number of selections in IES, IIMs, PSU's, Infosys, TISCO, L&T, Civil services and blah blah blah...But no prizes for guessing where our heart lay. As soon as decency permitted we all rushed to TIC, we danced , partied all night long . It was a journey down memory lane with gratitude and affection for our self-appointed guardians during our college days, a token of which was a sari for Didi and a pair of jeans and T-shirt for Thakur from all of us. And, yes, Mahatam Singh a.k.a Thakur too swayed with the peppy numbers, buoyed by our invigorating presence and some spirit (pun unintended).

Question

1. What do you think: was Thakur 'marketing' or 'selling'? Defend your answer.

Notes

Marketing Environment

Section - Two

CONCEPTUAL FRAMEWORK

To facilitate a better debate on the cases in this section, a quick exploratory review of the marketing environment along with areas that need discussion are recapitulated briefly as follows:

- The marketing manager studies external forces that directly or indirectly influence an organization's acquisition of inputs (personnel, financial resources, raw materials, information) and generation of outputs (goods, services, ideas).
- Within the rapidly changing global picture, marketers must monitor **six major environmental forces**: **competitive, economic, political, legal and regulatory, technological** and **socio-cultural**.
- The marketing environment presents a never-ending series of opportunities and threats. The major responsibility for identifying significant changes in the macro-environment falls to a company's marketers. More than any other group in the company, marketing managers must be trend trackers and opportunity seekers.
- A good number of opportunities are found by identifying **trends** (directions or sequence of events that have some momentum and durability) and **mega-trends** (major social, economic, political and technological changes that have long-lasting influence)
- Business managers carry out **environmental scanning** to collect information about forces in the marketing environment. Scanning involves observation; secondary sources such as business, trade, government and general-interest publications; and marketing research. The Internet has become a popular scanning tool since it makes data more accessible and allows companies to gather needed information quickly.
- **Environmental analysis** helps managers in assessing and interpreting information obtained in scanning. A manager evaluates the information for accuracy, tries to resolve inconsistencies in the data and if warranted, assigns significance to the findings. This information helps marketing managers predict opportunities and threats associated with environmental fluctuation.
- Marketing managers may assume either a passive, reactive approach or a proactive, aggressive approach in responding to these environmental fluctuations. The choice depends on the organization's structures and needs, and on the composition of environmental forces that affect it.
- All businesses compete for customer's rupees. A marketer, however, generally defines **competition** as other firms that market products that are similar to or can be substituted for its products in the same geographic area. These competitors can be classified into one of four types:
  - **Brand competitors**
  - **Product competitors**

- **Generic competitors**
- **Total budget competitors**

- The number of firms, controlling the supply of a product may affect the strength of competitors. The four general types of competitive structures are **monopoly**, **oligopoly**, **monopolistic competition**, and **pure competition**. Marketers monitor what competitors are currently doing and assess changes occurring in the competitive environment.
- General economic conditions, buying power, and willingness to spend can strongly influence marketing decisions and activities. The overall state of the economic fluctuates in a general pattern known as the **business cycle**. The stages of the business cycle are **prosperity, recession, depression,** and **recovery**.
- Consumers' goods, services, and financial holdings make up their **buying power**, or ability to purchase. Financial sources of buying power are income, credit, and wealth. After tax, income used for spending or saving is **disposable income**. Disposable income left after an individual purchases the basic necessities of food, clothes, and shelter is **discretionary income**. Factors affecting buyer's willingness to spend include product price, level of satisfaction obtained from currently used products, family size, and expectations about future employment, income, price, and general economic conditions.
- The **political** and **legal and regulatory forces** of the marketing environment are closely interrelated. In the politico-legal environment, marketers must work within the many laws regulating business practices and with various special-interest groups. The political environment may determine what laws and regulations affecting specific marketers are enacted and how much the government purchases and from which suppliers. It can also be important in helping organizations secure foreign markets.
- State legislation affecting marketing activities can be divided into procompetitive legislation—laws designed to preserve and encourage competition and **consumer protection laws** that generally relate to product safety and information disclosure.
- **Industry self-regulation** represents another regulatory force; marketers view this type of regulation more favorably than government action because they have more opportunity to take part in creating guidelines. Self-regulation may be less expensive than government regulation and its guidelines are generally more realistic. However, such regulation generally cannot ensure compliance as effectively as government agencies.
- **Technology** is the application of knowledge and tools to solve problems and perform tasks more efficiently. Consumer demand, product development, packaging, promotion, prices, and distribution systems are all influenced directly by technology. In the technological arena, marketers should take account of the accelerating pace of technological change, opportunities for innovation, varying R & D budgets and the increased governmental regulation brought about by technological change.
- **Socio-cultural forces** are the influences in a society and its culture that result in changes in attitudes, beliefs, norms, customs, and lifestyles. Major socio-cultural issues directly affecting marketers include demographic and diversity characteristics, cultural values, and consumerism. Changes in a population's demographic characteristics, such as age, income, race, and ethnicity, can lead to changes in that population's consumption of products.
- Changes in cultural values, such as those relating to health, nutrition, family and the natural environment have had striking effects on people's needs for the products and therefore are closely monitored by marketers.
- In the **natural environment**, marketers need to be aware of raw materials shortages, increased energy costs and pollution levels and the changing role of governments in environmental protection.
- **Consumerism** refers to the efforts of individual, groups and organizations to protect consumer's rights. Consumer rights organizations inform and organize other consumers, raise issues, help businesses develop consumer-oriented programs, and pressure lawmakers to enact consumer protection laws.

Strategic BPO Location Analysis: Identifying Global Locations

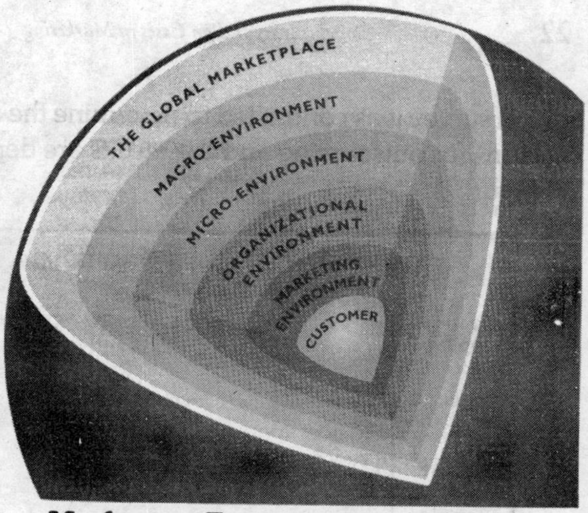

Marketing Environment Case - 2

Purpose of the Case

The idea is to assimilate the relevant concepts at work and analyse in light of the following issues:

- How to analyse environmental factors prevailing in different countries for arriving at suitability for starting a business?
- How do demographic, economic, natural, technological, political and cultural developments affect a service organization?

One of the most significant developments of the new millennium is IT-enabled services (ITES), a refined version of the long-accepted concept of "outsourcing". However what exactly is ITES? In simple terms it is the delegation of one or more IT-intensive operations to an external provider, who in turn administers and manages the selected business process based upon defined and measurable performance metrics. The long-standing understanding of services as 'being produced and consumed at the same place' stands absolutely nullified as most BPO companies provide services to customers situated thousands of miles away.

Global outsourcing is being recognized by business executives as a strategy to help companies focus on core capabilities and provide bottom line benefits. Fast eroding bottom lines in a global recessionary economy and the cost competitiveness of overseas ITES services providers is increasingly making global giants meaningfully examine them as attractive IT-enabled services outsourcing providers. As more and more companies turn to "specialist" players to handle significant portions of their in-house functions and activities, global outsourcing is taking the form of a major trend.

Reasons of outsourcing

1. Reduce overheads, free up resources. Avoid capital expenditure. Improve efficiency.
2. Offload non-core functions
3. Get access to specialized skills
4. Save on manpower and training costs. Reduce operating costs
5. Improve speed and service
6. Establish long-term, strategic relationships with world-class service providers to gain a competitive edge
7. Provide value added services and increase customer satisfaction

A survey was conducted to determine the major reasons for outsourcing and the results are depicted in Figure 1.

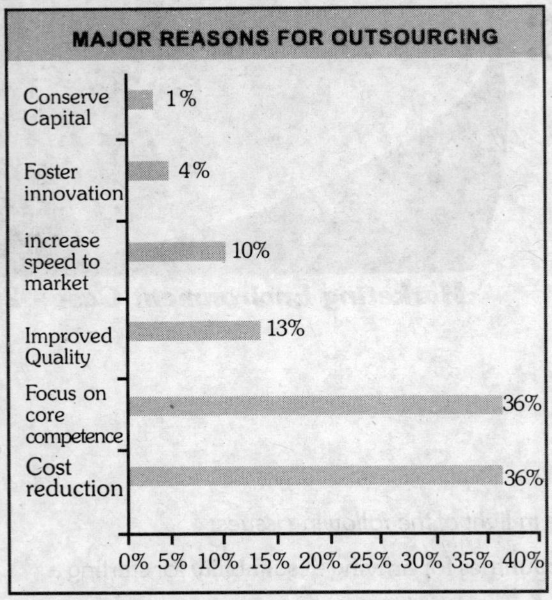

Figure 1: **Major Reasons for Outsourcing**

(Source: The 2001 Outsourcing World Summit, Michael F. Corbett & Associates)

As is clear from Figure 2, India is very cost efficient on parameters like personnel, property and General & Administrative expenses. The extra cost incurred in long distance communication is greatly offset by the other factors. In fact, as we can see from above table, overall operating costs in India are one-fifth of what they are in USA. Therefore cost cutting emerges as the one biggest factor for driving the industry, but as the industry in low-cost destinations matures and skill sets of BPO employees improve the reasons for the outsourcing decision are bound to change.

Comparison of the operating costs of India as a percentage of US costs

US$ Cost per full time employee	USA	India	India as % of US costs
Personnel	42927	6179	14
G&A Expense	8571	1000	12
Telecom	1500	2328	155
Property rentals	2600	847	33
Depreciation	3000	1500	50
Total expenses	**58598**	**11854**	**20**

Figure 2: **Comparison of the operating costs of India as a percentage of US costs**

Various companies can justify their outsourcing decision by citing any combination of the reasons mentioned above. But the outsourcing decision in itself is a complex process and due deliberation needs to be done before processes can be offloaded. An ideal decision making model to decide outsourcing should, as such, follow the decision tree (see figure 3).

GLOBAL MARKET SIZE

The BPO industry report for 2003-2004 by Gartner, shows that BPO services worldwide will grow from US$ 119 billion in 2000 to US$ 234 billion in 2005 at an 14.4 percent compound annual growth rate (CAGR). By 2005, the number of outsourced business processes will have doubled as compared to the existing numbers, the study states. Gartner's study by geography shows that the pattern of BPO is centered around the US market which in revenue terms accounted for US$ 70.6 billion of the overall industry (Figure 4). The trend is likely to continue till 2005 as the US is expected to outsource US$ 135.9 billion worth of business. The Gartner study also indicates that Europe, Asia Pacific, Japan, Canada and the rest of the world, will account for the remaining contributions.

INDIA'S OPPORTUNITY

An analysis of the Nasscom's Handbook Indian ITES-BPO Industry, 2004 clearly shows that the Indian ITES-BPO segment will experience growth in both the traditionally strong service lines as well as new, opportunity areas. Various service lines and their estimated size is detailed follows:

- **Customer care:** This deals with handling customer queries about various products and services, collection services, technical support etc Customer care and support services will continue to lead in terms of revenue generation, staying ahead of the ITES-BPO pack with a turnover of around US$ 1200 million in 2003-04. The 2002-03 statistics of the segment stood at US$810 million.

- **Finance:** Financial services are expected to experience the hottest growth, achieving revenues of US$820 million in 2003-4, up from US$510 million in 2002-03. No longer is it just entry-level work for Indian players in this service line. Service providers are moving into value-added domains such as insurance claims processing equity research and financial management.

- **HR services:** It started with processing of

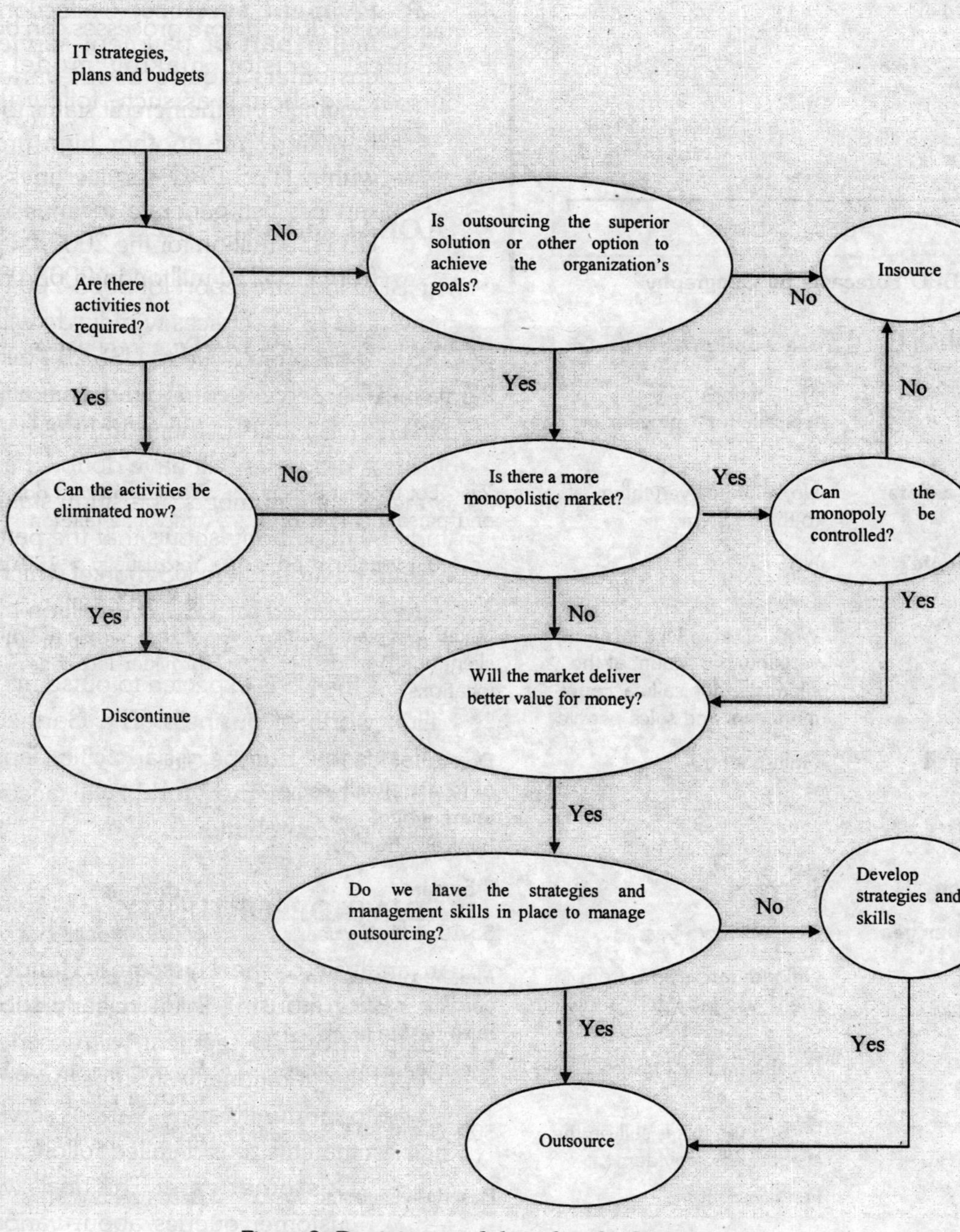

Figure 3: **Decision-model to decide Outsourcing**

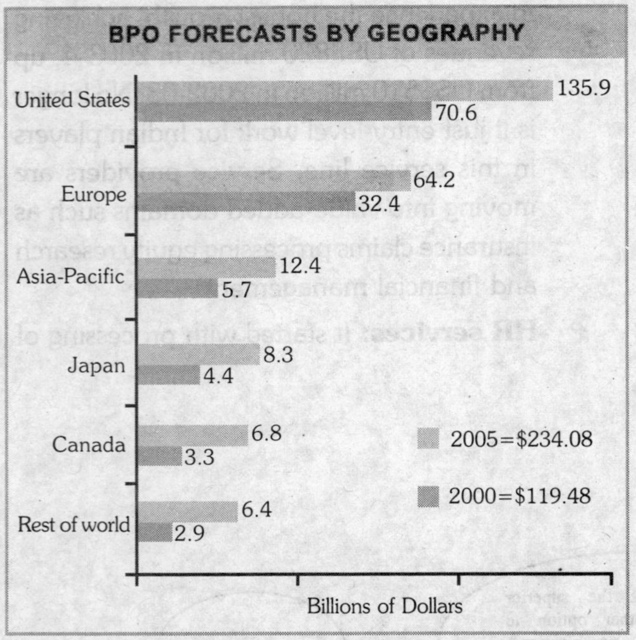

Figure 4: **BPO Forecasts by Geography**

employee welfare related applications and has now evolved to design and processing of core HR functions like recruitment and selection, performance appraisal etc. HR services outsourcing will also become a bigger piece of the overall ITES-BPO pie over the next year, offering a significant latent opportunity for the country's industry players. Revenues are expected to touch US$70 million during 2003-04.

- **Payment services:** Collections forms a major part of payment services where customers inquire about various things ranging from their credit status to grievance handling. Yet another high growth area within ITES-BPO service lines, payment services will generate revenues of around US$430 million for the 2003-04 period, up from US$210 million in 2002-03.

BPO Business Model	Transactional	Niche	Comprehensive
Number of processes	Transactions only, typically for 1 process	2-4 processes	10+ processes in a function; sometimes more than one function
Invest in client assets?	No, migrate everything to their system	Yes - but modest dollars and personnel take-on	Yes - significant dollars and employee take-on
Hire client's people?	No	Yes - but usually < 50	Yes, usually > 100s and often in the 1000s
Locations	Work at provider's location; very low headcount at the client site -typically account managers and sales people	Mixed, people at both client and provider locations	Mixed, people at both client and provider locations
Geographic spread	Multi-country	Domestic (> 80% of revenue) with some international (typically Europe)	Global
Contract duration	1-2 years	3-5 years	7-10 years
Contract value per year	$1-5 million a year	$5-10 million a year	$50-$100 million a year
Business model	Offload transactions from client, use provider's software	Make processes more efficient - reduce costs, raise service levels	Make functions more effective, introduce best practices
Accountability	For the transaction processing	For process outcomes	For cost savings for the entire function plus business outcome
Risk-holder	90% of the risk is still on the client, 10% provider	50% client, 50% provider	30% client, 70% provider
Metrics	Per transaction	Based on outcome	Based on outcome

Figure 5: **Different Kinds of BPO Players**

- **Administration:** Revenues from the admin-istration services segment are expected to go up to US$540 million during 2003-04, up from US$ 310 million in 2002-03. Administration continues to be a hot growth, highly competitive segment for Indian ITES-BPO companies.
- **Content development:** Usually considered to be a low margin service, high-end content development requires specialized skills and very few players in the Indian market can claim to offer these niche services. The content development services segment is expected to keep pace with the other leading ITES-BPO revenue streams by logging in a turnover of around US$520 million in 2003-04. Content development services include engineering and design services, digitization (GIS), animation, network management and biotech research.

Amongst BPO players there are different kind of service providers ranging from a single contact point operators to end-to-end solutions providers. Table-5 clearly depicts the difference between a single point service provider and a comprehensive, end-to-end solutions provider. It clearly reflects the kind of responsibility and accountability that a service organization needs to undertake to win the trust of its clients and forge a long term, mutually beneficial relationship.

Offshore Location Analysis

The objective of this project undertaken was to identify countries where any BPO company can look to setup and further expand operations over a time frame ranging from three to five years.

Methodology flowchart (NASPEC model of offshore Analysis)

All companies operate in a macro-environment of forces and trends that shape opportunities and pose threats. These forces represent "non-controllables", to which the company must monitor and respond. Companies and consumers are increasingly being affected by global forces. Within the rapidly changing global picture, any firm must constantly monitor six major forces: demographic, economic, natural, technological, political-legal, and socio-cultural.

Therefore the need was felt to design a strategic and robust model for scanning the macro-environment, and hence the NASPEC model was born (Figure 6). This model was formulated by us as a generic model that is applicable to any industry and any firm in the fast changing modern business scenario that aims to increase market share and achieve and sustain market leadership in any product or service category. The various stages of the NASPEC model are shown below as a flowchart.

NASPEC= Need **A**nalysis→**S**ampling→**P**reliminary **E**limination→**C**alibration

Stage I: Need analysis: Detailed in-depth interviews were carried out with top management representatives from leading BPO players with presence in India and a broad framework was sketched. This process ultimately helped in understanding and quantifying what a BPO considers important before it takes an off shoring decision.

Stage II: Sampling: In this stage based on outcomes of the previous step, and perception of industry players about various countries, a particular sample of countries was chosen on a judgmental basis. Countries like Iraq, Chechnya, U.S.A. were eliminated based on negative perceptions about such countries for reasons like war or high costs etc. The offshore prospects of 15 countries have been analyzed, all of which were the finalists in the 'preliminary evaluation'. Refer to Annexure 1

Stage III: Preliminary elimination: To decide whether a country qualifies as an offshore location or not, countries were eliminated based on the following criteria:

a) Political Issues and Governance: Issues

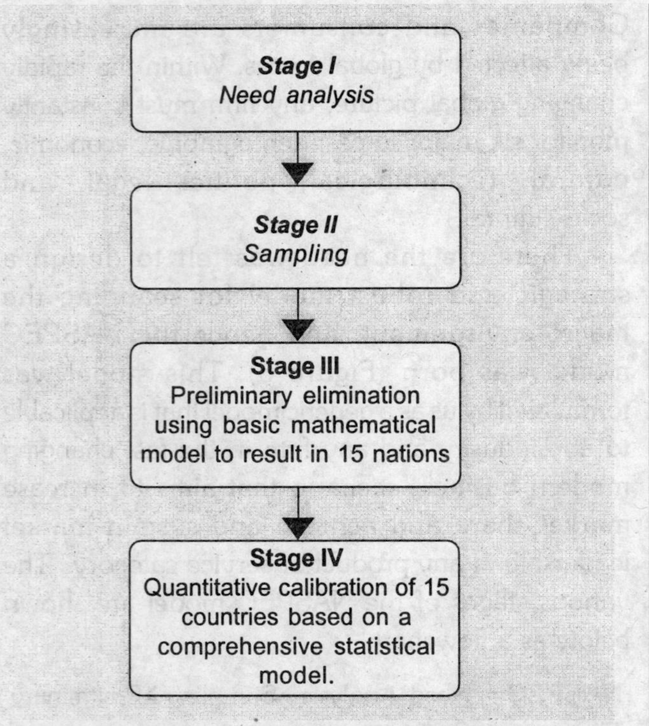

Figure 6: **NASPEC Model for Scanning Macro-environment**

such as political stability, macro level policy initiatives, corruption, legal system, licenses & permits and bureaucratic bottlenecks are factors that were considered. Corruption and bureaucratic bottlenecks were seen as 'irritants' but not 'impediments'.

b) Economic Considerations: Economic strength, though not directly related to the attractiveness of a country as an off shore destination, basic fundamentals such as GDP growth, stability of currency, foreign exchange reserves and inflation rate are indicators of a country's capability to develop its education and infrastructure and certainly affect any company's decision to invest in a foreign country.

c) Demographics/Labour Quality, numbers and cost of labor are the basic reasons to off shore business. Size of labor pools, skill sets available, and the education system that creates appropriate labour and per capita income determine a country's attractiveness. In addition, high levels of urban unemployment were indicative of a comfortable demand-supply ratio. Factors such as cultural affinity and language skills were perceived as major areas of strengths.

d) Infrastructure The basic assumption of delivering real time services to areas geographically distant from an off shore destination is sound infrastructure. Specifically, the size of international bandwidth and its costs becomes an imperative for BPO operations. Power production, though important, may not be as decisive as it would be in the manufacturing sector. Captive units could very well provide the basic requirement and redundancy levels required for BPO operations. It was also important for a country to offer several locations to set up a site. This would not only provide multiple expansion options within that country but also embed redundancy and business continuity to the in-country operations.

e) Business Environment-Comfort levels of conducting business in off shore locations could be gauged by the MNC presence in a country. Such presence may not be restricted to the BPO industry alone, but could be in other sectors as well. Other considerations would be the effectiveness of the legal system, labor laws, membership to ITO, historical relationship with western countries etc.

Stage IV: Calibration: Business model development and projection interpretation: A strategic business model was developed to compare and analyze all finalists. The model comprised of the following three broad categories (see Table 7):

1. Human Resource factors
2. Cost factors
3. Country specific factors

Each of these categories were assigned weights depending upon the importance they hold for any BPO company. 'Human Resource' category was assigned 40 per cent weightage owing to the importance it holds for the industry (Table 8). 'Cost' category was given a weight of 40 per cent. 'Country specific' factors aimed at judging the attractiveness of any country with respect to setting up and the subsequent operation of a BPO. Consequently this factor was given a weightage of 20%.

The final score for any country was calculated out of 100 for easier comparison and comprehension; higher the score more suited is the country for BPO operations.

KEY FINDINGS

Asian countries rule the roost as they capture all the top three positions in their Attractiveness index. In fact, four out of the top five nations are Asian. The only non-Asian nation to make it to the top five is Brazil (See Figure 8).

INDIA: WAY AHEAD OF THE PACK

India emerges as the 'numero uno' destination with a vast and talented labour pool, very low operational costs backed adequately by the government's initiative to promote the BPO industry. India's immaculate track record in the software industry further reinforces faith in foreign investors. In fact, 82% of U.S. companies ranked India as their first choice for software outsourcing. Bill Clinton has applauded India's brainpower: saying Indian-Americans run more than 750 companies in America's Silicon Valley. "You liberated your markets and now you have one of the 10 fastest growing economies in the world," said President Clinton.

Parameters	Attributes	Metric
Human resource factors	Availability	Unemployment in the 15-24 age group English speaking population Population in main city Technical graduates Non-technical graduates Total number of graduates
	Attrition	Industry specific attrition rate
	Cultural aspects	Cultural compatibility with the European Union Cultural compatibility with the US Accent
Cost factors	Infrastructure	Building Utilities Communication Transport Computers
	Labor	Compensation for Associates Compensation for Managers Meal allowance
Country specific factors	Tax structure	Corporate tax rate
	Cost indicator	Cost of living index
	Infrastructure	Number of I.T. parks
	Industry specific aspects	Tax exemption Fiscal incentives Existing major players BPO experience
	Intellectual property protection	Intellectual property rights

Table 7: **Criteria for Evaluating of Offshore BPO Location**

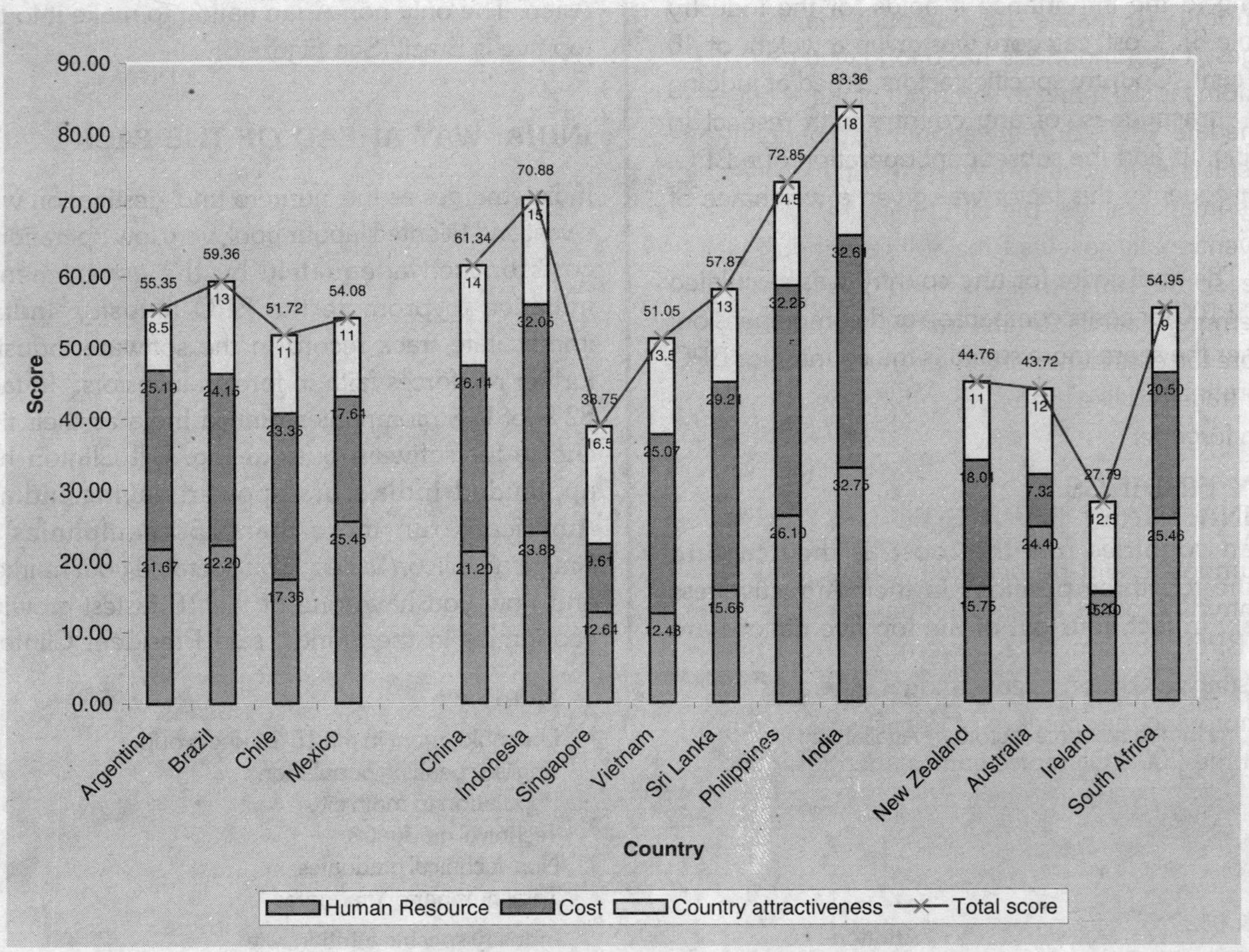

Figure 8: **Global BPO Location Attractiveness Index**

Software Technology Parks of India offer world-class infrastructure and various incentives and concessions to encourage foreign investment and promote software development in India. India has a very stable government with over 50 years of democratic rule, adding to the confidence of foreign investors.

PHILIPPINES: ALL GOOD THINGS COME IN SMALL PACKAGES

Not surprisingly, Philippines bagged the second spot owing to the low cost and culturally compatible workforce. American military presence for over a century in the country has led to an in-depth understanding of the U.S. culture, making it an ideal place for voice based American processes. The industry is exploding, with big names like Sykes, Convergys, Daksh, SPI Technologies and Accenture already operational and many more companies planning to open up centers in the immediate future. A little over 300,000 graduates pass out of Philippines every year maintaining a steady flow of talented workforce. But Philippines has a major disadvantage, it is a 'single location country', apart from Manila with a gross population of 14 million there is hardly any city which can offer the kind of scales that the industry needs to flourish on.

INDONESIA: UNSTABLE ISLAND ARCHIPELAGO

Indonesia is facing many problems ranging from communal tensions to an unstable government and economy. To realize the potential that numbers suggest it has, Indonesia has a long way to go. The economy is still trying to come out of the Asian crisis of the late 1990s and the sooner that happens the better it is for the country. With the software industry in its infancy stage, the BPO industry, which has conventionally followed the software industry, will take some time to switch to top gear. The government needs to take immediate measures to restore the confidence of foreign investors especially after tragedies like the Bali Bombing having still not been forgotten.

CHINA: GIANT RARING TO GO

If numbers could be believed, China is the only country that poses a genuine threat to India as the top BPO location. The government of China is investing $ 5 billion in educational programs aimed at improving the standard of English in the country. With the 2008 Olympics games lined up, China is on its way to become a prime location for any BPO. Tremendous infrastructural capabilities backed by the reputation of being a low cost economy further add to the attractiveness of the country. The entry of China in the World Trade Organization is further improving foreign investment in the country with 130 new research and development centers being opened up by western countries. It is also a very favorable destination for companies wanting to tap the Japanese and Korean markets.

BRAZIL: LATINO HEAT

Brazil emerges as the most preferred destination in Latin America owing to a stable government, good infrastructure and low operational costs. Brazil also scores on the resilience of its economy in times when most Latin American economies were crumbling. Other Latin American countries score almost identically owing to minor trade-offs in any of the three categories. Strong position as an industrial

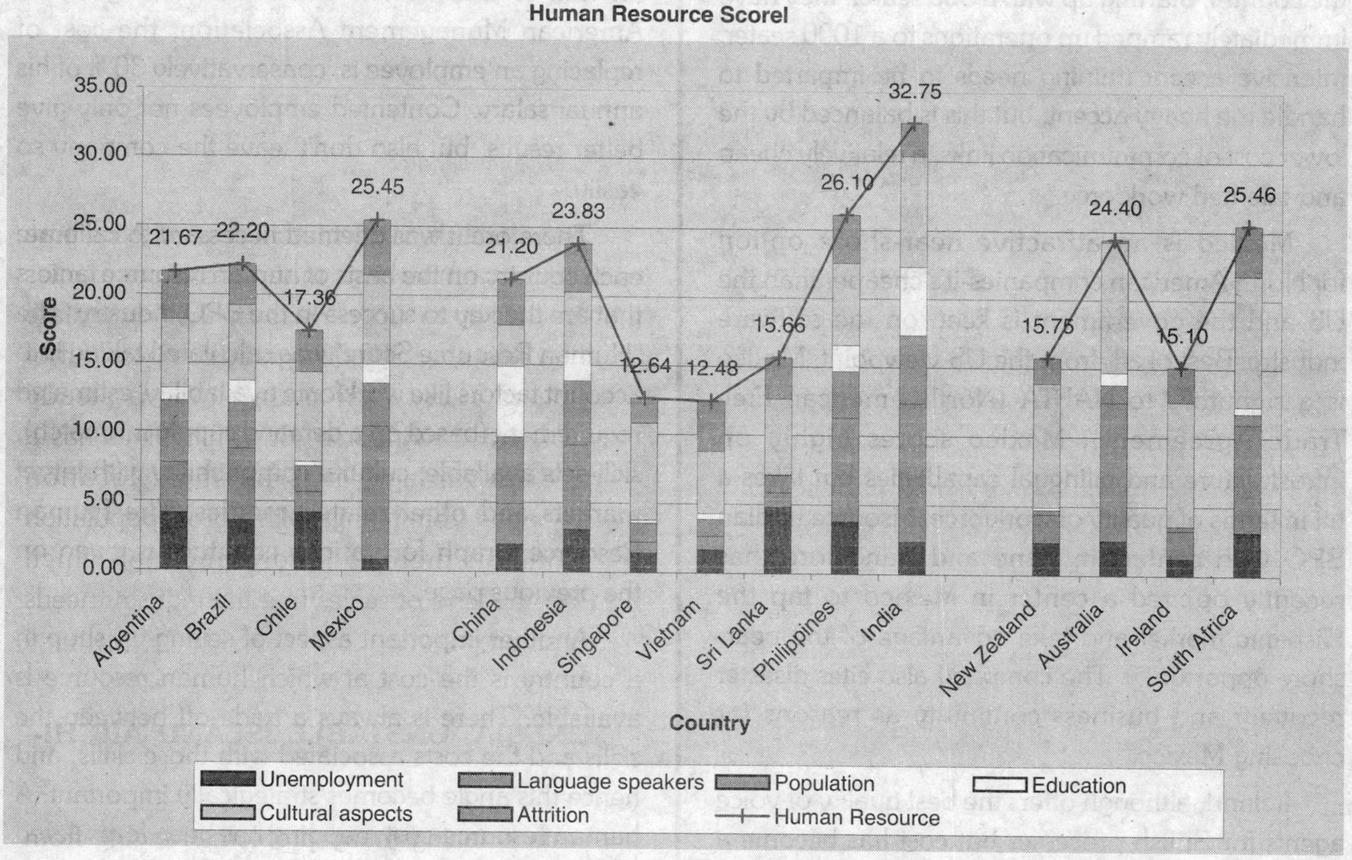

Table 8: **Human Resource Score**

economy backed by steadily increasing BPO experience makes it an ideal location wanting to capture the near-shore advantage and service the U.S. markets.

Amongst other countries that create an impact are South Africa, Mexico and Sri Lanka. South Africa strongly challenges its reputation of being an expensive location and comes up with a decent score. Geographical proximity to European markets and cultural compatibility are positives for the country. But, as of now, only 4 call centers exist employing more than 500 people. The AIDS pandemic gripping almost 30% of the South African population is although not a deterrent, but a cause of concern for companies as operational staffing policies of the company will have to be adjusted to cater to sporadic forced absence from work due to health reasons.

HSBC's recent foray into the island of Sri Lanka has dispelled all myths about security problems in the country. Starting up with a 500 seater, they have immediately ramped up operations to a 1000 seater. Intensive accent training needs to be imparted to handle the heavy accent, but this is balanced by the lower cost of communication links, a relatively cheap and talented workforce.

Mexico is an attractive near-shore option for North American companies-it's cheaper than the US and the government is keen on the software industry. Best of all, from the US viewpoint, Mexico is a signatory to NAFTA (North American Free Trade Agreement). Mexico scores highly on infrastructure and bilingual capabilities but takes a hit in terms of quality of workforce. Msource (Indian BPO with centers in Pune and Bangalore) has recently opened a center in Mexico to tap the Hispanic market and take advantage of the near-shore opportunity. The company also cites disaster recovery and business continuity as reasons for choosing Mexico.

Ireland, although offers the best quality of voice agents for British processes but cost has become a major factor playing against its attractiveness. Even the immense BPO experience the country has fails to overshadow Ireland's cost disadvantage. Consequently, Ireland ends up at the bottom of the rankings.

BPO: IT'S ALL ABOUT PEOPLE

The BPO industry stands on three pillars -technology, processes and people. Though technology and processes are keys to the business, people are the most important factor. Given the large workforce and the dependence on human interface in this business, the BPO service providers have many HR challenges to face. These challenges range from recruiting the right candidates, training them to suit the job to retaining them with the organization. Employee turnover is one of the biggest challenges that confront companies, today. It is not only difficult for the employer to let an employee go but twice as difficult for him to train a new recruit. According to the American Management Association, the cost of replacing an employee is, conservatively 30% of his annual salary. Contented employees not only give better results, but also don't leave the company so easily.

Therefore it was deemed necessary to calibrate each country on the basis of human resource factors that are the key to success in the BPO industry. The "Human Resource Score" was calculated taking into account factors like workforce availability, estimated requirement (based on a demand supply mismatch), skill-sets available, cultural compatibility with target markets and other related metrics. The Human Resource Graph for various countries is given on the previous page.

Another important aspect of setting up shop in a country is the cost at which human resource is available. There is always a trade-off between the skills and the costs associated with those skills, and hence this angle becomes strategically important. A human resource-cost mapping has been formulated and the results are detailed in Annexure 3.

CONCLUSION

The quest for competitive advantage is intense and global. Each company in an attempt to capture the biggest share of the BPO pie will expand its service offerings and venture into newer territories. A well-thought decision will be the difference between business excellence and mere survival. This study acts a pathfinder for venturing into unknown territory. The results of this study will prove beneficial for any BPO company aiming to strategically expand its global presence.

Questions

1. Assess how key demographic, economic, natural, technological, political and cultural developments affect a service organization.
2. Develop a mathematical model to calibrate the business opportunity for a financial company in a country of your choice.

Notes

Annexure I

Criteria for Preliminary Elimination

South America

COUNTRY	SELECTION	REASON
Argentina	**yes**	EFL-l2 transition, 89% urban population, services sector orientation- 66% of the GDP comes from the services sector., presence of major cities, infrastructure
Bolivia	No	Inadequate l1,l2, lack of infrastructure
Brazil	**yes**	Presence of major cities, good infrastructure, services sector orientation- 59%
Chile	**yes**	Services sector orientation-59%, technical skill availability, sound financial institutions
Colombia	No	Inadequate l1, l2, insurgency
Ecuador	No	Inadequate infrastructure
Falkland Islands	No	Low urban population
Guyana	No	Low urban population
Paraguay	No	Inadequate l1,l2
Peru	No	Low urban population
Surinam	No	Low total population
Uruguay	No	Inadequate l1,l2
Venezuela	No	Inadequate l1,l2, fragile political setup

Europe

Iceland	No	Low total population
Norway	No	Inadequate l1,l2
Finland	No	Inadequate l1,l2
Sweden	No	Inadequate l1,l2
Denmark	No	Inadequate l1,l2
Ireland	**yes**	High concentration of English speaking people around Dublin, service sector orientation-58%, good infrastructure
United kingdom	No	High cost of operations
France	No	Inadequate l1,l2, high labour costs
Luxembourg	No	Inadequate l1,l2, lack of infrastructure
Belgium	No	Inadequate l1,l2
Portugal	No	Inadequate l1,l2
Spain	No	High labour costs
Italy	No	High labour costs
Slovenia	No	Unfavorable political climate
Croatia	No	Weak financial setup
Bosnia and Herzegovina	No	Inadequate l1,l2 high security risk zone

Serbia	No	Inadequate l1,l2, security concerns
Albania	No	Low total population
Macedonia	No	Lack of infrastructure
Greece	No	Inadequate l1,l2
Germany	No	Good for high end knowledge based processes, high labor costs
Switzerland	No	Low total population, high costs
Austria	No	Inadequate l1,l2
Estonia	No	Inadequate infrastructure
Latvia	No	Low total population
Lithuania	No	Low urban population
Poland	No	Inadequate l1,l2
Czech Republic	No	High costs
Slovak Republic	No	Low total population
Hungary	No	Inadequate l1,l2
Romania	No	Weak infrastructure
Bulgaria	No	Inadequate l1,l2
Moldova	No	Low total population
Ukraine	No	Political instability
Belarus	No	Infrastructure, lack of political support
Andorra	No	Low total population
Liechtenstein	No	Low total population
San Marino	No	Low total population
Vatican City	No	Low total population
Monaco	No	Low total population
Malta	No	Inadequate infrastructure

Asia

Bangladesh	No	Poor infrastructure,
Bhutan	No	Low total population
Brunei	No	Inadequate infrastructure, low total population
Cambodia	No	Inadequate urban population
China	**yes**	Technical skills, infrastructure, government support
India	Yes	L1,l2 infrastructure, government support
Indonesia	**yes**	Good educational profile, good infrastructure
Japan	No	High costs
Laos	No	Low total population
Malaysia	**yes**	L1,l2 technical skills, financial structure
Maldives	No	Total population
Mongolia	No	Inadequate infrastructure
Myanmar	No	Inadequate infrastructure
Nepal	No	Inadequate infrastructure
North Korea	No	Inadequate l1,l2

Pakistan	No	Inadequate l1,l2
Philippines	**yes**	services sector orientation-53%, technical skills,govt support
Singapore	**yes**	L1,l2 good infrastructure, services sector orientation-67%
South Korea	No	Inadequate l1,l2
Sri Lanka	**yes**	L1,l2 cheap labor availability
Taiwan	No	Low population
Thailand	No	Low population
Vietnam	**yes**	Low costs, good infrastructure, technical skills

Others

Mexico	**yes**	Low cost, hispanic population, cultural similarity with the us
Canada	No	High cost
New Zealand	**yes**	English-speaking country, cultural similarity
Australia	**yes**	English speaking nation, infrastructure, cultural similarity

Glossary: L1: Number of people for whom English is the mother tongue, **L2**: Number of people for whom English is the second language, **EFL**: Number of people for whom English is a foreign language, **Urban population**: Percentage of the total population residing in cities, rural population is not being considered as possible skilled labor because of low population density in rural areas and lack of formal education., **Services sector orientation**: Contribution of the services sector to the GDP (around 60% is being considered as favorable), Presence of major cities: **Presence of cities** apart from the capital which have population more than 20,00,000, **Infrastructure** includes transport facilities, communication facilities, power generation figures and fair degree of industrialization that is in turn indicated by the contribution of the industrial sector to the nation's GDP.

Annexure II

Cost analysis

Monthly operational costs have been calculated based on the following parameters:

1. 250 associates
2. 30 managers
3. 5 IPLC links
4. Floor area requirement: 20,000 sq. ft.
5. Consumption of electricity: 50,000 units
6. Meal costs calculated on the basis of 1 meal per employee per day for 22 days.

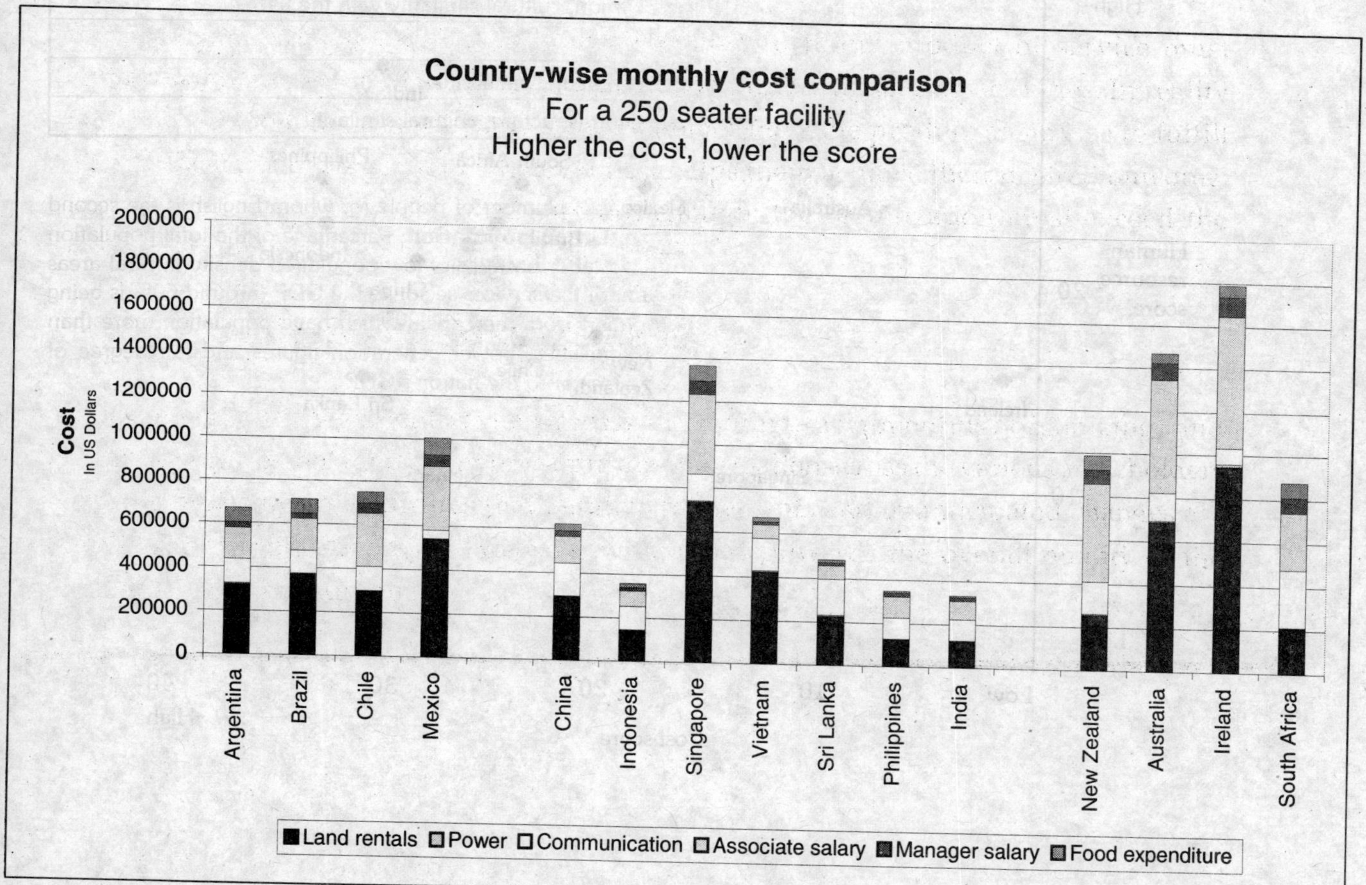

Annexure III

As is evident from the map below, various kinds of skillsets are available at differential costs. A company has to decide based upon its business requirements, what kind of skills it requires and what kind of money it can dole out for these skills. India and Philippines here also are at the top of the rankings. Low quality but relatively cheaper skills are available in countries like Vietnam, Chile and Sri Lanka.

Note: A high cost score indicates lower operational costs. Cost score is inversely proportional to operating costs

HUMAN RESOURCE - COST MAPPING

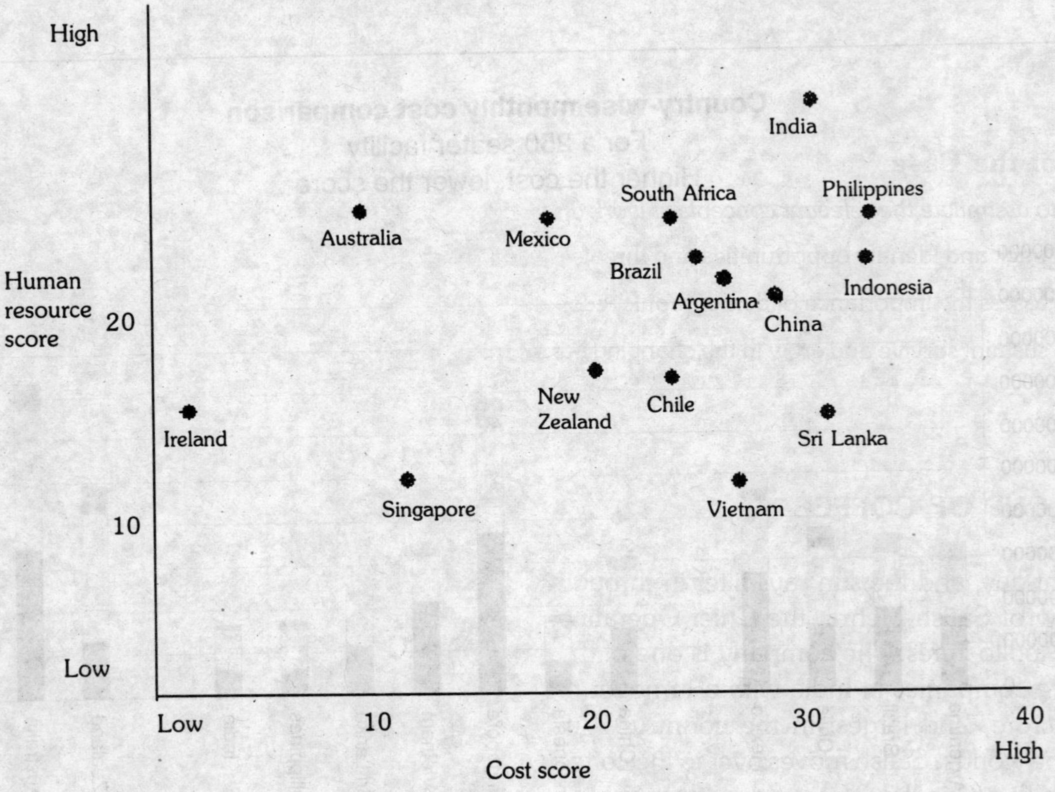

Apollo Tyres: Learning from Environmental Scanning

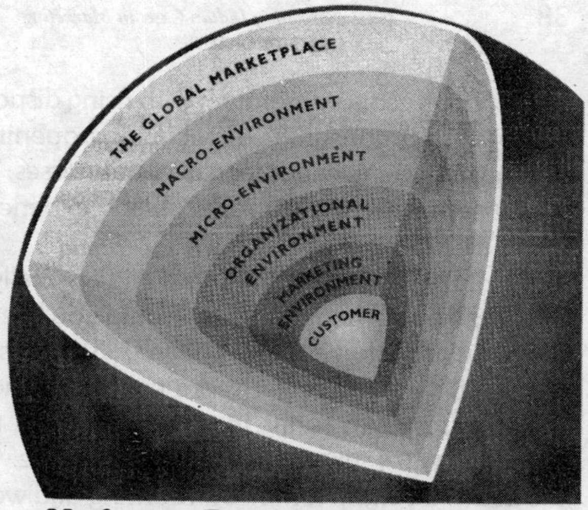

Marketing Environment Case - 3

Purpose of the Case

The idea is to assimilate the relevant concepts at work and analyse in light of the following issues:

- How to track and identify opportunities and threats in the macro-environment
- How to assess the importance of demographic, economic, political and technological factors
- How to sustain, survive and grow in the changing business milieu

OVER A CUP OF COFFEE

It is a bright day, and the sun rays filter in through the window of Satish Mehra, the Chief Operating Officer at Apollo Tyres. The company is one of the leading tyre companies in India with a turnover of Rs 2,600 crore, 2nd largest in the country, 17th largest in the world. . Satish moves over to the coffee machine to brew his third cup and turns it on. His door opens and Karan Sinha, the Strategy Head walks in with a worried look on his face. Satish looks at Karan and asks, "Why the worried look Karan, what's bothering you now?" "Worrying me? That's an understatement Satish, have you seen the kind of changes that are happening around us? It surely is a volatile business environment that we operate in" replies Karan. "Why what happened?" enquires Satish inquisitively. "There is change everywhere Satish, just look at it, the economy, political scenario, societal changes, technology booms, the way the environment is changing is overwhelming. We need to do something if we need to grow and maintain our position, otherwise we will get devoured by these changes in the environment," replies Karan. "All right I hear you but you need to relax first," quips Satish "Here let me pour you a cup of coffee and let's discuss this matter."

Satish pours Karan a cup of coffee and they both take a seat in the office. Satish notices the steaming cup on the table which lies untouched as Karan is too preoccupied with his thoughts. Satish thinks in retrospect about how vital Karan's contribution has been to the success of the company in all these years and his sincerity towards the organisation and ponders over what Karan has just said...

What Karan had just said was true. There were a lot of changes taking place in the macro environment which no one had really paid attention to and Satish realized the disastrous effects that this ignorance could have. The country was experiencing tremendous economic growth with rising disposable incomes and consumer expectations opening up new investment avenues for global businesses. There was a complete paradigm shift being experienced, ruminated Satish.

"I totally see your point Karan and am really glad that you have brought this up. Would you like some more sugar to go with that coffee?" "I am just fine, thanks, but would prefer more concrete action on these issues than sugar in my coffee right now," replied Karan with a hint of pun in his voice. "Meet me at 10 AM sharp tomorrow morning and we shall set up an agenda and an action plan to work on this." "That suits me fine Satish and I will see you tomorrow and let's get cracking on this." With this Karan leaves the office, feeling relieved.

THE MEETING

Satish hears a knock on his door and looks at the watch which just strikes 10. He smiles at the consistent punctuality that is Karan's trademark and motions him to come in. "Good morning Satish, are we ready to crack the environment this morning?" asks Karan. "Yes we are Karan, please have a seat." Karan takes a seat and dumps volumes of data on Satish's desk. Satish looks perplexed looking at the tonnage of paper that Karan has just

brought in and asks him that what it is. Karan tells him that he has collected data on the economic figures for India, the various policy changes of the new government and has various surveys which capture the changing consumer buying behaviors and perceptions. Satish flips through the data for a while and then looks at Karan and asks him "This is a lot of data here but how do we make sense out of all this ? If the GDP grows at 8% then how does it impact us ? If industrial growth is at 10% then what, and if any of these are lower than forecasted then what do we do ? The government has relaxed the cap on FDI into retail and R&D with so many other positive policy changes which would impact us, but how do we make sense out of all this?" "That is something I was hoping that you would help me answer, Satish because I am as overwhelmed by all this data as you seem to be," replies Karan. This data crunching is going to require a lot of time and I don't think we would be able to do justice to it with our current schedules especially with the Asia Pacific review due next week. Satish mulls over the scenario for a while and then says that it is a better idea to hire a consultancy for one of the aspects of the macro-environment and ask them to present their findings with the impact on their company. Karan seems delighted "That is a wonderful idea; so let's do it." They decide to allocate economic growth in India to Boston Consulting Group (BCG) and give a deadline of one week for the firm to present their findings.

After a week BCG presents their report on the macro-economic analysis and its impact on Apollo Tyres which is presented in the Annexure.

THE DILEMMAS

"Have you gone through the report yet Satish?" asks Karan as he walks into Satish's office holding a copy of the report himself. "Yes, I have and am impressed with their findings and analysis" replies Satish. "So am I and it is interesting to see the intensity of the impact that these economic factors in the macro environment have on our industry," says Karan as he puts the report on Satish's table. "I could have never imagined the high correlation that our industry has with these economic factors, it more so vindicates the importance of macro environment and scanning to survive in today's competitive business milieu. We need to tweak our strategy and maintain a long term strategic outlook keeping the macro environment parameters in mind."

They both then play with the econometric model provided in the report which forecasts the demand for tyres as well as the changes in it, based on the changes in the different economic parameters.

Changes in the macro environment and economy would impact business across the country and companies like Apollo Tyres and others will have to tweak and adjust their strategy accordingly. The question arises that what is the right strategy to fully exploit these changes. Already it is being said and shown in the case also how India is no longer dependent on monsoon for exhibiting robust economic growth (*Please refer to Annexure*) and still there is so much focus on the amount of monsoon we receive every year.

How should Apollo Tyres respond to these changes? What would be the right blend of strategising for them? If agriculture production increases then should they create and target new rural segments to market their tyres? Currently services sector contributes approximately 52% towards GDP but if the Business Process Outsourcing (BPO) paradigm in India bursts then what will be the impact on this contribution of services towards GDP. Also economic growth has a cascading effect on the macro environment where it impacts the consumers with changes in their disposable income, purchasing power and other cultural changes as an outcome of this. These are some questions that we as future managers would have to address in purview of the macro environment.

Questions

1. How do you think macro-economic analysis has a bearing on the company's marketing strategy?
2. How should Apollo Tyres "tweak" and adjust its strategy to stay in step with the incipient changes in macro environment and economy?
3. What are the straws in the wind that could change the future direction for Apollo Tyres? Give examples.

ANNEXURE : The Report for Apollo Tyres

Methodology

The methodology adopted is to identify factors and parameters imperative to driving economic growth in the country and identify which ones out of this impact the tyre industry by conducting statistical correlations. After the selection of final factors an econometrics model has been developed in the case which takes the various economic parameters as an input and gives an insight into the demand for tyres in the varied segments viz. total tyre, bus and truck tyre, passenger car tyre, light commercial vehicle (LCV) tyre, tractor tyre, etc. The research conducted for the case has been sourced from various secondary sources, Government of India, Respective ministries, IBEF, CII, Automotive Tyre Manufacturers Association (ATMA), etc. Various statistical tests like F-statistic, R-square and Independent R-square have been performed to vindicate the accuracy of the model.

The Indian Tyre Industry

The tyre industry is an Rs 13,000 crore industry. The fortune of this industry depends on the agricultural and industrial performance of the economy, the transportation needs and the production of vehicles. While the tyre industry is mainly dominated by the organised sector, the unorganised sector holds sway in bicycle tyres. Ever since the first Indian tyre company, Dunlop Rubber Company (India) was incorporated in 1926, the tyre industry has grown rapidly and today it is a Rs. 13,000 crore industry. India has 2.61 lakh villages, connected by 6.23 lakh Kms of metalled roads and 9.81 lakh Kms of unmetalled roads. These villages are linked to small towns and cities. There is a daily traffic of over 4.12 lakh trucks, 1.27 lakh buses, 7.23 lakh cars, and thousands of taxis, two-wheelers, three-wheelers, tractors and animal -drawn vehicles on Indian roads.

There exists a vast potential for the tyre industry in India. The fortune of the tyre industry depends on the agricultural and industrial performance of the economy, the transportation needs and the production of vehicles. Hence, this is a very sensitive industry, which has to adapt itself to a highly volatile environment. While the tyre industry is mainly dominated by the organised sector, the unorganised sector holds sway in bicycle tyres. The major players in the organised tyre segment consist of MRF, Apollo Tyres, Ceat and JK Industries, which account for 63 per cent of the organised tyre market. The other key players include Modi Rubber, Kesoram Industries and Goodyear India, with 11 per cent, 7 per cent and 6 per sent share respectively. Dunlop, Falcon, Tyre Corporation of India Limited (TCIL), TVS-Srichakra, Metro Tyres and Balkrishna Tyres are some of the other players in the industry. MRF, the largest tyre manufacturer in the country, has strong brand equity. While it rules supreme in the industry, other players have created niche markets of their own.

To sum up, the tyre industry is highly raw-material intensive, with raw material costs accounting for 70 per cent of the cost of production. Fortunately for the industry, the rubber and carbon black prices have taken a beating recently, which means lower costs for the tyre industry. The export-import policy allows free import of all types of new tyres and tubes. However, import of retreaded tyres, either for use or for reclamation of rubber is restricted. This has led to used tyres being smuggled into the country under the label of new tyres.

The Indian Economy

The Indian economy has made great strides in the years since independence. In 1947 the country was poor and shattered by the violence and economic and physical disruption involved in the partition from Pakistan. The economy had stagnated since the late nineteenth century, and industrial development had been restrained to preserve the area as a market for British manufacturers. India embarked on a series of economic reforms in 1991 in reaction to a severe foreign exchange crisis. Those reforms have included liberalized foreign investment and exchange regimes, significant reductions in tariffs and other trade barriers, reform and modernization of the financial sector, and significant adjustments in government monetary and fiscal policies.

** Prepared by: Boston Consulting Group*

The reform process has had some very beneficial effects on the Indian economy, including higher growth rates, lower inflation, and significant increases in foreign investment.

Real GDP growth was 6.8% in 1998-99, up from 5% in the 1997-98 fiscal years. The far reaching economic reforms undertaken since 1991 have unleashed the growth potential of the Indian economy. A series of "Second Generation reforms" aimed at deregulating the country and stimulating foreign investment have moved India firmly into the front ranks of the rapidly growing Asia Pacific region.

Relationship between Transport and Economy

There is a strong relationship between economic development and transport demand. Economic growth implies both an increase in goods transport and more mobility, resulting in an increase in passenger transport. Apart from the relationship between income, on the one hand, and production and consumption, on the other, other developments (e.g. changes in the scale and/or scope of production and reallocation of production from a global scale) influence transport demand. The transport system helps to make the economy tick. Good transport is needed to get people to work and many jobs are based on extensive travel. Transport is also a major contributor to the economy in its own right. Road transport, vehicle manufacturing and related industries alone employ a major chunk of the population. Good transportation is vital to the movement of goods and services and thus has a direct impact on economic growth and productivity. Thus if the transportation requirements of the country are affected by the economic growth, it has a direct impact on the demand for tyres as tyres form a major component of the transport requirements of the country and both are not mutually exclusive. Thus economic growth increases transport requirement which ultimately impacts and increases the demand for tyres.

Demand for Tyres

The demand for tyres comes from three segments — original equipment (OE) makers, replacement and exports where the replacement market is the primary driver of demand, followed by the OE segment. Exports account for less than 10 per cent of the total demand. As with any other auto-ancillary product, realisation and profitability in the OE segment is relatively lower compared to the replacement market. The demand from the OE segment depends on automobile production, while the flow of demand from the replacement market hinges on the automobile output in the recent past. The OE segment is a major source of demand in the passenger car market, followed by the two-wheeler and tractor segments. In the passenger car market, the OE segment accounts for about 60 per cent of the total demand, while in the two-wheeler and tractor segments, its contribution is about 50 per cent.

The demand for tyre has been derived from the annual tyre production data for all the tyre manufactures in India as shown below. The table below gives the figures for the tyre demand[1] from the year 1996 to 2004. The figures are in lacs nos.

Year	Total Tyre Demand	LCV Tyre Tyre	Bus Truck Car Tyre	Passenger Total	Tractor Tyre	Industrial
1996	278.94	11.66	76.2	32.6	22.37	0.95
1997	297.65	17.98	80.15	38.13	19.89	0.66
1998	310.59	18.3	79.79	41.8	19.77	1.43
1999	370.48	19.17	78.35	45.71	21.47	1.37
2000	414.13	19.8	87.93	60.54	24	1.72
2001	424.71	21.08	86.12	68.13	23.15	2.19
2002	435.14	23.52	84.74	74.81	22.55	2.14
2003	515.85	28.44	98.63	85.44	24.2	3.09
2004	546.9	32.71	108.21	99.59	24.05	2.95

[1] Source: Automotive Tyre Manufacturers Association

Macro Factors

The factors chosen to monitor and quantify the macro environment are given below. These factors encompass the political, Economical, Social and Technical Movements in India and are hypothesized to have an impact on the tyre industry in India.

- **GDP**
- **GDP Per Capita**
- **Monsoon**
- **Inflation**
- **Transport**
  - **Highways**
  - **Roads**
  - **Vehicles**
- **FDI**
- **Crude Oil**
- **Sensex (FII)**
- **API – Agriculture Production Index**
- **Food grain Production**
- **IIP – Index of Industrial Production**
- **Infrastructure**
- **Interest Rates**
- **Wages**
- **Industrial Index**
- **Employment**
- **Savings**
- **Population**

Macro Environment & Macro Economic Overview

This section lists the historical movement of the chosen macro environment factors for about a decade taking cognizance of the developments of the same post liberalisation in India

Year	[2]GDP Real (Absolute) Crores	[3]GDP Growth rate real (%age)	[2]GDP per Capital growth rate (%age)	[4]Monsoon (%age)	[5]API	[5]Food Grain Production (million tonnes)	[2]Inflation (CPI) %age	[6]Total FDI $ Mill	[2]Total Employment (Lakh persons)	[7]Population (million)
1996	899563	7.3	8.8	103	157.1	180.42	9.2	4892	275.25	934
1997	970082	7.8	2.8	102	163.2	199.44	7.2	6133	279.41	966
1998	1016595	4.8	5.8	105	154.6	192.26	13.1	5385	282.45	984
1999	1082748	6.5	14.4	96	163.7	203.61	4.7	2401	281.66	1000
2000	1148368	6.1	19.37	92	176.9	209.8	4	5181	281.13	1014
2001	1198592	4.4	6.7	91	165.7	196.81	3.8	6789	279.6	1027
2002	1267833	5.8	4.5	81	178.3	212.85	4.3	8152	277.9	1037
2003	1318321	4	1.8	105	150.5	174.19	4.1	5639	272.05	1055
2004	1424507	8.5	7.1	87	179.6	212.05	5.5	16052	270.01	1073

[2] Source: Economic Survey Of India 2005[3] Calculated by taking the base as 100 for the year 1995 and then transposing the growth rates on the future years giving us a relative perspective of the GDP per capita growth on a base of 100[4] Source: India Meteorological Department, Monsoon measured in terms of percentage where the government has set a benchmark of normal average rainfall at 100% and releases monsoon figures in percentage terms by taking cognizance of this benchmark[5] Source: Ministry of Agriculture, India. API – Agriculture Production Index is an index of agricultural production (of 46 crops, including plantations) with base triennium ending 1981-82=100. The agricultural output is measured through this index with different weights being given to various types of crops.[6] Source: Confederation of Indian Industry (CII)[7] Source: Census of India 2004

Year	[8]Length of National Highway (Thous KMS)	[8]Length of Roads (Thous. KMS)	[8]Number of Registered (Thous. KMS)	[9]IIP Index of industrial production (Real)	[10]PLR Prime Lending rate (%age)	[2]Gross domestic savings (crores)	[2]Public Sector Emoluments (crores)	[11]Sectoral Contribution GDP in %age Agriculture	[11]Sectoral Contribution GDP in %age Industry	[11]Sectoral Contribution GDP in %age Services
1996	34.5	2302.5	33786	113.00	12	298747	21931	27	30	43
1997	34.5	2302.5	37786	120.00	12	317261	22219	26.6	30.4	43
1998	34.5	2328.3	41786	128.00	11	352178	25385	25.5	28.5	46
1999	49.6	2396.7	44875	133.00	8	374659	26254	25	28.5	46.5
2000	52	2416.1	48857.8	142.00	8	468681	30402	22.5	30.5	47
2001	52	2446.7	54991	149.00	8	490049	38223	22	30.8	47.2
2002	57.7	2483.3	58863	153.00	6.5	532274	38556	21	31.8	47.2
2003	58.1	2483.3	62210	162.00	6.25	642298	41929	20	30	50
2004	65.5	2563.1	64532	173.00	6	682176	43874	24	24.8	51.2

[8] Source: Ministry of Road, Transport & Highways[9] Source: Ministry of Commerce and Industry. The Index of Industrial Production (IIP) index comprises of 543 items of which 478 fall in the manufacturing sector, 64 in mining and one in electricity. The data for IIP has been normalized with taking base value for year 1995 (109.1), divided each by 1995 value & multiplied by 100[10] Source: Reserve Bank of India[11] India Brand Equity Foundation (IBEF)

Based on the findings and correlations conducted the final factors selected for the development of the econometrics model are: Year (Time), GDP Absolute, Inflation, Road Length, Index of Industrial Production (IIP), Service Sector Contribution and Population. GDP per capita was rejected since absolute GDP and population take account of GDP per capita. Monsoon & agriculture were rejected as the correlations are negative and the country is no longer dependent on monsoon as the year 2003-04 recorded GDP growth rate of 8.5% (highest ever) with lowest recorded rainfall of only 87%. National highway not selected as it is a subset of road length. Wages, Employment, PLR, FDI and Sensex were rejected due to low correlations though FDI exhibits tepid correlation with FII.

Econometrics Model

The model was developed to determine the demand of tyres in India based on the changes in the various macro and economic environment parameters. The model calculates the demand of tyres under various segments like Bus Truck, Passenger Car, Light Commercial Vehicle, Tractor and total tyre demand by taking an input of the various economic parameters, and derives the demand based on the changes in any of these seven variables thus giving a robust insight into how the changes in these macro-environment and economic variables impact the tyre industry as a whole and how Apollo Tyres Ltd. can formulate or goad their strategy by taking cognizance of the same. The model has been made by applying multiple linear regression and statistical tests are included later in the case to vindicate the model.

The regression equations derived from the model and which are used to get the demand are as follows:

Total Tyre Demand	32537.699130-18.60*Year + 0.00*GDP Real (Absolute) Crores + -10.27*Inflation conversion absolute with base=100 + 0.83*Length Of Roads (Thous Kms) + 1.96*IIP + 2.34*Population (million) + 30.03*Contribution Of Service Sector %age + 32537.70 (+/- 8.95)
Bus & Truck Tyre	5626.488375-2.91*Year + 0.00*GDP Real (Absolute) Crores + -1.42* + -0.04*Length Of Roads (Thous Kms) + 0.98*IIP + 0.20*Population (million) + 3.58*Services Contribution + 5626.49 (+/- 2.82)
Passenger Car Tyre	-9239.426567+4.73*Year + 0.00*GDP Real (Absolute) Crores + -0.50*Inflation + -0.03*Length Of Roads (Thous Kms) + 1.48*IIP + -0.24*Population (million) + -0.49*Services Contribution + -9239.43 (+/- 1.64)
Light Commercial Vehicle (LCV) Tyre	-10847.018630+5.48*Year + 0.00*GDP Real (Absolute) Crores + -0.36*Inflation + -0.08*Length Of Roads (Thous Kms) + -0.84*IIP + 0.15*Population (million) + 1.15*Services Contribution + -10847.02 (+/- 0.59)
Tractor Tyre	7102.601366-3.67*Year + 0.00*GDP Real (Absolute) Crores + -0.37*Inflation + 0.07*Length Of Roads (Thous Kms) + 0.55*IIP + 0.01*Population (million) + 0.92*Services Contribution + 7102.60 (+/- 1.20)

Consumer Behavior

Section - Three

CONCEPTUAL FRAMEWORK

To facilitate a better debate on the cases in this section, a quick exploratory review of consumer behavior along with areas that need discussion are recapitulated briefly as follows:

- While analyzing the buying behavior of consumers a marketing manger focuses on the decision-making processes and acts of people involved in buying and using products.
- Marketers study four factors in order to understand influencers of consumer while making a purchasing decision: **cultural** (culture, subculture, and social class); **social** (reference groups, family, and social roles and statuses); **personal** (age, stage in the life cycle, occupation, economic circumstances, lifestyle, personality, and self-concept); and **psychological** (motivation, perception, learning, beliefs, and attitudes). Hence, research into all these factors provides clues to serve consumers more effectively.
- Psychological influences determine people's behavior as consumers. The primary psychological influences on consumer behavior as mentioned before are perception, motives, learning, attitudes, personality and self-concept, and lifestyles.
- Individuals select, organize, and interpret information inputs (sensations received through sight, taste, hearing, smell) to produce their own meaning of packages, products, brands, and organizations. This understanding means their perceptions that affect their buying decision process.
- A motive is an internal force that drives a person towards those activities, which satisfies his needs or helps him in achieving his goals.
- Learning refers to changes in a person's thought process and behavior caused by information and experience. Marketers try to figure out the consumer's learning that influences what they buy.
- An attitude of consumers is their evaluation of a product, feelings for a product, and behavioral tendencies toward a product. It consists of three major components: cognitive, affective, and behavioral.
- **Personality** is the set of traits and behaviors that make a person unique. Self –concept is a person's perception of his personality. Research indicates that buyers purchase products that reflect and enhance their self-concept.
- **Lifestyle** is how one lives. Lifestyles influence consumer's needs, brand preferences, and how and where they shop.
- **Socialization** is the process through which a person acquires the knowledge and skills to

function as a consumer. The consumer socialization process is partially accomplished through family influences. A **reference group** is any group that positively or negatively affects a person's values, attitudes, or behavior. The three major types of reference groups are **membership**, **aspirational** and **disassociative**. In most reference groups, one or more members stand out as **opinion leaders** by furnishing requested information to reference group participants.

- To understand how consumers actually make **buying decisions**, marketers must identify who makes the final decision and who has input into the buying decision; people can be **initiators**, **influencers**, **deciders**, **buyers**, or **users**, and different marketing campaigns might he targeted to each type of person.
- Marketers must also examine buyer's levels of involvement and the number of brands available to determine whether consumers are engaging in complex buying behavior, dissonance-reducing buying behavior, habitual buying behavior, or variety-seeking buying behavior.
- The typical buying process consists of the following sequence of events: problem recognition, information search, evaluation of alternatives, purchase decision, and post-purchase behavior.
- Not all decision processes culminate in a purchase nor do all consumer decisions include all five stages. Problem recognition occurs when buyers become aware of a difference between a desired state and an actual condition. After recognizing the problem or need, buyers search their memories for information about products to help resolve the problem or satisfy the need.
- In the **internal search**, buyers search their memories for information about products that might solve the problem. If they cannot retrieve from memory enough information for a decision, they seek additional information through an **external search**.
- A successful search yields a group of brands, called a **consideration set**, that a buyer views as possible alternatives. To evaluate the products in the consideration set, the buyer establishes certain criteria by which to compare, rate, and rank different products. Marketers can influence consumers' evaluation by framing alternatives.
- In the **purchase stage**, consumers select products or brands on the basis of results from the evaluation stage and on other dimensions. Buyers also choose the seller from whom they will buy the product.
- After the purchase, buyers evaluate the product to determine if its actual performance meets expected levels. Shortly after the purchase of an expensive product, for example, the post-purchase evaluation may result in **cognitive dissonance**, dissatisfaction brought on by the consumer's doubts as to whether he or she should have bought the product in the first place or would have been better off buying another desirable brand.
- The marketer's job is to understand the buyer's behavior at each stage. The **attitudes** of others, **unanticipated situational factors** and **perceived risk** may all affect the decision to buy, as will consumers' levels of post-purchase satisfaction and post-purchase actions on the part of the company.

AVAL: Marketing to the 'Indian' Consumer

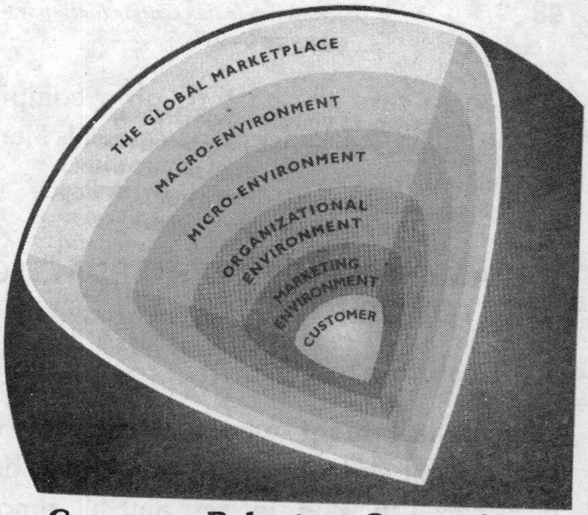

Consumer Behaviour Case - 4

Purpose of the Case

The idea is to assimilate the relevant concepts at work and analyse along the following lines:

- To discuss how consumer behavior in India has undergone visible changes especially post-liberalisation, i.e., early 1990s
- To examine what changes in marketing-mix may be necessary from the marketer's point of view

It was a 'happening' time at the Audio-Video Appliances Limited (AVAL), a Rs-2000 crore company into manufacturing and marketing of Home Appliances and Consumer Electronics. The company had done well for three years in a row now. The environment was bristling with nervous energy. All macro-economic indices were encouraging. Economic and Business journals were writing about the emergence of the great Indian consuming class.

AVAL's range of products included Air Conditioners (Window, Tower, Split and Cassette), Refrigerators (all sizes, styles and functionalities), Television (Plasma, LCD, Flat and Conventional). It had the technology, installed capacity and marketing savvy to produce and bring to market a host of other products in the Home Appliances and Consumer Electronics category.

Pramod Bhoop, the CEO, had faith in the core competence of the company (short time from conceptualizing a product to actually bringing it to the market). The professional skill of the Marketing team was well established over time. The distribution network was robust with distributors and dealers nurtured over 20 years. The only factor worrying him was a lack of insight into the Indian consumers' behavior in a fast-changing social, cultural, political and economic environment. The last decade has seen a transformation in the behavior of the Indian Consumer. In fact he was not sure whether the Indian Consumer was a single entity or as diverse as the socio-cultural kaleidoscope called India.

He had called a meeting of all his Business Heads in the afternoon to discuss the possibilities of new launches in the coming years. Perhaps even getting into new lines of business. Before that he wanted to carefully go through a compilation on the Indian Consumer prepared by his Marketing Team.

INDIAN CONSUMER: YESTERDAY, TODAY AND TOMORROW

1.0 Evolution

How India bought, what they bought, where they bought and when they bought was decided by a socialistic code of restraint till almost the 1980s. Every Indian was impressed upon the need to save, be austere and if one consumed conspicuously, the parents and even the society would possibly frown upon it. This was basically since employment opportunities were limited and per capita income grew at an insignificant 1% per annum.

Signs of change in the above became visible in the mid-80's, particularly after the Union Budget of 1985 bringing down the peak income tax rates to 50% from an astounding 97%. Launch of Maruti 800, emergence of a young and motivated professional class, increase in per capita income and urban household income, advent of cable and satellite TV etc.— all contributed towards a change in the urban consumer behavior. Imperceptibly, gradually but surely, these initiators of change made a dent in the hitherto rigid mindset of frugality and austerity. Vestiges of these still remain in the psyche of the Indian consumer but the intensity has come down. The process of change in the policy regime did not falter or reverse and it culminated into the watershed liberalization policy of the Government of India in 1991-92. There has been no looking back since then.

A plethora of goods and services now fill the platter of the consumer e.g., toiletries, cosmetics, durables, garments, food and beverages, two-wheelers, cars and the wherewithal for acquisition of all these through credit cards and a host of other financing choices. As a result, the consumer mindset has moved towards globalization but with a distinct Indian flavor. Few of the global and local features of the Indian consuming class are listed below.

Family: Though the consumption has grown, family plays a pivotal role in the decision making process, even sanctioning it. For any high-value purchase—a color TV, refrigerator, car, even holidays—the target consumer is the entire urban Indian family, not an individual. For a technology related product (mobile phones for example.), the children or the young adult in the family influence the decision-making.

Thrift & Frugality: Compulsive thrift has given way to 'affordable indulgence'. However, bargaining for rock bottom price still remains. Frugality is still a virtue. It holds true no matter what, where or to whom one is selling. The low-priced ice-cream cone by McDonald's is an invitation to lure in customers. Small pack sizes are *de rigueur* for all product categories be it soap, shampoo, or chips. Gillete sells its top-notch Sensor Excel shaving blade in a single-pack only in India. Throwaway culture has not set in completely, so be it color TV, Air Conditioner, Washing Machine or even cars, marketers have seen the strength and success of 'exchange offers'. Brands are welcome, but the Indian consumer won't pay a premium just for the intangible.

"Indian Flavor": As new products and services are introduced, local adaptation becomes a critical factor in success. International brands are forced to cater to our way of life. And so we have Domino's selling Hot Sams (samosa with Chettinad chicken or paneer), McDonald's introducing Maharaja Mac. Even a hint of beef and pork will spell doom for any food product. Nokia had to reinvent itself for the Indian market. Those that could not adapt to the Indian way, like Kentucky Fried Chicken have suffered initially, taken lessons and, hopefully, will survive the second round.

Advertising: Humor in advertising is appreciated as long as it does not cross limits. Being irreverent to the extent of lampooning one of the heroes is not welcome. Cricket sells and can be used to sell anything anywhere in the country.

Shopping Habits: The Indian consumer still prefers to shop at the street-corner kirana store for groceries rather than the new shopping malls. Apparel is still largely bought at the multi brand outlets rather than exclusive brand outlets. The only exception is footwear, where nearly 45 per cent prefer an exclusive brand store. But this is not true across products for shoes are bought in the brand outlets. But Indian retail habits are changing since organized retailers have now recognized the Indian shopper's inherent need for 'economy of purchase' as paramount.

Slow Pace of Change: The Indian consumer changes his behavior slowly. Companies who have succeeded have been patient with lot of staying power. Those who were in a hurry to make a quick buck or two have bitten the dust

2.0 What has Changed?[1]

According to marketing experts, the following five (the 'big five') have changed:

The Consumer: The consumer has changed dramatically, both quantitatively and qualitatively. It is irrelevant to argue that the so-called middle class is 15 or 250 million strong. The mistakes of quantification have seen the graveyards of brands, their businesses, and the aspirations of people who have been pink-slipped.

Today, the car is aspirational, not the two-wheeler; own homes are, not rented accommodation. Rural consumers lap up urban products and relate to the global village, delivered home through cable and satellite feeds, blurring the neat categorization of consumer segments.

Brands: Brands have thrived and products have been commoditized. Differentiation on the product-dimension is no longer anyone's preserve. Service remains a differentiator, but that too is gradually getting commoditized. It is important to witness the response imagery driven advertising targeting on altered psychographics and consumer aspirations. The Denim man does not need to try too hard. The Pepsi generation is wedded to irreverent fun. Product (including service) quality is a prerequisite; packaging is a critical marketing P. Distribution is a differentiator, but is vanishing quickly. Pricing, and margins, are only going one way— down. The positioning era has truly arrived.

Technology: The awe of technology is no longer there. Consumers demand it and dominate it. From 'low tech' soap-making to 'hi-tech' PCs@home, the Indian consumers demand quality, at lower prices, and at service levels that make many western marketers squirm. The Indian market has seen the arrival of world-class products. Refrigerators in real terms are almost at the same price as a decade ago. PCs cost less each year. We can call (and thankfully receive calls too) almost anywhere in the

world from our ten-year-old mobile services at lower costs. More for less.

Global Integration: Does anyone remember the "Lehar" in Pepsi or that Lifebuoy, the Great Indian brand, is actually an international one? Or that ColorPlus, Amul, and Oberoi are very Indian brands, with a taste of India, and we love them? Or that Maruti is still technically a PSU?

---

[1] *Adapted from an article 'Azaadi for Indian Consumer' by Saurav Adhikari in Business Today*

As global consumers we don't care anymore about the origins and lineage of the products as long as they satisfy our needs as consumers.

Less intervention from the State: Companies (and marketers) can enter (though less easily exit) most segments of the Indian economy, build brands, et. al. without having to obtain the cumbersome approvals. In earlier days, consumers' demands for more soap, cosmetics, or even cars would mean increase in licensed capacities and untold red-tape.

3.0 Consumer Demographics

3.1 Population Growth

The population of India will grow to 1.26 billion by the year 2016 despite a declining birth rate (See Table 1). The states contributing the maximum to this growth would be Bihar, Madhya Pradesh, Rajasthan, Orissa and UP. In 2016, these 5 states would contribute 55% of the country's population whereas Punjab and Haryana will contribute to 4% of country's population. The performance of the 5 states will have a significant influence on the consumption pattern in the country.

THE COMING EXPLOSION

The good news is that the population growth rate will drop from 1.3 percent to 0.5 percent. The bad news is that by 2016 India will be a country of 1.2 billion people. The mantle of the most populous nation on earth might well fail on us by then

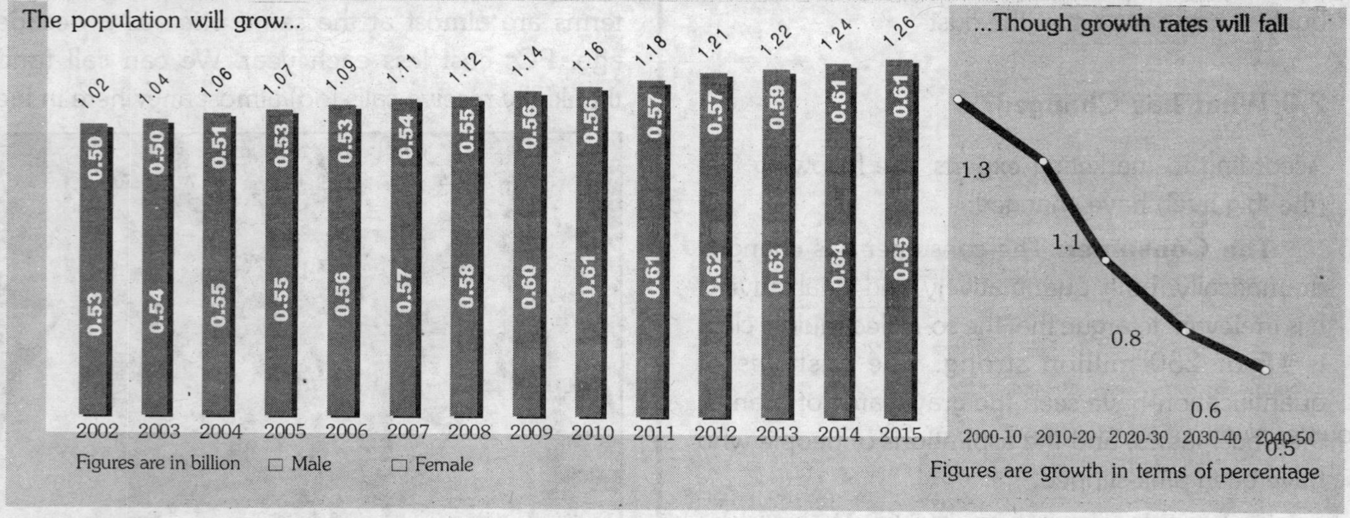

Source: Department of Education, Government of India

Table 1

India has a huge number of the young: a third of its billion population is accounted for by the just-born to the early- teen. That means a huge kids-and-teens market. That's great for business, but the fact that most drop out after 5-9 years of schooling is a big cause for concern in the overall scheme of India's well being - and for tomorrow's market (See Table 2).

Once again, these projections have to be seen in the context of education, occupation and income since sheer numbers do not translate into consumers.

3.2 The Consuming Class(es)

Table 4 gives break up of the different Socio Economic Classes (SEC) households with A1 as the top consuming class and E2 as the lowest for the year 2001. The socio economic classification remains skewed towards the bottom. 40% of the households are in SEC D with SEC B and C accounting for another 40%. There is room for marketing all kinds of goods from luxury goods targeting the 1.8 million SEC A1 households to small size, low value packaged goods targeted at SEC C, D and E.

THE INDIAN CONSUMER

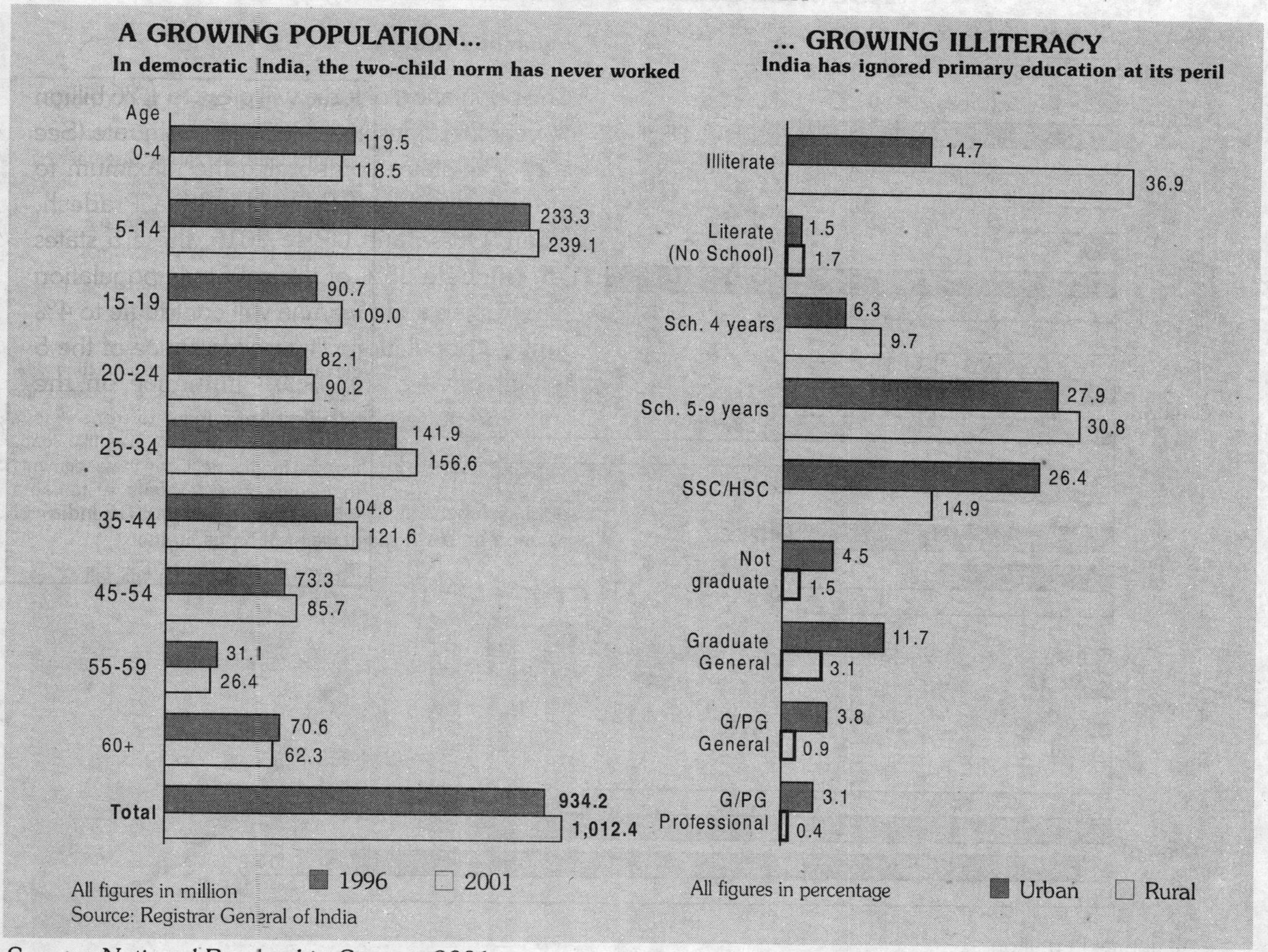

Source: National Readership Survey, 2001

Table 2

AGE-WISE BREAKUP OF POPULATION

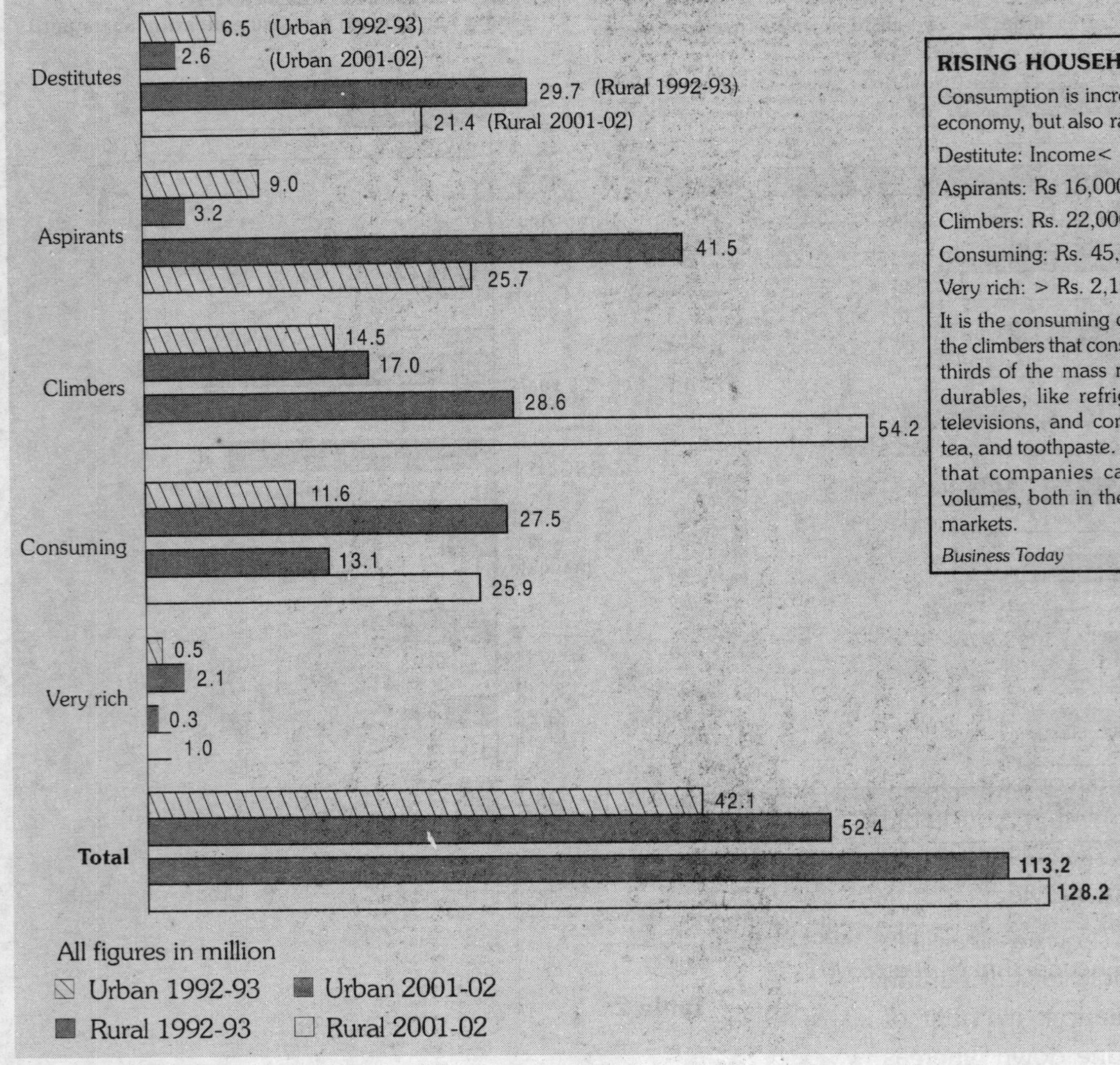

RISING HOUSEHOLD INCOMES

Consumption is increasing, powering the economy, but also raising disparities

Destitute: Income< 16,000 p.a.

Aspirants: Rs 16,000-22,000 p.a.

Climbers: Rs. 22,000-45,000 p.a.

Consuming: Rs. 45,000-2,15,000 p.a.

Very rich: > Rs. 2,15,000 p.a.

It is the consuming class and the mass of the climbers that constitute more than two-thirds of the mass market for consumer durables, like refrigerators and colour televisions, and consumables like soap, tea, and toothpaste. It is in these segments that companies can gain sustainable volumes, both in the urban and the rural markets.

Business Today

Source: National Council of Applied Economic Research

Table 2A

The Table 2A indicates age-wise breakup of the population for the years 1996 and 2005. The literacy or level of education has a direct bearing on the classification of the 'Socio Economic Class' (SEC) classification, which is used in segmenting the consumer class. High dropouts indicate more and more of the youth falling into the lower SEC classification. Projected growth of age-wise population is given in Table 3.

THE TOWERS OF OPPORTUNITY

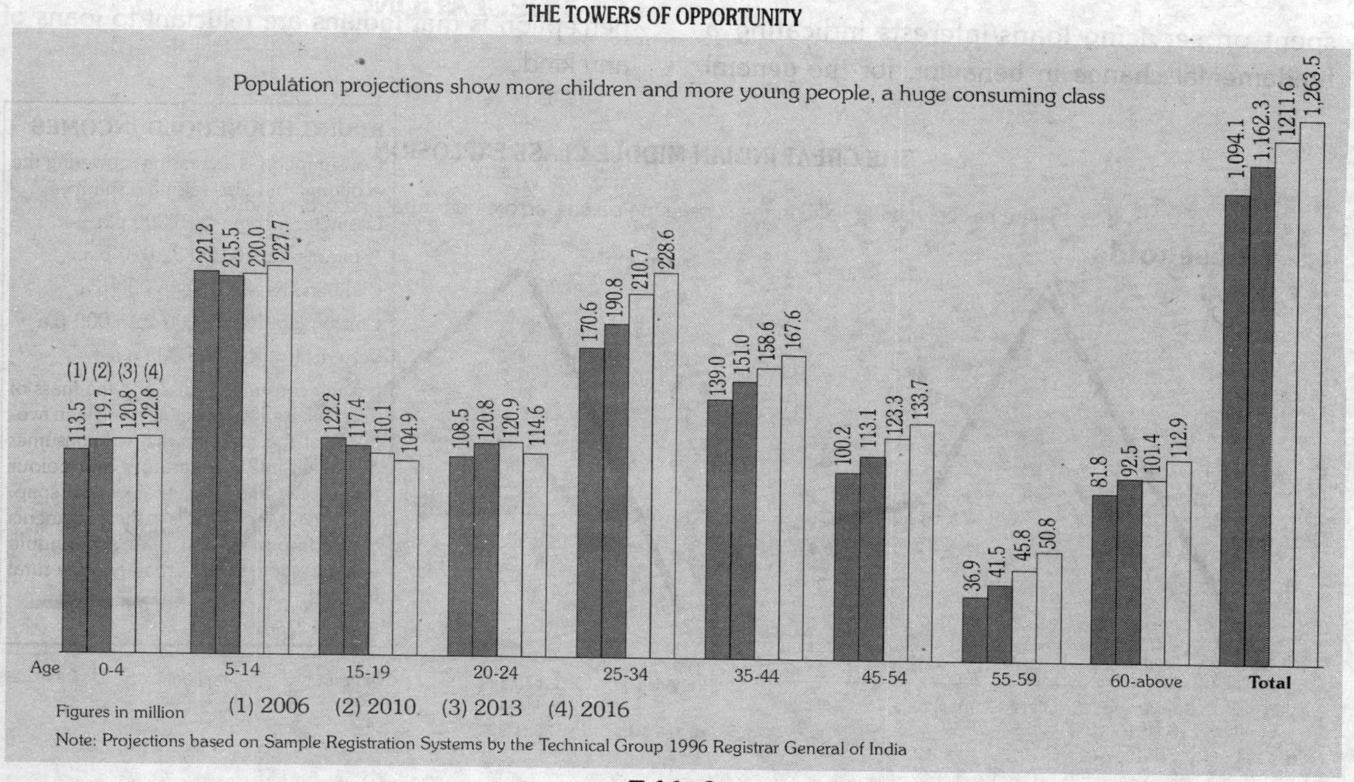

Table 3

The picture becomes clearer if we look at the growth of household in different SECs since 1994-95 and also the urban-rural divide:

The table 5 shows a clear shift towards the middle for both urban and rural population. Number of destitutes has gone down whereas the number of climbers and consuming classes has gone up substantially.

THE CONSUMING CLASS

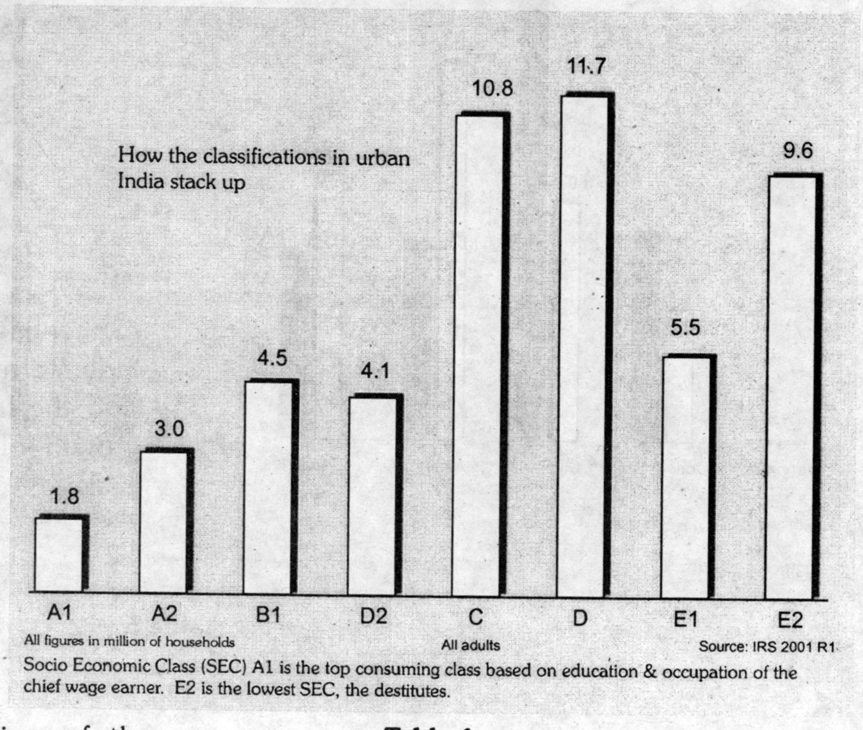

Table 4

3.3 Household Spending

Table 6 presents the spending pattern of an urban household. Food and general provision account for a substantial portion of spend in an urban household. Children's education, utility bills, transport and entertainment are other items that make up a significant portion of the spending. What is surprising is the amount spent on servicing loans/interests indicating a fundamental change in behavior, for the general perception is that Indians are reluctant to loans of any kind.

THE GREAT INDIAN MIDDLE-CLASS EXPLOSION

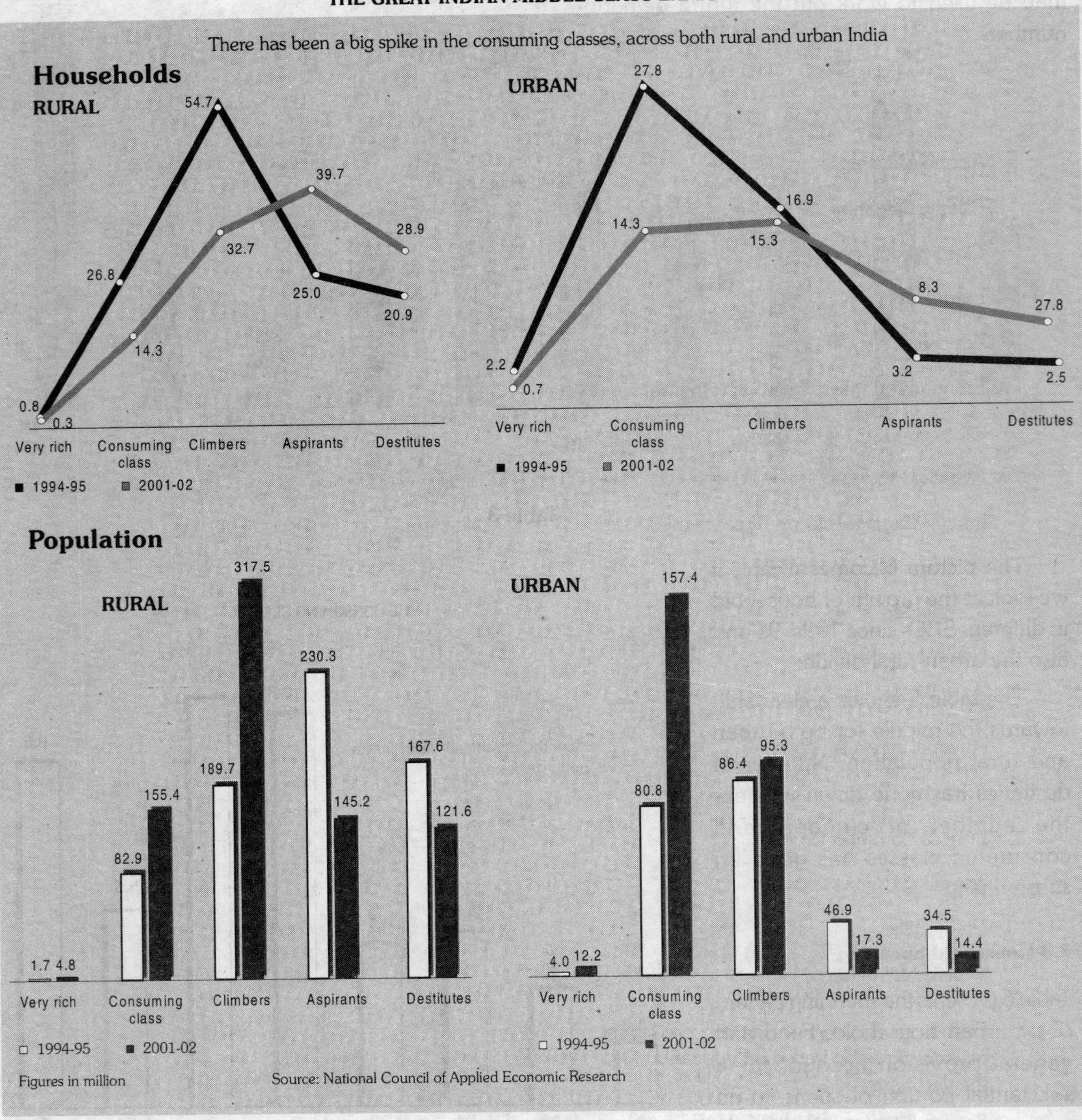

Table 5

The top 5 and bottom 5 products in Indian homes (urban and rural) are as per Table 7 which roughly correspond to the pattern seen in the SEC classifications. The SEC projections may be used to work out the future demand in numbers.

Except for toilet soaps and edible oils, there is a projected growth across FMCG and durables categories with maximum projected growth in wrist watches, CTV, Two-Wheelers and Fridges (Table 8).

	All	A	B
Alcohol/Beverages	528	530	470
Charity Donation	319	320	312
Clothes/Footwear	941	945	877
Eating Out	758	752	862
Education	1,550	1,535	1,789
Entertainment & Relaxation (other than eating)	540	549	429
Gifts	411	416	339
Hygiene Products	391	391	371
Interest Payments/Loan Repayment/ Installments/Premiums	1,755	1,775	1,623
Medicine & Doctor's Bills	527	520	623
Miscellaneous	1,419	1,444	1,004
Newspapers & Mags.	254	256	236
Servants, drivers, cooks	1,015	1,028	821
Personal care/cosmetics	518	515	318
Provision & Food	3,301	3,317	3,104
Rent & Maintenance	1,316	1,358	844
Travelling/Conveyance	1,342	1,351	1,192
Utility Bills	2,188	2,185	2,239
Vehicle Maintenance	860	860	858

Figures in Rs are average amount spent per month. Socio Economic Class (SEC) A1 is the top consuming class, based on education and occupation of the chief wage earner. E2 is the lowest SEC, the destitutes.

Source: Platinum 2001, ORG-MARG

Table 6: **Household Expenditure–Spending Pattern**

PRODUCT OWNERSHIP

Top Five Products In Indian Homes (per thousand homes)

Bicycle 534 | LPG Stove 265 | Pressure Cooker 303 | Radio 219 | B&W TV 289

The Bottom Five (per thousand homes)

Dishwasher 1 | Cooking Range 4 | CD Player 2 | PC 4 | Air-conditioner 4

Source: NCAER (Note: Assumes annual growth rate at 6.7% from 1995-96 to 2001-02 and 7.8% from 2002-03 to 2006-07)

Table 7

CONSUMPTION PATTERNS

Expected penetration levels per 1,000 households

WHAT WILL WE BUY?

The present and the future of the home-buys

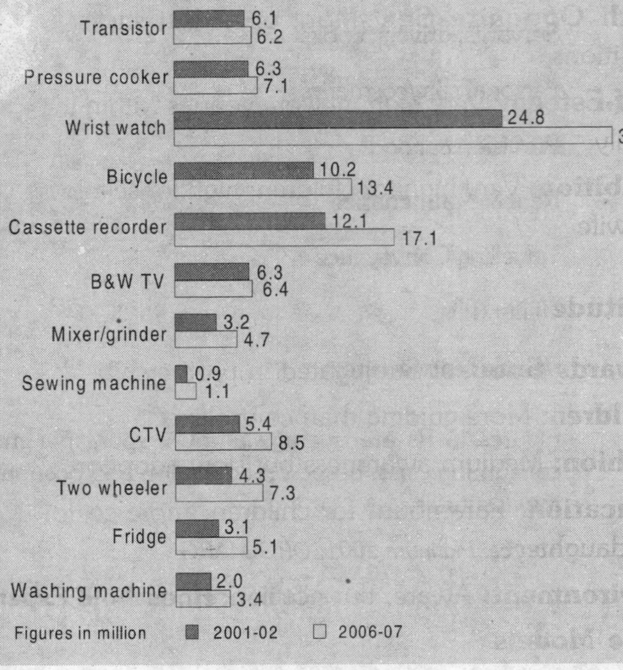

Table 8

4.0 THE MAN. WOMAN AND THE CHILD

An attempt has been made to profile the Indian of the new millennium (man, woman, the young adult and the child) based on numerous articles published on the subject.

The New Century Man

The Hedonist: The I, me, myself person. Everything is viewed through the soft-focus of self-interest, the what's-in-it-for me culture. Much time is spent toning and shaping the body. It is a time to create opportunity, even at other's expense. The each-man-for-himself attitude is getting strengthened as the age of multiparty rule displaces a strong centre. One can notice, cynical of the system and the rusting steel frame, men leaving for foreign lands in record numbers. Yet, *globalization is bringing unprecedented opportunities for the individual*.

Relationships

With Family: Flexible, but still the breadwinner

With Peer Group: Open, but male bonding is on the wane

With Opposite Sex: More open but sticks to traditions

Self-Esteem: Very high, newer avenues within the family

Ambition: Very high for children; high for self; low for wife

Attitude

Towards Spouse: Subjugated in partnership

Children: More guiding than controlling

Fashion: Medium awareness but slow adoption

Education: Paramount for children, more so for the daughter

Environment: Aware, but not concerned

Role Models

Professionally successful men

The New Century Woman

The Achiever: If they have it, they flaunt it. It is the *decade of the body beautiful*, what with an assembly line of consultants, parlors and beauty queens. Professionally qualified working women spread through the workplace, *many putting their career before all else*. The mother's role has changed from passive nurturing to active enabling. The male felt threatened and by millennium's end there was a distinct yearning for an unambitious "homely" bride. Though it isn't easy, *many women learned to balance careers and home*. In poorer families, women struck out as bus conductors, even auto-rickshaw drivers.

Relationship

With Family: Relaxed, accommodative and democratic

With Peer Group: Friendly but competitive

With Opposite Sex: Open but maintains a degree of rigidity

Self-Esteem: Moving towards the individualistic

Ambition: Sets high standards for children; high-to-moderate ambitions for self and husband

Attitude

Towards Spouse: Democratic; and seeking parity

Children: Nurturing, more of a friend

Fashion: High awareness but adopts selectively

Education: Paramount for children; more so for the daughter

Environment: Aware, but still indifferent

Role Models

TV personalities, her mother

The Modern Indian Teenager

One might think that today's teen is freer with the opposite sex. Possibly, unless it interferes with career. Today's teenager wants greater intimacy but is scared to get into relationship, because of the complexities involved. *The teenager is also very conscious of the fashion trends and easily adopts to the changing trends*. Role models are not paragons of virtue but self-made millionaires—or billionaires like Bill Gates, Mahindra Singh Dhoni or Sunil Bharti Mittal. *Personal grooming is very important*, not just to appeal to the opposite sex but for personal satisfaction.

They only want the best in life—be it the shopping mall, life partner, or the latest MP3-enabled music system. To most, computer literacy is almost like what job-work skills were to their parents. No wonder then that for these, the all-consuming philosophy is individualism. But all this doesn't make them insulated from the great Indian tradition of contradictions. Amidst the flash and the cash, religion is still a big draw. Temples, mosques, churches, and gurudwaras report more young people coming to worship than ever before.

The Modern Indian Child

Today's child is highly acquisitive—a marketer's dream but a parent's nightmare. The flip side is that she is also likely to be extremely spoilt. Wooden toys made by artisans are out, battery-operated Tajwanese gizmos are in. And it wants those products that offer instant joy and help identify with the peer group.

Like the child of yesteryear, *today's child occupies a central position in terms of exercising power in the family.* It also has vaunting ambitions, of being rich and famous, at a very young age. No longer do middle-class children say they want to be steam-engine drivers or bus-conductors: they are likely instead to say they want to be Shah Rukh Khan or Sachin.

For parents, getting their kids to the best school—not just educating them—has become a do-or-die affair.

5.0 THE CONSUMER OF THE FUTURE

Urban: She (He) is value-conscious, as ever, but also includes the brand in her (his) value metrics. She (he) is willing to pay a premium for the intangible, as long as the marketer can justify that it helps manage her (his) life better. She (he) buys virtually everything through a debit or credit card, largely at specialty retailers. She (he) invests heavily on health/house/life insurance premiums, and lives on hope built on the foundation of a professional education, an individualistic but family-rooted outlook, and a double-income household. She (he) prefers to listen to her (his) kind of music on FM radio, from any one of the three stations in its genre within the city's 20-odd channels, while tuning to another for traffic updates on her (his) drive to work and back. At home it is either news on the direct-to-home (DTH) enabled television or that sizzling sex-thriller late at night. She (he) gives in to the only child's demand for a holiday abroad, even while factoring in the upgrade to the C-class car next summer.

Rural: She (he) now buys a 200-ml shampoo bottle, the one that was advertised during last night's showing of *Lagaan* on Star. She (he) still enjoys when it rains, but the 24-hour paid electricity and a well-serviced tube well means the fields are well-irrigated even when the Gods play truant. Their two teenaged children go to a school in a nearby town, not in a tractor any more but that multi-utility vehicle the family bought two years ago. They return only late evening after computer lessons. Though she (he) still goes to the weekly haat to pick up vegetables and dry rations, what she (he) looks forward, possibly twice a year, is that 100 km drive to the big city to buy apparel, audio cassettes of her (his) favorite movies, and of course, that roller-coaster ride at the amusement park.

6.0 FORCES THAT MAY SHAPE FUTURE BEHAVIOR

Movement of 'Have Nots' to 'Haves': The society in India is in a ferment with caste, religion, economic and regional divides. The churning may empower and bring a vast populace of hitherto marginalized populace into consumer mainstream.

Quality of Life: As consumer (urban) stabilizes and becomes more mature, consumption per se will cease to be an end in itself. Consumers will start asking whether the new markets and products have created a better quality of life. There may be insistent demand for 24 hour electricity, pure drinking water from the utilities, a responsive healthcare and public transport system and services that help cope with daily struggle of living with dignity and comfort. Private enterprise will have to step in much like the Metro Rail for Mumbai, or the Apollos, Hindujas and Fortis in the healthcare business.

Consumer Rights: Consumer rights will gain momentum with active intervention from the courts and consumer groups. Consumers will demand and get quality of services or products. There will be more and more pressure to conform to the promised deliverables responsibly.

Greater speed of urbanization: Urbanization has moved at great speed in Independent India (Table 9). Increase in the number of Urban population and social changes like consolidation of nuclear families, living away from family, urban singletons, an increasing proportion of senior citizens would alter the needs and behavior of the Indian consumer.

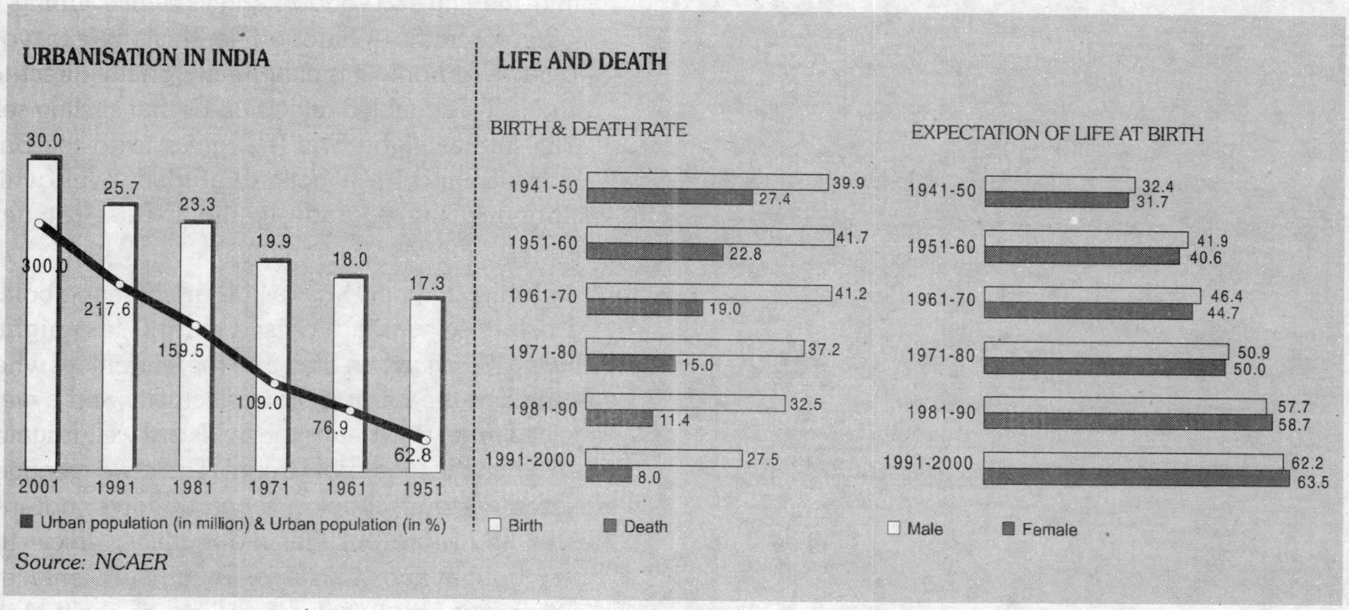

Table 9

Putting down the report, Pramod thought for a while. He started framing questions in his mind that he wanted to put to his Business Heads.

Questions

1. Based on the report, and company's core competence, which new product seems to have maximum promise. Why?
2. What would be the plan to bring this product in terms of the 4 Ps. What should be the Segment, Target and Positioning of the product?

Notes

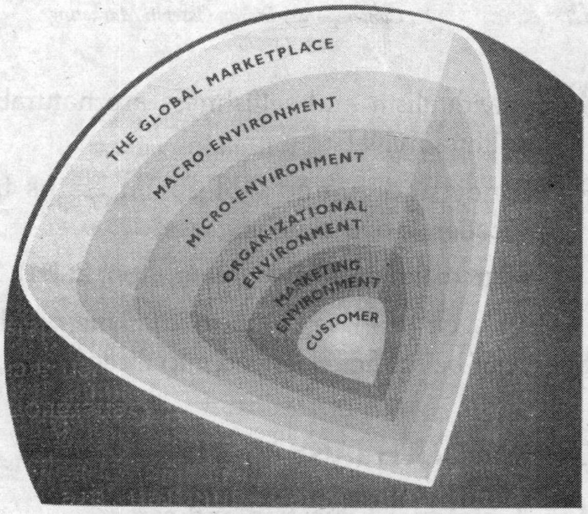

Consumer Behaviour Case - 5

The Changing Face of Youth in India

Purpose of the Case

The idea is to assimilate the relevant concepts at work and analyse in light of the following issues:

- How to employ the findings about changing youth behavior in marketing a product or a service?
- How to incorporate in on growing earning opportunities that youth enjoy, due to new, at times, unconventional career options?

Picture this: Cool dude, 19, walking down an empty stretch with a stylish body bag on his right shoulder. He stops over as he sees a portly- 40-something guy immersed waist-deep in the bonnet of his silver grey Mercedes convertible as one sees a cloud of smoke rising from the engine. The situation is just too much for the dude to resist. The young boy's expression gives the viewer an idea that something nasty has crossed his mind. The next instant one sees that while the Mercedes man is still occupied with the car, the real stuff has begun as the boy dumps his bag into the back seat of the Mercedes and confidently leans against the car asking for a lift. The trap is just too desirable to be missed and the viewer does not have to wait for long. Soon there is this bimbette in an open jeep who stops over as she inspects the car and the guy, and the viewer gets to hear the thought blurb "Nice Car!" The next moment, the girl asks the hunk if a lift is what he wants. The boy hops into the jeep but there are question marks in the girl's expression as she looks at the Mercedes guy who till now was fixing his car. But it's the dude's reply that puts everything else to rest. Sneeringly, he utters one word – "driver". And off they go leaving the man fumbling in frustration and disgust.

This is how the "*nayee peedhi*" of the youth is like. They are smart and selfish. To illustrate one of the best ways to define the contemporary Indian youth and his/her priorities, we find the following characteristics about them:

- They are bold, brash and more demanding than ever.
- They are decision-makers and want to command the spending power.
- For them smart work is the key, hard work is passé.

- Individualism and selfishness are natural for healthy survival.
- Money and symbols of social status take precedence over anything else.

(Source: *Indian Management*, April 2004)

But even in these characteristics the youth of today can be further classified into three stages:

EARLY YOUTH (AGE 13-21)

Key decisions: Education and career.

Influencers: Parents and peer groups

Consumption areas: Clothing, accessories, food, and entertainment.

Spending power: Rs1,000-2,000 p.m. (mostly provided by parents, some earn additionally)

Brands: Preferences are developed, but brand consumption is occasional and aspirational. So the average college goer wants to own Levi's but does not necessarily have to have wardrobe full of them. If a similar style and fit is available he will buy it. Prefers "Café Coffee Day" over "Barista" purely on price. Always looking for value for money.

Opportunity: To develop more products at affordable price for this category.

MIDDLE YOUTH (AGE 22-28)

Earlier if one had a job, one was called an adult. Now with few young people shouldering the responsibility of family, the money they earn is more disposable income especially with BPO jobs coming in good numbers.

Key Decisions: Career and relationships.

Influencers: Peer groups and workmates.

Spending power: Rs 7,000- 40,000 p.m.

Consumption areas: Personal clothing, accessories, food, and entertainment. And consumer durables

Brands: Can finally afford the brands he aspired for in early youth, with own money. Evaluates Café Coffee Day vs. Barista over service quality, ambience, not just price. Seeks few good factors and expression of identity through choice of brands consumed. But is also value conscious.

Opportunity: To keep innovating so that the brand is relevant and trendy.

LATE YOUTH (AGE 29-?)

Even after marriage and kids, people aspire to look and feel young through their choice of clothes, entertainment and outlook.

Key decisions: Career advancement of children.

Spending power: Given household expenses, the spending power remains equal to or less than what it was at the middle youth stage. Also many would be taking up home and car loans, and pay for children education.

Consumption areas: Household + kid products + personal clothing and accessories.

Brands: A mix of status and fun brands depending on personal beliefs. In some areas one may look for functionality and values while in others one may look for luxury.

Opportunity: Develop and position brands that are fun and spirited as opposed to being boring and conventional. But that should not appear foolish, for example a 35-year-old trying to pass off as 18. A successful example is a rash of lounge bars aimed at 30-somethings who want night-outs, but want to avoid noisy discos where they would be considered 'uncles' and 'aunties.'

Gone are the days when youngsters in India meekly accepted the choices made by the parents. Exposure to media, advent of new technologies, education, etc. has made the current lot highly brand conscious with strong brand preference. Today's youth seem to come in all shapes, sizes and attitudes. So before a company markets to youth, or any one for that matter they need to understand what makes them tick? Most marketing experts advise that a marketer must walk with them not walk on them in his shoes while dealing with youth.

The fact that today's consumer is a lot smarter and confident can be understood from the experience of Sony Entertainment Television (SET). SET conducted a research and during the focus group discussion (FGD) among Sec A, women suddenly threw up a winning idea. Observers at these FGDs noticed a new sub-text emerging from all the talk: a new woman who was growing tired of *saas-bahu* routines. This group saw itself as capable both at home and work; if they were housewives, they were so by choice, not circumstances. Armed with this insight, Sony scoured the world for a show that might address this audience. And there boomed the concept of 'Jassi Jaisi Koi Nahi'. It is common knowledge now that Jassi has set new cash registers for SET.

(*Source: Indian Management, March 2004- Article on Theme Market Research, Page 37*)

COMPARISON WITH AMERICAN YOUTH

A study appearing on Generation Y about their new attitude at work in the *USA Today* has been featured in *The Hindustan Times* dated Nov. 23, 2005. The study observes that they're young, smart, brash. They may wear flip-flops to the office or listen to ipods at their desk. They want to work, but they don't want work to be their life. This is Generation Y, and the first wave is just now embarking on their careers - taking their place in an increasingly multigenerational workplace.

Who is Gen Y

There is no consensus over the exact birth dates that define Gen Y, also known by some as echo boomers and millennials. But the broadest definition generally includes those born between 1977 to 2002. Generation X was born roughly 1965 to 1976. Narrower definitions put Gen Yers as those aged 16 to 27, born from 1978 to 1989. This narrower view is based on the thinking that as the pace of change in society accelerates, the time frame of a generation gets shorter.

Generation Y is moving into the labour force during a time of major demographic change, as companies around the world face an aging workforce. Sixty-year-olds are working beside 20-year-olds. Freshly minted college graduates are overseeing employees old enough to be their parents. And new job entrants are changing careers faster than college students change their majors, creating frustration for employers struggling to retain and recruit talented high-performers.

Unlike the generations that have gone before them, Gen Y has been pampered, nurtured and programmed with a slew of activities since they were toddlers, meaning they are both high-performance and high-maintenance. They also believe in their own worth.

Conflict areas

- In the workplace, conflict and resentment can arise over a host of issues, even seemingly innocuous subjects such as appearance, as a generation used to casual fare finds more traditional attire is required at the office.
- And then there's Gen Y's total comfort with technology. While older workers may expect a phone call or in-person meeting on important topics, younger ones may prefer virtual problem solving.
- Conflict can also flare up over management style. Unlike previous generations who've grown accustomed to the annual review, Gen Yers have grown up getting constant feedback and recognition from teachers, parents and coaches and can resent it if communication from bosses isn't more regular.

Gen Y markers

- **They have financial smarts:** After witnessing the financial insecurity that beset earlier generations stung by layoffs and the dot-com bust, today's entrants into the workforce are generally savvy when it comes to money and savings. They also care about such benefits as retirement plans.
- **Work-life balance is tops:** Unlike boomers who tend to put a high priority on career, today's youngest workers are more interested in making their jobs accommodate their family and personal lives. They want jobs with flexibility, telecommuting options and the ability to go part time or leave the workforce temporarily when children are in the picture.
- **Change, change, change:** Generation Yers don't expect to stay in a job, or even a career, for too long - they've seen the scandals that imploded Enron and Arthur Andersen, and they're skeptical when it comes to such concepts as employee loyalty. And they believe in their own self-worth and value enough that they're not shy about trying to change the companies they work for.
- **High expectations of self:** They aim to work faster and better than other workers.
- **High expectations of employers:** They want fair and direct managers who are highly engaged in their professional development.
- **Ongoing learning:** They seek out creative challenges and view colleagues as vast resources from whom to gain knowledge.
- **Immediate responsibility:** They want to make an important impact on Day 1.
- **Goal-oriented:** They want small goals with tight deadlines so they can build up ownership of tasks.

WHAT'S NEW

New & Unconventional Career Options

Indian youth is ready to walk down a different path.

There is a large mass of young people who have no memory of pre-liberalized India. To them Gandhi and Nehru are nothing but historic characters. The youth of today don't want to confine themselves to respectable and secure life; they want something different, something more. They are not worried about jobs but rather they are looking for as to how to choose a path that fits in with one's own individual identity. They are making choices based on instincts rather than survival. and are ready to change the rules of the game.

Youth

Today's youth are discovering new, unconventional routes to the same God. Earlier the kids were expected to secure their career by making it to the best of professional colleges. And thus began India's eternal affair with medicine and engineering, the two career choices that defined the aspirations of every middle-class student in India. By the early 1990's, MBA had joined the list. But now things are changing; there are new undercurrents and for the first time, questions are being raised about the medical-engineering route to success. There are strong reasons for this change. Firstly, there are 'achiever' parents who are open to a wider range of possibilities as they are financially secure enough to allow their children to take some risks and make some mistakes. These 'achiever' parents believe they must guide, but not goad and they are happy to see their offsprings become 'actualisers', those who pursue their dreams and maximise their true potential.

The youth of today is thinking beyond becoming engineers, doctors and MBAs; for them the definition of achievement means something else. Slowly but surely more professions are joining the preferred list of youth. Professions which were regarded as unconventional and 'cheap' earlier, but which now offer good money and prospects have become acceptable. Popularity graphs of careers like mass media, hairdressing, fashion, interior or accessory designing, bartending, DJ, personal grooming, etc are gaining people's recognition and achieving heights. Personal satisfaction is high on the agenda of youth in India and setting up small enterprises seems to provide these young individuals with flexibility and greater sense of achievement

Usage of Internet

The next generation Internet users i.e. today's youth, prefer IM (Instant messenger) over email (which they find old-fashioned now) to communicate with their peers and this development has implications for the workplace of the future and for marketers as well. This Internet generation of young India, having access to latest gizmos and gadgets, can spread information through IMs to their friends at enormous speeds if they like or dislike a food-joint, movie, music video, T-shirt label and so on; word-of-mouth publicity had never been so swift and effective.

Most of the young adults in the age group of 18-24 are students. So they keep in touch with their peers. They are generally online 6-8 hours. They find interest in random surfing and chatting with strangers. They can even connect online on projects, instead of having face-to-face meetings. A 25-slides PowerPoint presentation can be divided up among 5 students with real-time collaboration, thus, ensuring that things remain in synchronization. Instant messaging allows them to exchange files of all kinds including audio and picture. IM is fast becoming the most preferred application on the Internet for the youth demographic. As per reports published in *Businessworld* of 28th June 2004, there are 10 million unique users a month in India on MSN and 5 million users on Yahoo Messenger. In fact, 50% of these users are students. This has serious marketing implications as you can't bullshit this new generation because the new savvy customers will not only sift through an offer and reject it if there is nothing in it but also message it to all Tom , Dick and Harry if an experience does not live up to its expectations.

MSN Messenger	Yahoo Messenger	
≈ No. of users of all MSN services in India: 12 million.	q No. of users: 5 million.	
≈ Age profile: 18-24 yrs.	Age profile:	
≈ 50% are students	Age (Yrs.)	%
≈ 88% are single	14-17	0.60
≈ 67% are online everyday	18-20	9.90
	21-24	20.70
	25-29	33.10
	30-34	21.20
	35-44	4.30
	45>	3.20
Source: *Businessworld*, 28 June, 2004		

Table I: Users of the Messenger

IM is a kind of metaphor reflecting the mindset of the new millennium youth. The cool thing about the IM as per the youth of today is that a person can chat in real time even as several other things can also be done simultaneously. The Internet lingo like 'asap', 'btw', 'lol' have even become a part of our daily lives. Life has to be lived in the fast lane and today's youth consider slow typers as a huge turn off.

CREDIT CARD USAGE

India's latest tryst with BPOs and other jobs have had a huge impact on consumerism in youth. Money is not reckoned as a serious problem.

A cursory look at Table-2 quickly shows the tremendous job opportunities available to today's youth.

The youth of today is increasingly becoming financially independent thus allowing the marketer to design products for them as now they possess a credit card with no supervised spending limit. Levi-Strauss India, a leading jeans marketer, has tripled its sales in Bangalore city in last 3 years (2000-

03 period) and they believe this is largely due to the effect of disposable income coming into the hands of 18-22 age group employed in BPO jobs. A leading bank in India believes that India adds around 3 million young earners in the age group of 20 to 24 annually. These first-time earners account for 7-8% of its credit card base of 1.4 million. The bank has launched a special mini visa card, which is 43% smaller than the regular card and is being positioned as a cool accessory. This card offers discount at popular retail outlets and hangouts frequented by people. (Source: *Businessworld*, 28 June 2004, Page 50)

According to India Infoline, the ITES-BPO segment registered a growth of 59% in 2002-2003 to reach US $2.3 billion and is projected to grow 54% to $3.6 billion in 2003-04. Approximately 90% of the workforce in this service is below the age of 25 and earns Rs 10,000 per month on an average, therefore the purchasing power of this lot is not less than Rs.2,200 crore annually. The mantra of these guys is "live for today, hope for tomorrow and splurge tonight".

Sectors	No. of Jobs	Qualifications Required	Pay (Rs/ p.m.)
Items	1,00,000	Under graduate	7000/- 14000
Insurance	1,00,000	Under graduate with IRDA certification	10,000
Retail	1 milion	Under graduate	4,000

Table 2: Job Opportunities in the New Emerging Sectors

BPO is just one example of this mammoth market creation, which has wide exposure and purchasing power. There are huge and similar job creations happening in various emerging sectors like retail, insurance and banking, etc.

SPENDING PATTERN

Around 54% of India is estimated to be under the age of 25 years, however, the consuming class that is the target of most youth lifestyle brands numbers approximately 16 million.

In India, all the companies are eyeing the middle class because of its increasing spending power. The middle class youth is very important in this game plan, as this is the segment, which is ready to go to any extent in order to make its dreams come true. Even the media pundits have realized the fact that the consumer of today is growth engine of tomorrow.

The good news for the marketer is the youth of today is very aware of brands and their influence in a family purchase is high. Anything related to technology, they are the ultimate decision makers.

Let's look as how a college-goer reacts to the prestige–price permutation. For a college-goer, who gets an average pocket money of Rs. 1,000-2,000, certain branded products go beyond his reach. So, while brands may be attractive shopping at street-market is equally cool. A study claims that 58% of apparels for young women and 42% for young men are unbranded. This is where the smart marketers have to create an opportunity for themselves. To cater to this segment Airtel, which estimates 40 million young customers, has launched Rs.50 and Rs.100 recharge cards. Levi's is another company which launched its 'street wear' range.

Even though this college-goer is not able to spend grands on the brands but as per the study done by NFO, only 23% of U.S. teens think that being cool means intelligent, whereas 77% of Indian teens think so. The inference that can be made is that the Indian youth doesn't only concentrate on brands but gives due importance to the product as well.

There is another important consumer segment viz. 'the young at heart'. Unlike other countries, where clubbing (going to clubs) is a teen and young phenomenon, in India it is embraced by moneyed 40-plus something. These middle age consumers are living out their lost youth and it is reflected in their grand consumption.

THE NEW TREND

With this whole new look and attitude of the youth, the face of the middle class has also changed. This changed outlook has become evident and more visible by the trends that have taken place in the last five decades, which shows how the middle class of today has evolved over the period of time. Yesterday's conspicuous consumption has become the new age necessity. Interestingly enough, there is an upheaval across age groups. Let's look at the lowest common denominator, or the symbol of middle class, and the symbol signifying change. This lowest common denominator has risen from being the proverbial Bajaj Chetak during the late 1970s and all through the 1980s to a Maruti in 1990s.

This whole change and evolution has been on account of a lot of reasons like the liberalization of trade, new working opportunities, and attitude towards attaining a lifestyle living. All these factors have covered a wide spectrum of our being—from 'working' to 'living' to 'earning' and 'spending'.

These developments hint at the new emerging definition of the middle class. If we look at this new customer from the marketer's perspective, we can see the changes in the mindset of today's consumer from the following table:

Evolving Symbols of the Indian Middle Class

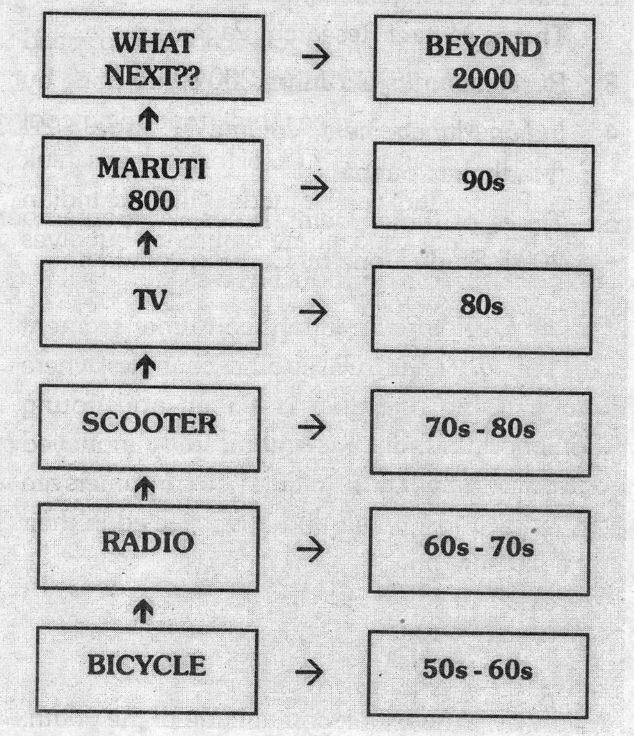

Source: ***Indian Management,*** April 2004

This changed mindset of today's consumer gives a new definition of the middle class consumer of today. This 'new middle class' is a definition shaped by a new set of people who are hungry and want to move up, do better, and make a mark. With this hunger inside the individual and the desire facing the Indian household, there is a lot of pressure to maximise the monthly domestic income. Aspirations are running just as high among women as they have decided to generate finances for the family with or without a formal office to go to. The woman of the family wants to make money for a better lifestyle. It is not a surprise then that today India has the largest population of working women in the world. Both the adults in the family work towards more money with the 'nayee-peedhi' of today becoming independent and actively involved in lifestyle shopping, the role of children in buying decisions for their products, which were earlier bought by

Three consumer types across 3 generations of India

	Traditionalist (60s/70s) Pre-liberalization	Transient (80s/90s) Liberalization	Millennium (2000s) Pre-liberalization
	Security Conformity Family	Freedom Individuality Work	Meaning Personal style Personal pleasure
Mindset	Obligation Discipline Risk-avoidance Moderation	Entitlement Self-indulgence Risk-taking Excesses	Accountable Self-control Risk-management Balance
Motto	I want my children to be better off than mine.	I want to be better off than my parents.	I want to enjoy
Accompli-shment	What I've done for my family?	What I have and own	What I do?
Obsession	My country?	Myself	My society
Purchase	Functionality	Statement	Enjoyment
Behavior	Is it good for my family?	Is it good for me?	Is it good for me and my society?
Role of	Information	Enticement	Entertainment

Source: Madhukar Sabnavis, *Indian Management*, Volume 41, Issue 7, 2003

mummy or papa is quite visible. Today's children are also independent when it comes to making choices and developing an attitude.

To support this, a survey conducted by Cartoon Network, covering 3206 kids in the age group of 7 to 14 years of age and an equal number of women across 14 cities in India revealed the following:

So, the results of the study reveal a pretty clear picture of as how the children of the new millennium are so different from the children of 90s. Today, the children are aware, they watch television, they have Internet access and are provided with full freedom by their parents to make choices and pursue their dreams.

KIDDO CREDO	
On their marks	90% say that good grades are critical.
Humse badkar kaun?	71% want to outperform friends.
Mai Hoon!!	83% want to be the most popular student in the class.
Date, set, GO!	18% have boy / girl friend.
The Great Outdoors	69% play outdoors for just an hour / day.
They have got the look	52% feel a conscious need to look good.
Guns and poses	35% boys choose the toys as the best buy.
	44% girls choose soft toys as the best.
Main doc banoonga	30% boys, 44% girls want to be doctors.
Early to bed?	45% don't follow the 10 pm go-to-bed deadline.

Source: *Times of India*, 23 September, 2004, Study Done by Cartoon Network

Questions

1. Taking due cognizance of the changing demographic and psychographic profile of urban Indian youth, divide the class into groups of 5 students each and design appropriate market-mix strategies for the following products:
   1. Lingerie
   2. Western Movies
   3. Fitness and health equipment.
2. Design a 'Business Model' for a marketer who wants to open an outlet to sell T-shirts to urban Indians.

   Let's say, these T-shirts can be embossed with customised messages through special machines, which can deliver such product in an hour. The cost of embossing a message and the T-shirt is Rs. 100.

References

1. *Indian Management*, April 2004
2. *Indian Management*, March 2004- Article on Theme Market Research, Page 37
3. *Businessworld*, 28 June, 2004
4. *Indian Management*, Volume 41, Issue 7, 2003 (Madhukar Sabnavis)
5. *Times of India*, Delhi Times, 23 September, 2004, Study Done by Cartoon Network

Notes

Notes

Segmentation, Targeting and Positioning

Section - Four

CONCEPTUAL FRAMEWORK

To facilitate a better debate on the case in this section, a quick exploratory review of segmentation, targeting and positioning along with areas that need discussion are recapitulated briefly as follows:

- Marketing managers employ target marketing through **market segmentation**, **market targeting** and **market positioning**. Their focus is on targeting markets at four levels: segments, niches, local areas , and individuals.
- Marketing managers try and locate those individuals or organizations who have needs for products in a product class and have the ability, willingness, and authority to purchase such products. Marketing professionals look for commonalities and differences in the market while addressing the issue of marketing a product or service.
- Marketing managers usually employ a five-step process when selecting a target market:
  - Step 1 is to **identify the appropriate targeting strategy**. The undifferentiated strategy is effective in a homogeneous market, whereas a heterogeneous market needs to be segmented through a concentrated targeting strategy or a differentiated targeting strategy. When using a concentrated strategy, an organization directs marketing efforts toward a single market segment through one marketing mix. With a differentiated targeting strategy, a Marketing Manager directs customized marketing efforts at two or more segments.
  - Step 2 is **determining which segmentation variables to use**. Segmentation variables are the characteristics of individuals, groups, or organizations used to divide a total market into segments. The segmentation variable should relate to customer's needs for, uses of, or behavior toward the product.
  - Step 3 is to **develop market segment profiles**. Such profiles describe the similarities among potential customers within a segment and explain the differences among people and organizations in different markets segments.
  - Step 4 is **evaluating relevant market segments**, which requires that several important factors - including sales estimates, competition, and estimated costs associated with each segment - be determined and analyzed.

- Step 5 involves the actual **selection of specific target markets**. In this final step, the company considers whether customer's needs differ enough to warrant segmentation and which segments to focus on.

- Certain conditions must exist for effective market segmentation. First, customers' needs for the product should be heterogeneous. Second, the segments of the market should be identifiable and divisible. Third, the total market should be divided so that segments can be compared with respect to estimated sales, costs, and profits. Fourth, at least one segment must have enough profit potential to justify developing and maintaining a special marketing mix for that segment. Fifth, the firm must be able to reach the chosen segment with a particular marketing mix.

- Segmentation variables for consumer markets can be grouped into four categories: **demographic** (e.g., age, gender, income, ethnicity, family lifecycle), **geographic** (population, market density, climate), **psychographic** (personality traits, motives, lifestyles), and **behavioristic** (volume usage, end use, expected benefits, brand loyalty, price sensitivity).

- **Product positioning** refers to the decisions and activities that create and maintain a certain concept of the firm's product in the customer's mind. Product position is the result of customers' perceptions of the product's attributes relative to competitive brands.

- The real motive of a Marketing Manager behind undertaking a positioning exercise is to design his company's offering in such a manner that it occupies a distinctive place in the mind of target segment, and thus successfully create a customer focussed value proposition by giving strong reasons to target market as to why they should buy his product/service.

- When a brand possesses unique characteristics that are important to some buyers, positioning it to avoid competition is appropriate. It is important to avoid positioning a product so that it competes with sales of the company's existing products. Companies can also increase an existing brand's market share and profitability through **product repositioning**. Repositioning can be accomplished by making physical changes in the product, changing its price or distribution, or changing its image.

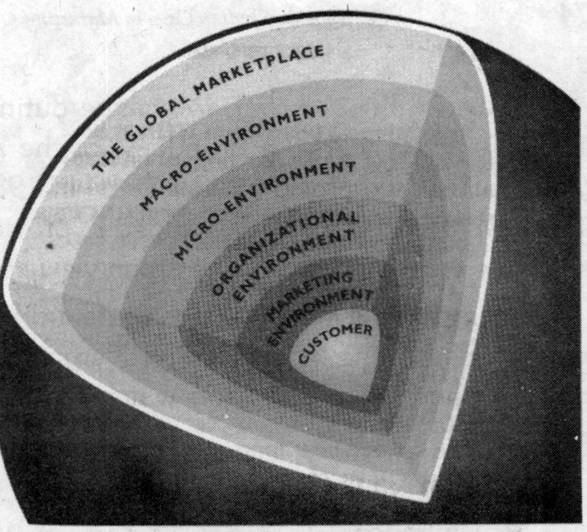

Zee Telefilms Limited

Breaking the Jinx

Purpose of the Case

The idea is to assimilate the relevant concepts at work and analyse in light of the following issues:

- To focus on how a TV Channel has to keep alert and attuned to the evolving tastes of the audience as dictated by changing demographics and psychographics, to stay aloft
- To appreciate how segmentation, targeting and positioning concepts apply to the Zee's turnaround in terms of Television Rating Points (TRPs)
- To debate whether a TV Channel can hold its own for relatively a long period or is it a slippery deal always

Zee Telefilms has come a long way since October 1992, when it launched India's first Hindi General Entertainment Channel, Zee TV. After its success in the initial years, Zee lost its position of market leader to new players like Sony TV in 1995 and Aaj Tak in 2000. Star TV also improvised its programming content after 2000 which had a major impact on Zee TV's market position as their TRPS began to fall and their advertising revenues dropped considerably.

Celebrating 10 years of world class entertainment

Pradeep Guha, the CEO of the company, feels that they need to improve their programming content to capture the mind share of the new Indian consumer. This is a study of how Zee Telefilms managed and developed its products so as to regain their position of being the market leader.

THE HISTORY OF INDIAN TELEVISION

Although television was introduced into India in 1959, for almost two decades the government of India used the national network, Doordarshan, as an instrument of social change, and produced programs which focused on issues like national integration, agricultural development, literacy, education, health and family welfare.

Indian viewers had to make do with DD's chosen fare, which was dull, non-commercial in nature and directed towards education and socio-economic development.

However, things began to change during the 1980s, starting with the broadcast of the Asian Games which were held in New Delhi in 1982. In 1984, DD Metro channel was added to provide an exclusive entertainment for the urban viewers.

During 1980's there was no segment of viewer but one - the Grand Indian Family. Everybody from grandmother to the grandson watched the same programmes:

- Ramayana
- Chitrahaar
- News
- Hum Log

Till late 1980's, Doordarshan was the biggest player in the television channel industry, in fact the only player. Segmentation of viewers was unheard of and considered a social taboo. The genesis of the Hindi mass entertainment channel would then take us back to 'Hum Log' and 'Buniyaad' that were launched in 1984, which took the country by storm and were some of the earliest successes of the mass entertainment genre or rather the beginning of it in India. Then came what was arguably the biggest TRP chartbuster of all time, Ramayana in 1987-1988 followed by a dose of Mahabharata in 1989 and 1990, which ensured our generation knew the mythology arguably well. The costume and wig renting business was further kept alive by historicals like Tipu Sultan.

PRIVATE CABLE & SATELLITE TELEVISION

The true birth of the Indian Cable & Satellite Industry happened when urban Indians learnt that they could watch the Gulf War on CNN, who was the first foreign programmer to enter India. In the years that followed Satellite TV came to India in early 1990s when Star TV was launched in 1991 with 4 channels; however the market was not ready to accept wholeheartedly as the channels were all in English and the mass of the viewership of India was Hindi speaking.

In India, most homes were single TV homes. Hindi was and still is the preferred language for consuming entertainment across India (except the four Southern states) and that makes Hindi General Entertainment Television an intensely competitive space.

With the coming of elections in 1998, news became big news. Prannoy Roy's Star News became the first independent news channel which later evolved into NDTV. A year later, during the 1999 elections, Zee too had set up its independent news channel and both were fast gaining in popularity.

And the next thing we all know, in the year 2000 KBC became the new acronym for a successful comeback, not only for the channel but for the host as well. The show quickly became the biggest hit on Indian television. Hosted by the megastar of Hindi cinema, Amitabh Bachchan, KBC, and catch-phrases from the show such as 'lock kiya jaye,' 'computer-ji,' 'pucca,' and 'fifty-fifty,' became popular parlance in India. Then of course came in the Balaji 'K' series that have endured even till the ultimate game show started airing its sequel. Also, Aaj Tak arrived in the same year. And lately we have seen all the reality shows that have promised to find the best singer, pop-star, movie star, comedian, dancer, roadie and what not!

In the 21st century, the television industry has become more specific. In this competitive market, channels are targeting specific viewers. The Hindi and English speaking markets are separated. So now dad has a Star Sports and ESPN to watch cricket; CNN and BBC to watch international news, Aaj Tak to watch national news. Kids have their Hungama channel and Cartoon Network; the teenage daughter has MTV and Channel V and of course the grandmothers and mothers have their dose of daily soaps on general entertainment channels. (See Table 1). Along with these, we also have the religious channels like Aastha in the Hindi segment and GOD TV in the English. Table-1 provides the channel bouquets of the major players of the Indian cable & satellite industry

However, content remains king on the general entertainment channels. With new avenues for entertainment, not to mention other niche channels eating into their pie, the task seems to be getting tougher. At the end of the day, the focus is to bring in the moolah and the audiences.

	Star	Zee	Sony	Others
General Entertainment	Star Plus Star One	Zee TV	Sony	Sahara One
Movies Hindi	Star Gold	Zee Cinema	Set Max	B4U Movies
Movies English	Star Movies	HBO/ZeeStudio		
News Hindi	Star News	Zee News	NDTV Hindi	Aaj Tak Channel 7, India TV, Rashtriya Sahara
News English			NDTV News	Headlines Today
News (Business)		CNBC/CNBC Awaaz Zee Business	NDTV Profit	Bloomberg
Education	National Geographic		Discovery/Animal Planet	
Kids Channel	Disney/ Hungama	Cartoon Network POGO	Animax/ Nickelodeon	
Sports Channel	Star Sports	Zee Sports	Ten Sports	ESPN
Music General	Channel V Star World	Zee Music/VH1 Zee Cafe	MTV	B4U Music
Entertainment (English)				
Adventure Channel		Reality TV	AXN	
Lifestyle Channels		Discovery Travel & Living	Zoom Times Group	
Fashion Channels		Trends		FTV

Table 1: **Channel Bouquets of Major Indian Cable & Satelite Companies**

THE ZEE STORY

Zee Telefilms Ltd was founded in October 1992 as a content supplier for Zee TV - India's first Hindi satellite channel. It was promoted by Subhash Chandra, one of India's leading entrepreneurs, who sought to establish Zee as an 'infotainment' company focused on the convergence of media and communications. In the early 1990s, Subhash Chandra came out with the experimental Zee TV the (3 hour) Hindi channel on the cable platform and drove the market wild. There was the era of Banegi Apni Baat, the era of 'Tara' (it refused to end) and subsequently 'Amaanat' and the Ramsay's

Zee Horror Show over the span of the 1990s. Early in Zee's history, Subhash Chandra and the Star group of companies entered into a joint venture for television broadcasting in India. When News Corp Limited acquired the satellite distribution business of Star, News Corp de facto became a partner of Zee. To further develop the relationship, News Corp and Zee subsequently co-founded Siticable one of the leading cable distribution networks. In March 2000, after a six-year joint venture, Zee bought News Corp's stake in both the broadcasting business and Siticable.

With the increasing purchasing power of the Indian consumer and the demand for more variety, new domestic and international channels entered the industry offering a wide range of programming content across different genres. Zee too launched new channels to cater to the needs of the Indian consumer from time to time such as Music Asia in 1997 (now known as Zee Music). Zee Telefilms has a variety of channels in its bouquet which includes Zee TV, Zee Cinema, Zee News, Zee Music, Zee Studio, Zee Cafe, Zee Marathi, Zee Bangla, Zee Punjabi, Zee Gujarati, Zee Business, Zee Sports, Smile TV and Trendz as well as CNBC in English and CNBC Awaaz in Hindi and HBO which became a part of the Zee bouquet as a result of their collaboration with Turner International.

In 1998, the company took two major steps: Zee TV was launched in USA and the first Zee Cine Awards function was organized. Zee also became the first company to provide Internet services over cable.

Despite all these initiatives, Zee was fighting a losing battle against the newly launched national and international channels by the Star and Sony group in the late 1990s (See Exhibit 1). To revive itself, Zee entered into a joint venture with Turner Ltd., a wholly owned subsidiary of Warner, in December, 2001, which garnished its bouquet with international channels like CNBC, Cartoon Network and Zee MGM (now known as Zee Studio).

Market Share of Viewership in 1997

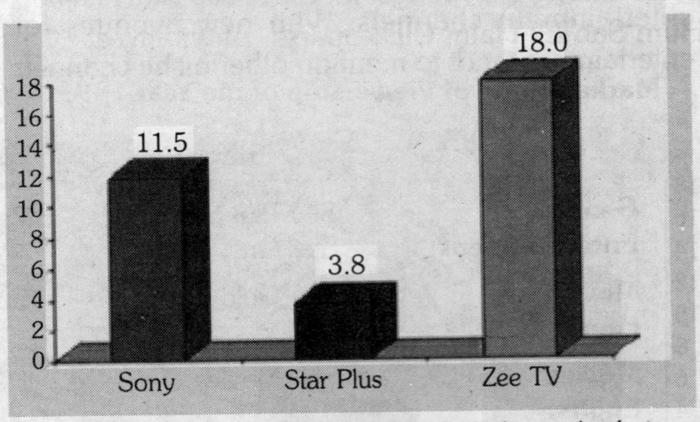

Source: Television and Media Research, Industry Analysis

Exhibit 1

As in 2005, the performance of Zee Turner Ltd. (ZTL) still remains a mixed bag with some of its channels like Zee Cinema, Cartoon Network and HBO being market leaders in their respective genres. However, its flagship channel, Zee TV, is ranked third behind Star Plus and Sony Entertainment.

THE DOWNFALL OF ZEE

As the journey of Indian television began, also happened the evolution of Indian audience. The channels always had to exceed the viewer expectation or else there was always someone waiting in the flanks to take their place.

Life was not that simple anymore; the ground was heating up and the viewer was demanding more and more. The expectation of the viewer was no longer restricted to the core product as in the time of Doordarshan, but it was growing over a period of time and so the marketer needed to think through different levels - the ability to delight the customer and gain his loyalty.

While most of the serials during mid-1990s were identifiable, contemporary and aspirational to the average viewer it was Zee's 'Amanat' which had a relatable backdrop and touched the emotional chords of the viewer.

However, by 1999, Sony had surged ahead on the back of a slew of new and refreshingly contemporary shows. Sony was hitting the right notes among the younger lot especially with Heena, Hum Sab Ek Hain, CID, Sparsh, Alpviram, etc.

Market Share of Viewership of the Year 1999

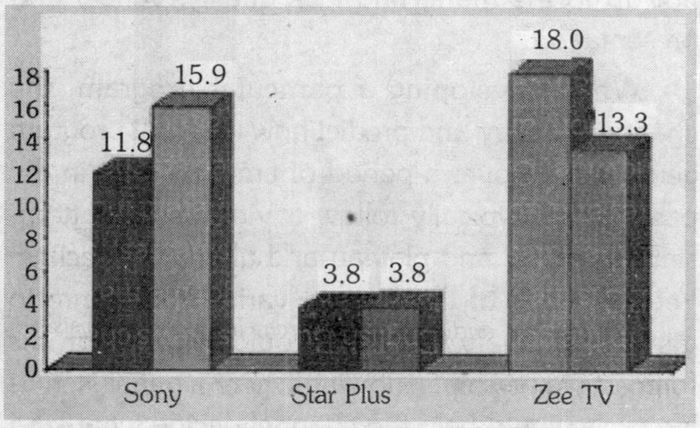

Source: Television and Media Research, Industry Analysis

Exhibit 2

The great Indian middle class remained conventional, careful, cynical and glued to the cable television with its fictional weepy soaps. The two went on well, till *Kaun Banega Crorepati* happened in 2000. It became such a phenomenon that between 9 and 10 in the night you didn't find many on the roads, cinema halls or public places. Hooked to Star TV, millions across the nation watched with bated breath who is going to be the next lucky one. *Kaun Banega Crorepati* was a show which caught the imagination of the man in the street and took Star Plus to the No. 1 position. Ever since, Star has retained its position in the market.

But the popularity of the brand Zee had gone down considerably. Zee, being weak in its programming and content gave ample opportunity to its competitors like Star and Sony to become major crowd-pullers in the prime time slots. As a result of this, Zee was unable to grab the TRPs.

It is important to note that the demand for a channel from the end-consumer is also strongly affected by the overall look, feel and presentation of the channel. Zee's quality of presentation being inferior to its competition reduces the demand for the channel. The channel failed in capturing the mindshare of the consumers which led to a fall in their market share.

In the general entertainment category, Star Plus was the market leader since it had the largest viewership. It still does. Star's strategy is largely two-pronged: defending its current market share while at the same time come up with new innovations in order to expand its viewership. Sony Entertainment and Zee TV are the major challengers of Star Plus, and are constantly at battle with each other for the number two position. Sony has an edge over Zee because of its better quality of content and programming over Zee.

Market Share of Viewership of the Year 2005

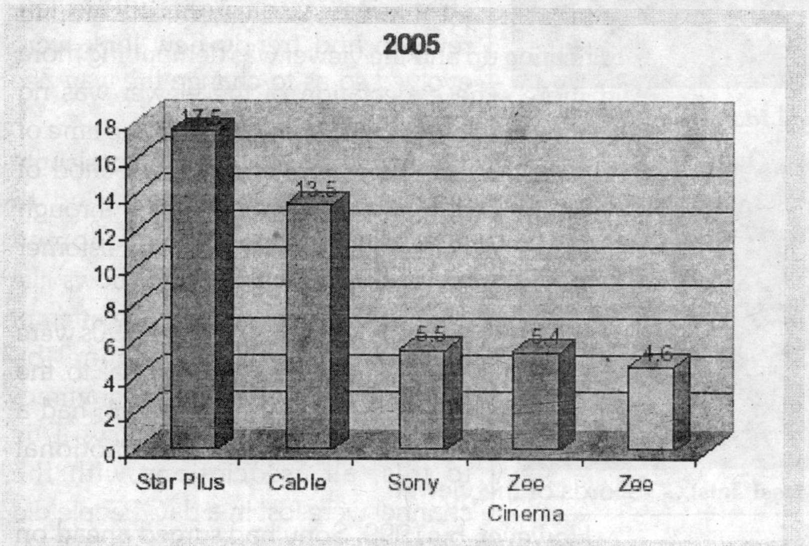

Source: Television and Media Research, Industry Analysis

Exhibit 3

ZEE'S UNDOINGS

Most industry experts believe that Zee did not realize that people watched shows with which they can vicariously associate with. As they could not capture the mindshare they began declining in the TRP ratings from 1998 onwards. TV media experts believe *people watch programmes, not channels*.

Zee lagged behind Star and Sony in both market share and capturing the mindshare. Of these, the mindshare factor is the more crucial one, since Zee should have tried to first make an impact on the consumer's mind and believe that the market share will follow thereafter as a natural corrolory. Zee has also lacked innovative ideas over the years, and this was indicated in the competitor strategies, where both Star (with KBC in 2000 and KBC 2 in 2005) and Sony (with *Indian Idol in 2004-05*) made a huge impact on the viewers and to an extent raised the bar of the Indian television scenario.

Internal competition within the Zee bouquet is also prevalent. This can be seen in the competition between Zee Studio and HBO in the English Movies channels and CNBC and Zee Business in the English Business News channels. CNBC's presence as leader in the market prevents Zee Business to get a better penetration, viewership, and revenues.

The viewership of a general entertainment channel like Zee TV depends largely on what type of programs people like to watch in such channels. It is seen that a substantial number of people tend to like programmes of more than one type. So the success of such channels will depend on how well they can cater to the demand of the consumers with varying tastes, as well as the variety in programming content of the channel. People perception about Zee is that it has very low brand visibility. Its programmes are not up to the mark; and lack quality, variety and presentation.

*'Kyunki Saas.... '*Star TV

'Indian Idol'– Sony TV

'KBC'-Star

'Jassi Jaisi...' -Sony

When developing a particular program, the channel must try and predict how well that program genre will do over a period of time. As seen in the past, genres typically follow a Viewership pattern-start, increase, and plateau and ultimately decline. Yet the shape of this pattern varies from genre to genre and analyzing thus would help programs forecast viewership. Knowing where a genre is in its life cycle would help the channel decide what kind of shows to put up. However the shape of the life cycle can be affected by the activities undertaken by the channels in terms of promotions as well as tricky twists in the program.

ZEE REACTS

It's been a long haul back on the upward curve for Zee Telefilms but things are certainly moving north for the network. Zee TV has kicked off its initiatives from ground up, by having a re-look at the channel positioning, presentation and the marketing strategies in the year 2005. The revamp and trendy new look were evolved so as to change the way Zee TV was sold.

After the KBC-*saas bahu* onslaught in 2000, an injured Zee tried to retaliate by a series of doomed gimmicks, like introducing shows like *Sawaal Dus Crore Ka.* Or the attempt to revamp the entire channel by throwing out all existing programmes and introducing 26 new shows. Due to this, all associations with the channel were lost in a day. People did not like it either and according to Ashvini Yardi, senior VP programming, 'People felt it was not the same Zee anymore.'

Then Zee pushed ahead with 'different' serials like *Astitva- Ek Prem Kahani*- about an older woman marrying a younger man. Zee, always a mass-viewed channel, was trying to be 'elitist'. The channel also revamped some of its popular shows like *Kareena Kareena* and *Antakshari* by keeping in mind the youth taste. The grandeur of *Zee Cine Awards* and the presence of Bollywood badshah Shah Rukh Khan were used to unveil brand new logos for the whole Zee network.

Saath Phere, the soap that presented an unconventional heroine, has been Zee TV's best find in the recent times
Source- www.indiatelevision.com

shows like 'Saat Phere'- the 'unconventional' story of a girl's search for her unique identity and 'Kasam Se'.

But the trick that really clicked for Zee TV was a revamped *Sa Re Ga Ma Pa* which became the channel's top-rated show. Sa Re Ga Ma Pa has been around for several years as one of Zee's most stable, well-regarded music talent shows. But Ashish Kaul says 'No one expected the show to come up with a mixture of salt, pepper, spice and masala that it did in Challenge 2005.'

The extensive repackaging of Sa Re Ga Ma Pa to fight the rival talent hunts turned out to be a masterstroke for ZeeTV
Source- www.indiatelevision.com

TRP Ratings of Channels in the Year 2006

Channel	Key properties	April-May average ratings combined
Star Plus	Kyunki..., Kahaani..., Kasauti...	12.64 TVR
Star One	Laughter Challenge, Mano Ya Na.., Kya Hoga..	2.61 TVR
Zee TV	Saath Phere, Kasamh Se	4.44 TVR
Sony	Idol final & Idol Muqabla, Fear Factor, CID	3.36 TVR
Sahara One	Cricket, Woh Rehne Wali.., Hanuman (film)	2.76 TVR
Sab TV	Caravan (film), Idol Takka Tak, Wah Wah, Lo Kal..	0.52 TVR

Source: TAM Peoplemeter System TG: CS 4 years + Markets: Hindi Speaking Markets
Period: 2/4/06 to 6/5/06 (www.indiatelevision.com)

The idea or new thought in the year 2005 was to make the channel look younger and more vibrant. Research findings showed that Zee had started looking a little jaded and hence the logo and the look of the channel was changed. Since the change in packaging there has been a considerable change in the mindsets of the viewers.

Zee TV has surged ahead of Sony Entertainment Television with the charge led by a couple of popular shows and afternoon movies. Even in the prime time band it has jumped in ratings with

Zee TV has shifted its focus to shows like 'Sa Re Ga Ma Pa Challenge' and 'Business Baazigar' where the former can be said to counter Sony's 'Indian Idol 2' and the latter to counter Star's 'Kaun Banega Crorepati 2'. They are also introducing a comedy show 'Johny Ala Re' to counter 'The Great Indian Laughter Challenge-Dwitiya' of Star One in June 2006.

Drawing inspiration from the success that some of the low-budget movies have drawn on the tube, Zee has initiated a number of movie projects, with each costing the company approximately Rs 10 million. The themes range from thriller, comedy, real life drama and love.

The films are being made, keeping in mind the various target groups and hence attempting at all the popular themes. The channel started airing these movies on weekends from August 2005 which also could be looked at as another strategy to fight KBC 2.

With Pradeep Guha at the helm of marketing, an area Zee TV is seriously looking at is to tap events. The channel has already unveiled a new property, *Zee Astitva Awards* - honoring women achievers – in the year 2005. Instead of plotting a marketing splash with this event, what Zee has done here is a strategic attempt to woo the female segment. Zee has already given its *Zee Cine Awards* a global positioning.

Furthermore, Zee Telefilms has been undertaking a restructuring for its English channels over the last six to seven months in 2005-06. One of the results of this is that Zee Café is doing local initiatives.Other offerings that have been launged are 'After Hours', which looks at the latest happenings in the Mumbai social circuit, and 'Simply Style' that is about fashion and 'Bombay Talking'-the show which looks at the glamour of Bombay. For the first time ever, a channel has taken the initiative to bring an exclusive English drama with Indian content to connect with the Indian audiences, whose preferred language may be English but ethos is still uniquely Indian.

But that's not all with the English language channels from the Zee stable. Zee Studio, formerly known as Zee MGM, too is undergoing a programming change with the aim being to showcase blockbusters like 'The Aviator' and 'The Hours'. If Zee Telefilms senior VP and business head of English channels (Zee Café, Zee Studio and Zee Trendz) Neil Chakravarti is to be believed, then in the near future the movie channel is all set to take on competition head on from HBO and Star Movies by airing one new movie daily. They also plan to re-launch Zee Trendz, their lifestyle channel taking the mindset of the Indian consumer into consideration.

In the genre of English Business News channels, CNBC is the world leader and has got the maximum and the latest happenings of businesses, stocks, shares and ups and downs of the different industries worldwide. CNBC is the most respected channel in its category and as of now, CNBC has come up with the Indian version of its channel by launching the channel in Hindi version in the name of CNBC Awaaz.

Zee Telefilms has made a sincere attempt to re-established its position in the market, from a channel which had been in the ratings wilderness for six years, by keeping in mind the social and psychological factors that affect the Indian consumers' buying behavior. As Ashvini Yardi, Senior Vice President, Programming puts it, 'The audience should get the feeling that it is *their* story'.

Question

1. Do you think Zee is getting its equation right in terms of segmentation, targeting and positioning? Is there room for second-guessing?

Notes

Notes

Marketing Research

Section - Five

CONCEPTUAL FRAMEWORK

To facilitate a better debate on the case in this section, a quick exploratory review of the marketing research function along with areas that need discussion are recapitulated briefly as follows:

- Students must realize that tomorrow if they get a job as a "market researcher", their job-content would include systematic research design, collection, interpretation and reporting of information. Their purpose is to help their marketing managers solve specific problems or take advantage of business opportunities. An MR person helps in making well-informed decisions not based on guesswork.
- Let us see how your job as a MR person will help the company. To implement the marketing concept, marketers need information about the characteristics, needs, and wants of target customers. Your job as a Marketing researcher is to furnish practical and unbiased information so that your company can better its marketing performance.
- One major task given to a market researcher is to discover market opportunities. Once the research is complete, the MR guy must carefully evaluate its company's opportunities and the markets into which it should enter. If the company is already in the market, as an MR guy you should help marketing managers prepare the sales forecasts based on estimates of demand.
- Three developments make the need for marketing information greater now than at any time in the past:
  - The rise in global marketing
  - The new emphasis on buyers' wants, and
  - The trend towards non-price competition
- Companies can conduct their own marketing research or hire other companies to do it for them. For conducting a good marketing research is should be characterized by scientific method, creativity, multiple research methods, accurate model building, cost-benefit analysis, healthy skepticism and an ethical focus.
- To maintain the control needed to obtain accurate information marketers approach marketing research as a process with five logical steps:

1. **Locating and defining problems or issues**. To launch a research study, problem or issue definition, a good market researcher should focus on uncovering the nature and boundaries of a situation or question related to marketing strategy or implementation.
2. **Designing the research project**. In the second step, marketing researchers design a research project to obtain the information

needed to address it. This step requires formulating a hypothesis and determining what type of research to employ to test the hypothesis so the results are reliable and valid. A hypothesis is an informed guess or assumption about a problem or set of circumstances. The type of hypothesis being tested dictates whether an exploratory, descriptive, or causal approach will be used to gather data. Research is considered reliable if it produces almost identical results in repeated trials; it is valid if it measures what it is supposed to measure.

3. **Collecting data**. Two types of data are available to a market researcher i.e. Primary and Secondary. Primary data are observed and recorded or collected directly from respondents; secondary data are compiled inside or outside the organization for some purpose other than the current investigation.

4. **Interpreting research findings**

5. **Reporting research findings**

- In conducting research, an MR guy has to decide whether to collect their own data (i.e. Primary Data) or use data that already exist (i.e. Secondary Data). Sources of secondary data include an organization's own database and other internal sources, periodicals, government publications, unpublished sources, and online databases. Methods of collecting primary data include sampling, surveys, observation, and experimentation.
- Next Marketing Researcher should select representative units from a total population known as **Sampling**. In **probability sampling** every element in the population being studied has a known chance of being selected for study. **Non-probability sampling** is more subjective than probability sampling because there is no way to calculate the likelihood that a specific element of the population being studied will be chosen.
- Marketing researchers employ sampling to collect primary data through mail, telephone, online or personal interview surveys. A carefully constructed **questionnaire** is essential to the success of any survey. In using observation methods, researchers record respondents' overt behavior and take note of physical conditions and events. In an experiment, marketing researchers attempt to maintain certain variables while measuring the effects of experimental variables.
- To help marketers in effective decision making, it's important that a market researcher interpret the research data and report the findings properly—the final two steps in the marketing research process. **Statistical interpretation** focuses on what is typical or what deviates from the average. After interpreting the research findings, the researchers must prepare a report on the findings that the decision makers can understand and use. Researchers must also take care to avoid bias and distortion.
- Now a days many firms have developed a framework for the management and structuring of information gathered regularly from sources both inside and outside the organization by using computer technology known as **marketing information system (MIS)**, Database is a collection of information arranged for easy access and retrieval. A **marketing decision support system (MDSS)** is customized computer software that aids marketing managers in decision making by helping them anticipate the effects of certain decisions. Online information services and the Internet also enable marketers to communicate with customers and obtain information.
- To carry out their analysis, planning, implementation and control responsibilities, marketing managers need a marketing information system (MIS) which has four components:
  - An internal records system, which includes information on the order-to-payment cycle and sales reporting systems
  - A marketing intelligence system, a set of procedures and sources used by managers

to obtain everyday information about pertinent developments in the marketing environment

- A marketing research system that allows for the systematic design, collection, analysis and reporting of data and findings relevant to a specific marketing situation
- A computerized marketing decision support system that helps managers interpret relevant information and turn it into a basis for marketing action.

- There are two types of demand: market demand and company demand. To estimate current demand, companies attempt to determine total market potential, area market potential, industry sales and market share. To estimate future demand, companies survey buyers' intentions, solicit their salesforce's input, gather expert opinions, or engage in market testing. Mathematical models, advanced statistical techniques and computerized data collection procedures are essential to all types of demand and sales forecasting.
- Eliminating unethical marketing research practices and establishing generally acceptable procedures for conducting research are important goals of marketing research. Both domestic and international marketing use the same marketing research process, but international marketing may require modifying data-gathering methods to address regional differences.

Notes

Rockwell Automations: Researching Customer Perceptions

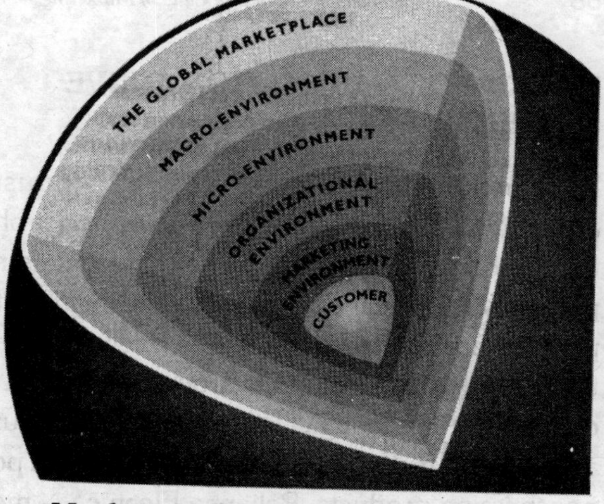

Marketing Research Case - 6

Purpose of the Case

The idea is to assimilate the relevant concepts at work and analyse in light of the following issues:

- How to use market research tools for ascertaining buying behavior towards various attributes/qualities for an industrial marketing outfit?
- How to fine-tune deliverables in order to meet customer expectations better based on market research findings?

AUTOMATION INDUSTRY

The automation industry is a knowledge-based industry. It is also a powerful growth engine that is supporting the economy in a big way. The industry itself is very dynamic in nature because no two customers are having same requirement and hence no two customers can be offered a same solution. It requires a lot of customization in terms of offering customer the solution so as to satisfy his requirement.

Another major factor though intangible up to an extent is to build confidence in customers to win order from him. A wrong selection of product/system may prove very costly for the customer because if by any chance the system fails, the entire production is stopped and may prove to be a very costly one. Therefore any company that claims to minimize these problems is really a bright light of hope. But the product/company will be able to find its right fate only when the efficacy and safety of the product is established and accepted by the Industry. It is only then that the customer will be able to understand and enjoy the benefits of such solutions/systems.

In a systems job, though price of a system plays quite an important role but it is not the only thing that matters to the customers. Through this study we intend to find, the factors that may play a decisive role in customer's mind at the time of awarding one out of many companies with their order. It is very important to understand what these other factors are and how much weightage does the customer assign to these factors.

This case is intended to be used as a basis for class discussion rather than as an illustration of either effective or ineffective handling of the situation. Authored by Dr. Mukesh Pandey.

ROCKWELL AUTOMATION DRIVE SYSTEM INDIA

Rockwell Automation is a global industrial automation company providing power, control and information solutions, which help customers meet productivity objectives. Leading brands and strategic partnerships uniquely qualify Rockwell Automation to deliver industry solutions around the world. The company brings together leading brands in industrial automation, including Dodge® - mechanical power transmission products, Reliance Electric™ - motors and drives, Allen-Bradley® - controls and engineered services and Rockwell Software® - Factory Management Software.

The company is also a leading provider of contact management technologies and applications; marketed under the Rockwell First Point Contact brands that help companies more efficiently manage interaction with their own customers. Global technical and customer service is an integral part of Rockwell Automation, with nearly 5,600 distributors, system integrators and agents serving customers in 80 countries.

In India, Rockwell Automation Drive Systems is the fourth largest supplier of custom engineered drive systems. It undertakes the automation of complete lines, which not only requires synchronization of various sections of the whole process but also needs complete customisation. High degree of expertise, is as such needed, to detect which of the lines are useful in producing different material/products and thus requires different engineering specifications.

Drive System involves using of not only drives but also other automation components like PLC (Programmable Logic Controller), MMI, Encoders, Communication Network, I/Os and several other bought out parts like Panels for mounting Drives etc. It also has to take care of other customer requirements as well. Drive System is a critical component as it is one of the few departments in the field of automation, which uses products of other departments as well.

THE COMPETITION PROFILE

1. Siemens: It has very aggressive pricing to gain market share. It strongly leverages their solution capability, using India as a "Centre of Excellence" to serve Asia Pacific market, thus leveraging their strong manufacturing base in India. Siemens is also planning to invest $ 500 Million for expanding Indian operations in near future.
2. Asea Brown Boveri: ABB is the Market leader in Drives and Drive Systems. The operations and marketing of ABB has been found to be very aggressive in Metals and Paper industry with aggressive pricing. India is their "Center of Excellence" for Metal Industries.
3. Schneider: Since 2000 onwards, Schneider has become very aggressive in Drives and TSX Range of PLC Products. Its major focus being localization, Schneider is acquiring local manufactures and thus promoting the locally designed/branded products. Again being an aggressive player in OEM Markets, it offers very flexible offers based on volume but it hasn't had much success till date.

COMMISSIONING MARKET RESEARCH

Faced with new aggressive competitive players, Rockwell conducted a research study to find out where they stand vis-à-vis their competitors in terms of customers' perception, with the following objectives:

1 Understanding Customer's value prospective, so as to satisfy him better.

2 Improve the business penetration in Drive System industry segment.

3 Partner with customer to maximize their value chain.

4 Rockwell also focussed on improving the business penetration in Drive System industry segment with the aim of becoming a market leader in the segment.

Through this study, the company was also aiming to find out if any correlation existed between the perception of the buyer and the category he was representing.

Towards this end, Rockwell decided to first ascertain if the attributes/qualities that a buyer values varied across different segments or remained the same. As such, different factors that Rockwell decided to evaluate were short-listed as follows:

1. Buying behavior across the different types of industries viz. Metals, Pulp and Paper, Tire & Rubber, Infrastructure, Converting Lines and Fibres.
2. Buying behavior across End User/OEMs.
3. Buying behavior across Economic Buyer/ Technical Buyer#/both.
4. Buying behavior across the size of the company viz. < 700 Crore, > 700 Crore and < 2500 Crore and > 2500 Crore.
5. Importance that the end users assign to OEM's specification and vice versa.
6. Customer's approach in selecting an automation vendor.
7. The customer's viewpoint on the best method to judge company's capabilities.

Economic Buyer is the person, who has a real decision making power.

Technical Buyer is the person, who mainly acts as a gatekeeper. He mainly short-lists 2 to 3 suppliers out of which the economic buyer decides finally.

SCOPE OF THE STUDY

Rockwell Automation Drive Systems short-listed the following six Industries, namely

1. Metals
2. Fibre
3. Pulp and Paper
4. Tire and Rubber
5. Converting Lines
6. Infrastructure

This selection was done because Rockwell is serving mainly the above six industries in India right now.

Ensuring representativeness of sample: Out of the above-mentioned industries also, 'metals' are the biggest consumer/buyer of Drive Systems and were thus given maximum focus. To ensure representativeness of the sample selected, companies from above six segments were selected in proportion to their offtake from Rockwell. Since, the metals segment companies were buying more than 50 per cent of the Drive Systems, around 50 per cent of the interviews were conducted in Metals industries.

DESIGNING QUESTIONNAIRES

Rockwell prepared a questionnaire on the basis of their objectives and conducted number of personal interviews, in order to gather data for the same. The Systems jobs are generally big in size and require technical expertise as such both the deciding authorities viz. The Economic Buyer and The Technical Buyer were interviewed. The final Questionnaire that was administered after pretesting is enclosed as per Annexure-1.

MAJOR FINDINGS/DEVELOPMENTS

On the basis of the study conducted followed by a thorough analysis, Rockwell came to a number of important findings, viz.

1. Rockwell found that the top six factors viz. performance, support, past performance, reliability & ruggedness of the system, dependability and price influence almost 80 per cent of the customer's buying decision.
2. Another important finding was that price is an important criterion, but performance and past performance together are more important then the price.
3. OEMs were found to be more price sensitive then the end users. At the same time, Paper and CPI were the two segments that were found to be very price sensitive.

4. Since the Drive Systems deal with complete systems job, influence of Technical Buyer is high. At the same time, Rockwell found that, advertisement; newsletters are not important players in getting orders. Recommendations & Past Performance were found to be more important, thus corroborating the old saying that "A satisfied customer is your best unpaid salesman."
5. A very interesting finding that came up was that the entry barriers were quite high due to factors like performance and past performance.

Questions

1. Should Rockwell continue with its differentiation strategy rather than fighting on price in new, aggressive competitive scenario?
2. How can Rockwell satisfy and retain the price-sensitive OEM buyers?
3. What kind of promotional programs do you suggest Rockwell should undertake?

ANNEXURE 1

QUESTIONNAIRE

1 Name of Organisation

2 Activities OEM ( )

End User ( )

3 Type of industry Metal Fibres Infrastructure Pulp & Paper Tyre & Rubber Consumer Product

4 Name of the Person Visited

5 Designation

6 Whether Economic Buyer Technical Buyer Both

7 Size of the Organization

8 Major Automation System Suppliers

		Approx. %
RAIL	( )	( )
ABB	( )	( )
Siemens	( )	( )
C T	( )	( )
L&T	( )	( )
Others	( )	( )

9 How would you like to grade the above mentioned criterion while making the purchase decision. Total = 100

A Performance ( )
B Brand Image ( )
C Support ( )
D Past Performance ( )
E Consultant's / Project Builders' Recommendation / End Users' Recommendation ( )
F OEM's Specification ( )
G Accesability of Sales & Support ( )
H Reliability / Ruggedness (in terms of Products / System) ( )
I Total Cost of Ownership ( )
J Upgradability ( )
K Approachability / Responsiveness ( )
L Dependability (in terms of Service / Team) ( )
M Price ( )

10 In a new project how do you select a control vendor

A Website ( )
B Advertisement ( )
C Newsletters ( )
D Catalogues ( )
E Recommendation by OEM / Consultants ( )
F Past Performances ( )

11 Best method of knowing Company's Capability

A Exhibition ( )
B Advertisement ( )
C Mailers ( )
D Salesmen ( )
E References from people in similar industries ( )

12 Frequency of RA salesperson calling you

13 Do you know the complete range of products supplied by Rockwell?

Notes

Product

Section - Six

CONCEPTUAL FRAMEWORK

To facilitate a better debate on the cases in this section, a quick exploratory review of the product ingredient of the marketing mix (consisting of product, distribution, promotion and price) along with areas that need discussion are recapitulated briefly as follows:

- Product is the first and most important element of the marketing mix in the hands of a marketing manager. The basic concepts and relationships must be understood to make effective product decisions.
- A product is a good, a service, an idea or any combination of the three. It includes functional, social and psychological utilities or benefits. A **good** is a tangible physical entity. A **service**, in contrast, is intangible. It is the result of the application of human and mechanical efforts to people or objects. An **idea** is a concept, philosophy, image, or issue. Ideas provide the psychological stimulation that aids in solving problems or adjusting to the environment.
- Marketers classify products in several ways. In terms of durability and reliability, products can be **non-durable goods**, **durable goods**, or services. On the basis of the buyer's intentions, we can have **consumer products**, industrial goods and business services, etc. Consumer products can be subdivided into convenience (staples, impulse goods, emergency goods), shopping (homogeneous and heterogeneous), specialty (cars, stereo components, photographic equipment) and unsought (life insurance, encyclopedias) products.
- Business products or **industrial goods** can be classified as installations, accessory equipment, raw materials, component parts, process materials, MRO (maintenance, repair and operating) supplies, and business services.
- A product item is a specific version of a product that can be designated as a distinct offering among an organization's products. A **product line** is a group of closely related product items that are considered a unit because of marketing, technical or end-use considerations.
- The composite, or total group of products that an organization makes available to customers is called the **product mix**. The width of the product mix is measured by the number of product lines the company offers. The depth of a product mix is the average number of different products offered in each product line.
- Marketers uses **product life cycle** so as to study how product items in an industry moves through four stages: **introduction, growth, maturity** and **decline**. The life cycle concept is used to

ensure that the introduction, alteration and termination of a product are timed and executed properly. The sales curve is at zero at introduction, rises at an increasing rate during growth, peaks at maturity and then declines. Profits peak toward the end of the growth stage of the product life cycle.

- The life expectancy of a product is based on buyers' wants, the availability of competing products and other environmental conditions. Most businesses have a composite of life cycle patterns for various products. A good marketing manager manages existing products and develops new ones in a company, which have a direct relation with keeping the overall sales performance at a desired level.
- Customers who eventually accept a new product do so through a five-stage adoption process. The stages of the product adoption process are as follows:
  - **Awareness**. The buyer becomes aware of the product.
  - **Interest**. The buyer seeks information and is receptive to learning about the product.
  - **Evaluation**. The buyer considers the product's benefits and decides whether to try it.
  - **Trial**. The buyer examines, tests or tries the product to determine if it meets his or her needs.
  - **Adoption**. The buyer purchases the product and can be expected to use it again whenever the need for this general type of product arises.
- A product manager's functions include line extensions and product modification, new-product development and product deletions. Organizations must be able to adjust their product mixes to compete effectively and achieve their goals.
- A product mix can be improved through line extension and through product, quality, functional or aesthetic modifications as indicated herebelow:
  - A **line extension** is the development of a product closely related to one or more products in the existing line but designed specifically to meet different customer needs.
  - **Product modification** is the changing of one or more characteristics of a product. This approach can be effective when the product is modifiable, when customers can perceive the change and when customers want the modification.
  - **Quality modifications** relate to a product's dependability and durability.
  - **Functional modifications** affect a product's versatility, effectiveness, convenience or safety.
  - **Aesthetic modifications** change the sensory appeal of a product.
- Developing new products can enhance a firm's product mix and add depth to the product line. A new product may be an innovation that has never been sold by any organization; a product that a given firm has not marketed previously, although similar products may have been available from other organizations, or a product brought from one market to another.
- Before a product is introduced, it goes through a seven-phase new-product development process as follows:
  - In the **idea generation** phase, new-product ideas are generated. These may originate from internal or external sources.
  - In the process of **screening,** ideas are evaluated to determine whether they are consistent with the firm's overall objectives and resources.
  - **Concept testing**, the third phase, involves having a small sample of potential customers review a brief description of the product idea to determine their initial perceptions of the proposed product and their early buying intentions. For a single product idea, an organization can test one or several concepts of the same product.
  - During the business analysis stage, the

product idea is evaluated to determine its potential contribution to the firm's sales, costs and profits.

- **Product development** is the phase in which the organization determines if it is technically feasible to produce the product and if it can be produced at costs low enough to make the final price reasonable. To test its acceptability, the idea or concept is converted into a prototype, or working model.
- A limited introduction of a product in geographical areas chosen to represent the intended market is called test marketing. Its aim is to determine the extent to which potential customers will buy the product.
- Finally, in the commercialization phase, full-scale production of the product begins and a complete marketing strategy is developed.

Product differentiation is the process of creating and designing products so that customers perceive them as different from competing products. Product quality, product design and features, and product support services are three aspects of product differentiation that companies consider when creating and marketing products.

Notes

Scorpio from Mahindra: Geared up for Success

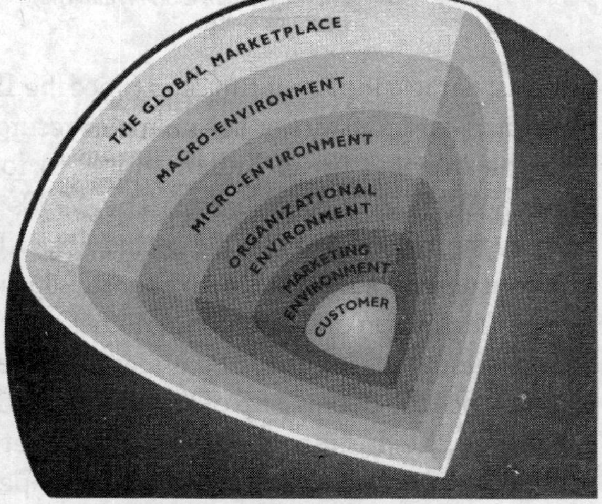

Product Case - 8

Purpose of the Case

The idea is to assimilate the relevant concepts at work and analyse in light of the following issues:

- How is new product development process initiated?
- What constitutes a successful product launch?
- How can a value proposition be strengthened with strategic branding?

From the singsong rhythm of the bullock cart to the jet-age, India has traveled a long way, It was in 1898 that the first motorcar rode down India's roads. From then till the First World War, about 4,000 cars were directly imported to India from foreign manufacturers The Hindustan Motors (HM) was set up in 1942 and in 1944, Premier Automobile (PAL) was established to manufacture automobiles in India. However, it was PAL who produced the first car in India in 1946, as HM concentrated on auto components and could produce their first car only in 1949.

Today most international car manufacturers have entered the Indian market. As it is one of the fastest growing economies in the world and it's automobile industry is one of the fastest growing in Asia With the opening of the economy since 1991, and with Quantitative Restrictions being removed, imports have become more liberalized. A growth in production of over 16 per cent in the year 1999 - 2000 and an estimated growth of 20 per cent in 2001 - 2002 have led to an increased supply of cars. With globalization and increasing purchasing power, Indian consumers are demanding the latest in automobiles and automotive technology.

As India provides excellent global technologies, most international Car Manufacturers can access these through joint ventures with India. In fact, many international brands of cars, which are produced in India, contain more than 70 per cent locally produced parts. Most multi nationals have started exporting components made in India to their other plants around the world, thus increasing investment to make India a major manufacturing base.

It was left to another company, Mahindra and Mahindra (M&M) to manufacture sturdier utility

This case is intended to be used as a basis for class discussion rather than as an illustration of either effective or ineffective handling of the situation. Authored by Dr. Mukesh Pandey.

vehicles, namely the American Jeep.Since the 1980s, the Indian car industry has seen a major resurgence with the opening up of Indian shores to foreign manufacturers and collaborators.The 1990s have become the melting point for the car industry in India. The consumer is king. He is being constantly wooed by both the Indian and foreign manufacturers. The Indian automobile industry had undergone a radical change since the opening up of its economy in 1991. By 1997, the Indian automobile market was probably one of the most open and competitive automobile markets in the world, with all major global players having a presence there. New models like Maruti's Classic, Alto, Station WagonR,Hyundai Santro, Ford's Ikon,Fiat's Palio, the new look Mitsubishi Lancer etc.are all being launched with an eye on the emerging market.

Some interesting facts about the Indian Automobile Industry:

- India is the 2nd largest two-wheeler manufacturer in the world
- India is the 2nd largest tractor manufacturer in the world
- India is the 5th largest commercial vehicle manufacturer in the world
- India is the 3rd largest car market in Asia.

The automobile industry in India offers significant employment opportunities. The automobile industry including component industry employs 0.45 million people directly and around 10 million people indirectly.

The auto industry recorded a turnover of US$ 10 billion while the auto-component industry recorded a turnover of US$ 2.7 billion in 1999-2000.

- India's largest car-maker Maruti Udyog Ltd (MUL) was privatized in 2002 with Suzuki Motor Corporation moving into the driving seat after acquiring a majority stake and management control in the Maruti Suzuki joint venture .

POLICY INITIATIVES

Auto policy announced by the government in 2002 has opened the automobile sector to 100 per cent foreign direct investment and removed the minimum capital investment norm for fresh entrants. This will benefit manufacturers who are planning to enter the Indian market, particularly in the burgeoning motorcycle market.

- The new policy has taken into account the need to address emerging problems and make the auto sector WTO compatible.
- The policy is also in favour of providing excise duty concessions to small cars, multi-utility vehicles and low emission vehicles. It envisages India becoming a major hub for the manufacture of small cars and a global supplier of components. The policy also includes incentives to facilitate R&D.
- Import tariffs are to be fixed in a manner so as to promote manufacturing in India, as opposed to mere assembly, without giving undue protection to domestic industry. While ensuring a balanced transition towards open trade, the automotive tariff structure will be reviewed periodically to prevent India from becoming a 'dumping ground' for international rejects.

OPPORTUNITIES

- India enjoys a distinct cost advantage with respect to auto-ancillary manufacturing capabilities. While developed nation's labour cost component is 30-35 per cent of sales,

Indian labour cost is only around 8-9 per cent of sales.

- The number of vehicles manufactured in India has risen from 3 million units annually in 1999 to 5 million units in 2002. This has also led to an increase in domestic demand for automotive components.

MAJOR PLAYERS IN THE INDIAN AUTOMOBILE (CAR) MARKET ARE

- Maruti
- Hyundai
- Tata
- Ford
- Hindustan Motors
- Mahindra & Mahindra(M&M) etc

In the car industry 90.2 per cent share is held by Economy segment and the rest is held by mid size and Luxury segment.

In the arena of cars, A-segment cars, which have been the leaders in terms of volumes and grew at the rate of 55.2 percent in the year 1999, were having a reduced growth rate of 34.2 percent in the year 2001. It was found that the fastest growing segment (growing at the rate of 42.9 per cent) in year 2001 was semi luxurious cars or B segment cars. And the luxurious car segment i.e. C segment cars were also growing at a healthy rate of 14.2 percent in that year. However, super premium cars termed as segment D and E cars, were not growing at such healthy rates and did not offer volume in terms of number of cars sold.

MULTI UTILITY VEHICLES: CUSTOMER'S NEW FANCY

The multi-utility vehicle (MUV) as the name suggests can be used for transporting goods as well as passengers over medium and small distances The name Multi Utility Vehicle (MUV) is derived from the vehicles used by the US Army in World War II called "General Purpose" vehicles due to their variety of uses. American Motor Company (later acquired by Chrysler Corporation) introduced the MUVs to the world with brand "Willys".

The MUV is used in transporting smaller loads over medium and small distances, providing low fixed and operating costs in comparison to LCVs. It can be used for transporting both goods and passengers. Apart from these it can be converted into an ambulance, a minivan, a pickup van or leisure vehicle.The army is a major consumer segment. It uses MUVs for variety of uses like mounting recoil-less guns, transporting explosives, towing equipment like DG sets, gun carriers, etc.

Earlier MUVs neither got much attention from the customers nor have they tried to do so. About the only attention they have got is from the government, and that has not always been of the good kind. But all this is changing now with the MUVs suddenly catching the fancy of the market and manufacturers, including global majors.

They can be classified as

Soft tops (or canvas / PVC tops)

Hard tops

Pick-ups

The conventional UV market was too small in India, the percentage of MUVs in the total car market still accounts for a meager 16 per cent as compared to say 51 per cent in the US markets and 40 per cent of the Asian markets. Hence, there still exists a large gap in demand for these vehicles in the context of above ratios. In the US markets, the MUV market is as big as the passenger car market.

Production in Indian Industry can be seen from the graph

MAJOR PLAYERS IN THE INDIAN UV MARKET ARE:

Mahindra & Mahindra: Their product range includes

- Jeep
- Scorpio
- Marshal etc.

Tata: Their product range includes

- Tata Safari
- Tata Sierra

- Tata Sumo

Toyota: Their product range includes

- Toyota Qualis

MARKET DYNAMICS

In the 1990's,the sales of soft tops MUVs were found to be stagnating. Hard top vehicles were garnering market share. The urban market was showing more potential for vehicle sales and UVs were gaining higher acceptability in urban cities. The competition was getting tougher with international UVs entering the market. And also operating in the urban market meant competing with cars.The market was moving from traditional multi utility, non-luxurious vehicles to luxurious vehicles. UV as a percentage of the overall passenger car market was just 16 per cent in 2001; this simply meant that for attaining the volumes,a vehicle should be designed beyond UVs in terms of competitive framework.

CONSUMER PERSPECTIVE FOR UV

A study conducted to understand the UV customer by advertising agency 'Interface Communication' revealed the following criterion of consumer buying process

- Customer preferred big size as it stands for status.
- Consumers seek latest technology.
- Customer wants the sheer thrill and passion of driving an SUV but at affordable prices.

Indian Car Market

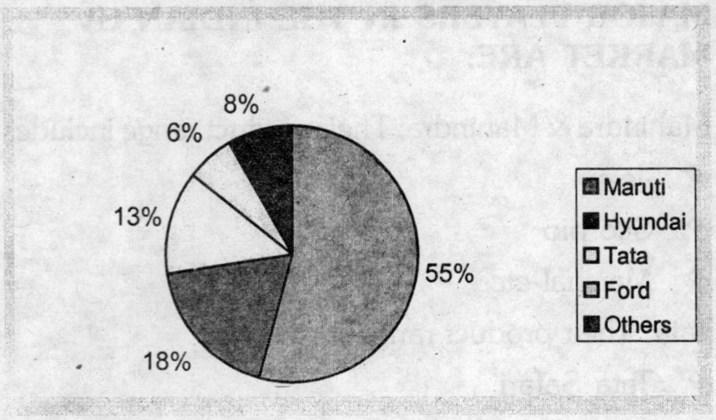

source - siam.org

Segmentation of the Cars

Category	Models
A segment	Omni, Maruti 800
B segment	Fiat Uno, Maruti Zen, Maruti Alta, Maruti Wagon R Hyundai Santro, Daewoo Matiz, Tata Indica,
B+ segment	Fiat Palio
Lower C segment	Maruti Esteem, Ford Ikon, Fiat Siena, Opel Corsa, Daewoo Nexia, Hyundai Accent, Tata Indigo, Hindustan Ambassador
Upper C segment	Opel Astra, Honda City, Toyota Corolla, Mitsubishi Lancer
D segment	Skoda Octavia, Opel Vectra, Toyota Camry, Ford Mondeo, Honda Accord, Mercedes C class
E segment	Mercedes E class
Luxury segment	Mercedes S class

Category	Models
Economy segment (up to Rs.0.25mn)	Maruti Omni, Maruti 800,
Mid-size segment (Rs.0.25-0.45 mn)	Hindustan Ambassador, Fiat Uno, Zen, Hyundai Santro, Tata Indica, Wagon R, Alto
Luxury segment (Rs.0.45-1 mn)	Maruti Esteem, Honda City, Mitsubishi Lancer, Ford Ikon, Opel Astra, Fiat Sienna, Opel Corsa. Hyundai Accent, Maruti Versa, Skoda, Tata Indigo
Super luxury segment (Above Rs. 1 mn).	Hyundai Sonata, Honda Accord, Toyota Corolla, Toyota Camry, Opel Vectra, Ford Mondeo, Mercedes Benz and other imported models

- Power of the vehicle is a differentiating factor in the customer mind.
- Luxury served as a very important parameter.
- They feel that international vehicles define imagery.

- SUVs like Pajero, Land Cruiser and Prado are seen as urban vehicles for the rich and famous.
- Consumers aspire to own these vehicles as the imagery of these vehicles has become very desirable
- The Key Consumer Insight that emerged from all the consumer analysis and which was used for strategy development was "Consumers want to consume premium imagery at prices affordable to them.

Car Production in India

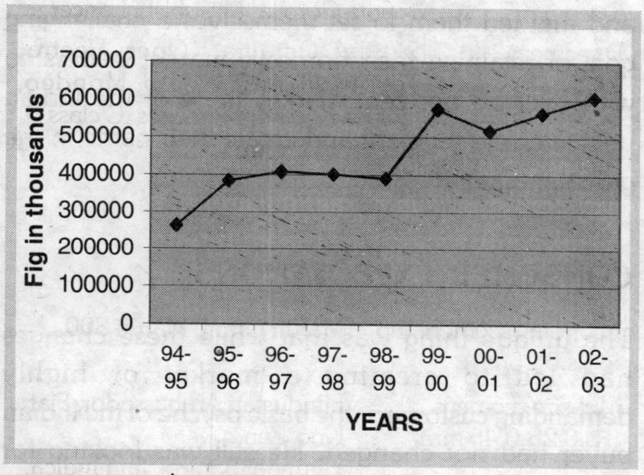

source - www.siam.org

MAHINDRA CONTEXT

In late 1990's Mahindra, a leader in the UV segment, was fast witnessing loss of market share. Global players were entering the auto market and aggressively launching products. The Mahindra share of business was largely from the semi urban and rural markets of India. A large contribution of

Car Market Scenario

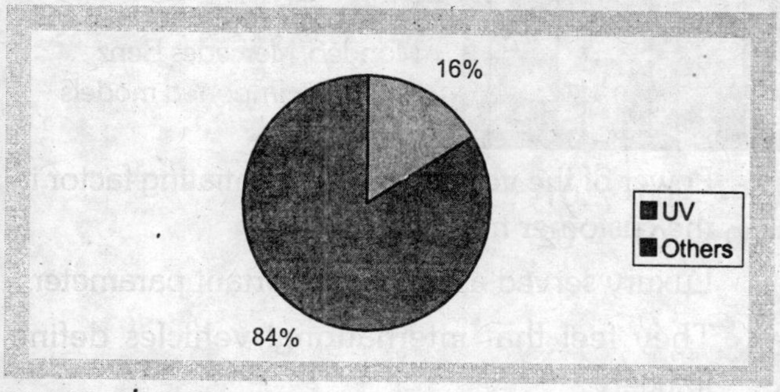

source - siam.org

Mahindra sales also co me from institutional sales-army, police, paramilitary gro-ups and other institutional gro-ups. Though Mahi-ndra had a wide product portfolio, what it was lacking was products that catered to the modern urban consumer needs. The markets where Mahindra was strong were stagnating. The urban markets where it did not have a product to offer were seeing all the growth and action.

The Mahindra image was a big barrier as well. Though it had positives as rugged, tough, reliable, economical vehicles, the brand was not seen as modern or technologically advanced. The negative parameters were : uncomfortable, rough, not easy-to-drive, rural imagery, down market, fuddy-duddy, etc

When Mahindra started to lose its market share because of above mentioned problems they decided to launch a product with the following objectives:

1. To create a new segment and retain market domination
2. To differentiate offering (vis-a vis MNCs)-i.e. to provide an excellent value proposition to the customer
3. To optimize project costs

Countrywise penetration of MUV's to total cars market

Korea	49
China	54
Thailand	67
Indonesia	80
Philipines	63
Asia average	40
India	16
USA	51

In the UV market there existed a gap that wasn't tapped. There was no SUV in the country that the masses could buy.Based on consumer research, Mahindra found that to make SUVs a mass concept in India -UVs needed to be seen as comfortable, easy-for-city-driving and should have imagery comparable to international brands.

India: Company market share in MUVs

Company	FY97	FY98	FY99	FY00	FY01	FY02
M&M	71.6%	52.2%	58.0%	58.7%	44.9%	46.2%
HM	3.1%	6.6%	4.1%	2.2%	1.9%	2.7%
Maruti	2.7%	2.6%	4.5%	7.3%	4.9%	4.8%
Bajaj Tempo	8.6%	5.8%	5.3%	5.1%	3.9%	4.2%
Telco	14.0%	32.7%	28.0%	26.7%	24.4%	21.7%
Toyota	-	-	-	-	20.0%	20.4%

source - mahindra.com

This marks the beginning of Scorpio story, Scorpio story started in 1997 with a vision - a vision to continue the domination of the Utility vehicle (UV) market in India; to be a global niche player. This vision also clarified that M&M would focus on the niche UV market and, hence, would not directly participate in the car market.

Its founders passionately believed that Indians are second to none. They had a dream: to make M&M known worldwide for the quality, durability and reliability of its products and services and at the same time play an active role in the development of the nation. The current management held this dream and vision as an integral part of their existence

UV Production in India

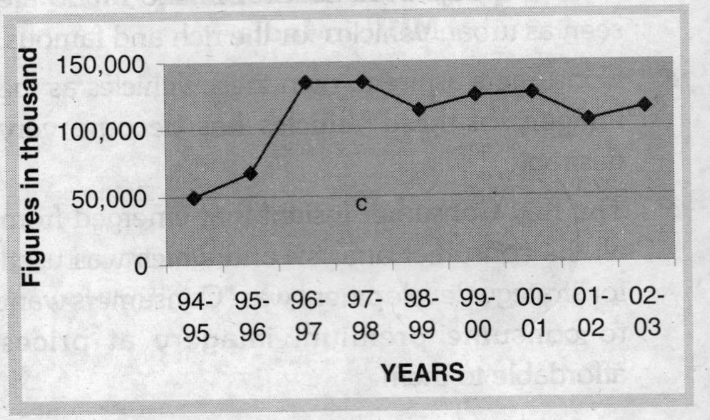

source - siam.org

and that led them to set themselves a challenging goal of retaining their domestic market leadership with over 50 per cent market share of the Indian utility vehicle segment and create their name in the global market.

CONSUMER EXPECTATIONS

The unique thing was that while these changes had led to creating a market of highly demanding customers, the basic psyche of the Indian buyer had not changed. He still was looking for Value for Money, VFM, in terms of low unit cost, operating economics packaged with modern style and robust design.

Car Production vs UV Production

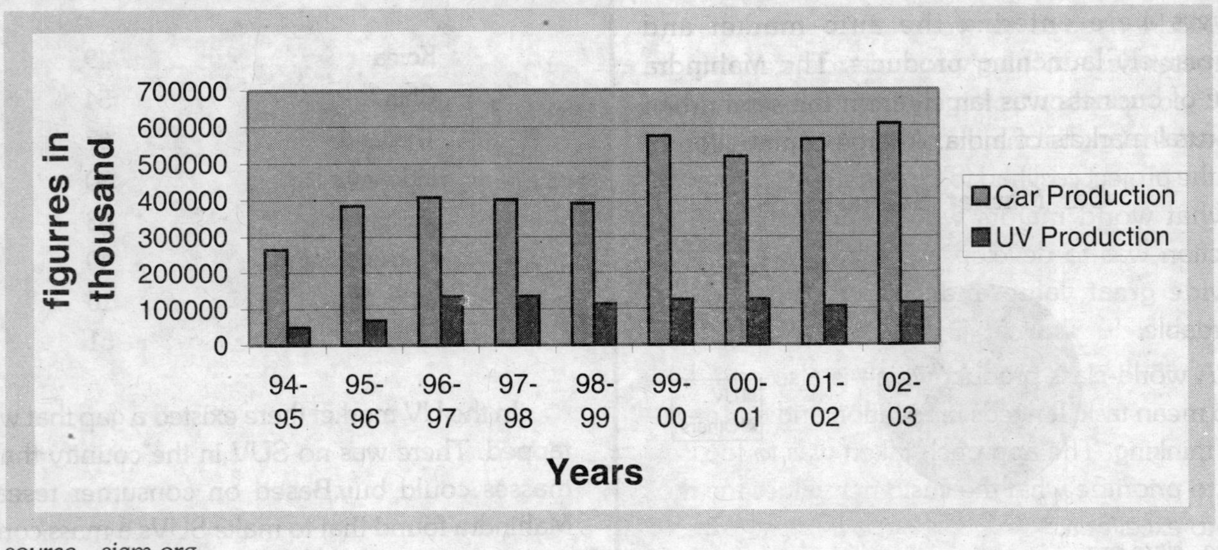

source - siam.org

Company wise market share of MUV in India

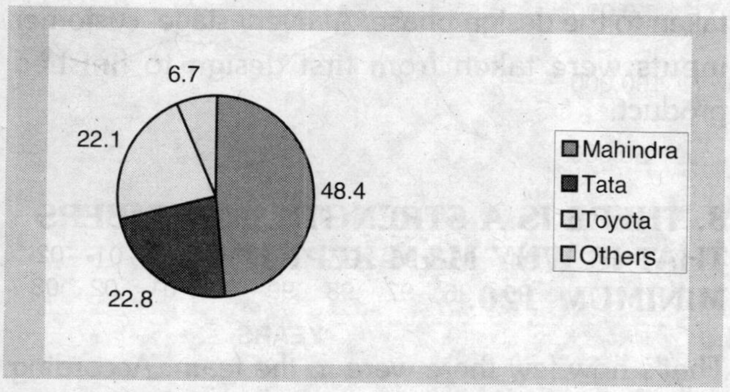

source - siam.org

STRATEGIC INTERFACE WITH THE MARKET

With the above reality as a backdrop, M&M defined a two-pronged strategy for the Automotive Sector:

- Continue to dominate the rural and semi-urban market with a range of products catering to the needs for low-cost mass transportation needs.
- Develop a strong presence in the fast growing urban markets with a range of value for money products.

To compete against the global players and also to meet its goal of developing a strong presence in the urban market, M&M embarked on Project Scorpio.

M&M needed to work to its strengths and competencies. To find ways of side-stepping the MNC competition for it did not have the deep pockets that global majors did. The implication was that the project cost had to be optimised to a fraction of what world majors would spend. The other direction was to develop a product, which would provide great value and hence would be very affordable.

A world-class product which is also affordable is no mean task. It needs innovation and out-of-the-box thinking. The approach taken was to focus on and to prioritize what the customer values the most and to excel at it.

PROJECT SCORPIO: CREATING A WORLD CLASS, YET INDIAN PRODUCT

M&M developed a new product to meet the above objectives and to create a world class product. Key achievements of the product development process were as follows:

- A unique process called IDAM (Integrated Design and Manufacturing)
- Best in the world tie-ups but in-house execution
- Customer focus from thought to finish
- A cross-functional, co-located, young, lean team
- Lowest Project Costs
- Intensive Testing
- All,new Manufacturing Set up

It is easier to make what you can sell than to sell what you have made. That was the guiding force of IDAM

Integrated Design and Manufacturing (IDAM), is a product development process, which was adopted by M&M to streamline the delivery of a world class, zero-defect, trouble-free product to the customer. It encompasses the entire value chain starting and ending with the customer. This outside-in approach ensures that the product is designed around the customer and not vice versa.

Unlike the traditional department structure, the IDAM team consisted of cross-functional teams, co-located in the IDAM Centre in Mumbai. These teams had cross-functional strengths that covered every aspect of product development, from 'Design & Development, Testing & Validation and Manufacturing' to 'Vendor Development and Marketing.'

1. GLOBAL ALLIANCES FOR BEST OF THE WORLD INPUTS

M&M tied up with the best in the world in their respective areas of the global auto industry. Fukui, Japan for the Press shop. Fuji, Japan for the Dies. Korean company Wooshin for body shop. Fori Automation, USA for the tester line for

Project Scorpio: Milestones

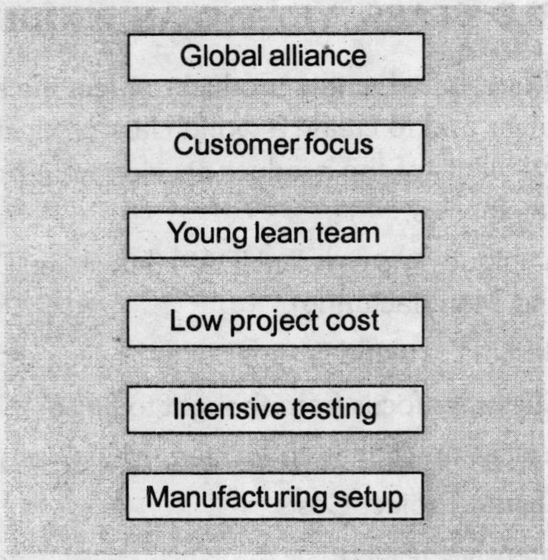

final assembly. Durr Germany for the paint shop. Lear, USA for Seats and interiors. Visteon, USA for exteriors. Samlip, Korea for suspension and BEHR, Germany for AC. M&M tied up with Renault for petrol engines.

M&M facilitated the development of these aggregates and played the role of an integrator. The vendors set up facilities in and around the factory. The end result was a fully indigenous product with international quality at affordable price. The most heartening of it all was the fact that not only was M&M a staunch follower of the IDAM concept but even logistic support companies, vendors and dealers bought into it wholeheartedly. This synchronicity in commitment aided efficient implementation and guaranteed success. Mahindra didn't compromise on international quality and at the same time ensured that the product was fully Indian.

2. CUSTOMER FOCUS- FROM THOUGHT TO FINISH

The first step was to trap customer requirements and map the market potential of the various vehicle categories. For this purpose, the in-house team visited the market and met customers from various segments. As a result, key buying factors were evolved through the Quality Function Deployment process (QFD). These customer requirements were then converted into product specifications and were taken to the design phase. At every stage, customer inputs were taken from first design to finished product.

3. THERE IS A STRENGTH IN NUMBERS THAT IS WHY M&M KEPT IT TO MINIMUM 120.

That's how few there were in the team. According to industry standards that figure was scandalous. But it worked. And the management knew it would. This team had an average age of 27 so while there was immense drive Project Scorpio had just 120 people. These people worked in tandem, round the clock to develop a product unsurpassable in its design and manufacturing. The IDAM team for Scorpio was divided into 19 cross-functional design teams with people from design & development, testing & validation, marketing, manufacturing and supplier development.

4.LOW PROJECT COST

A project cost of 120 million US Dollars may seem to be high. But it's only a fifth of what a world major would have spent on a similar-sized project. A typical ground up, new platform project would have cost 500 million dollars. This low cost was achieved by a series of innovative decisions.

5.INTENSIVE TESTING

Seventy four vehicles were built only for testing. Then using the Simultaneous Testing & Examination Process (STEP), they were tested and re-tested. To check every component till only the best combination of form and function was left. Then the vehicle itself, as a whole, was put through the NOVA-C (New Overall Vehicle Audit-Customer) system to measure the overall quality of the production process itself. Thus, the Scorpio was put through some of the most grueling tests.

6. MANUFACTURING SET UP

A world-class manufacturing facility spread over 120 acres with a capacity of producing 40,000 units on a 2 shift basis was set up in Nashik with an investment of USD 120 million.

Infrastructure-wise, three new, state-of-the-art lines had been set-up for Scorpio:

1. A fully automated press shop set-up with help from Fukui of Japan with Dies imported from Fuji, Japan to ensure quality output delivery.
2. The jig and fixtures in the body shop were developed with Wooshin of Korea, also on an automated line, equipped with CMM to ensure a high quality final output with excellent fit and finish.
3. A state-of-the-art Trim Chassis Final (TCF) line with a world class tester line, built in collaboration with Fori Automation USA for vigorous testing from the wheel alignment to squeak and rattle test. The paint shop was set-up in collaboration with Durr of Germany. The final assembly and testing is done on the TCF line. The programmed logistics and flexible manufacturing system can accommodate a large number of variants in the product mix. This fully conveyorised system with minimum handling and effort combined with continuous improvement training for the workers ensures a quality product at the end of the line.

MARKETING STRATEGY: TO CREATE A MARKET CATEGORY

The following objectives were set for Scorpio:

First year of launch

To capture 22 per cent of the premium hard top market in F03 (9 months)

- To sell 12,000 Scorpios in F03 (9 months)
- To increase Mahindra unaided brand recall score by 22 points (defined in terms of Brand Track study scores)
- To make Scorpio brand recall score to achieve 50 points

Within three years of launch

- *To capture 45 per cent of the premium hard top market*
- To sell 24,000 units in F04
- To make Mahindra emerge as a true urban player

Strategic Branding Approach

Therefore, as a strategy it was decided that Scorpio would not take the traditional UV imagery of tough, off-roading and 4x4. A 4x4 approach would be a very niche category and would not generate numbers. To appeal to a car buyer, the Scorpio needed to be seen as a car that offers much more. A Scorpio had to be seen as providing car-like driving pleasure and at the same time providing the edge over cars in space, power, style, fuel efficiency, luxury and comfort. In short, to provide status of a Pajero (international SUV) at the price of midsize car. The Scorpio product package offered - Superior technology, Dynamic Looks, Car-like product and great value for the price.

Value Proposition for Scorpio

To capture the identified need gap, the value proposition of Scorpio was defined as -

'Car plus'

Rational benefits: World class vehicle, good looks, car like comfort, great value Emotional benefits: Ownership experience of thrill, excitement and power Relational benefits: Young,modern, premium, city companion / extension of lifestyle. Brand Promise: 'Luxury of a car. Thrill of an SUV' This brand positioning addresses the key consumer insight and the product delivers the promise. The position is also a unique proposition, which will help the brand have a distinct image in the consumer's mind.

Baseline - "Nothing Else Will do"

The baseline captures the essence of the brand, which is superiority and uncompromising attitude. It also summarizes the spirit behind the making of the Scorpio.

Brand Strategy - Parent brand relationship defining A study of international brand names was done and a classification of brand names of midsize cars and SUVs was done into groups. International brand naming trends and strategies were analyzed. New names were generated. These brand names were researched massively first by qualitative techniques and then by quantitative techniques. The name that emerged as most popular, and which was also the most liked name internally at Mahindra was SCORPIO.

Brand Endorsement Strategy

The relation between Scorpio and the mother brand Mahindra was also deliberated upon. The strategy chosen for Brand Endorsement was - Scorpio from Mahindra - shadow endorsement, one which does not shout "Mahindra." The Mahindra brand image was not modern and young. There was a need to create a strong distinct modern brand. Hence Mahindra as a Masterbrand could not contribute towards enhancing the Value Proposition. Yet Mahindra had to provide source reassurance. Also, the distribution would be through Mahindra dealerships. Hence it became a shadow endorser.

Advertising and Promotions Strategy

The creative strategy was to drive home the 'Car Plus' positioning forward. There was a need to leverage on product strengths. And a need to establish car plus story. Hence the product was to be the hero in all communications. The tone and manner was to help associate the brand with the modern and urban lifestyle. The TVCs as well as the press still-shots were shot in Australia to provide an international city feel. This brought in the international, premium, up-market association for the brand.

Media Strategy

Role of Media

- Dramatic and high impact launch
- High visibility
- Push brand image even by the media vehicle

Building impact through multiple-media

- PR, Mass Media, Direct Marketing, Events

Public Relations

Pre-launch excitement and buzz was created by a full blown PR program. Media coverage on the IDAM process, the people behind the Scorpio, the obsession, the world class technology, etc set the tone for the hyped up launch. PR was also the first tool used for launching the Scorpio. The coverage of the launch was massive. It got four cover stories.

Mass Media

'While the media targets would be achieved through the right selection of the media mix, the Scorpio media posture was to ensure that Scorpio was present on the decided media but 'with a difference.' Scorpio would use media innovations to create differentiation on the traditional media and do things in a 'bigger and better' manner.

Customer Relationship Management (CRM)

CRM as a tool was used to create positive word-of-mouth, to monitor customer experiences and generate referrals. A series of CRM activities were implemented with regular direct communication, events and customer research. The CRM plan included a welcome Pack on filling up Scorpio Club (Top Gear) form, satisfaction surveys, Events, Festive offers, Rewards Program, etc.

Pricing Strategy: to be a premium brand yet having universal appeal

Scorpio was to compete with the midsize cars like Hyundai Accent, Ford Ikon, Opel Corsa, Maruti Suzuki Esteem on the one side and UVs like Toyota

Qualis, Tata Safari and the Tata Sumo on the other. Scorpio adopted the penetrative pricing strategy positioned in the psychological price barrier of Rs. 5 -7 Lakhs.

Distribution Strategy - Serve less markets at a time but serve them well

Since the Scorpio was targetted at an urban clientele it needed a stronger ditribution presence in Metros and urban areas. Hence, the distribution channel had to focus on providing an appealing experience for modern car buyers and on offering international standards of auto retail.

Phased Launch

The Scorpio was launched in a phased manner - first in Metros (Mumbai, Delhi, Bangalore, Chennai). Twenty cities were included over a period of 4 months and within a year 50 cities were covered. This ensured attention to main markets and to ensure that initial production of the vehicle could match demand. Dealerships were revamped prior to launch in a particular city.

Showroom Experience

The showroom revamp was centred around the intention to provide a uniform customer experience at all the touch points and to provide the customer with a unique "experience" and not just a "product". Therefore the back office would remain outside the customer's line of vision because the customer would be concerned with the product and not with the paperwork.

Infrastructure

Thirty-five showrooms across the country were redone entirely with the same look and identity and a décor built around movement, technology and sportiness. The theme focussed on giving the customer a memorable experience.

Response - The strategy delivered

Volumes and Market Shares: Scorpio achieved its targets on market share and achieved a volume of 12,000 vehicles in the first 9 months of its launch. Image: Scorpio advertising had a very high recall for the Mahindra brand as well as for the product. Apart from this, advertising actually positioned Scorpio as a powerful vehicle with a sporty look, solidly built with good cargo capacity amongst the premium car consumers and sports utility vehicle consumers. Overall response to the Scorpio was stupendous. The product was well received across the country and got rave reviews across media. More importantly the product and the strategy delivered in terms of the various objectives set before launch. Footfalls in the showrooms had been massive and demand had far exceeded supply of vehicles with a waiting period of three months.

Impact on Mahindra Image

The saliency of Mahindra increased considerably. Mahindra enjoyed stronger recall as a manufacturer of personal vehicles and stronger customer perceptions on the following attributes -

- Well-respected manufacturers
- Technologically advanced
- Suitable for city driving
- Great to drive
- Makes VFM vehicles
- Proud to own
- Makes good quality vehicles

Scorpio Brand Recall

In the SUV/MUV segment, Scorpio has the second-largest awareness and has emerged as a strong brand in the C & sub-C car segment, however as compared to Qualis, it needed higher recall. Scorpio advertising had been able to create a good impression on appearance and styling of the vehicle.

Scorpio buyer profile

Scorpio managed to pull out customers from the C segment of vehicles. The product, communication and the retail experience of the Scorpio passed the stringent test of luxury car buyers and the buyer profile was exactly as per the target profile. The strategy delivered with more and more small and mid-size car buyers choosing the Scorpio over the others.

Awards

The Scorpio was awarded various awards from various bodies. Mahindra achieved the objectives it set out to achieve. M&M has more than 39 per cent of market share in hard tops, sold 11,800 Scorpios in first nine months of operation and due to this campaign, Mahindra image improved.

SCORPIO IMPACT ON M&M

Scorpio was launched on June 19, 2002. At that time Mahindra was losing-market share and the share prices were also at an all time low at around Rs. 100. The Mahindra share of business was largely from the semi-urban and rural market of India and the markets where Mahindra was strong were stagnating. With the launch of Scorpio, things started looking up for Mahindra. There was an improvement in the bottom line as well as the return to the shareholder. The revenue for M&M Auto Sector increased from Rs. 1827 Cr. in F 02 to Rs. 2511 Cr. in F 03, a growth of 37 per cent. The profits before Interest and Tax (PBIT) too zoomed up from Rs. 102 Cr. in F 02 to Rs. 147 Cr. in F 03, an increase of 43 per cent. In F04 the scenario has further improved. The half-yearly results show a growth of 54 per cent in revenue and 218 per cent increase in PBIT. The share prices have outperformed the Sensex and Share prices had zoomed from Rs. 100 to Rs. 400 by December '03.As regards Mahindra image in the customers mind, the post launch study conducted gave the following improvements (Brand track Study - Nov 2002 - IMRB):

- The Mahindra saliency scores improved by 27 points among MUV/ SUV owners and by 29 points among all car-owners.
- The overall positive opinion about Mahindra also moved up by 18 per cent among MUV/ SUV owners and by 11per cent among all car owners.
- Mahindra Scorpio has fared excellently in overall opinion as against its key competitors.

FUTURE DIRECTIONS – WORLD CLASS PRODUCT GOES GLOBAL

Having done well in the domestic market, Mahindra and Mahindra is now moving forward on its path to become a global niche player. i.e, it is stretching its activities in foreign markets. "Car makers over the world have realized that India can design a car on its own and make it globally acceptable." (India is now the ninth country in the world to design a vehicle on its own) The company is in the process of negotiating joint ventures in markets like Spain, Italy, South Africa, Indonesia, Russia, Equador. .. for marketing of Scorpios.

Questions

1. Is Scorpio a new product or an example of line extension? Explain .
2. Evaluate the management decision to launch Scorpio.
3. What is your opinion of Scorpio as a brand name and its positioning in India?
4. Take another automobile company in today's competitive scenario and what can they learn from 'Project Scorpio'?

Notes

Notes

Amul: Milk Turns to Gold

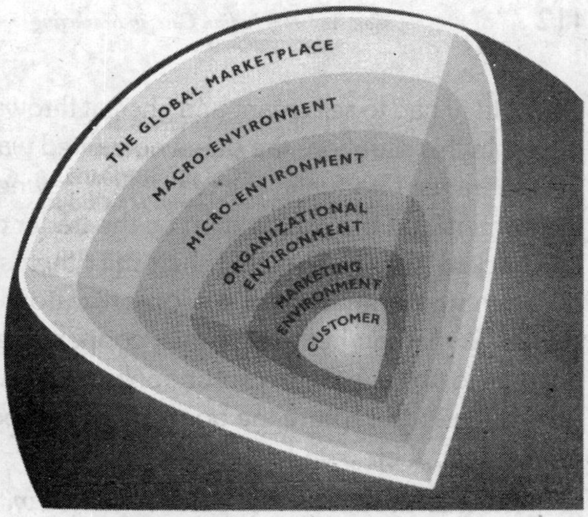

Product Case - 9

Purpose of the Case

The idea is to assimilate the relevant concepts at work and analyse along the following lines:

- To discuss how Gujarat Cooperative Milk Marketing Federation (GCMMF) created a competitive advantage over MNCs in terms of product variety, quality, packaging, sizes, etc. and built an enviable reputation for Amul as a symbol of excellence
- To focus on key factors that heralded White Revolution in India and what does the future look like
- To debate how Amul should approach markets optimally and compete with the milk products launched by other organizations in India

Almost till India's independence, milk producers had to travel long distances to deliver milk to the only dairy, the Polson Dairy in Anand; often milk went sour, especially in the summer season, as producers had to physically carry in individual containers. In winters, the producer was either left with surplus unsold milk or was forced to sell it at very low prices. It is important to note that milk is a highly perishable commodity that needs to be collected twice a day from each cow/buffalo. Moreover, the government at that time had given monopoly rights to Polson Dairy (around that time Polson was the most well known butter brand in the country) to collect milk from Anand and supply to Bombay city in turn (about 400 kilometers away). Polson agents decided not only the prices but also the off-take from the farmers by the season.

India ranked nowhere amongst milk producing countries in the world in 1946. In such a scenario, Gujarat Cooperative Milk Marketing Federation (GCMMF) was formed in response to the monopoly that existed since the time of colonial India. At that time, Polson Dairy was the biggest buyer of the milk being produced in Kaira. The revolution started as awareness among the farmers that grew and matured into a protest movement and the determination to liberate themselves. Over four decades ago, the life of a farmer in Kaira District was very much like that of his counterpart anywhere else in India. His income was derived almost entirely from seasonal crops and the income from milch cattle was undependable. The marketing and distribution system for the milk was controlled by private traders and middlemen. As milk is perishable, farmers were compelled to sell it for whatever they were offered.

Often, they had to sell cream and ghee at throwaway prices. In this situation, the one who gained was the private trader. Gradually, the realization dawned on the farmers that the exploitation by the trader could be checked only if marketed their milk themselves by forming some sort of an organization. The challenge that lay before the milk cooperative was not only to upstage Polson's monopoly on the supply side, but also to capture the booming milk products market with their own brand.

The milk producers' cooperative started with the aim of providing remunerative returns to the farmers and to also serve the interest of consumers by providing good value-for-money quality products. A Rs. 5 million plant to manufacture milk powder and butter was completed in 1955. In 1958, the factory was expanded to manufacture sweetened condensed milk. Two years later, a new wing was added for the manufacture of 2500 tons of roller-dried baby food and 600 tons of cheese per year, the former based on a formula developed with the assistance of Central Food Technological Research Institute (CFTRI), Mysore. It was the first time anywhere in the world that cheese or baby food was made from buffalo milk on a large, commercial scale. Another milestone was the completion of a project to manufacture balanced cattle feed. The plant was donated by OXFAM under the Freedom From Hunger Campaign of the FAO.

Starting with a single shared plant at Anand and two village cooperative societies for milk procurement, the dairy cooperative movement in State of Gujarat has in 2005 evolved into a network of 2.14 million milk producers (called farmers) who are organized in 11,615 milk collection independent cooperatives (called Village Societies). These Village Societies (VS) supply milk to thirteen independent dairy cooperatives (called Unions). AMUL is one such Union. Milk and milk products from these Unions are marketed by a common marketing organization (called Federation). GCMMF has 42 regional distribution centers in India, serves over 5,00,000 retail outlets and exports to more than 15 countries. All these organizations are independent legal entities yet loosely tied together with a common destiny. The growth of sales in GCMMF in last couple of years is as per Table 1.

Sales Turnover of GCMMF over the years.

Sales Turnover	Rs (million)	US $ (in million)
1994-95	11140	355
1995-96	13790	400
1996-97	15540	450
1997-98	18840	455
1998-99	22192	493
1999-00	22185	493
2000-01	22588	500
2001-02	23365	500
2002-03	27457	575
2003-04	28941	616
2004-05	29225	672

Source: www.amul.com

Table 1: **Sales Turnover of GCMMF over the years.**

For several years, the Kaira cooperative supplied milk and allied products without a formal distribution network leave alone a brand name. However under the leadership of Verghese Kurien the brand name Amul was formally adopted. When the need of a brand name for the Kaira Cooperative was felt initially, the word was circulated in Anand (the birth place of Amul) among friends and cooperative members. The name Amul was most probably suggested by a quality control expert in Anand. It was derived from"*amulya*", which in Sanskrit, Gujarati and many other Indian languages, means priceless, and implies matchless excellence. The name was short, memorable and easily pronounced. It could also serve as an acronym for the organization –the unusable KDCMPUL (Kaira District Cooperative Milk Producer's Union Limited) taken from Kaira Cooperative's full name which could be substituted by AMUL, standing for Anand Milk Union Limited. Although not the Cooperative's true name it unmistakably conveyed the desired meaning. Even though Amul products have been in use in millions of homes since 1946, the brand Amul was registered only in 1957. The difficulty in registration stemmed from the fact that the cooperative had to prove enough sales and advertisements before this common word could be established as a brand name of a dairy product.

From the very inception brand Amul stood for high quality products at reasonable prices. As an Indian name, it associated itself with pride in swadeshi goods. And over the years Amul as a brand has continuously delivered on the promise of quality products at reasonable prices, making that proposition stronger than ever. In a recent survey GCMMF was ranked amongst the top ten FMCG firms in the country while AMUL was rated the second most recognized brand in India amongst all Indian and MNC offerings. Interestingly, the Gujarat movement spread all over India and a similar structure was replicated (all are at different levels of achievement but their trajectory appears to be quite similar!). Two national organizations, the National Dairy Development Board (NDDB) and the National Co-operative Dairy Federation of India (NCDFI) were established to coordinate the dairy activities through cooperatives in all the States of the country. The former provides financing for development while the latter manages a national milk grid and coordinates the deficit and surplus milk and milk powder across the states of India. In the early nineties, AMUL was asked by the Government of Sri Lanka to establish a dairy on similar lines in Sri Lanka.

The story of Amul inspired 'Operation Flood' and heralded the 'White Revolution' in India. Amul besides being India's largest food products marketing organisation has become a symbol of the aspirations of millions of farmers creating a pattern of liberation and self-reliance for every farmer to follow. Out of the entire milk procured, approximately 40 per cent is sold as liquid milk and 60 per cent is converted to value added products like butter, ghee, dairy whitener, milk powder and others.

The range of products marketed by GCMMF is as follows:

1. Breadspreads

- Amul Butter
- Amul Lite Low Fat Breadspread
- Amul Cooking Butter

2. Cheese Range

- Amul Pasteurized Processed Cheddar Cheese
- Amul Processed Cheese Spread
- Amul Pizza (Mozarella) Cheese
- Amul Shredded Pizza Cheese
- Amul Emmental Cheese
- Amul Gouda Cheese
- Amul Malai Paneer (cottage cheese) Frozen and Tinned
- Utterly Delicious Pizza

3. Mithaee Range (Ethnic sweets)

- Amul Shrikhand (Mango, Saffron, Almond Pistachio, Cardamom)
- Amul Amrakhand
- Amul Mithaee Gulabjamuns
- Amul Mithaee Gulabjamun Mix
- Amul Mithaee Kulfi Mix

Amul's Range of Products

4. UHT Milk Range

- Amul Taaza 3% fat Milk
- Amul Gold 4.5% fat Milk
- Amul Slim-n-Trim 0% fat milk
- Amul Chocolate Milk
- Amul Fresh Cream
- Amul Snowcap Softy Mix
- Amul Taaza Double Toned Milk

5. Pure Ghee

- Amul Pure Ghee
- Sagar Pure Ghee
- Amul Cow Ghee

6. Infant Milk Range:

- Amul Infant Milk Formula 1 (0-6 months)
- Amul Infant Milk Formula 2 (above 6 months)
- Amulspray Infant Milk Food

7. Milk Powders:

- Amul Full Cream Milk Powder
- Amulya Dairy Whitener
- Sagar Skimmed Milk Powder
- Sagar Tea and Coffee Whitener

8. Sweetened Condensed Milk:

- Amul Mithaimate Sweetened Condensed Milk

9. Fresh Milk:

- Amul Taaza Toned Milk 3% fat
- Amul Gold Full Cream Milk 6% fat
- Amul Shakti Standardised Milk 3% fat
- Amul Smart Double Toned Milk 1.5% fat

10. Curd Products:

- Amul Masti Dahi (fresh curd)
- Amul Butter Milk
- Amul Lassee

11. Amul Ice creams:

- Royal Treat Range (Rajbhog, Cappuchino, Chocochips, Butterscotch, Tutti Frutti)
- Nut-o-Mania Range (Kaju Drakshi, Kesar Pista, Roasted Almond, Kesar Carnival, Badshahi Badam Kulfi, Shista Pista Kulfi)
- Utsav Range (Anjir, Roasted Almond)
- Simply Delicious Range (Vanilla, Strawberry, Pineapple, Rose, Chocolate)
- Nature's Treat (Alphanso Mango, Fresh Litchi, Anjir, Fresh Strawberry, Black Currant)
- Sundae Range (Mango, Black Currant, Chocolate, Strawberry)
- Millennium Icecream (Cheese with Almonds, Dates with Honey)
- Milk Bars (Chocobar, Mango Dolly, Raspberry Dolly, Shahi Badam Kulfi, Shahi Pista Kulfi, Mawa Malai Kulfi, Green Pista Kulfi)
- Cool Candies (Orange, Mango)
- Cassatta
- Tricone Cones (Butterscotch, Chocolate)
- Megabite Almond Cone
- Frostik - 3 layer chocolate Bar
- Fundoo Range - exclusively for kids
- SlimScoop Fat Free Frozen Dessert (Vanilla, Banana, Mango, Pineapple)
- Health : Isabcool

12. Chocolate & Confectionery:

- Amul Milk Chocolate
- Amul Fruit & Nut Chocolate
- Amul Eclairs

13. Brown Beverage:

- Nutramul Malted Milk Food

14. Milk Drink:

- Amul Shakti Flavoured Milk

15. Ready to Serve Soups:

- Masti Tomato Soup
- Masti Hot & Sour Soup

GCMMF is India's largest exporter of dairy products. A large quantity of products, are exported every year for the huge population of Non Resident

Indians. GCMMF has not only been accorded a "Trading House" status but also received the APEDA Award from Government of India for excellence in dairy product exports for the from 1997 to 2005. They have posted more than 50% growth in the volume of consumer pack exports which reflects strong and growing consumer faith in Amul brand. The Long Life milk has been very well accepted in the UAE and Singapore markets. UHT milk has been launched in Hong Kong and Sri Lanka market. They have also made a successful beginning in export of ghee to Australia. The major exports in consumer packs are Amul Pure Ghee, Butter, Shrikhand, Full cream milk powder, Mithaee gulabjamun, Skimmed milk powder, Nutramul brown beverage, Infant milk food, Cheese, malai paneer. In bulk packs Amul skimmed milk powder and full cream milk powder are exported extensively.

GCMMF has been able to create entry barriers for its competitors through its low procurement cost due to extremely efficient management of its supply chain. GCMMF's competitor Nestle procures 600,000 litres of milk per day which is hardly 10% of Amul's capacity. The enactment of the Milk and Milk Products Order (MMPO) prescribes state registrations to plants producing between 10,000 to 75,000 liters of milk per day. Plants producing over 75,000 litres per day have to be registered with the Central Government. These requirements for new capacities have restricted large private players from making significant investments in this product category.

The supply chain of GCMMF consists of 7 levels (Figure 2). The farmers provide the milk (basic raw material) to the co-operatives. From these co-operatives the milk goes to all dairies that AMUL has all over Gujarat. After the products are made in the dairies, these are supplied to various depots. From these depots various distributors are serviced who then supply to the retailers. From these retailers the final consumer buys the finished products.

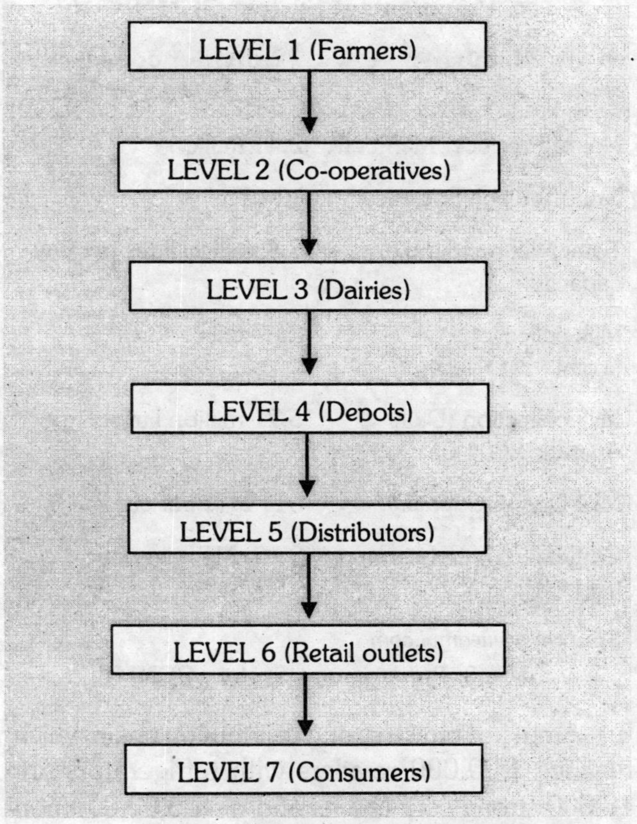

Figure 2 : **Supply Chain of GCMMF**

Information Technology (IT) has played a significant role in developing the Amul brand. The logistics behind co-ordinating the collection of some 6.7 million litres of milk per day from 110,000 plus separate Village Cooperative Societies throughout Gujarat and then storing, processing and producing milk products at the respective 12 District Dairy Unions, are awesome (See Table 3). The installation of 3000 Automatic Milk Collection System Units (AMCUS) at Village Societies to capture member information, milk fat content, the volume collected and amount payable to each member has proved invaluable in ensuring fairness and transparency throughout the whole Amul organisation. In 1996 Amul was one of the first major organisations in India to have a website. This site has been used both to develop an intranet of Amul distributors as well as a cyber-store for consumers, one of the first examples of e-commerce activity in India.

Procurement System-GCMMF

Members:	**12 district cooperative milk producers' Union**
No. of Producer Members:	2.41 million
No. of Village Societies:	11,615
Total Milk handling capacity:	7.4 million litres per day
Milk collection (Total - 2004-05):	2.08 billion litres
Milk collection (Daily Average 2004-05):	5.71 million litres
Milk Drying Capacity:	511 MTs per day
Cattlefeed manufacturing Capacity:	2340 MTs per day

Source: *www.amul.com*

Table 3: **Procurement System-GCMMF**

Amul has built a strong distribution chain which, reaches 1,00,000 retailers with refrigerators and 18,000 strong cold chains and over 5,00,000 non-refrigerated retail outlets. It controls the milk and butter outlets and since these also stock ice creams Amul has an advantage over competitors such as Nestle in butter and HLL in ice creams. GCMMF undertakes a census of all retail outlets to evaluate customer perceptions and distribution efficacy of their network. Interestingly, this is being done by wholesalers in their respective territories at their own cost. The co-operative has plans to service 1 million retail outlets by end of 2005. Distributors of AMUL divide their area into number of routes keeping in mind the number of outlets on the route, the maximum that they can service in a day and the ease with which they can service them in the best possible manner. These routes are serviced twice a week, with each route allotted specific day in the week for being serviced. Every day in the morning the distributor's salesman goes on the specific route to get the order from the outlets and returns by noon. Then outlet wise bills are made, stock is loaded in the rickshaw and the outlets are supplied the required goods. A point to note here is that, a single rickshaw can service a maximum of around 40-45 outlets, in a day.

The Federation has developed competence in distributing fresh products on daily basis. This is equally true of long life products held at ambient temperature, products requiring deep-freezing during storage or transportation, and products that require zero degree temperature. This established competence is, and will continue to be, an essential element in building synergies among product lines and in ultimately creating superior economies of scale.

The success of Amul's advertising and brand building process is attributed to its 'thumb-sized girl', the Amul Butter Girl. The first time it climbed on to hoardings, it created a great curiosity and since then has continuously put a spell on the masses. Call her the Friday to Friday star. Round eyed, chubby cheeked, winking at you, from strategically placed hoardings at many traffic lights. She is the Amul moppet everyone loves to love. How often have we stopped, looked, chuckled at the Amul hoarding that casts her sometime as the coy, shy Madhuri, a bold sensuous Urmila or simply as herself, dressed in her little polka dotted dress and a red and white bow, holding out her favorite packet of butter.

GCMMF considered that, advertisement & promotion (a la FMCG) is not enough of value addition and hence the advertising budget was always kept relatively small as compared to the industry average. Instead, GCMMF preferred a lower price with emphasis on efficiency in advertising. In this context, GCMMF does umbrella branding of all its products. It has not created sub- brands for its various products thus working within an ad spend of less than 1% of its sales. This has given Amul a huge advantage in advertising cost vis-à-vis its private sector competitors who, on an average spent 8% to 9% of their sales on advertising. Interestingly, the advertising has centered on building a common identity (e.g., a happy & healthy "cartoon" AMUL girl) and evoking national emotion (e.g., the key advertising slogan says "AMUL - The Taste of India"). This helped translate the core and extended identity of brand to all its products and makes product extension much more easy and with high probability of launch success. The major focus of Amul brand building process through advertisements has been the use of humour, through its regular topical stories and the proposition of healthy happy family/ individuals because of quality products, in its print advertisements and TVCs. Some of the Amul topicals till date have been given in Annexure 1.

GCMMF entered Delhi's liquid milk market in 2005 much to the discomfort of National Dairy Development Board subsidiary Mother Dairy, which enjoys a monopolistic position in the Delhi's milk market. Meanwhile, in one of its recent initiatives, GCMMF has floated a second brand in the health food drinks (HFD) market called Amul Shakti with an aim to pitch it directly against market leader Glaxo SmithKline Beecham's (GSK) Ltd's Horlicks. Priced at a slight premium over Horlicks—Amul Shakti will be launched in 2006 as a health beverage (in the white segment) across the country at Rs 110 for a 500gm jar against GSK's Horlicks at Rs 108.50 per 500gm. The brand was earlier being test-marketed in the North-East. The brand will be soon promoted through a multimedia advertising campaign and a consumer promotion. The co-operative will in the meantime continue to market its other HFD brand Nutramul, which is priced at Rs 80 for a 500-gm jar. The HFD market in recent years has remained stagnant though GSK's attempts to relaunch its flagship brand Horlicks are believed to have revived the market to some extent.

GCMMF has come out with a new product — coffee-based *gutkha* without the harmful tobacco — which is expected to hit the market very soon, though the exact date for the launch has not been fixed yet. The company has decided to apply for a patent after putting the product through several in-house tests. The coffee-based *gutkha* is originally the idea of GCMMF managing director B M Vyas. The product has been developed by the research and development wing of GCMMF using coffee beans.

GCMMF has already initiated talks with the ministry of railways to set up Amul parlours at 6,800 railway stations spread across the country. If all goes well, these parlours are expected to turn out to be big revenue earners for the co-operative. There is a huge potential for safe and reliable milk and food products at railway stations and the government has thus evinced interest in the project.

The marketing managers of GCMMF realise that there is a steady increase in consumer expectations and product and service quality is rapidly becoming the minimum threshold for consumer acceptance. It is important to note that to achieve and maintain competitive advantage, innovation in product design and delivery are increasingly essential and GCMMF must innovate at each stage in their value chain i.e. production, procurement, processing, marketing and branding.

As everywhere else, the market trend in India is towards the growing importance of fresh products. The coming years will see increasing volumes being generated from fresh milk, Long Life Milk, curds and the like. There is no doubt that Amul's milk procurement and processing capacity is unparalleled in the country and the region and they have a brand equity that is unsurpassed in the food business sector but they must constantly create and update their competencies in these products so that they can lead, set and exceed market expectations.

Question

As an Indian name, Amul is strongly associated with swadeshi food and flavour. Of late there is a big rush in India for Western & Oriental cuisine due to the associated values of fun, independence and lifestyle. Big MNC and Indian food-marketing companies like McDonalds, Subway, Pizza Hut, Dominos, various ice-cream giants and now Mother Dairy itself are expanding their reach in a big way. What kind of product strategies do you recommend for GCMMF in such a competitive scenario?

Annexure - 1

Virender Sehwag's triple century against Pakistan, April '04

On Vanilla Coke-2004 — Vivek Oberoi

On Dr. Singh's election as PM

Politicians' sons in the Parliament election race - April'04

Obituary on Bollywood's well-loved comedian Mehmood July '04

On Athens Olympics 2004

Indian car market flooded with new entrants April 2000

Controversy raised by Maneka Gandhi on drink of milk April 2000

One of the first Amul hoardings

Notes

Notes

Brand Management

Section - Seven

CONCEPTUAL FRAMEWORK

To facilitate a better debate on the cases in this section, a quick exploratory review of the brand management function along with areas that need discussion are recapitulated briefly as follows:

- A brand is a name, term, design, symbol, or any other feature that identifies one seller's good or service and distinguishes it from those of other sellers. A **brand name** is the part of a brand that can be spoken. A **brand mark** is the element that cannot be spoken. A **trademark** is a legal designation indicating that the owner has exclusive use of a brand or part of a brand and others are prohibited by law from using it. A **trade name** is the legal name of an organization.
- **Branding** is a major issue in product strategy. A marketer understands that branding is expensive and time-consuming, and can make or break a product. A brand is a complex symbol that can convey many levels of meaning.
- Brand managers formulate brand strategy based on, whether the brand is a functional brand, an image brand or an experiential brand.
- Branding helps buyers identify and evaluate products, helps sellers facilitate product introduction and repeat purchasing, and fosters brand loyalty.
- **Brand loyalty** is a customer's favorable attitude toward a specific brand. Marketers constantly focus on building brand loyalty because if it is strong, customers may consistently purchase a particular brand when they need a product in this product category. The three degrees of brand loyalty are brand recognition, preference, and insistence as elucidated herebelow:
  - **Brand recognition** exists when a customer is aware that the brand exists and views it as an alternative purchase if the preferred brand is unavailable.
  - **Brand preference** is the degree of brand loyalty in which a customer prefers one brand over competing brands and will purchase it if available.
  - **Brand insistence** is the degree of brand loyalty in which a customer will accept no substitute.
- **Brand equity** is the marketing and financial value associated with a brand's strength. It represents the value of a brand to an organization. The four major elements underlying brand equity include brand name awareness, brand loyalty, perceived brand quality and brand associations.
- A **manufacturer brand**, initiated by the producer, ensures that the firm is associated with its products at the point of purchase. A **private**

distributor brand is initiated and owned by a reseller, sometimes taking on the name of the store or distributor. Manufacturers combat growing multiple brands. A **generic brand** indicates only the product category and does not include the company name or other identifying terms.

- When **selecting a brand name**, a marketer should choose one that is easy to say, spell, and recall and that alludes to the product's uses, benefits, or special characteristics. Brand names can be devised from words, letters, numbers, nonsense words, or a combination of these. Brand names are created inside an organization by individuals, committees, or branding departments, and by outside consultants. Services as well as products are branded, often with the company name and an accompanying symbol that makes the brand distinctive or conveys a desired image.
- The best brand names suggest something about the product's benefits; suggest product qualities; are easy to pronounce, recognize and remember; are distinctive; and do not carry negative meanings or connotations in other countries or languages.
- Producers have to protect ownership of their brands through registration with the relevant authorities. A company must make certain the brand name it selects does not infringe on an already registered brand by confusing or deceiving consumers about the source of the products. In most countries, brand registration is on a first-come, first-serve basis, making protection more difficult.
- Major problem faced by many brand managers is **brand counterfeiting** in the form of fake products is becoming increasingly common and can undermine consumer's confidence in a brand.
- Brand managers brand their products in several ways. **Individual branding** designates a unique name for each of a company's products. **Family branding** identifies all of a firm's products with a single name and **brand-extension branding** applies an existing name to a new or improved product.
- **Co-branding** is the use of two or more brands on one product. It is a popular branding method in a number of processed food categories and in the credit card industry. The brands may be owned by the same company or by different companies. Effective co-branding profits from the trust and confidence customers have in the brands involved. To avoid confusion marketers must ensure that brands have a complementary fit in buyer's minds. Co-branding sometimes allows an organization to differentiate its products from those of competitors. It can also take advantage of the distribution capabilities of the co-branding partners.
- Brand manager uses many **brand-building tools** which comprise advertising, public relations and press releases, sponsorships, clubs and consumer communities, factory visits, trade shows, event marketing, public facilities, social cause marketing, high value for the money, founder's or a celebrity personality and mobile phone marketing (m-commerce).
- Through a licensing agreement and for a licensing fee, a firm may permit another organization to use its brand on other products. **Brand licensing** enables producers to earn extra revenue, receive low-cost or free publicity, and protect their trademarks.

Eureka Forbes Limited

Turning a Friend for Life

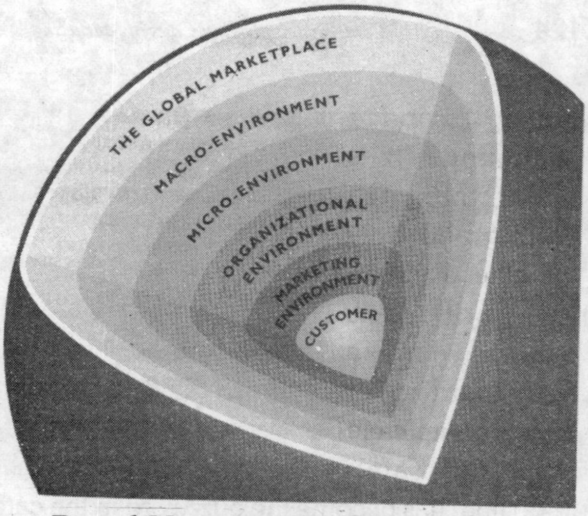

Brand Management Case - 10

Purpose of the Case

The idea is to assimilate the relevant concepts at work and analyse along the following lines:

- To discuss how Eureka Forbes built the Aquaguard brand in India and what were the critical success factors
- To focus on the stratagems which can help the brand increase its lead over and above the competition
- To debate how the brand will grow and mutate over the long term

The birth of the purified drinking water market in India began over twenty years ago when the first Eureka Forbes Eurochamp (as its salesman is proudly called) set out to knock his first door. The product that the modern Indian families welcomed into their home was Aquaguard, India's first water purification system.

Unlike developed countries, where the main pollutants in household drinking water are harmful chemicals, in India, pollutants are three-fold: sediment, chemicals and the most critical - bacteria and viruses. Aquaguard was specifically customized to deal with them. Despite having an effective product it was a bold step to take for Eureka Forbes. Exploratory research had indicated that few people realized the threat from invisible bacteria and viruses in clear, safe-looking water. They simply bought candle filters to remove the sediment that they could see and found no need for the more expensive water purifier. Undeterred, the indomitable army of Eurochamps persevered with its mission.

Many doors have opened since then. Aquaguard is the leader in the ultra violet (UV) water purification systems market with a 70% share and is available in over 500 cities. Purified drinking water is one of the fastest growing consumer product categories. With only 23% of 57 million urban households and almost none of 136 million rural households tapped, the surface has barely been scratched.

Under recent developments, an extensive nationwide research study indicated that boiling the water was accepted as the customer's benchmark for safety. Doctors also actively promoted it, especially in times of illness. As the leader, Aquaguard has staked its claim to the high ground by embarking on a program to demonstrate how electronic

boiling (branded 'e-boiling+') is better than just boiling and how the other stages in its purification process make Aquaguard water 'more completely pure and safe'. 'e-boiling' has become the buzzword in the category and the market has begun to expand.

A high level of awareness about spreading of the multiple waterborne diseases and constantly rising pollution levels highlights the importance of consumption of safe drinking water. Need for water free from all kinds of dirt, germs and chemicals is becoming the order of the day. Awareness about being healthy and preventing yourself from any kind of water related infection is paramount and safe drinking water is sought after. With an increase in awareness, the water purifying companies are booming through proving solutions to people about safety aspects. Packaged water, water purifying equipments, water-cleaning medicines, etc are having a positive and a high growth rate indicating a change in the attitude of the masses towards the consumption of safe drinking water.

Not surprisingly, various companies involved in water purification and water treatment are cashing in on the opportunity by aggressively marketing their products. But, in spite of the tremendous potential for expansion and growth, the water purification industry has not had an easy time, partly because a water purifier is still not considered a consumer durable and partly because of issues of pricing, low margins and technology.

The real competition lies with the bottled water industry (Exhibit 1). Colloquially called the mineral water industry, the bottled water industry is a symbol of new lifestyle emerging in India. While a large segment of the population is struggling to get access to potable water supply, a new generation - especially in the urban areas - is getting accustomed to bottled water paying handsome prices.

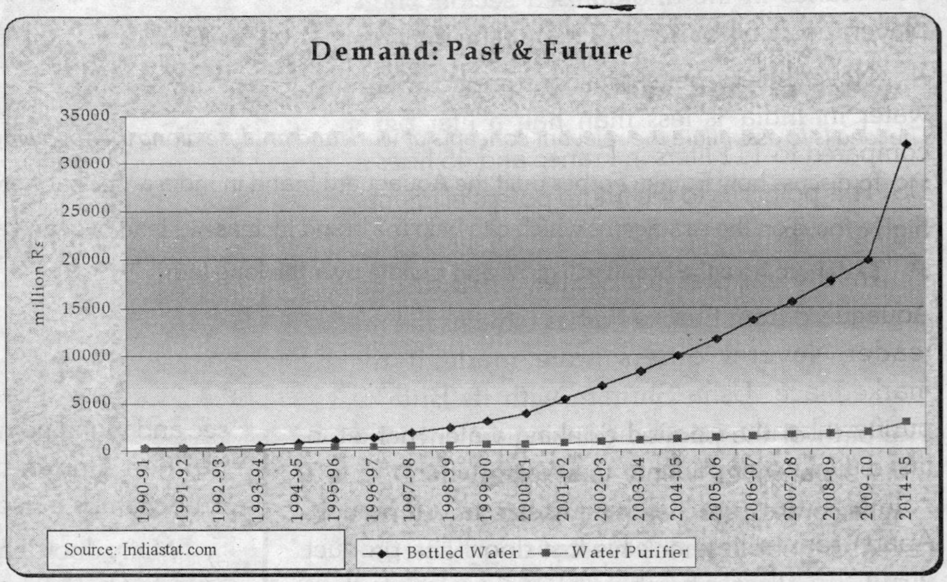

Source: Indiastat.com

Exhibit 1: **Demand of Bottled Water Vs Water Purifier**

The phenomenal increase in demand for bottled water from just 2.0 mn cases in 1990-91 to 68 mn cases presently is being boosted further by

the concern and need for safe drinking water. What is amazing is that people are prepared to pay Rs 10 for a liter of simple water - especially when the cost of material input is negligible. The cost of packaging can be as high as 15% to 35% of the price of the product.

The growth rate of the bottled water market was around 20% a year in 2003 (down from 50% to 60% earlier). At this growth rate, the Rs 7,000 mn per year market is estimated to overtake the soft drinks market soon. Multinationals, Coca-Cola, Pepsi, Nestle and others are trying to grab a significant share of the market. There are more than 180 brands in the unorganised sector. The small players account for nearly 19% of the total market.

Nevertheless, per capita consumption of bottled water in India is less than half a liter per year, compared to 111 liters in France and 45 liters in the US. This points us to the future potential beyond the high growth.

In the market for water purifiers, while Aquaguard from Eureka Forbes remains the market leader, several others have made it to the marketplace. Usha Shriram with its Brita water purifier already established, has launched India's first digital water purifier - the Waterguard Digital in collaboration with Brita GmbH of Germany. Apart from killing disease-causing bacteria and virus the filter claims to dissolve hazardous organic pollutants, to ensure safe drinking water. Other features include a cartridge life indicator (on the LCD screen) detachable spill tray lamp life indicators and a computerized monitoring system (to control the purification process). Another company, Proctor & Gamble (P&G) has also been planning to launch its international brand Pure - a water purification product. The product has been developed is close consultation with CDC (Centre for Disease Control and Prevention) and USAID. The product is expected to be highly useful for developing countries such as India. Hindustan Lever (HLL) also forayed into the water business, with its water purifier device called Pure. It can be attached to the kitchen tap to purify potable water at minimum cost. HLL plans to take the purifiers to small metros, towns and cities so that it does not remain an urban phenomenon. Water purifiers (residential segment) is a Rs. 5 to 6 bn industries, with Aquaguard cornering more than 50% of the market. The rest is divided among Kent RO, Pentair, Ion Exchange and others.

An indicative data is hereby provided which puts forward the facts w.r.t. the consumption pattern of the mineral water as well as the Water purifying systems. Also, the market growth rates are provided to understand the potential prospects in the respective product lines. (Exhibit 2)

Year	Bottled Water	Water Purifiers
1990-91 - 1996-97	33.80%	16.00%
1996-97 - 2001-02	31.10%	19.80%
2001-02 - 2006-07	20.50%	10.20%
2004-05 - 2009-10	15.00%	11.00%

Source: Indiastat.com

Exhibit 2: **Average Growth rate Bottled Water vs. Water Purifiers**

The story of Aquaguard is indelibly linked to the story of the Eurochamp. Eurochamp has become the face of Eureka Forbes. It has contributed almost 100% in the success span of the company. The greatest challenge in driving the strategy of doorstep demonstrations and education lay in finding a sufficient number and quality people to accomplish this task across the country.

Were it not for him reaching out to customers in their homes, the brand might never have existed today. The company has achieved an iconic standing in the Indian market through the grit and tenacity of its salesforce. This dedicated group of people understands customer requirements, tailors presentations to them, demonstrates, handles queries, persuades, installs, collects money and backs sales with service. Training, re-training and customer care activities are its hallmarks. Aptly termed Eurochamps for their pivotal role in the process, they serve as consultants and advisors to customers. Eureka Forbes believes that supplying a product and getting paid for it is not the end of a relationship but the start of a valuable association. Eureka Forbes is constantly looking at providing products and services and focusing on customer satisfaction. The company's slogan is appropriately summed up in three words: 'Friend for Life'. It religiously adheres to this mantra in every facet of its business. This unwavering customer focus and unique business model have been crucial to its progress.

Thus Eureka Forbes chose the direct selling option - a distinct plus over competitive retail branding. The Eurochamp has become the most identifiable face of the brand in the customer's home. This business model has enabled the company to pioneer and lead several other categories whose latent potential it also recognized way ahead of their time.

"Is it Aquaguard water?" has become a commonplace expression today, with Aquaguard being virtually generic to the category. Over fifteen million Indians trust only Aquaguard for their drinking water and it is present in over 35 countries. Committed to being a true 'friend for life' to its customers Aquaguard is dedicated to providing them with products of the highest quality. It is the only brand with an international Water Quality Association (WQA) endorsed carbon block that removes pesticides. It is manufactured in ISO: 14000 and 9000 certified factories and tested and certified by over 100 Indian and international laboratories. Aquaguard is also certified by the Indian Standards Institute.

Aquaguard has an expansive service operation, comprising of 3,000 company-trained technicians, supported by call centers, customer care representatives and mobile service vans.

Aquaguard's advertising focused on encouraging customers to call the Eurochamp to know more, and on making them more receptive to him when he knocked. Eureka Forbes was the first direct sales organization in the world to use advertising in this manner. To enlighten the customer, the Eurochamp was well-trained to expertly use the demonstration and a sales aid detailer. This was his primary tool and included water facts, the need for purification supported by newspaper cuttings on water-borne diseases and pollution, an analysis of existing purification methods and endorsements by laboratories and institutions.

FACTS

- Every minute 23 Indians drink a glass of Aquaguard filtered water.
- Over 14 million homes in India have witnessed an Aquaguard demonstration in the last 20 years.
- UNICEF has used Aquaguard water test kits for its field sampling in India.
- Aquaguard has featured models in its advertising who have gone on to becoming famous celebrities in the field of politics, modeling, acting such as Nitesh Bharadwaj, Aditi Govitrikar.

Source: www.eurekaforbes.com

Using an umbrella as a symbol of protection, Aquaguard made special efforts during the monsoon when water-borne diseases were at their peak. Simultaneously, free service camps played a critical role in ensuring that customers' units functioned efficiently.

Gradually the brand's efforts bore fruit and Aquaguard gained acceptance. Focus then shifted to building trust with its unique reassurance of 'safe water or no water at all'.

The health of children was a key concern and was also the primary motivator for purchase. Aquaguard capitalized on its leadership to emphasize that mothers trusted only Aquaguard when it came to drinking water for their children. 'Mother and child' became one of the brand's most enduring images.

Other initiatives included a free water bottle offer to address a common customer's concern about pure drinking water when away from home. Special advertising in cookery magazines to encourage cooking and washing of vegetables in Aquaguard water, plus glow signs at restaurants, using filtered Aquaguard water, were all part of this initiative. The brand associated itself with prominent serials and used innovations such as in-programproduct exposure and a safe water awareness tag-on to episodes. As a responsible leader, Aquaguard created a special schools program to educate children on the hazards of drinking unsafe water. The brand used a series of themes such as 'The story of a virus', 'Mr. Cleany' and 'Water right. Child bright' that involved innovative games and video-based aids to drive home this point. In this way, the company has reached more than 200,000 students in over 500 schools thus far. About 30% of these homes have requested for demonstrations.

Free water kiosks have been set up at parks for senior citizens, charitable medical clinics, schools for physically challenged children, public places like beaches, theatres and auditoriums and during times when calamities strike such as earthquakes and cyclones. Aquaguard sponsors seminars on water related subjects and has instituted an award for path-breaking research in microbiology on water-borne diseases.

Question

1. With increasing education levels, and awareness of water-borne diseases, reasons to drink clean, uncontaminated, purified water are getting increasingly established amongst Indian population. How would you, as a "Marketing manager" of 'Eureka Forbes ensure that your company gets a higher and ever increasing market share and not lose out to companies supplying bottled water?

Notes

Pidilite Industries Limited:

Brand Bigger than the Company?

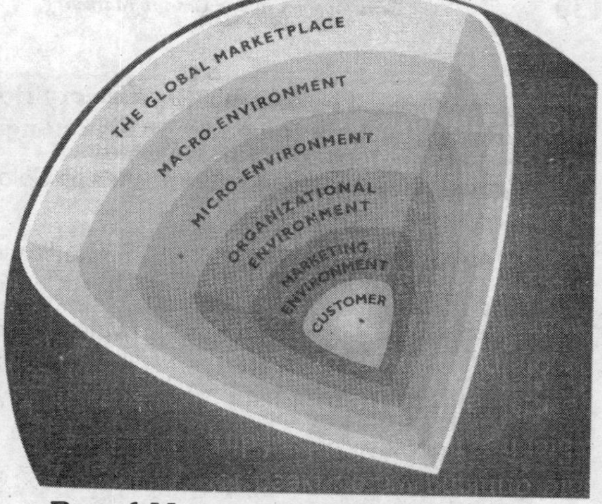

Brand Management Case - 11

Purpose of the Case

The idea is to assimilate the relevant concepts at work and analyse along the following lines:

- To discuss how the brand Fevicol has grown over the years and what have been the critical success factors making it one of the most trusted brands in the country
- To focus on the possible courses of action open to the management for building on the success of Fevicol
- To debate how a company should not be constrained by a single brand - single product strategy

Pidilite Industries Limited (PIL), the flagship company of Parekh Group of companies since its inception in 1959, has been a pioneer in the manufacture of branded bazaar and specialty chemicals. PIL has recorded an excellent export performance with some of the products having been accepted well in international markets like Europe, USA, Middle East, Africa, Asia, Australia and Japan. It manufactures adhesives (polyvinyl acetate, synthetic rubber based cyanoacrylate, epoxy, hot melt and polyurethane adhesives, synthetic gums and glue stick); construction and paint chemicals (water proofing compounds and coatings, tile fixing adhesives, lime binders and strainers); art materials (acrylic, poster and water colors, crayons and glitters); industrial and textile resins (based on polyvinyl acetate and acrylic; SBR lattices; finishing and sizing agents) organic pigments and preparations (violet and emulsions), etc. The diversified product range of the Group caters to disparate fields like furniture, footwear, paints, printing inks, textiles, leather, paper, automobiles, plastics, electronics, packaging, construction, defense, etc. They are also used extensively in households, offices and educational institutions, as shown in Exhibit 1.

Consumer goods business is characterized by the two pillars of brand equity and distribution reach. In adhesives, brand loyalties are high and demand is relatively price insensitive, as adhesives account for an insignificant proportion of the total cost of the end product for which they are used. Construction/ paint chemicals, pigments, resins etc are typically sold in bulk to industrial buyers. Meeting technical specifications as per the user's requirement and consistency in quality play an important role. As per the report published on August 8, 2003, by Parag Parikh Financial Advisory Pvt. Ltd. (http://www.ppfas.com/investindia/week/2003/aug08.htm) the adhesives and sealant market, is estimated at

Stationery Rang	Acron Range	Fevicry/Hobby Idea Range	Maintenance Range	Fabricare Rnge	Kids Art Range
Fevicol MR	Rangeela	Acrylic Colors	Fevikwik	Ranipal Stain Off	Safe Finger Paints
Fevicol YAA	Wax Crayons	Solvent based Glass Colors	All Fix	Ranipal Facric Whitener	Safe Bold Crayons
Fevigum	Paper Glitters	Water Based Glass Colors	Shoe Fix	Ranipal All White	Fun Coloring Marker
Fevistik		Stik-on Colors	Zorrik 88		No Spill Pot
Prime Notes		No-Stich	Brite-0		Powder Color
Prime Correct			Candle Making kit	Roberts Liquid Polish	
Primestik		Mould and paint	Roberts Wax	Polish	
		Glass painting kit	Motomax Kit		
		Feviart magazine			
		Stencils			

Exhibit 1: **Product Range of PIL**

Rs 5 billion. Pidilite is the leading player in the segment. Other major players are Vam Organic, Mafatlal Dyes & Chemicals (MDC), Kitply and Ciba Specialty. Industrial & textile resin is a Rs3.5 billion market. Pidilite has a 13% market share in this industrial segment. Organic pigment is a Rs 4.5 billion market, with a large presence of the unorganized segment. In the organized market ColourChem, Ciba Specialty, Sudarshan Chemicals and Pidilite are the major players.

Pidilite has gradually expanded its branded product portfolio, which earns higher margins and has come to be recognized as a leading FMCG player. Consumer and Bazaar products (as they refer to the segment) accounts for over 65% of the company's turnover. All its brands are either No. 1 or No. 2 in their respective product segments. *Fevicol, Parcol, Fevibond, Fevikwik, Pidifix, Pidivyl, Pidiseal, Acrolyte, Fevicryl,* etc are some of its leading brands. The company has launched several new products in the last few years like *Fevistik Super glue stick. Feviseal EasiMix epoxy putty, Acron art materials, Prime tape, Pidifin water proofing system and Wudfin wood polish* in the consumer product segment. Moreover the brand has become synonymous with the name of the category. When Fevicol entered the Market in 1959. It was primarily focused on the need for a good adhesive for carpenters. The carpenters earlier used a mixture made out of animal extracts to make an adhesive. This process was not only time consuming but also it could not be mass manufactured. Fevicol was the first synthetic adhesive to cater to this need.

> ***Madhukar Balwantray Parekh, MD, Pidilite Industries says:***
>
> "*Fevicol* has become a household name due to several reasons. First, because it is a good product introduced at the right time in India and secondly it was promoted at the end user levels such as carpenters and households. Intense sales promotion and user contacts consolidated our standing. Sound advertising strategies when there was none in this category further strengthened our position besides our excellent trade relations."

Source: Chemical Business, June '99, Vol.13, issue 6, p25, 4p

To reduce dependence on one product and drive growth, PIL has over the years been continuously innovating and introducing new products as well as making synergistic acquisitions. As on 2006, the company has a leading presence in consumer products like glue, tapes, art materials and other similar kinds of niche segments. At the same time the acquisition of well-known brands like Ranipal (a fabric whitener), M-Seal (a sealant) and Steelgrip (an electrical insulation tape) are likely to keep the company's growth momentum intact. PIL has also entered the construction materials category with Dr Fixit range of products, which is an entirely new but related category, and is already building relationships with architects, builders, masons etc. The notable feature is that there is no other player in the organized sector like PIL with a presence in all these categories across the country. Its competition is mainly from regional players and small firms in the unorganized sector along with a few large companies like Jubilant Organosys and Camlin, that too in one area of business only.

The market share of Pidilite in the domestic adhesives field is about 60% and Fevicol contributes over 50% of the company's revenue (Exhibit 2). This dependency on Fevicol has always been a concern to Mr. Parekh, MD, PIL. for a long time. Over the years there has been a clear strategy shift from the company relying only on the Fevicol brand. Now it is trying to diversify its product portfolio by creation of strong brands and reducing the dependence on Fevicol sales for profits.

Exhibit 2: Break-up of PIL's Revenue		2001	2002	2003
Specialty Industry Chemicals	Others	1	1	1
	Agency	2		
	Industrial Adhesives	9	8	8
	Organic Pigments	10	9	9
	Industrial Resins	11	11	10
Consumer & Bazaar Products	Art Material & Others	4	5	5
	Construction Paints Chemical	10	12	13
	Adhesives and Sealants	53	54	54

Source: Annual Report, 2005, PIL

Exhibit 2: Break-up of PIL's Revenue

As per PIL's Annual report 2005, their products are sold in over 4 lakh outlets across the country giving it an unparalleled reach in its industry segments. This is a huge entry barrier for potential competition and also helps the company drive growth of acquired products that may have had the potential as brands but previous owners lacked distribution capabilities. The company is increasing distribution in smaller towns where the furniture market is likely to mushroom once benefits of economic growth percolate downwards. In early 21st century the company has also entered new markets like South Asia, Africa and Europe with products such as adhesives, art materials and industrial chemicals.

Pidilite's performance has been steadily improving; the average growth rate for last ten years has been 13.13% for sales and 19.35% for profits. The steady growth of Sales and Profits in last decade can be observed from Exhibits 3 and 4. One of the main growth drivers of PIL has been the steady growth of Indian GDP, as the company's products are used in a wide range of industries most of which have a strong correlation with the economic activity in the country. Growth in housing has also shown a big boost to the company as Fevicol and Dr Fixit, are used mainly in furniture making and

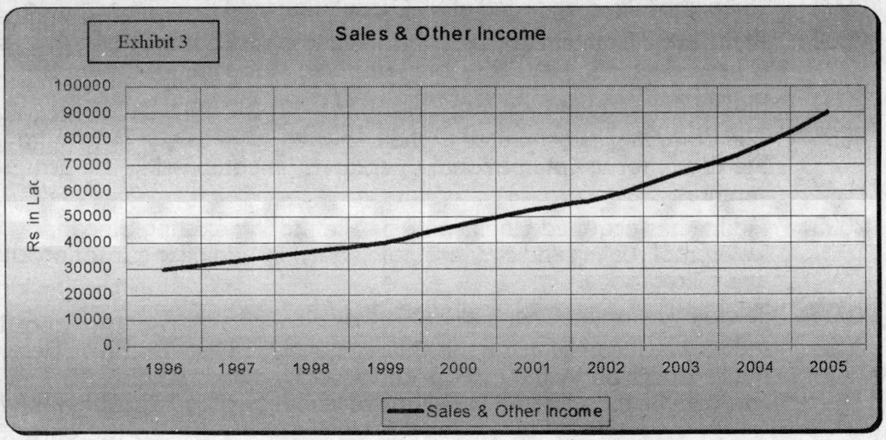

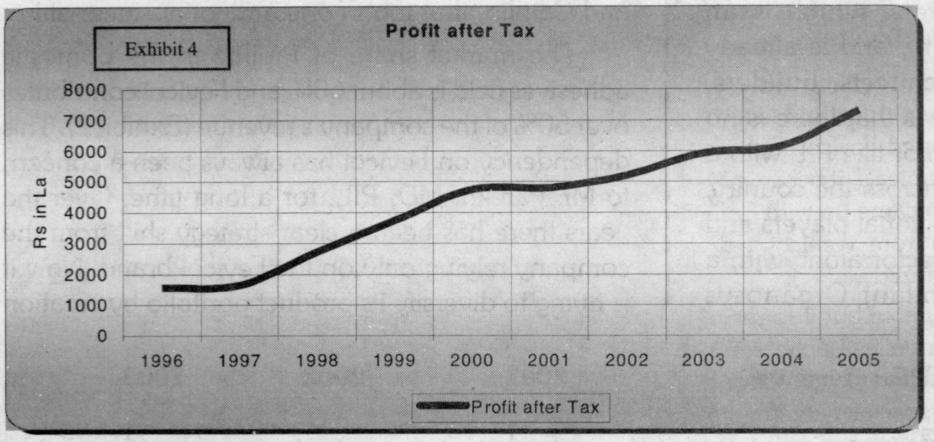

Source: Annual Reports, 1996-05, PIL

wall repairs respectively, which go hand in hand with the growth of the housing industry. A rise in disposable income in the country, especially semi-urban areas, has also added a new set of people into the consumers of furniture – thereby increasing Fevicol sales as well. New products such as construction chemicals, paint chemicals, student stationery and adhesives for the rubber and foam industry are likely to drive growth and further reduce share of Fevicol. Further, export markets will also add to the growth of the company in the years to come. Acquisitions of products have been and are likely to be a growth driver for the company. All acquisitions are in related segments, are paid for in cash and can grow faster due to the company's extensive distribution network as compared to that of the previous owner.

Through constant investment in R&D and by following the path of innovation the company has today established itself. The path from a single brand to a multi-branded establishment is highlighted in Exhibit 5

Year	Achievements
1959	Plants commissioned for Acron brand of pigment emulsion
1965	FEVICOL, established as carpenter's preferred choice of synthetic adhesive
1973	First company in India to start production of violet pigment
1984	Consumer Products Division is born. Plans to set up a nationwide distribution chain
1989	Fevicryl acrylic colors transform fabric and multi-surface painting market
1993	Pidilite makes a maiden public offering of equity shares
1995	Plants in Mumbai & Vapi acquire ISO 9001; plant at Mahad acquires ISO 9002 certification
1997	Fevicol ranked among the Top 15 Indian brands (by FE Brandwagon Year Book, 1997)
1999	"Ranipal", leading brand of optical whitener, acquired
2000	"M-Seal", leading brand of epoxy compounds, acquired
2000	Fevikwik "fish" commercial wins Golden ABBY for the best TV Commercial of the Century in India
2000	Fevicol campaign wins Silver ABBY for the Campaign of the Century in India
2001	Dr. Fixit range of Construction Chemicals launched
2002	"Steelgrip", leading brand of PVC insulation tape in India, acquired
2002	At the 2002 Cannes Awards, considered to be the Oscar of the advertising world, Fevicol 'Bus' TV commercial wins a Silver in the category for Household Maintenance Products
2004	Pidilite has acquired the 'Roff' brand of Construction Chemicals
2005	The Company incorporated a wholly-owned subsidiary in Singapore , under the banner "Pidilite International Pte Ltd.", for its international operations, encompassing the acquisition of overseas companies and joint ventures.
2005	Pidilite has acquired Chemson Asia Pte Ltd, an existing Singapore-based in the business of manufacturing waterproof coating and emulsion paints, thereby adding to its existing, and rapidly-growing construction chemicals and paints range.
2005	Taken over Jupiter Chemicals in Dubai.
2005	Pidilite has incorporated a subsidiary, namely "Pidilite Do Brasil Desenvolvimento De Negocios Ltda", in Sao Paulo, Brazil, on May 10, 2005, and a wholly-owned subsidiary, "Pidilite Middle East Limited", as an offshore company in the Jebel Ali Free Zone of Dubai on May 18, 2005, for its international operations.

Madhukar Balwantray Parekh's views on competition:

Fevicol already have the experience of dealing with Mowicol in the past, it's nothing new. It had existed as a product of Hoechst for many years (until about 1975-77) after we started Fevicol. Subsequently, after the emergence of Mafatlal Dyes & Chemicals, it became Mahacol, an MDC product about 19 years ago. Calico came up with Calibond and for the past 13 years there is competition from Vamicol. So, competition has always been there and it has never fazed us.

Mowicol may have restarted in Mumbai but it forms only a small part/ activity of a large company. It has virtually disappeared from the overseas market. If the total set up of Clariant and Colour-Chem is observed, one would realize that it is an industrial specialty company and not a bazaar consumer company like ours. Our growth has a different dimension now and industrial specialties are only a small part of Pidilite. Consumer and bazaar segments make up a large part (60%) of PIL.

(Source: Chemical Business, June '99, vol.13, issue 6, p25, 4p)

Although Fevicol was a first mover in this category, it faced competition on two fronts, Small-scale sector, which was unorganized and multinationals like the German major Hoechst Dyes and Chemicals, which has been manufacturing Movicol white glue internationally since the early 1940s. On both the fronts Fevicol was able to beat the different brands because of closer association with the carpenters. To further strengthen its position among the carpenters in 1975 Fevicol launched bi-monthly magazine "Fevicraft" showcasing furniture designs – a practice that continues till date.

The competition for Fevicol is from the likes of Kitcol, Vamicol etc at the product form level. At the Product category level Fevicol itself is a competitor to many of its own brands itself like Feviquik, Fevigum, Prime tapes etc. This poses a serious question of cannibalization to the Fevicol Brand and as a whole company. At the generic level again on can see that Fevicol brand competes with other brands of PIL like M-seal, Dr. Fixit etc. At the Budget category we again see that since all stationary products fall into this category again the whole stationary division of Pidilite is a competitor of Fevicol, other that that the Camlin, and Asian paints who produce Wood finish are the competitors in the budget category to the target segment which is the carpenters.

The Fevicol story began in 1989, when a TV commercial showed six half-naked men and one elephant, which was completely naked! The ad became a super-hit!

Piyush Pandey, the man who designed this ad for Fevicol, has since then been coming up with more and more bizarre ideas to promote the brand. This ad threw the 30 yr old brand into public consciousness and today 8 out of 10 carpenters are loyal to Fevicol.

"They wanted me to talk of molecules and things, but consumer would not get it. Fevicol to me is a brand with a smile on its logo," says Piyush Pandey in an interview to Times Now, a TV Channel.

Source: Times Now Feb, 2006

Since its launch, Fevicol has stood for the convenience and ready to use property as against the animal based resin available then. Over the years, being a very conservative company Pidilite never focused on the brand issues of Fevicol, but rather focused on the core marketing issues, which actually in turn built the brand. There has been constant advertising through print media (Exhibit 7), but the image of the brand increased only after it started to campaign on TV. With the success of the various ads on TV made by Ogilvy & Mather Advertising, India, the brand has evolved over time and now is one of the most respected brands in the country

Pidilite's advertising reached a high pitch in the mid-eighties. The "*dum lagaake haisha*" campaign which translated the logo of elephants trying to break the Fevicol bond into a television commercial was the beginning of efforts that unleashed a spiel of creative energy on the brand. The commercial starts with two wooden blocks joining together using Fevicol... six well built men along with an elephant try to break the Fevicol bond by pulling it using a rope... an ordinary looking man with a Fevicol can in his hand says, "*maante hi nahi, kitni baar samjhaya, ye*

Exhibit 6A-1

Fevicol ka jod hai tootega nahi". In the end along with the elephant they all fail to break the bond. (Exhibit 6A-1)

After mid nineties, the brand has risen above the physical bonding of tables and chairs and is bonding with the carpenters. – It launched its "*pakade rehna-chodna nahin*" campaign (Exhibit 6B) The objective of the campaign was not to let the well established carpenter bond break. Featuring carpenter at work, the commercial goes like this. A group of carpenters are at work. However, their attention is divided between their work and a TV set, where a man hanging over a chasm is clinging on to a woman for dear life. "*Pakde rehna*," the woman screams. "*Chodna nahin*," the man pleads. The workers watch as the couple on screen keep up the "*Pakde rehna-chodna nahin*" strain for an incredibly long period Fed up with the melodrama, one of the carpenters gets up in disgust. "*Arre, yeh bhi koi* film *hai*!" he exclaims Wanting to continue with his work, he walks over to the TV and picks up a can of Fevicol placed on top of it Instantly, the man on screen plummets. Surprised, the carpenter peers at the can of Fevicol he has picked up. Slowly, he turns and eyes another TV, atop which a tub of Fevicol is perched. The man on screen is still dangling over the chasm. "*Chodna nahin...*"

Exhibit 6B

In 2005, Fevicol attempted to capitalize on its brand property of 'bonding' by extending it from the tangible benefit associated with Fevicol to an intangible level. This appeal is more abstract in nature trying to incorporate people from all walks of life instead of just carpenters. For example, the bus commercial (Exhibit 6C-1). Starting with a shot of a man as he is perched atop a moving vehicle, swaying slightly from side to side. The camera focuses on one side of him to show his co-passengers huddled together. Cut to the inside of the vehicle, people are occupying every inch of space The camera shifts focus to the front of the truck, with men plastered against the bonnet An aerial shot of the vehicle lumbering down the stretch, overflowing with people from all sides Cut to the back of the truck, the Fevicol logo is seen. 'The ultimate adhesive.' The truck continues its journey with its clinging passengers.

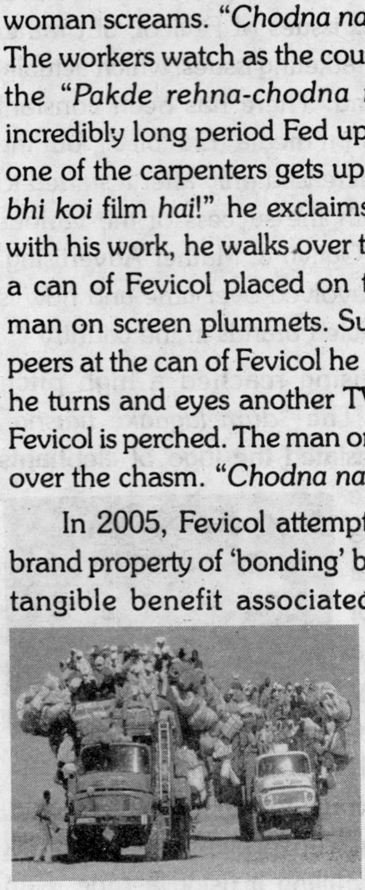

Exhibit 6C-1

Pidilite

The communication by the ads of Fevicol has been very strong time and again, although the theme had been very relational initially i.e. the carpenters

Exhibit 7: **Print Ads (Fevicol)**

at work being shown but at a later stage the link has been abstract and the people from all walks of life are shown in the ads. This helps in relating to all the people and reinforces the fact that Fevicol is present in the lives of all kinds of people of India. (Exhibit 7) The promotional activities are not just confined to television, Fevikraft - a bi-monthly magazine for carpenters has aided to establish goodwill with the prime users. Recently, it formed a carpenters club, Fevicol Champion Club, which meets three times a year. The brand Fevicol has earned its stripes well and is counted among most trusted brands in the country (Exhibit 8)

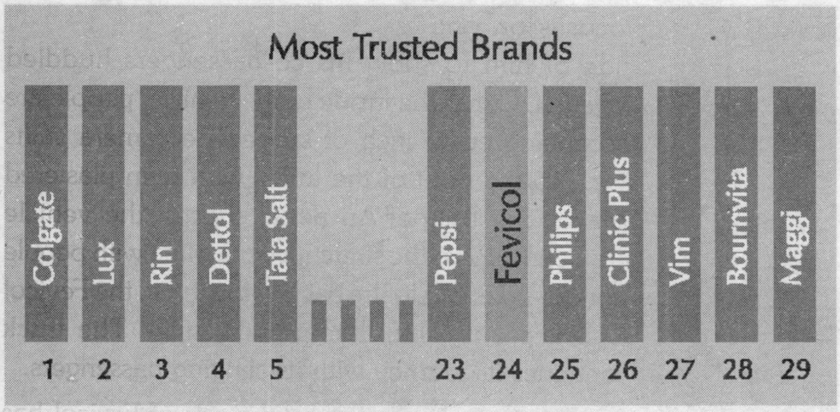

Source: The Economic Times Decempber 15, 2004

Exhibit 8

Over time, tight economic conditions, a need for growth, and other factors forced PIL to rethink their "one brand-one product" policy. Recognizing that one of their most valuable assets is Fevicol, PIL has since decided to leverage Fevicol by introducing a host of new products under the prefix 'Fevi' some of whom target new segments, whereas some belong to entirely new product categories. However, PIL is increasingly realizing the pitfalls of depending too much on a singular brand name "Fevi" and is making efforts to create new brands in its stable.

Questions

1. Does Fevicol qualify as a brand bigger than the company? What might be the implications of this? What are the possible solutions?
2. Comment: Should the brand Fevicol be extended? If yes, then when, where, and how should this be done?

Note: The information gathered in this case is obtained from online edition of various publications - Business Standard (BS), The Economic Times (ET), The Financial Express (FE), The Hindu Business Line (HBL), Hindustan Times (HT), The Times of India (TOI) - copyright protected by the respective publishers.

Notes

Sales Management

Section - Eight

CONCEPTUAL FRAMEWORK

To facilitate a better debate on the cases in this section, a quick exploratory review of the sales management function along with areas that need discussion are recapitulated briefly as follows:

- The sales representative is the company's link to its customers and it is he or she who brings back to the company much-needed information about the customer.
- **Personal selling** is finding prospects, persuading them to buy, and keeping customers satisfied.through paid personal communication.
- A sales person, either consciously or unconsciously, moves through a general selling process as he or she sells products. In prospecting, the salesperson develops a list of potential customers. Before contacting prospects, the salesperson conducts a **pre-approach** that involves finding and analyzing information about prospects and their needs.
- During the **sales presentation**, the salesperson must attract and hold the prospect's attention to stimulate interest in and desire for the product. If possible, the salesperson should handle objections as they arise. During the closing, the salesperson asks the prospect to buy the product or products. After a successful **closing**, the salesperson must follow up the sale.
- Being a marketing manager you should consider which types of salespeople will sell the firm's products most effectively. The three classifications of salespeople are order getters, order takers, and support personnel:
  - **Order getters** inform both current customers and new prospects and persuade them to buy.
  - **Order takers** seek repeat sales and fall into two categories: inside order takers and field order takers.
  - **Sales support personnel** facilitate selling, but their duties usually extend beyond making sales. The three types of support personnel are missionary, trade and technical salespeople.
- **Sales force management** includes five steps:
  - Recruiting and selecting sales representatives
  - Training the representatives in sales techniques and in the company's products, policies and customer-satisfaction orientation
  - Supervising the sales force and helping representatives to use their time efficiently
  - Motivating the sales force, and balancing quotas, monetary rewards, and supplementary motivators

- Evaluating individual and group sales performance

- A great amount of Human Resource insight is required to build an effective sales force.
- Effective salespeople must be **trained** for an accurate analysis and customer management. No approach works best in all circumstances but most trainers agree that selling is a seven-step process: prospecting and qualifying customers, pre-approach, approach, presentation and demonstration, overcoming objections, closing, and follow-up and maintenance.
- **Compensation** of salespeople involves formulating and administrating a compensation plan that attracts, motivates, and retains the right type of salespeople. **Motivation** of salespeople should allow the firm to attain high productivity. Managing sales territories focuses on such factors as size, shape, routing, and scheduling. To control and **evaluate sales force performance**, sales managers must use information obtained through salespeople's call reports, customer feedback, and invoices.
- **Sales promotion** is used by marketers to identify and attract new customers, introduce new products, and increase reseller inventories. Sales promotion techniques fall into two general categories, consumer and trade as elaborated below:
  - **Consumer sales promotion** methods encourage consumers to trade at specific stores or try a specific product. These sales promotion methods include coupons, demonstrations, frequent-user incentives, point-of-purchase displays, free samples, money refunds and rebates, premiums, cents-off offers, consumer contests and games, and consumer sweepstakes.
  - **Trade sales promotion** techniques can motivate resellers to handle a manufacturer's products and market those products aggressively.

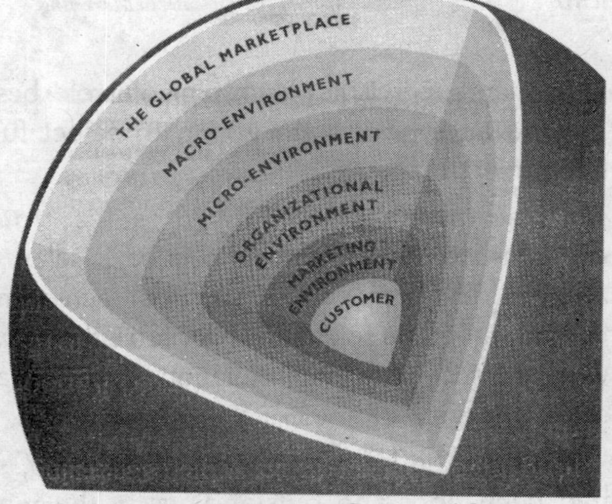

Sales Management Case - 12

Polar Electrical Appliances Limited

Dilemma over Sales Contest

Purpose of the Case

The idea is to assimilate the relevant concepts at work and analyse along the following lines:

- To focus on the ways to motivate sales force and keep them motivated
- To weigh the pros and cons of organizing a sales contest among the sales personnel

Joydeep Banerjee was working as General Manager of Polar Electrical Appliances Limited (PEAL) and was based at Company's head office at Calcutta. PEAL manufactured and distributed a complete line of electrical motors, pumps, parts, switch–gear and accessories and had made a significant mark amongst the channel partners and customers primarily due to its focus on quality and 'value-for-money' pricing. Joydeep recommended a sales contest to improve declining sales performance. This was his response to first-quarter results that saw sales fall substantially below quota. Joydeep believed that a sales contest would, among other things, provide an incentive to get sales upto or beyond territorial quotas.

PEAL's marketing operations were spread in four Eastern states of India viz. West Bengal, Orissa, Assam and Bihar since 1991. In 2004, PEAL started operation in 3 major districts of Andhra Pradesh viz. Vijaywada, Hyderabad and Vishakapatnam. As on 1st April 2006, its sales force of forty persons operated out of four branch offices located in respective state capitals and thirteen Area offices located at Kolkata, Siliguri, Guwahati, Patna, Dhanbad, Jamshedpur, Ranchi, Cuttack, Bhubaneshwar, Vijaywada, Hyderabad and Vishakhapatnam. The Area Sales Managers used to sit at respective state capitals The "Profit Centre operations" of complete state were being looked after with the support of Area Sales Managers. Most of the sales persons were "diploma engineers" having an average job experience of 9 years in engineering industry. The Company had however recruited qualified, experienced , graduate Engineers in recent past. Joydeep believed that in the rapidly changing conditions of industry, a band of technically competent supervisors played a pivotal role, besides serving as a pool from which to select future department managers.

Traditionally in PEAL, sales force's compensation plan consisted of a basic salary and a bonus. The bonus was based upon achievement of territorial quota sales and collection targets, which was set by Joydeep in consultation with the Branch sales manager.

During the last 6 months of Year 2005, sales had been poor and outstandings in the market increased substantially. Competitors also became aggressive in their pricing and promotional effort, and increased their reach to smaller towns.

Joydeep proposed a sales contest which would, in his opinion, motivate sales personnel to achieve their quotas. The details of the contest were as under:

(a) The duration of the contest would be 2 months called the "Scheme period".

(b) There would be a weekly sales volume quota for each salesperson determined by Joydeep and respective branch manager.

(c) Each of the thirteen branches would also have a branch sales volume quota for this "Scheme period".

(d) A cash bonus of Rs.1000 each week would go to the sales person exceeding his/her quota by the greatest percentage. This would be calculated every week. Joydeep wanted to use "total sales volume" instead of percentage but settled for the percentage eventually.

(e) Each sales person who achieves the "Scheme period" quota would get a bonus of Rs. 2,500.

(f) A cash bonus of Rs. 5,000 would be paid to the sales person exceeding his "Scheme period" sales quota by the greatest percentage. This would be calculated at the end of "Scheme period" i.e. after 2 months. Bonus of Rs. 3,500 and Rs. 2,500 would go to sales persons in second and third places respectively.

(g) In the competition amongst branches, the branch exceeding its quota during "Scheme period" by greatest percentage would receive Rs.10,000 as prize, which would be shared equally among the sales persons associated with that branch. Second and third places in the inter branch competition would receive Rs. 7,500 and Rs. 5,000 respectively.

(h) All sales persons, who achieve their quotas and those who are to receive bonuses at the end of the quarter, would be invited for a grand Award function at Hotel Taj Bengal, Calcutta, a leading 5–Star hotel. The award would be handed out by Mr. Sandeep Singh, the Managing Director of PEAL.

When Joydeep formally proposed his plan for a sales contest, many objections were raised. All these objections related to usual objections in sales contests like disappointment and frustration amongst sales persons who would not win, disruption in normal pace of work, over-aggressiveness amongst some people, the likely fall in sales during the period succeeding the contest and so on.

Joydeep felt that a contest would correct the poor sales performance, raise and kindle a competitive spirit amongst its sales force, give them an opportunity to get their achievements recognized, and raise the morale of the entire sales force.

In spite of murmurs of disagreement, Joydeep scheduled a meeting of his staff and branch managers to discuss the merits and mode of implementation of conducting a sales contest.

Questions

1. Should PEAL go ahead with a sales contest to motivate its sales personnel to better sales performance? Why or why not?
2. Should individual performance based contests be run concurrently with group-performance based contests? Why or why not?
3. Could you suggest some other proposal to motivate sales personnel to achieve their sales quotas? Give your reasons with details of the proposal, as to how it would be better than the sales contest.

Notes

Notes

Assam Farm Fresh Tea
Handling Sales Pressures

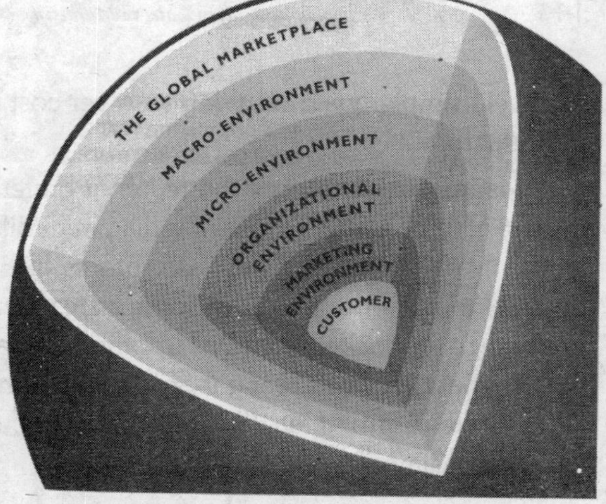

Sales Management Case - 13

Purpose of the Case

The idea is to assimilate the relevant concepts at work and analyse along the following lines:

- To discuss how should Assam Farm Fresh Tea (AFFT) strike a balance in its 'push' and 'pull' policies to enable sales personnel function in a result-oriented way
- To focus on the major decision areas and activities that make sales force management as an important determinant of a firm's success
- To debate how Kapoor, Sales Officer, AFFT will position himself between Shah Bhai and his bosses

India is the largest producer and consumer of tea in the world. It consumes the largest quantity of tea in the world, accounting for nearly 14% of global retail volume sales. Although the annual tea-leaf production has been around 800 million yet India ranks 7th in value terms, due to relatively low unit prices. Black standard tea constitutes nearly 80% of value sales, although green tea is steadily rising in popularity. Geographically, tea is widely consumed in the North, East and West of India, and is popular with a wide variety of social classes and consumer age groups. Offering a hot cup of tea to a visitor is a part of the inherited tradition in Indian homes.

The tea plantations were started in the middle of the 19th century under the British management. The farm ownership, however, is fragmented. Tea plantations in India are concentrated in the North-East i. e. Upper Assam, West Bengal. In the South, regions of Kerala and Tamil Nadu produce tea. The North- Eastern region with 82% of area accounts for 76% of total tea production. In the North East, the yield is lower but quality of tea leaf is superior. The foothills of Darjeeling stretching along the Bhutan border up to the Assam border and the areas of Arunachal Pradesh, Meghalaya, Nagaland, Orissa, Sikkim and Uttar Pradesh have abundant tea-plantations.(Source:www.agriculture-industry-india.com/agricultural-commodities/tea.html). Large players own the gardens whereas the smaller, local ones purchase the produce and then process it. However, the manufacturing cost of the local tea manufacturer turns out to be lower because the tea leaves are not only processed in smaller quantities as they intend to cater only to the local market but the processing also is done in a relatively simpler way; resulting in lower cost to the manufacturer.

It is important to note the regional preferences in taste of tea. Different areas of India prefer different kinds of tea. Some like dust tea, others like good quality loose flavoured tea. In some states there is a preference for packet as well as unbranded tea. The eastern states of West Bengal and Orissa consume 'CTC broken' form of tea. (Source: www.agriculture-industry-india.com)

There is a high brand preference observed in the product tea across all the segments. However, brand loyalty is missing in the economy and mid premium segment. Therefore there is a fierce price competition in these segments. Since tea is a highly differentiable product, its prices vary a lot depending upon the consumer segment to which it is targeted. For example, tea brands in the economy segment range from Rs. 19 to Rs. 35/250gm whereas specialty teas are priced as high as Rs. 375/250gm. The premium and specialty segments command a good number of brand loyal consumers therefore the prices tend to be of hardly any importance to such consumers. Thus prices in these segments are more indicative of the value they provide to the consumer than the cost incurred by the manufacturer.

The tea market lends itself to benchmarking the complexity of the FMCG set of products. The product necessitates packing of a type, which ensures the freshness of the tea (flavour and fragrance) as well as secure packaging to prevent loss. The tea market can be divided into various segments on the basis of the pack sizes. Available pack sizes range from 50 grams to 2 kgs. India shows preference for small pack sizes, which can be seen from the absence of I kg and 2 kg packs from the rural market. The smaller packs of 50 grams and less exhibit an increasing trend with their respective contributions increasing from 32% to 45% from 1995 to 2000 respectively. (Source: Packaging Industry In India www.globus.cam.com) whereas in urban India the preference is for 200/250 grams, which contributes 48% to the total market. The pack types prevailing in the industry today are jars, bottles, boxes, sachets, pouches, strips, envelopes and tins. Poly pouches introduced in 1985 have captured 12% of the tea market from the loose tea segment as they were not only cost-effective, but were also effective in retaining freshness. (Source: Packaging Industry In India www.globus.cam.com)

Small, local players, through regional brands, have been sipping away the market share of such bigwigs as Tata Tea and Hindustan Lever. Local brands penetrate better due to better knowledge of the requirement of the people in the area and superior knowledge of the area as such. National brands, on the other hand, are most of the times unable to provide the exact blend of the tea required by the people and also have to deal with difficult logistics due to poor transport infrastructure. Therefore superior knowledge of the area helps local players reduce their costs. Local brands are usually managed by the families and employ very little outside labour. This also helps them to keep their overheads low. They hardly spend anything for marketing the product except for some small promotional schemes launched here and there thus keeping the overheads low.

In addition, higher promotional outlays have also affected the profitability of large and medium-sized players. Of the 680 million kg of tea consumed in India, about 44 per cent is in packet form and the rest, loose. Though this consumption level seems substantial, the packet tea segment has not grown over the past few years. Owing to this and waning brand loyalty, players have been aggressively competing for market share. (Source: 'Small brands, strong brew', Author: C.Raja Rajeshwari, www.hindubusinessline.com 2003)

Large players have been combating the declining trends in market share by stepping up their marketing efforts and broadening their range of offerings to straddle different price points. The national level players have rolled out new products straddling different price points. For instance, to combat price competition, Tata Tea launched Agni Sholay, a low-priced packet tea. It has been active at the premium end too, rolling out Temptation and Tetley, targeted at the quality-conscious consumer. These launches have helped transform Tata Tea from a player with a predominant presence in the mid-priced segment to one with a broader presence across the price spectrum. Hindustan Lever, on the other hand, has adopted the strategy of putting greater marketing muscle behind its tea business and rationalising its portfolio of brands. In 2003, HLL made an attempt to revitalise the tea business, which has suffered owing to the heavy price competition from the local players. HLL relaunched and consolidated all its tea offerings under the umbrella brands — Brooke Bond and Lipton. The Brooke Bond brand now encompasses Taaza, Red Label Tea and Taj Mahal. Taaza has been shifted from the Lipton to the Brooke Bond brand. (Source: 'Small brands, strong brew', Author: C.Raja Rajeshwari, www.hindubusinessline.com 2003). Players have also been trying to create new differentiators for their brands. For instance, Duncans launched a new tea brand — Marybong Mystique, positioning it as a handpicked premium Darjeeling tea. Duncans has also tweaked the brand's packaging. While its Runglee Rungliot brand is available in packet form, Marybong Mystique comes in higher-end chestlets. (Source: 'Small brands, strong brew', Author: C.Raja Rajeshwari, www.hindubusinessline.com 2003)

Duncans, has entered into retailing loose tea, and has opened Duncans Tea House in West Bengal, a retail outlet which allows consumers to blend different varieties of tea. This is to cater to the consumers who prefer 'bush-to-cup' tea. (Source: 'Small brands, strong brew', C.Raja Rajeshwari, www.hindubusinessline.com 2003)

In such a scenario, a mid-size player in the tea business called Assam Farm Fresh Tea has launched a new attractively packaged leaf tea, called 'Valley's Pride'. The company has a turnover of Rs 210 crore and has been there in the Indian market since last 35 years. It has made its mark because of its quality of tea, aroma and 'value for money' pricing however the business is getting extremely competitive now. Since last 5 years, the company has also started procuring fruit drinks, jams and jellies from contract manufacturers under strict quality-control norms and started branding and distributing them through their existing channel partners.

The sales of Valley's Pride have not picked up in Gujarat and Maharashtra despite aggressive selling on field. Orders from distributors are not coming. No wonder Kapoor, the Sales officer, is very worried. His boss, Vijay Desai has been screaming at him, for low sales achievement. To make matters worse, the nearest competitor, Brakes Bond is launching another leaf tea 'Green Darjeeling' next month. Assam Farm Fresh Tea's distributors were facing resistance from retailers as they said four other brands were well established and 'Valley's Pride' was not even getting trials. Although, sales of 'Valley's Pride' has picked up in Northern India i.e. U.P, Rajasthan, Uttaranchal,

Punjab and Haryana but Kapoor's territory is primarily 'dust tea'.

Kapoor pressurized as well as emotionally cajoled with great difficulty, that too after spending three very taxing days of forced convincing, his Ahmedabad distributor Shah Bhai to somehow take three tons of tea with the promise that advertising will start soon and his stocks will be liquidated.

When Desai saw order of three tons only, he was disappointed and told Kapoor that Shah Bhai being a key man must have taken five tons at any cost, at least four tons is a must. Desai also expressed shock on unsold two tons of 'tetra-pack drinks' lying with Shah Bhai as unsold inventory. Kapoor explained that this was unwanted stock but had to be pushed on the insistence of Food division. In fact, Kapoor told him Shah Bhai was dispatched four tons of 'Valley's Pride' plus some fruit drinks, jams and jellies to complete truckload on the insistence of C&F agent.

Shah Bhai called up immediately on receipt of truck and was very-very upset. Kapoor told him that the boss had ordered him to do so and he will adjust later. On opening the consignment, Shah Bhai not only found wrong products but also unwanted pack size composition. He wondered how would he sell 1 kg packs when demand in his territory was skewed towards 250 gram packs. Also, he had received wrong flavors of fruit drinks, which according to him didn't sell, in his territory.

Shah Bhai in desperation asked Kapoor for a scheme, which the latter had no authority to disburse. Desai kept on calling Kapoor on phone, complaining of stuck money, space and inability to rotate money. Kapoor reminded Shah of the display windows he provided with full payment of lighting for a year and asked him to switch customers to their brand and also push his products when the customer comes for buying other household goods.

Retailers also complained of company constantly trying to push unordered, low-demand products along with ordered ones. Desai told Kapoor 'push' was necessary and there is no need to extra-empathize with dealers as launches are done on scientific demand assessment basis and as such dealers must take interest. Kapoor is stuck between bosses and dealers who are getting restive and do not like Assam Farm Fresh Tea's policies.

Questions

1. Imagine you are Kapoor who is stuck between his channel partners and bosses. What would you do in such a situation?
2. List how you would like to make channel partners like Shah Bhai especially inclined to push your company's products to the customers. Where is AFFT going wrong?

Distribution

Section - Nine

CONCEPTUAL FRAMEWORK

To facilitate a better debate on the cases in this section, a quick exploratory review of the distribution ingredient of the marketing mix (consisting of product, distribution, promotion and price) along with areas that need discussion are recapitulated briefly as follows:

- A marketing manager who looks after the **channel of distribution** directs the flow of products from producers to customers in order to make products available at the right time at right place, and in the right amounts. He coordinates with various groups of people and the organizations to develop smoother flow of the product through the channel. These individuals and organizations are called channel members.
- **Marketing intermediaries**, or **middlemen** link producers and consumers in most channels of distribution. Of the two major types of intermediaries, **retailers** purchase products and resell them to ultimate consumers, and **wholesalers** buy and resell products to other wholesalers, retailers, and business customers.
- The most important **functions performed by intermediaries** are passing on the information to marketers, promotion of the product at the point of purchase, negotiation with the ultimate customer, ordering the product, financing the customer for short period, risk-taking and payment.
- **A** marketing manager's choice of channel of distribution affects all other marketing decisions. Hence, **marketing-channel decisions** are among the most critical decisions facing the management.
- Two different types of marketing channels are developed for **consumer products** and **business products**. Within these two broad categories different marketing channels are used for different products. It is generally seen that marketing channels for consumer products provides greater efficiency than the direct selling.
- A direct distribution channel is common in **business marketing**. Also used are channels containing industrial distributors, manufacturer's agents, and a combination of agents and distributors. Most producers have multiple or dual channels so the distributing system can be adjusted for various target markets.
- Depending upon the company's overall marketing strategy, a marketing manager can choose any one or the combination of more than one from **intensive distribution** where producers strive to make a product available to all possible dealers **or selective distribution** where only some outlets in an area are chosen to distribute a product **or exclusive distribution** which

usually gives one dealer exclusive right to sell a product in a large geographic area.

- Each channel member performs a different role in the system and agrees to accept certain rights, responsibilities, rewards, and sanctions for non-conformance. Channels function most effectively when members co-operate; when they deviate from their roles **channel conflict** can arise.
- A marketing manager should select appropriate intermediaries and train them. He should motivate them to build a long-term partnership that will be profitable for all channel members. He should bring changes to channel arrangements when market conditions change. All these activities lead to an effective channel management.
- A marketing manager should integrate various marketing channels to bring various activities under one channel member's management. Vertical integration combines two or more stages of the channel under one management. The **vertical marketing system** (VMS) is managed centrally for the mutual benefit of all channel members. Vertical marketing system may be corporate administered, or contractual. **Horizontal integration** combines institutions at the same level of channel operation under a single management to form **horizontal marketing system**. Another new trend has been **multi-channel marketing system**.
- After setting up a distribution channel, a marketing manger looks into the **physical distribution**, or **logistics** which refers to the activities used to move products from producers to customers and other end users. These activities include
  - **Order processing**
  - **Inventory management**
  - **Materials handling**
  - **Warehousing**
  - **Transportation.**
- A marketing manager should look at the efficiency of physical distribution system as a way to reduce costs and improve customer satisfaction. Within the marketing channel, physical distribution activities are often performed by a wholesaler, but they may be performed by a producer or retailer, or outsourced to a third party.
- Physical distribution functions account for about half of all marketing costs and have a significant impact on customer satisfaction. Effective marketers are therefore actively involved in the **design and control of physical distribution**.
- Physical distribution affects every element of the marketing mix - product, price, promotion and distribution. To satisfy customers, marketers consider customer's changing needs and shifts within major distribution function. They then adapt existing physical distribution system for greater effectiveness.

Eveready: Building a Strong Network

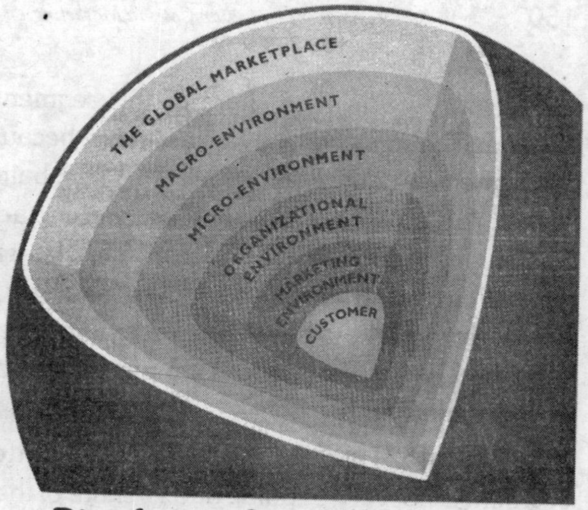

Distribution Case - 14

Purpose of the Case

The idea is to assimilate the relevant concepts at work and analyse in light of the following issues:

- To focus on how a company builds its distribution muscle to be able to serve a large consumer universe
- To learn when do innovative upcountry marketing programs actually translate into sales

Ask any Indian consumer to name a brand of batteries, and 9 out of 10 will spontaneously say "Eveready". The *Economic Times'* recent all India survey ranked Eveready at No.19, on strength of brand. This makes it bigger in sales than brands such as Cadbury's, Surf, Close-Up, Parachute, Godrej, Amul, etc.

The Indian battery market size, as per industry estimates, is around 1400 to 1500 crore rupees and is projected to grow at 5 to 7% per annum. Eveready industries, Indo National and Lakhanpal National are the major players in India. The top global players like Duracell and Energizer have strong presence in India.

The price-sensitive Indian consumer continues to prefer using the low-priced dry cell batteries (99% of total usage) as against high global usage of alkaline batteries. Eveready dominates the dry cell (carbon-zinc) battery market and is poised to grow its market share aided by its strong brand equity and unmatched distribution reach.

A dry cell battery basically converts chemical energy into electrical energy. Based on the size, the dry cell batteries are classified into three categories — UM1 (large-sized batteries), UM2 (medium-sized batteries) and UM3 (pencil-sized or AAA-sized batteries). Batteries are either paper or metal clad. Paper-clad batteries, suitable for high-drain applications and prone to leakage, are cheaper than the metal-clad ones.

UM1 or large-size batteries are primarily used in transistor radios and torchlights. The demand for this battery flows primarily from the rural areas where transistor radios and torchlights are widely used. Thus, the demand for this battery depends on agricultural incomes. Thanks to the good monsoon and the resultant improved farm income levels, the UM1 segment recorded an impressive growth in early

21st century years. The share of this segment has been declining steadily over the years because of the higher use of the UM3, or the AAA-size, batteries. The growing offtake of electronic gadgets has increased the demand for AAA batteries. The UM1 batteries' share in the total dry cell battery production has been dropping over the past three years, from about 85 per cent to about 60 per cent (Figure 1).

The UM2, or the medium-sized batteries, segment is not very popular, and its share of the total declined from about 4 per cent in 1996-97 to 2.7 per cent now. The UM3 (AAA-sized) batteries recorded the highest growth rate over the last four years. The share of this segment in the total improved from 20 per cent in 1994-95 to 37 percent in 2003-04. This segment is slated to grow at a healthy 10-12 per cent. Given the nature of application, the demand for this battery comes primarily from the urban areas.

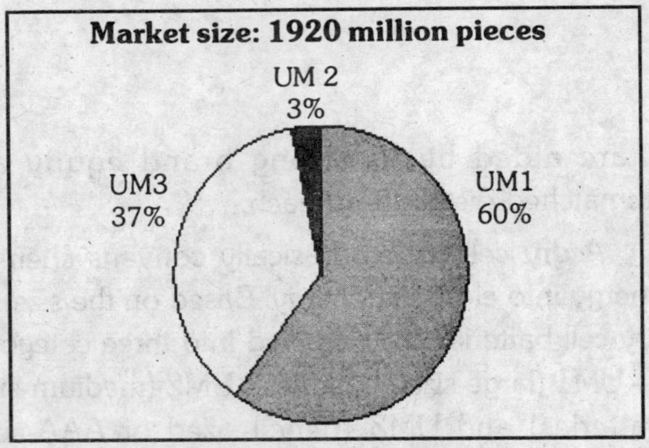

Figure 1: **Market composition**

Eveready is the market leader, followed by Indo National (Nippo brand), and Lakhanpal National (it enjoys a strong position in the UM3 segment). Geep Industrial Syndicate is a marginal player but with significant presence in the UM1 segment. Although its presence is limited to a few northern States but with the acquisition of its production facilities and brand name, Geep has now come under resourceful Gillette's fold. BPL, the latest entrant, has managed to carve a place for itself in the fast-moving AAA segment through their Excel range.

Apart from size, dry cell batteries can also be categorised into zinc and alkaline batteries, based on the electrolyte used. The alkaline battery costs twice as much as the traditional zinc cell. The higher pricing is because of the relatively higher cost of production as also the better and lasting performance. BPL, the only listed company producing both alkaline and zinc carbon batteries, sells its alkaline batteries at around Rs 20 per piece, while its zinc battery is priced at around Rs 7 per piece.

Alkaline batteries are typically suited for high-drain applications, such as portable cassette players (walkman) and cameras. Given the prohibitive cost,

(Numbers are indicative)

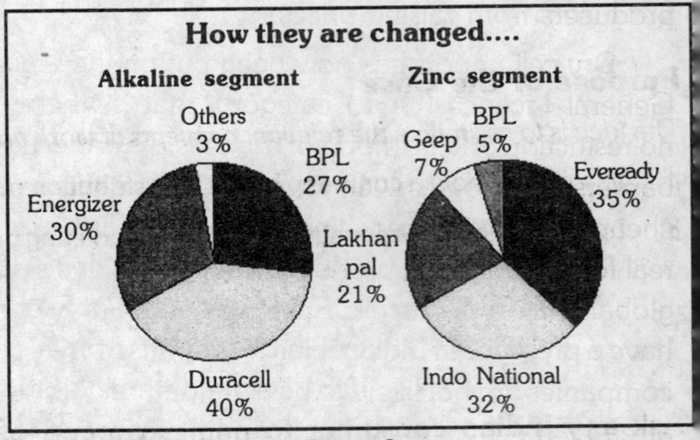

Figure 2

the alkaline battery segment has not really taken off in India. This battery now accounts for less than 3 per cent of the total battery demand. In stark contrast, alkaline batteries are popular in developed economies. In the US, they have over 70 per cent of the total battery market, while in Europe the ratio is marginally lower at a little over 50 per cent. In India, BPL and Duracell are the only major manufacturers of alkaline batteries. (Figure 2) The alkaline battery production is capital-intensive. BPL invested Rs 130 crore to set up the alkaline battery unit with a capacity of about 75 million units.

Given the market conditions and the 20-million-unit alkaline battery segment, setting up exclusive alkaline battery lines is not economically viable. However, since Lakhanpal National and Indo National have the technological backing of Matsushita Electric, they can access this technology if they so desire. With the easing of import norms the two companies can also import and market alkaline batteries from their collaborator.

The dry cell battery industry is highly raw material intensive, with their costs accounting for over 50 per cent of the turnover. The major raw materials used for the manufacture of dry cell batteries include zinc, carbon rods and manganese dioxide. Of the lot, zinc is the major input, accounting for about 35 per cent of the total raw material cost; therefore, zinc's price movements would have a significant impact on the margins of dry cell manufacturers. Negligible differences in product appearance and quality, and the competitive pressure in the industry have prevented domestic producers from raising prices.

Dry cell import has now been put on the Open General Licence (OGL) category, that is, there is no restriction on the import of dry cells. As protection barriers are progressively dismantled, the threat of cheaper imports from China and South-East Asia is real for the domestic producer. On the positive side, global majors Duracell, Energizer and Panasonic have a presence in Indian. Hence, imports from these companies are not likely to be a major threat as they already have a presence in India. Duracell, for instance, has production facilities in India and leverages the distribution network of its subsidiary — Indian Shaving Products. Energizer, owned by Ralston Purina, has a presence in India through a tie-up with Eveready Industries. Matsushita Electric, owners of Panasonic and National brands, has teamed up Lakhanpal National and Indo National. While domestic majors are comfortably positioned in the present environment, a further reduction in the import tariff could heighten the competitive threat from cheaper imports.

Eveready Industries India Ltd (EIIL) is heralded as the market leader of India when it comes to dry cell batteries and flashlights. It produces over 1 billion batteries per annum. and is the market leader in the battery market in India with a 46% market share. It started its operation in India in the year 1905. The first dry cell batteries were imported from USA and sold in the major cities of the country. These batteries were primarily used in imported torches. Today, EIIL has a turnover of more than Rs.900 crore and has a diverse product portfolio ranging from carbon zinc batteries, alkaline batteries, flashlights and rechargeables, packet tea under the Greendale brand and bulk tea.

In 1939, the company set up its first battery plant in Kolkata. This was followed by another battery manufacturing plant in Chennai in the year 1952. It was only logical for the company to set up a torch manufacturing plant to boost up the market for batteries. Accordingly, a torch manufacturing plant was set up at Lucknow in the year 1958. Today it is one of the largest torches manufacturing plants in South East Asia. The plant manufactures the full range of brass, aluminum and plastic torches, which have helped EIIL, not only attain market dominance in the flashlight industry but also increased the per capita consumption of battery and thus expanded the battery market. Today more than 50% of all batteries produced in the country are consumed in Flashlights making it the largest consumer of batteries. With a 70% market share of organized flashlight market, the dominance of EIIL in the dry-cell battery market is a foregone conclusion.

Success in any business depends upon anticipating changes and being ready for them. The late '60s saw an upsurge in the ownership and usage of transistor radios in the country. To meet this new requirement EIIL's Research and Development team designed a battery specifically for transistors. Called a transistor battery, it had a leak-proof construction to safeguard expensive transistors from damage. This was a milestone in the history of the dry-cell industry as this battery was the first Leak Proof battery in the country. This product was a runaway success and was later upgraded to a heavy-duty construction in the 90s to address the new power requirements for Cassette tape Recorders and Boom boxes.

Various independent market studies suggest that rising battery usage in modern devices such as toys, cameras, portable music players, FM radios, remote control, etc will drive demand for batteries. Anticipating the high power needs of the new equipment, EIIL launched India's first Zinc-chloride pencil battery in the Mid 80's. By early 90s the consumption of these 'AA' (pencil batteries) had started rising sharply and it was then that Eveready launched its memorable "Give Me Red" advertisement campaign. This campaign advertisement has been often quoted as one of most memorable campaigns run in Indian media. The advertisement campaign was targeted at the new generation youth, the prime user of equipment like personal stereos and cameras.

The success of its products in the marketplace would not have been possible without the emphasis the company placed on state-of-the-art technology and stringent quality control measures. Technological leadership has long been the driving force of the company. EIIL has always had one of the most advanced Research and Development centers. Recently, its Central Testing Laboratory at Chennai received NABL (National Accreditation Board for Testing and Calibration Laboratories) accreditation under Ministry of Science and Technology, Govt. of India, thereby making it the only company in India to be accredited with the same. The State-of-the-art Computerized Testing Laboratory has complete range of facilities to test dry batteries as per National and IEC Standards.

Keeping its commitment of providing the highest quality, EIIL, today has launched rechargeable batteries for cellular and cordless phones as well as alkaline batteries in the AA and AAA sizes. Imported from Japan, the alkaline batteries are aimed at discerning consumers who use equipment that require long-lasting digital power. To tap the urban market, new premium flashlights have been launched.

Year	Milestones of EIIL
1905	National Carbon starts its Indian operations with sale of batteries imported from USA.
1926	Eveready Company India sets up the first arc carbon factory at Canal Road, Kolkata
1934	Eveready Company incorporated as a private company on 12th November
1939	Camperdown Works – first modern battery plant established at Cossipore in Kolkata
1941	Union Batteries merges with Eveready Company and the name is changed to National Carbon Company
1951	Renamed as Union Carbide India Ltd, a subsidiary of worldwide multinational, Union Carbide Corporation
1959	Name of the company changed to Union Carbide India Ltd.
1995	Sale of shares of Union Carbide Corporation in Union Carbide India Ltd to Mc Leod Russel (I) Ltd. belonging to the Williamson Magor Group and a new name - Eveready Industries India Ltd (EIIL)
1996	Mc Leod Russel (India) Ltd, merged with EIIL, bulk tea business brought into EIIL fold
2000	Bishnauth Tea Company merged with Eveready Industries India Ltd
2005	Brand Eveready completes hundred years

Eveready Industries India Ltd, currently has three strategic business divisions, namely

Batteries

Batteries itself contains three successfully established brands:

- **Carbon Zinc:** Eveready is the world's third

largest producer of carbon zinc batteries, selling close to 1 billion primary batteries every year. Eveready carbon zinc batteries dominate the Indian market and are available in all standard sizes and technology types.

- **Rechargeables:** Playing the role of a future technology leader, Eveready not only markets rechargeable batteries and chargers but is also the sole Indian player in the organized segment. Eveready Recharge AA NiCd and AAA NiMh batteries, can be recharged up to a thousand times and therefore result in huge savings. With the penetration of cordless telephone instruments into Indian households Eveready Recharge is also marketing cordless phone batteries. Here, it brings to the customers the reliability and assurance that safeguards the performance of their handsets and also assures a longer standby and talk time.

- **Alkalines:** The recently launched Eveready Alkaline battery is well geared to meet the power demands of the next generation of digital equipment such as MP3 players, personal compact disc players, digital cameras and new-age toys. EIIL imports these batteries from world-renowned manufacturers, who have amongst the best manufacturing facilities in the world.

Flashlights

Eveready is the largest manufacturer of flashlights in South Asia. The trusted 'Jeevan Sathi' brass torch has been a constant companion over generations. The Company also has a comprehensive range of metal and plastic flashlights including lanterns and rechargeable lights to cater to every need. In the remotest corner of this country as the sun sets, it's always an Eveready flashlight that lights up hamlets and homes with the promise of life renewed.

Tea

Since it's beginning in 1868, the Williamson Magor Group has gone on to become one of the largest tea producers in the world. In 1996 Eveready Industries India Ltd. launched packet tea under Greendale. Greendale teas are marketed under four variants, Tez, Premium Gold, Jaago and Classic. And in a short period of five years Greendale has made a niche for itself in the highly competitive packet tea industry of India.

Since EIIL does not have the license to market its products under Eveready outside India, Bhutan and Nepal, it was imperative to identify a new brand name for the export market. Accordingly, brand Lava was launched in 1999. The launch of Lava marked the entry of Eveready Industries India Ltd. into the global market. Lava commenced its worldwide journey with its launch in Sri Lanka, Bangladesh and Mauritius and then moved on to the more distant markets of Middle East, Africa, Latin America, USA and United Kingdom, and became a well-recognized brand in the markets of Sudan, Ethiopia, Nigeria, Djibouti, Eritrea, Qatar, Egypt, Yemen, UAE and Bahrain. To promote the Lava brand in Ethiopia, company selected the legendary long distance runner and Olympic gold medal winner, Haile Gebre Selassi as the Brand Ambassador.

Indeed, Lava has made its presence felt in 15 countries in less than 36 months. In order to be a comprehensive supplier of the global battery market, company has expanded its product range to include the Heavy-Duty series, the Super Heavy - Duty series and even the Alkaline series. The Lava portfolio spans the entire range of sizes - D, C, AA, AAA and 9V in both Carbon Zinc and Alkaline segments. Following in the footsteps of Lava batteries, EIIL has also launched Lava Flashlights in two segments - the Heavy Duty Range comprising all brass focusing flashlights, and the Contemporary Range comprising Aluminum and Plastic.

The most important factor that has contributed to EIIL's dominance as a No.1 brand has been the investment it made in developing a formidable distribution network across the width and depth of India. Apart from the traditional urban distribution system comprising of distributors, stockists and retailers, it reaches out to the villages of India through a unique rural van distribution system. Today, EIIL products are available in more than 2 million shops with the company's own distribution systems catering to 6 lakh retail outlets through more than 4,000 distributors and 1000 exclusive vans painted with the Eveready logo and messages

Eveready understood that being present is the first step in building a brand. Eveready's distribution system has evolved over the years to ensure that products are distributed as widely as possible, to be available for consumers to purchase as close to their homes as they can. Company have over 15 Sales Branches, one for each major State Capital. Products are distributed from more than 44 warehouses across India. Over 4000 distributors cover the markets and have 1000 dedicated distribution vans carrying products to outlets. The Distribution network reaches 600,000 outlets directly, and including indirect coverage, reaches 1,800,000 outlets. The company has largest distribution network of more than half a million retailers directly and nearly two million indirectly from fifteen branches and forty-four depots spread all over India.

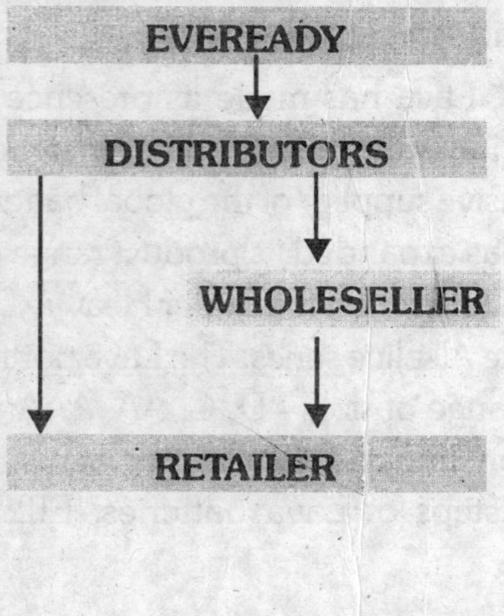

The Organisation Structure of sales department of EIIL is as follows:

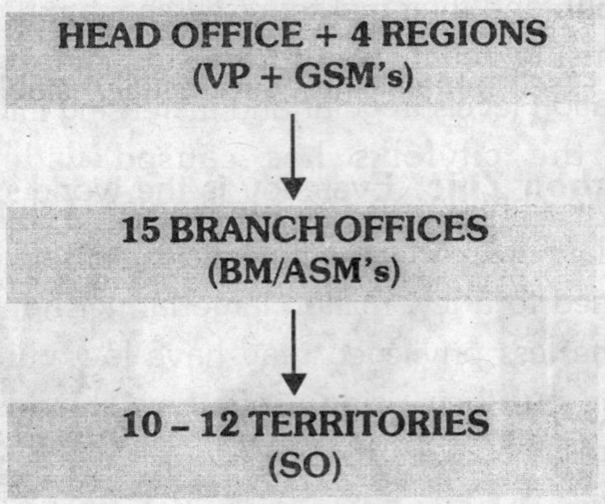

At a time when the battery industry was flickering on falling growth, EIIL painted the rural landscape red, and flashed rising volumes on the strength of an interactive campaign. The battery industry registered a negative growth in 2004 but Eveready India bucked the trend, pushing its market share from 38% in 1999 to 42% in 2001 i.e. a neat 4% volume growth, according to an ORG-Marg survey.

EIIL realised that remote areas where electricity was non-existent and torches are a mainstay and where white batteries were in use are the main rural markets and thus it wanted a larger penetration there. EIIL found out that those villages and small towns, which were once inconsequential dots on maps, are now getting the attention of global marketing giants and media planners. Thanks to globalization, economic liberalization, IT revolution, Indian diaspora, female power, and improving infrastructure, middle class rural India today has more disposable income than urban India. The advent of commercial and market–oriented farming, with the help of modern agricultural technology, necessitated the use of manufactured inputs like fertilizers, pesticides and high yielding varieties of seeds.

According to NCAER, by 2006-07, the lowest income class (i.e. Rs. 25,000 & below) will shrink by than 60 per cent. The higher income classes are likely to double by 2006-07. This apparently is the result of development work, which happened under the five-year plans, and other special programmes such as land reforms, rural electrification, rural communication and credit facilities.

EIIL and their market research team found out that rising reach of audio-visual media, rising education levels, regular and increasing interaction with the cityfolks has caused widespread lifestyle changes in the rural areas. Contrary to popular perception, the potential rural market is not confined to a few million large farmer households but the less privileged may have low purchasing power, but their rising aspirations should not be underestimated.

Eveready's two-tier system of distribution began with appointment of distributors in large towns, which was then extended to distributors in smaller towns. The 'Van Stock Point' concept allowed picking up of stocks of small town distributors and then reaching out to hinterland villages. However, in quest for greater coverage, van zones became too large, as such a need arose to address the bigger markets separately. The result was that EIIL had local Eveready representation for bigger markets thus time was freed for the van to cover deeper markets

The strength of Eveready lay in its strong distribution network, which the company had developed over the years. An internal survey showed that traditional print and electronic media campaigns barely reached 30 per cent of the target population, Eveready opted for a different tack. Lending a helping hand to this initiative was 'Ogilvy Outreach' the rural initiative arm of O & M, who thought of devising promotional campaigns using local themes in their regional languages.

Eveready realised that organized media can reach its rural target group to the extent of 40%; the rest 60% of its rural target group remains untouched. Eveready has traditionally been very strong in "Rural Mela" participation. O&M rural assisted Eveready in increasing their brand awareness in rural areas by organizing film festivals, game shows and many other simple activities ensuring consumer interaction.

Host of "commonsense but impact" activities were started by EIIL. To begin with, Eveready used the adage 'ful ful masala', which is usually meant for the power of a battery. The ingredients that go in to make a battery is termed as `masala' by the rural folk. Eveready also planned games, which would all relate to light and strength, communicating power...essentially Eveready power. All these activities involved fun, interaction and even prizes for the participants so that there remains a very high brand recall in their mind.

Packaged on the punch line 'Kaun banega Eveready Mahashaktimaan', EIIL began an onslaught of festive bonanza with dangals (wrestling matches), bull worker - signifying power - arm wrestling matches, nautankis, with folklore interwoven with brand properties like power and strength and even filmy hungamas with free tickets to action movies.

With campaigns right through UP, Bihar and MP, covering over 4,000 villages and 30 odd districts, from 1999 to 2001, Eveready has gained about 43.9 per cent of the market share in the rural segment in 2001. These initiatives in the rural segment contribute over 65 per cent to the company's total battery business.

Eveready is currently focusing on display at the point of sale. They are also reworking their packaging to enhance display. Eveready is the only company with a 20-piece display as compared to the other companies who have a 10-piece display, to get more shelf space. Eveready was the first company to start the concept of packing the batteries with the torch, despite a lot of criticism and bottlenecks and now every other battery company follows it.

In early 2000s, Eveready tied up with the promotion of "Shanghai Knights" which was branded around the Eveready truck, which is seen in the Eveready TV commercial.

The branch teams get excited with these promotions.

Eveready has an enormous distribution system, with 1000 vans operating across India. The whole system is based on Eveready reaching the inaccessible areas, which they do either by vans or by stockists (4,000 odd stockists). EIIL has a unique system of rural coverage wherein an exclusive, painted van makes weekly, fortnightly or monthly calls based on sales potential of the respective territory. The van makes 50 to 60 calls per day on an average thus an Eveready product is brought fresh to the door of the retailer.

Retail outlets in India grow at the rate of 8%. According to experts, whoever gets the farthest in distribution has a competitive edge in user preference; this is particularly true in rural India. Therefore the need of doubling its reach in by 2010 is high especially when the distribution network remains stagnant. Eveready reaches 600,000 retail outlets once, twice or sometimes even four times a month directly, however, work is on to make that a million for deeper entrenchment across the country.

Questions

1. Design a marketing channel for EIIL given that vast rural areas of India are remote and inaccessible, infrastructure facilities like roads, warehouses, communication system and credit facilities are inadequate, villages are highly dispersed.
2. It's a statistically researched fact that high rate of illiteracy added to the inadequacy of mass media impedes reach to a majority of India's population. In such a situation, how would you use the distribution channel for promoting goods of EIIL?

Notes

Wardha Soap Company: Taking on Price Undercutting

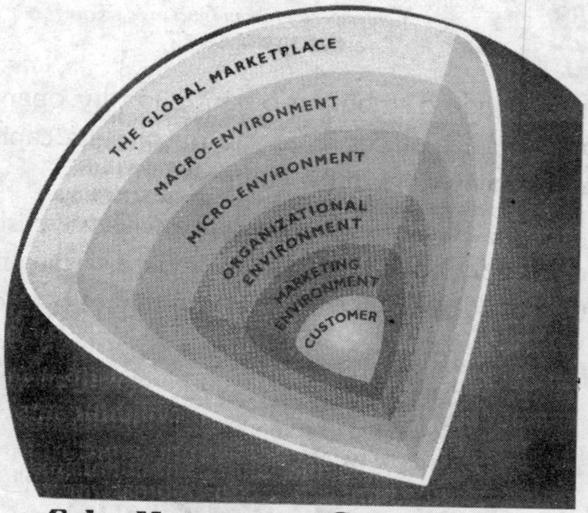

Sales Management Case - 15

Purpose of the Case

The idea is to assim late the relevant concepts at work and analyse along the following lines:

- To focus on how to monitor the operation of a distribution network effectively
- To reason out whether it is prudent to eliminate wholesalers from the distribution channel with a view to control prices better

Wardha Soap Company (WSC) was established in 1979 by an ex-fertilizer company chemist Ramneek Bhai Patel, who had to quit his job in one of the Fertilizer companies in Kota due to sudden demise of his father and elder brother in an accident. As on 2006, the company has grown into one of the leading manufacturers of soaps and other related washing products. With brands like Super-Clean and Fresca, its products enjoy a high reputation in the market. It's TV ads depicting mother-child bonding built around the theme of success in exams, sports and extra-curricular activities coupled with hummable jingle has made Wardha's brands a name to reckon with. The company's head office was in Ahmedabad, however the factory was situated in Wardha, Gujarat. WSC was created almost singlehandedly by Ramneek Bhai, who got inspired by the success of Karsan Bhai Patel of Nirma fame. He seemed almost convinced by the philosophy that in a predominantly agrarian economy like India there will almost be buyers if you can provide 'value-for money" without compromising on quality.

With a population of over 100 crores, India represented one of the largest soap and detergents markets in the world. Rapid growth of population, urbanization, rising incomes and media proliferation had helped the company to progress still further both in production and sales. The highly fragmented soap market was dominated by low-priced products made by small-scale manufacturers in different parts of the country. There were few established players like Hindustan Lever, Procter and Gamble, Godrej, Henkel too but they had low market shares and were predominantly urban in nature.

During the 80s, the company had not only spent a sizable amount on market research and development activities, but had also established a

This case is intended to be used as a basis for class discussion rather than as an illustration of either effective or ineffective handling of the situation. Authored by Dr. Mukesh Pandey.

nation-wide distribution organization by opening branch sales offices in all the major state capitals and leading cities of the country.

One of its branch sales offices was established in 1986 in Indore in Madhya Pradesh. This office functioned under the direction and control of a Rohit

Vyas who was working as company's Marketing Manager. Rohit who was assisted by five Sales Officers stationed one each at Indore, Bhopal, Gwalior, Jabalpur and Raipur and an Accounts staff.

The company distributed its products in Madhya Pradesh through stockists and wholesalers both to about 6,000 retailers. The stockists dealt exclusively with the products of the company in all the abovementioned five different areas of the market. They were authorized by the company to sell the products both to the wholesalers and to the retailers. Each stockist had two or three salesmen who frequently called on the retailers and sold the company's products. With a view to offering better service to its dealers, the company had agreed to bear the expense incurred by these stockists in appointing salesmen and also in performing other services to the company usually allowed on sales. The company also often sent their own salesmen to assist the stockists in selling.

Besides stockists, the company had appointed about 100 wholesalers. These wholesalers distributed a variety of products of different companies also besides Wardha products. In appointing these wholesalers there was mutual agreement between the company and the stockists. The wholesalers sold the company's goods to the retailers, who in turn sold them to the customers. Every wholesaler received 3.5 percent commission on purchases, subject to the condition that an order be placed for a minimum amount of Rs. 6,000.

In addition to paying a commission, the company provided stockists and wholesalers with promotional aids such as free cable and press advertisements, hoardings, wall paintings, handbill facilities and in-shop display material. The company also gave a guarantee that it would be willing to take back any non-saleable or damaged stock.

In return, the wholesalers were required to:

(a) Make frequent and regular visits to the retailers and replenish their stock.

(b) See that the company's products were properly displayed.

(c) See that the POP material and window displays were properly maintained in all the shops.

(d) Send periodical reports suggesting improvements and modifications on the present sales methods of the company.

(e) Maintain good relationships with the company's salesman and retailers.

(f) Sell the goods at the Company's listed price.

The five salesman of the company looked after five different sales territories of the market. They made frequent visits to the retail units and inspected whether the retailers are getting material on time, in right quantity and pack sizes, whether wholesalers provided prompt service to the retailers, whether the company's products were properly displayed and whether the retailers and consumers were satisfied with the company's products and prices. Very often they accompanied the salesman of the stockists and booked orders. Each salesman submitted a weekly report to Rohit Vyas on his sales, distribution, promotional and monitoring activities in the field.

In 1995, the company's sales in the Indore branch amounted to Rs 9.5 crores, which compared very favourably with those of the previous years. However, the Marketing Manager received many complaints via the Company salesmen from some retailers, and from customers. It was reported that there was much undercutting by the wholesalers in the prices of the Company's products. Despite the Company's strong price-enforcement activities, many semi-wholesalers got the goods without the Company's knowledge and sold them either surreptitiously or openly at discounted prices.

The Marketing Manager investigated the problem. His investigation showed that there was keen competition among the Company's wholesalers, which led to undercutting. Many wholesalers passed on to the retailers their entire 3.5 per cent commission and were satisfied with meager "Annual Target Bonus" and the value recovered out of the empty cases which they got after distributing soaps to the retailers. Some of the wholesalers sold their products to semi-wholesalers who had no separate establishments of their own. There was a tendency among this semi–wholesalers to evade sales tax on the products, which amounted to 4 per cent and to sell below Company's listed prices.

Each wholesaler handled a wide range of brands and products like tea, biscuits, toothpaste, soaps, shampoos, salt, spices etc. of different companies and so the undercutting of prices in Wardha Soap products and the consequent loss of certain percentage of profit did not affect their profitability very much.

The quick disposal of goods by the wholesalers at rates below the Company's listed prices prompted the retailers also to cut prices. Since most of the retailers got credit facilities from the well-established wholesalers, they were tempted to dispose of the Wardha products quickly at lower prices and invest the amount on other profitable items. Soon this gave rise to competition among the retailers. By April 2001, the products of Wardha Soap Company were sold at prices much lower than the company's listed price in all the retail shops, which created confusion in the minds of consumers. The retailers generally preferred to buy from the wholesalers at lower prices rather than from the Company or stockist's salesmen. As such, the Company salesmen during their routine calls found it difficult to book orders.

DISTRIBUTION MANAGEMENT

Rohit Vyas feared that if this state of affairs were to continue, it might affect the reputation of the Company's products. He was also afraid that the wholesalers might lose their interest in selling the Company's products, due to their loss of profit margin. He felt that the Company should get the cooperation of the retailers and make them realize the company's genuine interest in stabilizing prices and offering better service.

The salesmen of the Company advocated elimination of the wholesalers. In their opinion, the Company had already established its reputation by having stable and fixed prices all over the country, and it would be suicidal for the company to lose control over its prices.

Rohit Vyas recognized that direct selling would result in many advantages from the point of view of better control over prices, better relations with retailers, and increased effectiveness of sales promotion. The Company was also in a strong position to take its products to any part of the market. At the same time, he felt that there would be many difficulties in eliminating the wholesalers. He felt that it would be difficult to depart from the traditional methods of distribution through wholesalers, who had given valuable service to the Company in the past, especially in its initial stages, when the branch sales office had no control over the supply of the Company's products because of transport and communication bottlenecks. The wholesalers purchased goods in bulk, as and when they were available, stocked them in their godowns and helped the Company in distributing the products throughout the year. Furthermore, the wholesalers had helped the Company to market its products in rural areas with a population of less than 15,000 where due to administrative and logistical difficulties, the Company could not take its products.

Rohit Vyas also feared that the wholesalers, if eliminated, might take up distribution for competitive products and companies, which would adversely affect the Company's sales. He also realized that the wholesalers had long-term emotional bonds with most retailers, supplying them with a variety of products of different companies and providing credit facilities, which the Company could not provide.

Questions

1. What are the deficiencies in the existing distribution system of the Company? How can Rohit Vyas rectify them in view of WSC's long-term business objectives?
2. What steps would you recommend Rohit Vyas to overcome the problem of establishing Company prices?

Notes

Pacific Pneumatic India Limited

Dwindling Distributors' Margins

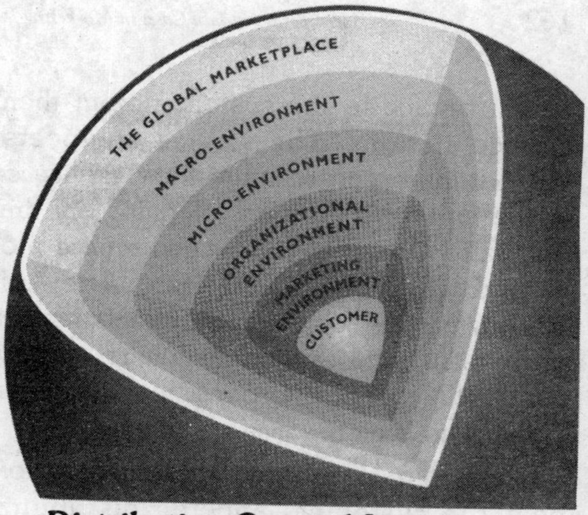

Distribution Case - 16

Purpose of the Case

The idea is to assimilate the relevant concepts at work and analyse along the following lines:

- To discuss how a company should keep its distributors happy for smooth running of a business
- To focus on the need for a company to keep a tight leash on outstandings while operating with an extensive distributors' network and how can a delicate balance
- To debate the best course of action open to the Resident Engineer, Namit Sharma

Pacific Pneumatic India Ltd. (PPIL), is the pioneer of pneumatic technology in India. Established in 1968, by its parent company, Pacific Pneumatic Inc., Boston, as on financial year ending 2006, the Indian operation yields Rs. 250 crore turnover per annum. With the parent company holding 51% stake and no other shareholders individually holding more than 6% of the equity, PPIL is a professionally managed Company, with 48% market share.

The Company deals in pneumatic equipment that cater to virtually every industry. In India, it has three factories located at Ahmedabad, Nagpur and Surat. Also, the entire product range of Pacific Pneumatic – Boston and its subsidiaries and sister concerns all over the world, is available in India. This import trading is handled from the International Trading Centre located at New Delhi.

PPIL sells its products through a distribution network (175 distributors all over the country). It has four regional offices at Mumbai, Calcutta, Delhi and Chennai along with a string of branch offices in every State capital and Area Offices in all major industrial cities all over the country, to perform the sales and service functions. In addition, there are three marketing managers at the corporate head office – to co-ordinate the activities of different product lines with the factories (both domestic and abroad). The regional managers and the marketing managers report to the General Manager (Marketing), who in turn reports to MD

Each Senior Sales Engineer/Resident Engineer/ Sales Engineer,is responsible for smaller business territories within a region. The sales personnel are posted either in the Branch office or in Area Sales offices. The service engineers normally operate from the regional office. The distributors provide the actual service to the customer from their own service stations. The service engineers help the distributors to manage their service centres in the form of spare parts planning and training. They also attend to complicated service problems as and when the need arises. The Assistant Manager's main job is to co–ordinate the activities of the sales and service engineers. Finally, the Regional Manager is responsible for the operation of the entire region.

The purpose of the Area offices is to be as near the customers and the distributors, as possible. Each Area office is headed by a Resident Engineer and a team of 2 to 3 sales engineers reports to him. A Resident Engineer is ultimately responsible for all the administrative and functional activities of the Area sales office. His functions include:

- Leading a team of Sales Engineers to set and achieve sales targets profitably

  Billing through a distribution network:
  - Assisting distributors to collect orders from customers
  - Managing distributors' inventories
  - Payment collection from distributors
  - Helping distributors to maintain their service commitments
  - Training of distributors' sales & service personnel
- Application engineering for finding out new uses of existing products
- Exploring market potential for new product launch
- Keeping the regional office informed of the competitive activity in the territory
- Organizing sales promotion events in conjunction with the distributors

Namit Sharma, one such Resident Engineer at Jalandhar, is looking after the Company's business in the State of Punjab. He reports to the Regional Manager (North), Delhi. The entire business in Punjab, is billed through five distributors. Namit, during the first three years of his stay in Punjab, had efficiently organized the sales set-up in the State. PPIL's business in Punjab, has been growing at a rate of 43% which was much more than the industry growth rate of the State for the last two years. However, recently, Namit has started facing some problems, which threaten to jeopardize all the good work done by him earlier..

PPIL has specific and strict guidelines for the appointment of distributors and their functioning. These guidelines are:

- The distributor has to furnish a security i.e. a bank guarantee of Rs. 5 lakhs to PPIL.
- He must be financially capable to invest at least Rs. 7 lakhs at any point of time, in PPIL's products. Depending on the potential of the customers a distributor is catering to, he has to maintain certain minimum stock (to be advised by the concerned Regional Manager).
- The agreement with the distributor is renewable after every 2 years.
- The distributor has to keep atleast 3 sales persons at his expense.
- The distributor has to maintain a service station and a trained service personnel, at his own expense. Under no circumstances, the distributor can charge more than the Company's authorized price, from the customers.
- The distributor is given 40% discount on the basic (list) price of the products. If he makes payment within 7 days, from the date of issue of the delivery challan, he is given a further discount of 5%. If he makes payments within 15 days, he gets a discount of 2.5%. Under no circumstances, is he allowed a credit limit of more than 1 month.

Operating under the above guidelines in Punjab, each distributor on an average, has the following monthly expenses for selling and servicing PPIL's products:

Namit, in the last financial year ending March 2006, achieved a sales turnover of little more than Rs. 4.85 crores from his 5 distributors. The contribution of each distributor was more or less the same.

ITEMS	COST (Rs.)
Fixed cost (apportioned to PPIL): Rent, Electricity & other miscellaneous costs	3,500.00
Sales personnel salary (for 3 salesmen on an average)	10,000.00
Service personnel salary (for 1 serviceman on an average)	3,500.00
Travel expenses for making sales & service calls	8,500.00
Freight and handling charges	4,500.00
Telephone, fax, courier, stationery, etc.	2,500.00
Others	5,500.00
TOTAL	38,000.00

On an average, the fortnightly turnover of a distributor on PPIL's products is Rs. 3 lakhs. Now the distributor avails an average credit period of 15 days. Thus, ideally in a no-inventory situation, the distributor is in a position to rotate Rs. 3 lakhs, invested at the beginning of the year, 24 times (2 times a month & 12 months in a year).

For each such cycle, the distributor earns say around 20%

Thus, the total earning for the distributor from PPIL, in the form of discount

= Rs. 3 lakhs* 20% * 24 = Rs. 14.4 lakhs per annum

Subtracting his initial investment of Rs. 3 lakhs, his net earning per annum = Rs. 11.4 lakhs. His earning per month by way of discount = Rs. 0.95 lakhs.

Subtracting his expenses, his operating profit on PPIL's product = Rs. 0.57 lakhs.

However, this is his earning in the ideal zero-stock case, where he sells out his entire stock within one fortnight. In normal circumstances, it takes one week for materials dispatched from the factories to reach the distributors at Punjab. However, the credit period starts from the date of issue of the delivery challan (that is the day when the goods are dispatched from the factory). Thus, the effective credit period for a distributor reduces to one week only. Again, due to poor sales forecasting, the distributor has to carry some dead stocks also. Also, he has to maintain buffer stocks of fast-moving items that the customers may require on a day's notice. In addition, he has to maintain inventory of spare-parts for his service centre. It is evident that in order to carry this extra inventory with a view to provide efficient customer service, the distributor has to invest more than Rs. 3 lakhs. The result of all this is that on an average, a distributor hardly makes any money.

With increase in business, the distributor has to keep more machine and spares inventory as buffer stock. The inventory carrying cost is nullifying the gains from new business generation. The distributors are complaining that their already meagre margin on PPIL's product, is further going down. To make their association with PPIL a more profitable venture, they are asking Namit to increase the timely payment discount to 20% along with extending the credit period to 30 days.

The General Manager is extremely finicky about timely collections. In fact, during the All India meeting in April 2006 of all Resident Engineers convened to review financial performance of last year, the Managing Director had very aggressively put his disgust and conveyed his non-compromising attitude towards outstandings going out of control in lots of territories.

What should Namit Sharma do?

Questions

1. What are the challenges facing the management in making a distribution network function without conflicts and glitches?
2. Put yourself in Namit Sharma's and prepare a report for the management presenting the distributors' case along with your recommendation.

Notes

Market Strategy

S e c t i o n - T e n

CONCEPTUAL FRAMEWORK

To facilitate a better debate on the cases in this section, a quick exploratory review of the market strategy planning function along with areas that need discussion are recapitulated briefly as follows:

- Marketing manager shapes the company's businesses and products with an aim to maximize the profits through the process of **market-oriented strategic planning**, wherein a firm develops and maintains a viable fit between the organization's objectives, skills and resources and its changing market opportunities.
- The managerial process establishes an organizational mission and goals, corporate strategy, marketing objectives, marketing strategy, and finally a marketing plan. To achieve its marketing objectives an organization must develop a marketing strategy, which includes identifying, and analysing a target market and developing a marketing mix that meets the needs of customers in the market.
- Marketing manager by strategic planning process designs the framework for a **marketing plan**, a written document that specifies the activities to be performed to implement and control the organization's marketing activities.
- Marketing managers doing strategic planning for a company starts with an **analysis of the marketing environment**, including economic, competitive, political, legal and regulatory, socio-cultural, and technological forces. These forces can affect the resources a firm can acquire and create favourable opportunities. Resources include **core competencies**, things a firm does extremely well - sometimes so well that it gives the company an advantage over its competition.
- A good marketing manager should try to take advantage of a market opportunity by identifying the right combination of circumstances and timing for an organization to take action to reach a particular target market. **Strategic windows** are temporary periods of optimal fit between the key requirements of a market and the particular capabilities of a firm competing in that market. When a company matches a core competency to opportunities it has discovered in the marketplace, it gains a **competitive advantage**.
- The goals of any organization should derive from its **mission statement** a long-term view, or **vision**, of what the organization wants to become. The mission statement answers two questions: Who are our customers? And what is our core competency? A well-formulated mission statement gives an organization a clear purpose and direction, distinguishes it from competitors,

provides direction for strategic planning, and fosters an organization-wide focus on customers. An organization's short- and long-term goals, which focus on the end result sought, guide the remainder of its planning efforts.

- Setting a **corporate strategy** entails four activities: defining the corporate mission, establishing strategic business units (SBUs), assigning resources to each SBU based on its market attractiveness and business strength, and planning new businesses and downsizing older businesses.
- Using corporate strategy marketing managers can determine the means for utilizing resources in the functional areas of production, finance, research and development, human resources, and marketing to reach the firm's goals. Corporate strategy planners are concerned with broad issues such as corporate culture, competition, differentiation, diversification, interrelationships among business units, and environmental and social issues.
- The next step in strategic planning is a consideration of **strategic business units (SBUs)**, which are divisions, product lines, or other profit centres within the parent company. A market is a group of individuals and/or organizations that have needs for products in a product class and have the ability, willingness, and authority to purchase those products.
- The percentage of a market that actually buys a specific product from a particular company is referred to as that product's market share. The marketing manager uses **market growth/ market share matrix** as a strategic planning tool to integrate a firm's products or SBUs into a single, overall matrix and to evaluate them in order to determine appropriate strategies for individual products and overall portfolio strategies.
- When marketing managers feel that current products and current markets have the potential for increasing sales they use strategies for intensive growth, which include-market penetration, market development and product development. Diversified growth occurs when new products are developed to be sold in new markets.
- While corporate, business-unit and marketing strategies all overlap to some extent; the **marketing strategy** is the most detailed and specific of the three. Marketing strategy is typically composed of two elements: the selection of a **target market** and the creation of a **marketing mix** that will satisfy the needs of the chosen target market.
- Selecting an appropriate target market may be the most important decision a company makes in the planning process because it serves as the basis for creating a marketing mix to satisfy the needs of that market. Marketing mix decisions should be consistent with business-unit and corporate strategies; they should also be flexible enough to respond to changes in market conditions, competition and customer needs. Different elements of the marketing mix can be changed to accommodate different marketing strategies.
- **Marketing planning** is done by marketing managers by systematically assessing marketing opportunities and resources, determining marketing objectives, defining marketing strategies and establishing guidelines for implementation and control of the marketing program. The outcome of marketing planning is the marketing plan, which outlines and explains all the activities necessary to implement marketing strategies. A firm should have a plan for each marketing strategy it develops. The marketing plan fosters internal communication among employees, assigns responsibilities and schedules, presents objectives, specifies how resources are to be allocated to achieve objectives and helps marketing managers monitor and evaluate the performance of a marketing strategy.
- Most marketing plans include many of the same components as outlined herebelow:
  - The **executive summary** is synopsis of the entire plan.

- The **environmental analysis** supplies information about the company's current situation with respect to the marketing environment, the target market and the firm's current objectives and performance.
- The **SWOT analysis** assesses an organization's strengths, weaknesses, opportunities and threats.
- The **marketing objectives** section states what is to be accomplished through marketing activities.
- The section on **marketing strategies** outlines how the firm will achieve its marketing objectives and achieve a competitive advantage, preferably a sustainable one that the competition cannot copy.
- The **implementation** section specifies how marketing strategies will be carried out by answering many of the questions about the marketing activities outlined in the marketing strategies section. Most marketing plans also detail how the results of the plan will be measured and evaluated.

A marketing plan is only as good as the information it contains and the effort and creativity that went into its development. Therefore, good marketing information systems and managerial judgment are important factors in creating a complete and workable marketing plan. Every marketing plan should be unique to the organization for which it is created. It should be also be flexible enough to be adjusted on a daily basis.

Notes

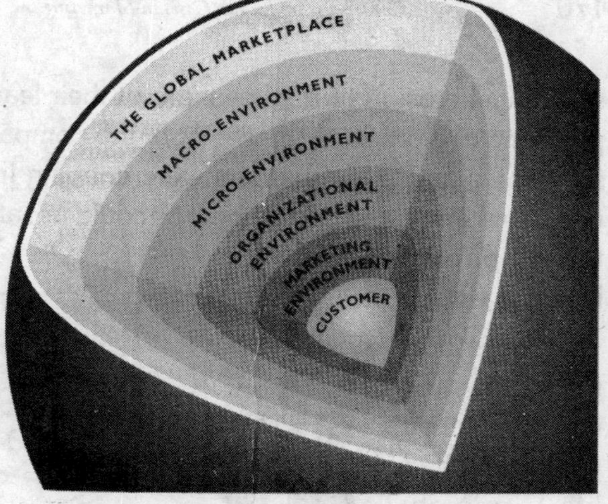

Kadilla Soaps Limited

Reacting to Competitor's Gameplan

Market Strategy Case - 17

Purpose of the Case

The idea is to assimilate the relevant concepts at work and analyse in light of the following issues:

- To focus on how Kadilla Soaps Ltd. should counter a product which though inferior is aggressive as far as sales promotion activities are concerned.
- To discuss how the formulation of a market strategy takes into account all major and minor factors that can affect the outcome of a market move, and how it is similar to defeating an opponent in a game of chess.

Mrs. Srinivasan was surprised. Once again, she looked at her boss's itinerary; he isn't supposed to be in office today, thought she. Sumit Bhatnagar was her boss and for the last 11 years she had worked as a Secretary to all Vice Presidents-Marketing irrespective of who was there in office in that hot seat. In the last 19 days, Sumit has untiringly crisscrossed the length and breadth of the country meeting all Sales Managers and top distributors and dealers across India. She knew from today onwards he was supposed to be on a weeklong leave with his wife and kids in Shimla. She herself had done their flight and hotel bookings at Shimla. Naturally she wondered why Sumit is back here in office when in fact he should have been in Shimla; it was different matter though her experience told her there must be something unavoidably urgent. Why else would Sumit cancel his trip so well planned in advance?

Sumit looked tense, as he entered the office; he was a bit too early to office given his usual routine and his propensity to put long hours in the evening. Sumit picked up the phone and briskly responding to the formal salutation told Mrs. Srinivasan, "Arrange a meeting with Rahul and Manish... immediately". She had normally not seen her boss, Sumit in any kind of anxiety over the years for he was a very calm, cheerful and vivacious young man in his early 40s. In her usual efficient manner, she located Rahul, GM-Sales and Manish, Brand Manager, and called them to be present in Sumit's office at 11 a.m. sharp with relevant reports and data that Sumit had instructed her for.

She vaguely thought, as the other two gentlemen, that the meeting was called because of a virtual panic situation as a competitive brand-Glint had launched a very attractive consumer offer. This had led to substantial erosion in market share of their leading profit making product-Amaze. Also, the company's sales force and trade partners were cribbing in no uncertain terms, and Sumit knew he could not afford to demotivate his own army.

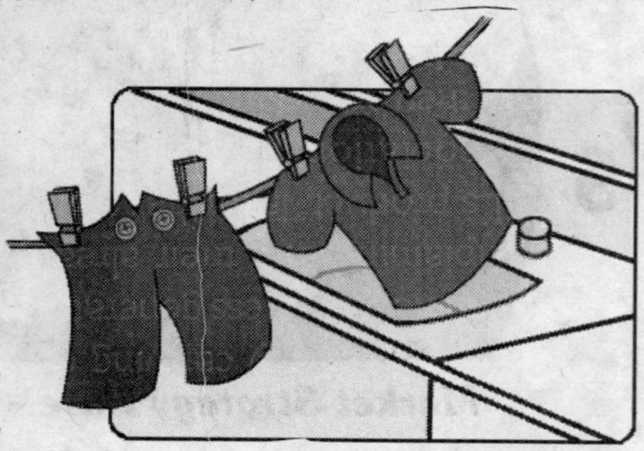

The mood in the meeting was grim but by then Sumit had his anxiety adequately controlled. However, without any preamble Sumit came straight to the point.

Sumit: It's weird, Rahul, I mean your Sales department has landed me in a fix. I have your competitor assessment report that you submitted last week with me. It's all bogus. Your evaluation of failure of the launch of Glint in carton packs is not right as far as I am concerned. Contrary to your report, their heavy consumer promotion seems to be paying off and that too bloody well. I have just come from an all India tour and I have seen it all with my own eyes. I have this latest ORG-MARG report with me; the fact is Glint has gained 22 per cent market share, mainly at our expense. On top of that there are various reports of the success of Glint promotional campaign. Are we sleeping?

Rahul: I admit that despite our initial assessment that Glint, in new carton packs, would be a failure, we now see that it is doing very well. You can't deny the fact that they are a major threat to our market share. They have a cheaper formulation and therefore they can afford such a heavy sales promotion. For the last week or so, I have been thinking of few options. The very first idea that comes to my mind is that to counter them we should introduce a second brand which would have an inferior formulation but comparable to them or may be marginally better as early as possible. We should promote this new product heavily, say at about the same level of expenditure as Glint. We can afford that kind of expenditure on promotions due the higher margin that we will make if we sell it at a price equal to Glint. We can even sell the product at a lower price than Glint.

Sumit: Well, Rahul I am willing to explore this alternative. Let's put a cross-functional team of marketing, production, sales and distribution guys on the job immediately, we should get a report in 10 days. Also, understand that while we know the formulation for such a product but then we have to procure materials and reschedule production. We may even have to procure some plant and machinery for that. Since, the proposal will have to go to the Board, even if I rush it, it is going to take at least a couple of months. Listen guys, I want my market share back to the previous levels within a month. Tell me how are you going to achieve this?

Rahul: Our Zonal Sales managers submitted a report to me last evening. According to the report, Glint is cutting into our sales with their new pack. In the last 5 years, this brand with their bulk packs constituted an insignificant part of the market. We must acknowledge that the main reason for their success is their very generous consumer offer; otherwise we would be fooling ourselves. Right now, I strongly believe we may not be able to achieve our sales targets. However, we can get back our market share soon if we also run an aggressive promotion campaign immediately.

Sumit: Rahul, please do not sound defeatist. You see, they can afford to spend more on promotion because they offer inferior formulation and in turn make higher margin by compromising on quality. Look at the positive side, our product is definitely superior; it is trusted by consumer and we have been there for ages. I think with the right strategy, we should be able to win back our market share.

Rahul: Sumit, you know it as well as I do it, in a bargain-conscious country like India, consumer promotion is a very effective sales medium to the retail stores and consumers. People love to lap up any freebies whether it makes economic sense or not. I am afraid that if they continue at this rate, we will find it very difficult to keep pressure on our sales force and achieve our targets. We must counter immediately with a promotion as heavy as theirs or else it will be very difficult to regain our market share.

Sumit: Well, your recommendation then seems to be that we enter the rat race and promote Amaze aggressively to the consumer. What about our time-tested strategy of offering less quantity due to our better product; it still makes better rationale to a consumer to get a powder which cleans twice as well despite applying so little quantity of it? Moreover, consumers are getting increasingly conscious of quality of fabric care of clothes that they so carefully choose to get their wardrobe in order. Do you think they will trust an inferior formulation in such a scenario? Don't you think, we should promote like we did in the past, emphasizing better product despite a bit higher prices; do'nt you think it makes better business sence to highlight better quality and consequently lot better value for money?

Rahul: I get really flustered when I see Glint campaigns all over the place; they seem to be all over TV, print and outdoors. Going through the reports, I am convinced that we need to step up our expenditure per tonne to at least the level that Glint is spending to make an impact and win back our market share. Otherwise we will not be able to sell our product.

Sumit: Manish, what do you think?

Manish: I disagree with Rahul, I think we should run a new advertisement campaign educating the consumer that such a heavy promotion by Glint itself proves the inferiority of their product. We should not dilute our No 1 position by stooping to the level of a substandard brand.

Rahul: Sumit, I have meticulously gone through the results of consumer promotion that Glint has run for the last four months. Their promotion has certainly been an outstanding success as one can see from the market share figures as well as the reports we have received from our sales team throughout the country. We have to be practical. We cannot keep articulating some nice fancy theories of brand values while someone takes our pants off in the cut-throat competitive jungle out there. I am not sure whether we can salvage the situation if we don't act right now. We should first get back our market share whatever the cost, financial or strategic. Therefore, I would like to immediately get an additional budget for promotion of Amaze. I promise you our market share back because we are better organized. We should be able to mount more effective promotions than theirs, provided that our gift is as attractive as Glint. This will mean about the same level of expenditure. For this I feel that you should cut down on theme advertising for Amaze and divert money to a consumer promotion scheme straight away.

Manish: Rahul, I am not sure I can second your opinion here. I feel that we should not indulge in such heavy promotional expenditure as Glint as this will get us into a vicious circle. We always sold Amaze on the basis of its superior formulation and performance and I see no reason why we should not continue to do so. In fact, we should shout even louder and focus consumer attention on this fact now all the more aggressively and sharply. We should highlight our superior product through heavier theme advertising. We should put as much of our money as we can into theme advertising to convince the consumer that when she buys Glint with gifts of such high value, she is bound to get an inferior product. For this, I would like to place all my money in TV, press, cinema, and point-of-sale material.

Rahul: Manish, how many consumers you think you will be able to reach through the media? Do you realise the efficacy of mass-media in our media dark country especially upcountry markets? I know our sales team will toil hard and put point-of-sale material in all places but we can cover only a very small fraction of our target through press, cinema and TV. Keeping in view the difficulties, cost and the inadequate reach of media for theme advertising in India, I suggest that we promote Amaze heavily and win back what we have lost. We have got to do this now. Otherwise Glint would do well mainly at our expense because we are the No. 1 brand in the market. I implore that we must start a consumer scheme, promoting Amaze at the level of Glint immediately.

Kadilla Soaps Ltd. (KSL) was a public limited company and was set up in 1979. The company had an authorized capital of Rs. 110 crores. The company was a leading marketing organization in the country and manufactured and marketed leading FMCG brands of household products.

KSL was a professionally managed company and for decades was well known for hiring talented MBAs from leading B-schools; it also had wonderful on-the-job training, job rotation and enrichment policies. It had a profit centre organization concept. Marketing was the coordinating function in the organization, and the marketing department had the profit responsibility for a particular product/product group. Washing Product was the major profit centre of the company.

The breakdown of the total turnover and contribution to profit of the major profits centers of the company is given in Exhibit 1. The company's main entry in the washing powder market, "Amaze" accounted for one third of the profits made by the Washing Products Group.

Total Turnover and Contribution To Profit

Total turnover (2005)	Rs.700 Crores
Group A turnover	Rs. 49 Crores (7%)
Group B turnover	Rs. 91 Crores (13%)
Washing products turnover	Rs. 420 Crores (80%)

Exhibit 1

The fabric washing market consisted mainly of two product groups: Washing Soaps and Washing Powders. Small-scale units operating in very small localized areas contributed more than 77% of the washing soap. These small-scale manufacturers operated on low overheads and also did not have any national distribution, and their products were generally sold within a radius of 200 kilometers of their plant locations. They mainly sold inferior quality washing soaps at a substantial price advantage. On the other hand, the production of washing powders was located entirely in the organized large-scale sector of the industry requiring greater technical know how.

The growth of this market since Amaze was introduced 11 years ago is shown in Exhibit 2. Although, in size the washing powder market was one-fourth of the washing soap market, it compared favorably in profitability because of its higher margins. The use of washing powders was restricted to the urban population and within the urban population it was concentrated in large towns. The potential for growth of washing powders was high in smaller towns; at the same time, the market in larger towns was highly competitive. Difficulties of distribution and the high cost of going to the smaller towns did not allow the manufacturers of washing products to employ their own distribution system in these towns. They left the transportation of stocks to the smaller markets to the wholesale trade channels.

Washing Powders Market Growth

Year	Index
1995	100
1996	180
1997	250
1998	310
1999	360
2000	400
2001	520
2002	650
2003	750
2004	820
2005	900

Exhibit 2

There were four main brands in the market: Amaze, Shine, Blanc and Glint. Amaze was the leading brand, and until April 2005, it enjoyed a market share of 82 per cent of the total washing powder market. Shine had a 9 per cent share, followed by Blanc with 6 per cent and Glint 3 per cent. Whereas Amaze, Shine and

Pack Sizes and Prices of Various Brands

Amaze/ Shine/ Blanc	Large	750g	Rs.50
	Medium	450g	Rs.35
	Small	250g	Rs. 20
Glint	Bulk	1 kg	Rs.65
	Bulk	2 kg	Rs.124

Exhibit 3

Blanc were sold in similar carton pack sizes, Glint was sold only in bulk until March 2005. Exhibit 3 gives the pack sizes and the prices of the various brands.

Technically, Amaze had a superior formulation and was accepted as a superior product by the consumer (as shown in various consumer researches). In quality, Shine and Blanc were practically at par and Glint was of the lowest quality with a technically inferior and hence much cheaper formulation. The margin after variable cost for the different brands is shown in Exhibit 4.

Margin After Variable Cost (Rs)

Amaze	10,500
Shine	11,500
Blanc	11,500
Glint	16,500

Exhibit 4

Amaze, Shine, and Blanc, as a part of their marketing strategy spent heavily on theme advertising and some consumer promotion. The consumer promotions run by these brands were mainly gift packs in which, some other company, product was given away free to the consumer along with the washing powder. These promotions were generally on the large pack and the expenditure incurred was around Rs.32, 000 per tonne as the cost of the gift.

Advertising and Promotional Expenditure (April 1995 to March 2005) in Rs.crore

	% of sales promoted with gift	Theme advertising	Promotion (gifts)	Total Advertising and Promotional expenditure
Amaze	20	4.50	2.00	6.50
Shine	80	3.00	1.00	4.00
Blanc	90	0.80	0.40	1.20

Exhibit 5

The gift pack promotions generally were limited to a single carton of the large pack, the large pack accounted for over 55% of the sales of all the brands. Exhibit 5 shows the level of advertising and promotional expenditure incurred by the three major brands.

In April 2005, the company manufacturing Glint in bulk packing launched Glint in two carton packs identical in weight, size, and price to the large and small cartons of the other three brands. The large carton was supported by an extremely heavy consumer promotion. The promotion was on five cartons of the large pack for which the consumer received a free, plastic bucket worth Rs.56, although, the cost of the bucket to the company was very much lower due to bulk buying. The redemption offer worked like this: On each large carton of Glint, a gift coupon was printed. Five of these gift coupons could be exchanged at the retail store for the free gift.

The launching of Glint in cartons did not involve any change in the product formulation, and the same product which went into the bulk pack was put into the carton packs. The promotion cost to the company was Rs. 7,500 per tonne for the gift alone. As a consumer offer, this was the most generous one ever given on washing powders by any manufacturer. The market share held between the four brands altered drastically over a period of four months. Exhibit 6 shows the market share of the various brands between April and July 2005.

Market Share by Weight (%)

	April	May	June	July
Amaze	82	76	73	66
Shine	9	8	8	8
Blanc	6	4	4	4
Glint	3	12	15	22

Exhibit 6

It may be noted that both Blanc and Glint were marketed by the same company and that after the promotion, this company's total market share rose from 9 per cent in April 2005 to 26 per cent in July 2005.

The introduction of Glint with this offer took the other manufacturers by surprise, especially KSL. Initially the marketing management of Amaze felt that Glint in carton packs would not be able to do well, as Glint had a technically inferior formulation and the consumer offer given, involved a very heavy purchase which would last the consumer easily for four months.

Questions

1. While looking at the market share figures of Amaze over the last four months, accompanied by a high-pitch sales promotion campaign by Glint, KSL management was in a quandary. Their need to act was urgent. What should Sumit and his managers do?
2. Based on the case facts, do a SWOT analysis for Amaze (washing powder from KSL) vis-vis its key competitors in the market. Should KSL intensify theme advertising to educate the consumers about its superiority over Glint or should it follow suit by aggresively launching a promotional offer for Amaze? Why?

Notes

Formulating LeasePlan's Car Remarketing Strategy

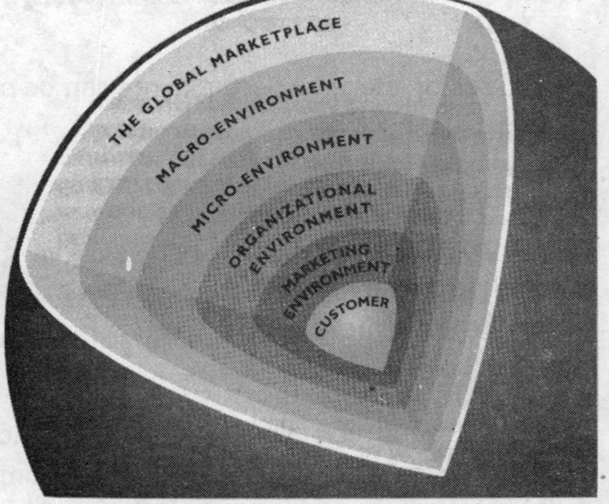

Market Strategy Case - 18

Purpose of the Case

The idea is to assimilate the relevant concepts at work and analyse in light of the following issues:

- To review the findings made by six management trainees during their research in used vehicle market in Delhi and surrounding areas, and how the same could be used by LeasePlan India Ltd. for reformulating its remarketing strategy for used cars and LCVs.
- To discuss how the management at LeasePlan should relook at the distribution of used vehicles as well as the price at which LeasePlan has to sell these vehicles to middlemen
- To appreciate various aspects of strategic marketing being applied in the case

In April 2005, Dileep Kaul – GM Operations, LeasePlan India Ltd. along with Babita Nihal Manager NCR region began a meeting to focus on Car and Light commercial vehicle (commonly known as LCV) remarketing strategy to be adopted by the firm in the next 3-5 years. Over a warm cup of coffee Dileep Kaul queried, "How are our management trainees doing with their field work, Babita? Have they actually been able to analyze the problem we are facing and come out with their findings?" "Actually Dileep, I wanted to discuss the same with you." Babita looked a little worried. "Their findings have further complicated our problem. We have to ascertain the relationship between different factors that they have found out which indicates that we may have to restructure our whole distribution system as well as the price at which we have to sell these vehicles to our middlemen so as to earn a maximum profit." Babita knew about the expectations that Dileep had from the group of management trainees that he had personally handpicked in the last 6 months from the top notch management schools in Delhi and also the fact that he was spending considerable time and passionate energy on this project. In the mean time Venu Gopalan just walked in after his marathon meetings at one of the top FMCG firm in India. Dileep joked, "I am called an Operation -guy, I wonder what do they call you, a FMCG-man, Durables-man or a Health product man." A light laughter prevailed in the room, which eased the prevailing tension. "Let's hope that Venu can help us in deciphering these complex report findings," Dileep continued with a clear sign of relief over his face.

Gopalan said, "See I have consulted for Maruti True Value long time back and have been in the

This case is intended to be used as a basis for class discussion rather than as an illustration of either effective or ineffective handling of the situation. Authored by Dr. Mukesh Pandey.

FMCG sector lately, let's see where I can be of help to you Dileep. Why don't we start with the market research that you guys have carried out? I am really excited to know more about it."

"Well, Venu you already know that since our inception in India since 1999, we grew up from mere 400 leased vehicles to more than 8,000 today. Our other fleet management related services in other 27 countries are quite old, but in India we worked really hard to increase our client base to more than 300 and dealer network to more than 470 across 11 cities. Our esteemed clients included Coca Cola India, TCS, and Cadence along with many others. We helped our clients choose from a variety of bundled services like: The Fleet Audit which encompassed studying clients' current fleet policy and methods of fleet acquisition and create a blueprint of an integrated solution that best fits the client's needs; Funding which provided financing as a part of fleet management package at interest rates that were competitive; Vehicle Acquisition and Delivery system for getting quotes, placing orders, registration, insurance, taxes, fitting accessories etc. of the client's vehicle and delivering it to the client's doorsteps along with preferred rates and extended warranties; Maintenance Management which was meant for the maintenance of client fleet through its entire lifecycle through a proactive maintenance schedule, carry out regular inspections and ensure that LeasePlan designated workshops give client the best maintenance required; Our enhanced Insurance & Accident Management which takes over and handles all matters pertaining to handling the insurance claims and accident repair of the leased vehicle with arrangement for replacement vehicles so that our client's employees can go about their business uninterrupted; Fuel Management which was a very helpful tool for our corporate clients to streamline and monitor their fuel expenses; Sale and Lease back policy which helped us to evaluate our client's fleet based on age and condition, and offer to buy client's fleet and lease them back with all our fleet management services."

"Wow! I thought Dileep was just an operation guy, now I realize he is even into much more non-operation work than I am." Gopalan bantered with a big smile. "Our competitors in India include Orix India Ltd., N2N from Maruti Udyog Ltd., Kotak Mahindra Financing, Sundram Finance and also GE capital fleet service," Babita continued with a detailed explanation about the competitor's product profile.

Dileep who has till now been sitting silent jumped into the discussion "In first week of April this year, we hired 5 management trainees from top notch B-schools in Delhi to put forward a market research primarily aimed at problem related to remarketing of the used vehicles. We follow a lease and remarketing process which can be seen from the flow chart. (See Exhibit 3). We were unable to realize the residual value of these used vehicles. Initially I wondered what could be the cause for this problem. Is it that the market is sluggish or are we not able to sell our vehicles to the right dealers? Why is there a fall in the resale price by the dealer, by quoting numerous factors like the internal or external condition of the vehicle? Is it the current market trend or our dealers are adding their own margins to churn more profits? Should we terminate our relationship with such dealers who are indulging in malpractices and start remarketing these used vehicles directly from our company or set up our own exclusive showroom network across Delhi? If that is done, what should be the functions to be performed by us, which should enhance the resale value of the vehicle, to fetch a maximum profit? Then what will be the cost that we will incur and benefit that we could derive from all this?"

"My goodness! Dileep I think you counted me a whole laundry list of your problems. Seems that I will be now working even overtime for you guys." Everyone burst into laughter, with Babita now turning the focus to the research "We hired the management trainees to study the characteristics of different used vehicle market in Delhi and nearby places like Noida and Gurgaon. Our trainees prepared a Questionnaire having 19 open as well as close-ended questions adopted an in-depth interview with a sample of 70 respondents for used LCV and 150 for used car dealers. Data so received was put on excel sheets for doing EDA (exploratory data analysis) like the findings were represented on Bar graphs and Pie charts." "Babita," Gopalan intervened, "If you don't mind, why not call these management trainees so that they can also actively participate in our exhaustive brainstorming session." "Oh! Sure Venu".

Ten minutes later all the MTs were explaining to the boardroom of their field work. "The sample that we chose was Non-Probability convenience sampling with area sampling (cluster sampling) involved, Since the sample of the entire used vehicle Dealers and Brokers were located in selected areas in Delhi like Karampura and Okhla. Our research also highlighted on:

- Vehicle having most preference among the used vehicle buyers.
- Resale Price of 1-5 year old vehicle in the used vehicle market and effect of different factors like the internal condition, external condition, comfort level and outstation vehicle on the resale price.
- Reseller behavior like their margin involved, functions performed by him like financing vehicles, refurbishment etc. and also time required for selling these vehicles and some other critical buying factors considered for a vehicle."

Trainees continued with their presentations: "From our research we came to know that, the light motor vehicle market could be broadly classified into three categories, i.e. Cars, SUV (Sports Utility Vehicle) and MUV (Multi Utility Vehicle). (See Exhibit 2). Cars are further broadly divided into four distinct segments according to their price (Ex-Showroom, see Exhibits 4 and 5). Segment A is completely owned by Maruti whose price ranges from Rs. 1.5 to 3.5 lakhs and is led by the most popular car Maruti 800. Segment B is also composed of the small sized cars ranging from the price range of about Rs. 3.5 to 4 lakhs. A new segment was introduced in the market, which covered the entire small and mid sized cars priced in the nearly Rs. 4 lakh range. C Segment has the largest variety of all and also has the largest price range of Rs. 4.5 to 6.5 lakhs. This segment covers all the mid and big sized Semi-Luxury cars in the market ranging form Esteem to Lancer. The Luxury segment or the Segment D is composed of expensive cars in the market, which may range upto the price of 40 lakhs or may be more. *(Source: The Auto Magazine)*

Used car market is unorganized overall as the share of the organized sector is very low as per date but is increasing at a faster pace especially in the Maruti True Value sector. The typical buyer mentality is that, the buyers want a good price while selling their car and hence they prefer Maruti True Value for selling their vehicles, while buying a used car the buyers want a car to be as good as the new one. Seeing the success of Maruti True Value Hyundai is starting its 'Real Value' outlets on a similar pattern. Ford Assured and Auto Mart are other leading companies in the organized sector trading in used cars. From our findings we interpreted that the demand of the used car is much more than the supply as the enquiries for buyers are more than those for the sellers (See Exhibit 11)."

"Who are this resellers and can you people please elaborate a little more about them and their modus operandi?" Venu was now totally engrossed in the discussion. "Well Sir, the survey conducted by us revealed that the used car market has a number of members who are involved in the car's resale. They can be either the:

Dealers as most of them are actively involved in the used car business and they have an average experience of upto ten years. Most of the dealers are brokers who do not take ownership of the vehicle but only pass the ownership from the seller to the buyer. They usually charge a commission in between and also do the resale after a little refurbishment to gain a huge margin ranging from Rs. 4,000 to

Rs. 1.2 lakh. The major problems faced by the dealers are the lack of parking space in the vicinity of their shops and the lack of customer awareness besides difficulty faced during reselling outstation vehicles.

Also are visible the Individual Vehicle Owners who are the ones having leased or contracted the vehicle for business purposes and once they recover the operating cost of the vehicle, they look forward to disposing it off and purchasing a new one. In LCV segment we also came across Transport Unions who are group of transporters involved in goods carrying freight handling (local or long distance) activities, working in a pool of 4-10 members. They act both as a buyer and the seller of used LCVs. Sometimes Companies also resell their current vehicle to dispose them and either lease or buy back new vehicle fleet.

"Good work done guys. But what about the customers of these used vehicles. Who are they and have you done any demographic study of them?" enquired Dileep. "Oh yes Sir. Customers from middle class segment are the majority buyers of the used cars. As they are mostly the first owners of cars and a new car means a huge investment for them that's why they turn to used car market. Most of the buyers go for a loan while purchasing a used car and they prefer a registration number of their own town due to ease of transfer and authenticity of prior ownership."

"But how do you find out which are the factors which affect the resale price of the vehicle and among them which one is the most dominant one?" Venu seemed to be a little puzzled now.

"Good question Sir. From our research we discovered that the resale price of the vehicle is affected by the factors as shown in Exhibits 6 and 7. We interpreted that the resale price is mostly affected by the age and the distance covered by the vehicle in its lifetime. A minor deviation of about 5-10% is also seen due to the features of the vehicle such as colour, accessories, condition of tyres and the condition of its external body (See Exhibits 6 and 7). In case of LCV some of the factors are totally different. We came to find out that the vehicle depreciates approximately by 20-25% in its first year of usage and about 5-10% in the years thereafter.

We have detailed out the different factors and their impact on decreasing the resale price of the vehicles. They are separate for both the LCV and the car segment as shown in Exhibits 6 and 7. We also came out with the best selling and the worst selling vehicles in both used car and LCV segment. (See Exhibits 8, 9 and 10).

"For the LCV segment intermediaries are what we have discussed, but this segment is divided into sub 1-ton, 2- ton, 4- ton and 6-9 ton segments. The used LCV segment is completely unorganized with no historical data available with us, but the buying behavior over the last two decades shows that the segment is growing at a rate of 10-15% year on year *(Source: Website of M&M India Ltd)* Also according to the latest TNS survey done in 2002, of every 100 passenger cars, 19 were second hand cars, but in 2005, the number has increased to 28.

"I can see that you guys have done great work, but I raise following questions to you: What is the reliability of these data and how much do you trust them? Second. What about the outstation vehicles? How much demand do they have in the market? If I go by your data it seems that, definitely the middlemen are playing a double game by quoting a lesser price to us and in turn selling it at a higher price to the actual buyers. Then, what do you guys recommend to us? What exactly should be our new or improved distribution system?"

At this stage, an uncomfortable silence prevailed in the Boardroom. Dileep who was already looking anxious asked for a concrete remarketing strategy to be adopted by LP and the way to calculate the value of its used vehicles, considering all the factors which will help increase the revenue for the firm.

Questions

1. What strategy can Dileep adopt which will maximize the revenue for the firm? He is also skeptical of the quantitative data and its analysis as done by the MTs. Analyse in light of fast changing macro and micro environment of the auto industry.

ANNEXURE

Exhibit 1: Distribution channel for used vehicle market (Cars and LCV)

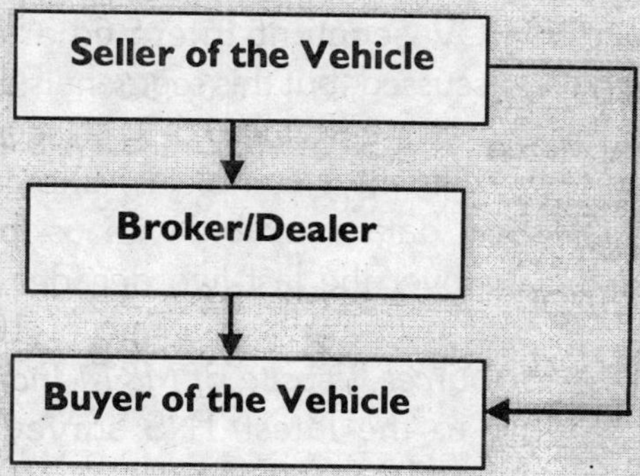

Exhibit 2: Market share of auto manufacturers in passenger car and LCV segment

Passenger Car Market Shares	
Hyundai	16.1%
Telco	11.5%
Maruti	57.1%
Others	15.3%

LCV Market Shares	
Tata Motors Ltd	49.5%
M&M	30.2%
Bajaj Tempo	8.1%
Eicher Motors	5%
Swaraj Mazda	6.1%
Others	1.2%

Source: SIAM

Exhibit 3: Lease Life Cycle

SALE AND LEASE BACK

This is the stage during which LeasePlan:

a. Formulate corporate fleet policy.
b. Identify and evaluate options for various levels of employees.
c. Negotiate with the Client.
d. Deliver the fleet at the doorstep.

OPERATIONS

Once the Fleet has been provided, the following operations are done by LeasePlan:

a. Operate and maintain fleet.
b. Track expenses.
c. Send monthly expense invoice of all the employees in a single document to its Client.
d. Performing frequent customer satisfaction survey.

REMARKETING

a. After contracted period vehicle comes back to LeasePlan
b. Assess market value of the Fleet and also the RV.
c. Invite bids from second hand vehicle dealers and resell vehicle to the highest bidder. Ensure resale value obtained is greater than or equal to RV to earn profit.

Exhibit 4: LAST FIVE YEAR EX-SHOWROOM PRICES OF CARS

Car Model	Ex-Showroom Prices** 2004	2003	2002	2001	2000
MARUTI					
Maruti 800	2.20	2.25	2.37	2.31	2.38
Gypsy	4.58	4.52	4.73	4.73	4.82
Zen	3.59	3.84	3.90	3.45	3.59
Alto	2.65	2.65	2.50	3.00	3.19
Wagon R	3.48	3.49	3.48	3.48	3.63
Versa	4.80	5.19	5.77	5.70	5.60
Omni	2.30	2.34	2.34	2.33	2.35
Baleno	6.30	6.70	7.20	7.50	7.68
Esteem	5.01	5.44	5.44	4.95	4.90
HYUNDAI					
Santro	3.20	3.57	3.55	3.61	3.53
Accent	6.20	6.52	6.21	6.33	6.83
Hyundai Sonata	12.50	13.50	13.80	13.59	
FORD					
Ikon	4.95	5.24	5.63	5.05	5.15
Mondeo	16.12	16.23	16.23		
TATA					
Tata Safari	7.96	8.66	9.99	9.99	10.10
Tata Sumo	4.40	4.42	4.48	4.88	4.75
Tata Indica	3.65	3.77	3.82	3.56	3.59
Tata Indigo	4.60	4.90	4.90	4.90	
Tata Siera				5.76	5.76
OPEL					
Opel Astra	9.50	9.70	8.64	8.80	8.20
Opel Corsa	5.25	5.30	5.50	5.63	6.00
Opel Sail	4.87	4.80			
FIAT					
Fiat Uno			4.05	4.18	4.18
Fiat Siena	4.59	4.52	4.73	4.75	4.75
Fiat Palio	4.36	4.20	4.10	4.10	4.18
MAHINDRA					
M&M Scorpio	6.15	6.32	6.32	6.32	6.41
M&M Bolero	4.88	5.10	5.20	5.79	5.83
TOYOTA					
Toyota Qualis	5.83	5.83	5.82	5.80	5.80
Toyota Camry	17.23	17.23			
Toyota Corolla	9.41	9.82	9.85		
HONDA					
Honda City	6.95	7.458	7.458	7.64	7.64
Honda Accord	15.13	15.25	15.49	15.49	15.5
CHEVROLET					
Optra	7.69	7.74			
Forestor	15.59	15.63			
Mercedes Benz	35.96	35.96	32.42	32.42	33.4
Ambassador	3.479	3.479	3.51		
Mitsubishi- Lancer	6.87	7.65	8.12	8.12	7.98
SKODA- Octavia	10.53	10.75	11.23	11.23	
Cielo			5.507	5.37	5.37

Exhibit 5: LAST FIVE-YEAR EX-SHOWROOM PRICES OF LCVs

Vehicle Model	Ex-showroom price for last 5 years** 2004	2003	2002	2001	2000
Tata 407	4.8	4.65	4.35	4.2	4
Eicher Canter	6.1	5.85	5.6	5.5	5.35
Tata 709	5.8	5.6	5.35	5.2	
Swaraj Mazda	5.85	5.65	5.5	5.45	5.3
BTL Tempo Traveller	6.05	6	5.8		
Tata 207DI	4.25	3.8	3.5		
M&M MaxPickUp	3.5	3.3	3.2		
Tata 1109	6	5.8	5.65		

**All Figures in Rs. lakhs

Source: Primary data collected by five management students

Exhibit 6: Premium Charged over the base prices due to additional features and other factors

FOR USED CARS

Factor	Upper value of range
Impact of A/C (Company fitted)	Rs. 5000-8500
Impact of A/C (Later Addition)	Rs. 4400-7500
Impact of Music system	Rs. 1500-3750
Impact of Power Windows	Rs. 2250-4000
Impact of Condition of tyres	Rs. 3500-5000
Impact of Colour of Car (Per cent of the car price)	2-4%

Exhibit 7: FOR USED LCV

Factor	Range of premium
Major Accident	Rs. 30,000-75,000
Minor Accident	Rs. 5,000-20,000
Riding Comforts	Rs. 10,000-75,000
Impact of Condition of tyres	Rs. 5,000-25,000

Source : Primary data collected by five management students

** Reseller premium charged based on each factor; for example reseller can charge anywhere between the range for the given factor.

Exhibit 8: Best selling cars in the secondhand market in descending order

Model	1st rank	2nd rank	3rd rank	4th rank	5th rank	6th rank	Total
Maruti 800	26	9	4	3	1	.	43
Maruti Wagon-R	13	21	19	1	2	.	56
Hyundai Santro	8	13	15	8	3	.	47
Maruti Zen	8	11	12	7	4	.	42
Tata Indica	4	.	4	5	2	1	16
Maruti Alto	3	4	3	2	.	1	13
Honda City	2	1	2	8	2	1	16
Maruti Esteem	2	.	2	9	1	.	14
Maruti Omni	1	7	4	4	2	1	19
Hyundai Accent	1	1	.	.	4	1	7
Total	68	67	65	47	21	5	

Exhibit 9 : Best selling LCVs in the secondhand market in descending order

Model	1st rank	2nd rank	3rd rank	4th rank	5th rank	6th rank	7th rank	Total
Tata 407	64					.		64
Eicher Canter	4	41	6	2	1	.		54
Swaraj Mazda		1	20	3	1	.		25
Tempo Traveller	1		1	2	4	2		10
Tata 709		13	8	8	2			31
Tata 1109			9	5	6			20
Tata 207DI			2	5	5	1		14
M&M Maxx			2	5	5	4		16

Source: Primary data collected by five management students

** For example out of 43 resellers trading in best selling car, 26 have ranked M-800 No. 1, 9 ranked it 2nd & 4 ranked it as 3rd best selling car.

Exhibit 10: Worst selling cars in the secondhand market in descending order

Model	1st rank	2nd rank	3rd rank	4th rank	Total
Fiat Palio	10	4	2	1	17
Opel Corsa	5	4	.	.	9
Daewoo Cielo	5	3	3	2	13
Opel Astra	4	2	6	.	12
Maruti Versa	4	2	.	.	6
Fiat Siena	2	8	1	1	12
Fiat Uno	1	3	2	-	6
Total	31	26	14	4	

Source: Primary cata collected by five management students

Exhibit 11: Buyer/seller enquiries per week

Statistics	Enquiries for Buyers of used cars (per week)	Enquiries for Sellers of used cars (per week)
Range	596	229
Minimum	4	1
Maximum	600	230

Statistics	Enquiries for Buyers of used LCV (per week)	Enquiries for Sellers of used LCV (per week)
Range	13	17
Minium	4	1
Maximum	600	230

Source: Primary data collected by five management students

Exhibit 12 Margins on LCVs

No. of Respondents	Lowest Margin*	No. of Respondents	Highest Margin*
45	6	37	10-15
12	10	15	15-20
10	10-15	10	20-30
3	2-5	8	35-40

Source: Primary data collected by five managemen students

* All figures in thousands

Price

Section - Eleven

CONCEPTUAL FRAMEWORK

To facilitate a better debate on the cases in this section, a quick exploratory review of the price ingredient of the marketing mix (consisting of product, distribution, promotion and price) along with areas that need discussion are recapitulated briefly as follows:

- **Price** is the value that you get in exchange of product/service. Price is everywhere. We pay 'rent' for our house, 'tuition fee' to our Math teacher and a 'consultation fee' to our doctor. The Indian railway and bus companies charge us a 'fare'; the local bank charges us 'interest' for the money we borrow. The price for driving our vehicle on a New Delhi Flyover is a 'toll' and the company that insures our car charges us a 'premium'. The visiting faculty from the industry charges an 'honorarium' to share its experience. The 'price' of a manager is a 'salary', the price of a sales person may be a 'commission', and the price of a worker is a 'wage'.
- Managers realize the importance of "Price" as a key element in the marketing mix because it relates directly to the generation of total revenue.
- Price is the only variable in the marketing mix that can be adjusted quickly and easily to **respond to changes in the external environment**.
- Profit = (Price/unit x Quantity sold) –Total costs.
- You can compete on either a **price** or **a non-price basis**. Non-price competition emphasizes product differentiation through distinctive features, service, product quality or other factors.(for example - the high-end mobile phones from Nokia or omnipresent after-sales service by Maruti)
- A great amount of economics insight goes in determining the right price. An organization must determine the demand for its product. Next, **price elasticity of demand**—the percentage change in quantity demanded relative to a given percentage change in price—must be determined. If demand is **elastic**, a change in price causes an opposite change in total revenues. **Inelastic demand** results in a parallel change in total revenue when a product's price is changed.
- **Breakeven analysis**—determining the number of units that must be sold to break even—is important in setting price. The point at which the costs of production equal the revenue from selling the product is the **breakeven point**.
- To use breakeven analysis effectively, a marketer should determine **the breakeven point** for each of several alternative prices. The determination makes it possible to compare the effects on total revenues, total costs and the breakeven point for each price under consideration.

- Eight factors enter into **price decision making**: organizational and marketing objectives, pricing objectives, costs, other marketing mix variables, channel member expectations, customer interpretation and response, competition, and legal and regulatory issues.
- When adjusting prices, business-to-business sellers take into consideration the size of the purchase, geographic factors, and transportation requirements.
- Producers commonly provide discount off list prices to intermediaries. The categories of discounts include trade, quantity, cash, seasonal and allowance.
- **Geographic pricing** involves reductions for transportation costs or other costs associated with the physical distance between buyer and seller. A price quoted as F.O.B. Factory means the buyer pays for shipping from the factory.(for example- the difference in the prices of coconuts in the south India and the north India)
- The six stages in the **process of setting prices** are (1) developing pricing objectives, (2) assessing the target market's evaluation of price, (3) evaluating competitor's prices, (4) choosing a basis for pricing, (5) selecting a pricing strategy, and (6) determining a specific price.
- When using **cost-based pricing**, the firm determines price by adding a fixed amount or percentage to the cost of the product. Two common cost-based pricing methods are **cost-plus** and **markup pricing**. **Demand-based pricing** is based on the level of demand for the product. To use this method, a marketer must be able to estimate the amounts of a product that buyers will demand at different prices. Demand-based pricing results in a high price when demand for a product is strong and a low price when demand is weak. In the case of **competition-based pricing**, costs and revenues are secondary to competitor's prices.
- A pricing strategy is a tool to adjust the revenues to meet the organizational objectives. The most common pricing strategies are **differential pricing, new product pricing, product-line pricing, psychological pricing, professional pricing,** and **promotional pricing.**
- After developing pricing strategies, firms often face situations in which they need to change prices. A price decrease might be brought about by excess plant capacity, declining market share, a desire to dominate the market through lower costs, or economic recession. A price increase might be brought about by cost inflation or overdemand.
- There are several alternatives to increasing price, including shrinking the amount of product instead of raising the price, substituting less expensive materials or ingredients, and reducing or removing product features.

Low Cost Aviation in India: Changing Realities

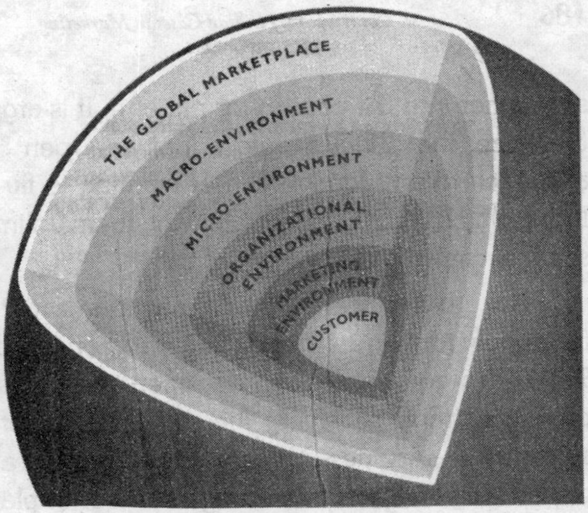

Price Case - 19

Purpose of the Case

The idea is to assimilate the relevant concepts at work and analyse in light of the following issues:

- How to put the fundamental changes happening in the aviation industry in proper perspective with a view to appreciate strategic market planning principles at work for making air travel more affordable
- How to assess the long-term sustainability of pricing as a competitive advantage for LCCs (Low Cost Carriers).

AVIATION IN INDIA

For many years in India air travel was perceived to be an elitist activity. This view arose from the "Maharajah" syndrome where, due to the prohibitive cost of air travel, the only people who could afford it were the rich and powerful. In recent years, however, this image of Civil Aviation has undergone a change and aviation is now viewed in a different light - as an essential link not only for international travel and trade but also for providing connectivity to different parts of the country. Until less than a decade ago, all aspects of aviation were firmly controlled by the Government. In the early fifties, all airlines operating in the country were merged into either Indian Airlines or Air India and, by virtue of the Air Corporations Act, 1953, this monopoly was perpetuated for the next forty years. The Directorate General of Civil Aviation controlled every aspect of flying including granting flying licenses, pilots, certifying aircrafts for flight and issuing all rules and procedures governing Indian airports and airspace. Finally, the Airports Authority of India was entrusted with the responsibility of managing all national and international airports and administering every aspect of air transport operation through the Air Traffic Control.

OPEN SKIES

A recurring demand often voiced by interested parties is that, in order to promote Travel & Tourism, India should adopt an Open Skies policy. It is argued that the current policy restricts the access of foreign airlines. As a result potential tourists are not offered a choice of airlines or seats when traveling to India. This problem is exacerbated during the holiday season when it is difficult, if not impossible, to get a seat either into the country or out of it. It is argued, therefore, that India should adopt an Open Skies approach to any foreign carrier wanting to fly into India, which literally means allowing them unlimited service, capacity and points of call.

The government owned airlines had their monopoly for almost four decades and on March 1, 1994, the government threw open the gates for private entrants satisfying the requirements of the scheduled services. Sensing a huge lucrative opportunity in this sector a large number of players jumped into the fray. The prominent among them were Jet Airways (JA), Sahara, Archana, East West, India International, NEPC, Modiluft and Damania.

WINDS OF CHANGE

The new trend of low cost aviation has been picking up immensely in the recent past. This new emerging trend has put the existing traditional airline agencies, both government owned and private, all over the globe to rethink their strategies and restructure their airfares.

A low-cost carrier (also known as a *no-frills* or *discount* carrier) is an airline that offers low fares but eliminates all unnecessary services. Low-cost carriers pose a serious threat to traditional 'full service' airlines, since full-service carriers cannot compete on price and, when given a choice, most consumers will opt for low price over other amenities.

NEED FOR LOW COST AIRLINES

For the first 10 years of deregulation the demand for scheduled passenger air transportation was driven by the constraints and confines of its providers – principally, the network air carriers. Network carriers were able to avoid cost-side pressures by focusing on revenue-side strategies – largely centered on the high-yield business traveler. That focus led to innovations like sophisticated global distribution systems, revenue management, and frequent flyer programs that helped the airlines segment demand. You are – or were – the linchpin in that strategy, as businesses and other time-sensitive travelers accounted for only 20% of network airline traffic, but for 80% of network airline revenue. This strategy worked because the business traveler grew accustomed to paying high fares and often did not have an attractive alternative to the high fare, and also because the airlines enjoyed a greater ability to control the number of seats available to discretionary travelers. In short, in the post-deregulation world, travelers – particularly business travelers – did have greater options than before, but, even with the impact of the occasional low-fare carrier, they were often at the mercy of major carriers when it came to price. In effect, demand for passenger service was driven, even controlled, by the supply that network carriers were willing to deploy in the market.

The above reasons and the price transparency that the Internet has created for all types of passengers have led to the emergence of a new breed of low-cost carriers. These developments have seriously compromised the ability of legacy carriers to charge higher prices to travelers on routes where they overlap with low-cost carriers. At the end of 2000 the demand for business class and other high-end products fell dramatically, as corporate managers became more cost-conscious.

Now low-cost carriers have proliferated and offer real, lasting competition to their network rivals. This generation of low-cost carriers has newer fleets, a better in-flight product, and better on-time performance and completion factors than the first wave of post-deregulation start-ups. The fare transparency delivered by the Internet and the expansion of low-cost carrier services has increased the price-sensitivity even of business passengers. The airline seat is rapidly becoming a commodity. The demand for more affordable air travel is quite robust. Increasing numbers of business travelers use low-fare airlines as a matter of corporate travel policy

Customers continue to fall into segments with regard to demand for products on offer (Exhibit 1). Not every airline will be able to satisfy every customer but the entrance of low cost airlines has pushed

CUSTOMER SEGMENTATION

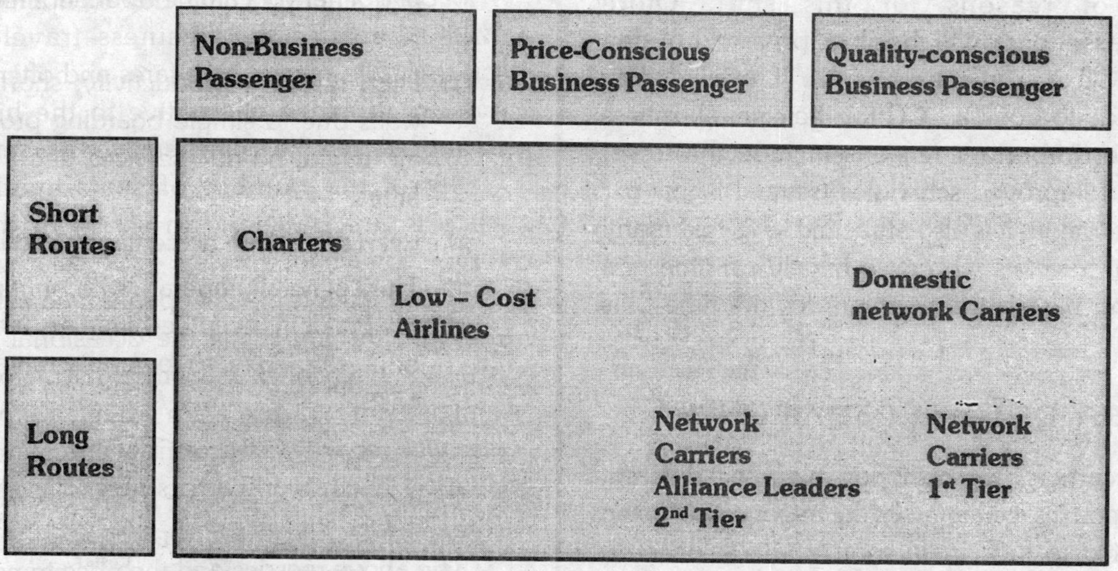

Source: AEA, IATA, Mercer analysis, Mercer Management Consulting © 2002

Exhibit 1: **Customer segmentation**

customer segmentation. There is a sharper focus for shorter routes and the target is the price conscious and quality conscious customer. This has led to stiffer competition for non-business passengers and price conscious business passengers.

TARGET MARKET[1]

The entry of these low cost carriers has several far reaching implications on the aviation sector of whichever country they have been launched in. It has to a very large extent influenced the mass transportation and domestic tourism industry. E.g., in a country of a billion people, the Indian aviation industry is puny. Around 12 million people who travel by air every year against 3 million people who fly everyday in the US, even though the population is one fourth that of India. The number of daily flights averages around 400 a day, as against 40,000 flights a day in the US. RyanAir amongst the low cost pioneers in Europe flies 25 million people in a year and still has less than 5% market share. In Malaysia, there are 12 million people who travel by air yearly, thus here is a nice big fat juicy market of around 200 million people which is equal to that of entire Europe. Now if the LCA's are able to tap even one-fourth of that large middle class and would persuade them to travel by air, there could be a rise by 5 to 6% in their capacity.

Comparing the Indian scenario with that of China we see that China leads India by a huge margin in terms of the number of air passengers. This can be seen from Table 2.

Aviation: India vs. China

Factor	China	India
Population (billion)	1.4	1.1
Air Passengers (million)	140	15
Number of LCCs	5	1
Middle-class population (million)	400	300
Longest route (hrs)	2.5	2.5
Growth forecast (per annum)	17%	25%

Source: Centre to Asia Pacific Aviation, Chartered Financial Analyst Dec. 2005

Table 2: **Aviation: India vs. China**

Initially, Low Cost Carriers (LCCs) were geared more towards holiday trips than towards business travel, due to the location of the airports, among other reasons. Based on research conducted by TQ3, business travelers are clearly starting to use

[1]Source: *Giving wings to 1 billion Indians* by R. Sugant, *Indian Journal of Marketing,* Vol. XXXIV, Number 11, Nov. 2004.

LCCs more often as time goes by. There are a variety of reasons for this shift. Quite often, passengers will book a private holiday with an LCC to acquire experience. If satisfied, they may decide to book a LCC for their next business trip. Other important reasons include the lower prices and improved schedules (several flights per day). In addition, it is also attracting to its fold many of the rail travelers who save hugely on time and don't mind paying the premium for the time thus saved.

STRATEGY OF LOW COST AIRLINES

Low cost carriers have been possible with a different set of economics. Unarguably, the major cost of flying is attributed to fuel, maintenance and salaries. In addition there are parking and landing charges as well, which are quite high. So how do RyanAir in Europe and Southwest Airlines in US manage to sustain low cost carriers? How does a low cost model work?

BUSINESS DESIGN FOR LOW COST AIRLINES

The "low cost carrier" business design can be defined by three key elements.

- Simple Product
  - No meals; drinks and snacks for free
  - Narrow seating (greater capacity)
  - No seat reservation; free seating
  - No frequent-flier programme
- Positioning
  - Non-business passengers, leisure traffic, price conscious business passengers
  - Short haul point to point traffic with high frequencies
  - Aggressive marketing
  - Secondary airports
  - Competition with all transportation carriers
- Low operating costs
  - Low wages, low airport fees
  - Low costs for maintenance, cockpit training and standby crews due to homogeneous fleet
  - High resource productivity; short ground waits due to simple boarding process, no air freight, no hub services, short cleaning times.
  - Lean sales; high percentage of online sales.
  - They generally operate with only one kind of aircraft in their fleet, such as Airbus 320s or Boeing 737s, to lower the maintenance costs.

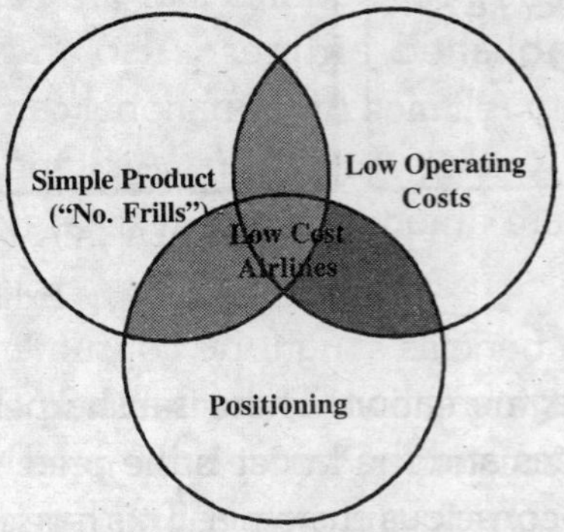

  - There is no business class just economy class; this increases the number of seats per flight.

INDIAN SCENARIO: AIR DECCAN, AIR SAHARA AND JET AIRWAYS

Jet Airways: Jet Airways took off with four Boeing 737-300's in April 1992 at Mumbai, as a 100% subsidiary of Tailwinds Ltd. A company registered in Cayman Islands (situated in northwest Caribbean islands) with Kuwait Airways and Gulf Air having a stake of 40% in the same. However the company's Indian promoter, Naresh Goyal bought the entire stake from the partners for an undisclosed sum and became the sole owner. By 2001, Jet Airways had a formidable fleet of 33 Boeing aircrafts to its credit.

Air Sahara: Sahara started its operations in December 1993, flying firstly between New Delhi-Mumbai sectors. By 2001, it expanded its flying routes to 12 sectors with nine Boeing aircrafts in hand. The carrier was able to succeed in satisfying its customers and won many excellence awards including Pacific Area Travelers Association Award (1997 and 2001), World Travel Market Global Award (1997), Diamond Award (1999) and International Food Services Association Award (1998). Sahara posted a turnover of Rs. 3.5 billion in the fiscal year 2001.

Low Cost Airlines: On 25th August 2003 Air Deccan, India's first low cost carrier operated its first flight on a metro sector. The airline is confident of 75% occupancy with passengers who are currently paying fares that are half of those of the established airlines. Also Indian Airlines subsidiary Alliance Air as national carriers' low cost airlines, GoAir, Air Arabia, Air One and foreign airlines are amongst others who are queued for a launch.

The benefits sought by consumers of different segments are shown in the Table 3. Thus it can be seen that customers whose basic need is to commute at a cheap fare and who cannot spend much time commuting by rail are the main customers of the low cost airlines. These customers do not desire other benefits like food, service and discounts from the airlines. From the above table it can be seen that sales/junior executives, traders, professionals, holiday travelers, housewives and students fall in this category.

AIR DECCAN

Air Deccan is a unit of Deccan Aviation Private Limited, India's largest private heli-charter company. Formed in 1995, Deccan Aviation Private Limited has carved a niche for itself in the Indian aviation scene with its reputation for providing speedy and reliable heli-services for company charters, tourism, medical evacuation, off-shore logistics and a host of other services. Air Deccan commenced operation with a vision to bridge the divide with those who fly and those who do not by introducing airfares that are lowest in the marketplace. As India's first (low cost-no frill) airline, Air Deccan has truly revolutionized air travel in India by not only making it affordable but has also leveraged the power of the Internet to simplify the entire process.

	FACTORS					
Segment	**Price**	**Timelines**	**Frequent flier programmes**	**Service levels**	**Image of airlines**	**Airline network (domestic & International)**
Top management		✓	✓	✓	✓	✓
Middle management		✓	✓	✓		✓
Sales/Junior. Executive	✓					
Businessmen	✓		✓		✓	✓
Traders	✓					✓
Professionals	✓	✓		✓	✓	✓
NRI's		✓		✓	✓	
Holiday travelers	✓			✓		✓
Housewives	✓					
Students	✓					✓
Conferences	✓					

Source: Turbulent Weathers; Pitch Case Study; September 2004

Table 3: **Benefits that various customers seek**

FARES AND RESERVATION

In pursuit of its aim to make air travel affordable to all, Air Deccan has introduced the concept of Dyna fares. The earlier a customer books a ticket, the lesser he pays. Fares go up as the date of journey nears. However, even on the date of journey its fare would still be lower than the regular fares of other Airlines.

Air Deccan has brought out several innovations in the domestic market for the booking of tickets. It is the first airline in India to have an independent and internet-based Computer Reservation System. Passengers are offered multiple modes of booking tickets on Air Deccan operated flights. Four types of booking modes are offered by Air Deccan:

- Internet-(www.airdeccan.net) Passengers can go on the internet and book their tickets online. Schedules, fares and availability can be checked on the Air Deccan website through the booking engine. To purchase tickets online, a credit card is required. The passenger, once a purchase has been made online, can print the ticket. If the passenger has provided an e-mail address, the passenger also receives an e-mail confirmation with the itinerary. In case the passenger is unable to print out the ticket while doing the online purchase, the passenger can use the PNR indicated in the e-mail confirmation to collect the ticket at the Air Deccan airport counters.
- Passengers can also book through the Air Deccan call center. They can call using any one of the listed circle numbers. Confirmed bookings through the call center require a credit card.
- Bookings can also be made through travel agents by paying cash. The travel agent will issue an E-Ticket. The E-Ticket will have the seal of the travel agent stamped on the ticket.
- Passengers can purchase tickets directly from Air Deccan Airport Counters by paying cash or through credit card.

Any booking made through the Travel Agent or the Air Deccan Call Center attracts a Transaction fee of 5% of the basic fare. This transaction is not applicable for bookings made directly through the Internet. Passengers who have booked on the Internet or through the call center must also carry a photo identification document. Passengers who cannot provide sufficient identification will be denied boarding.

Destinations: Air Deccan not only flies to all premier destinations in South India but also covers many major cites in the Northern India. In all it covers 34 destinations all over India which are as follows: Delhi, Surat, Ahmedabad, Baroda, Bhavnagar, Mumbai, Hyderabad, Belgaum, Goa, Kolhapur, Hubli, Mangalore, Coimbatore, Madurai, Bangalore, Chennai, Tirupati, Vijayawada, Vizag, Guwahati, Dibrugarh, Jammu, Vaishno Devi, Amritsar, Dehradun, Chandigarh, Lucknow, Kanpur, Jaipur, Bagdogra, Kolkata, Jabalpur, Bhopal and Nasik. (As on 20th Oct 2005)

Air Fares: Air Deccan starts issuing tickets at Re. 1 (Rs. 221 are charged extra in the form of fees and taxes). It claims to have sold a total of 1,36,311 tickets for Rs. 500 till 20th October 2005[1]. The earlier a customer books a ticket, the lesser he pays. Fares go up as the date of journey nears. However, even on the date of journey the fare will still be lower than the regular fares of other Airlines. A typical example of the comparison of Delhi-Mumbai fares of various airlines is shown in the following tables (See Table 3(a), (b) & (c)):

Jet Airways: Economy class

Days in advance	Fare in Rs.
Normal fares	7956
15	4755
21	3845
30 days super apex	3795

Fare structure as on 20th November 2004

Table 3 (a)

Indian Airlines: Economy class

Days in advance	Fare in Rs.
Normal fares	7969
7	5304
21	3518
28	2730

Fare structure as on 20th November 2004

Table 3 (b)

Sahara Airways: Economy class

Days in advance	Fare in Rs.
Normal fares	7070
15	4756
20	3845
30	3795

Fare structure as on 20th November 2004

Table 3 (c)

From the tables above it can clearly be seen that the fares of Jet, Sahara and Indian Airlines are almost the same on Delhi – Mumbai route. All these airlines also offer various discount schemes like frequent flier scheme, night fares, apex fares, senior citizen fares, etc to attract the passengers.

Air Deccan: Fares as seen on 27th November 2004

Date	Fare	Date	Fare
29th Nov. 2004	3550 (F)	3rd February	2850 (A)
30th Nov. 2004	3550 (F)	10th February	2550 (A)
19th Dec. 2004	3550 (A)	15th February	2200 (A)
2nd Jan. 2004	3400 (A)	1st March	2200 (A)
8th Jan. 2004	3200 (A)	30th March	2100 (A)

(F) => Tickets not available; (A) => Tickets available.

Source: www.airdeccan.net

Table 5: **Air Deccan: Fares as seen on 27th November 2004**

The table 5 shows the ticket availability and the fare to be paid for Delhi – Mumbai route by Air Deccan on various dates. We see that the Air Deccan fares are 30% to 40% cheaper as compared to the fares of other carriers. Also the tickets for Air Deccan are available on short notices even in the peak Christmas season.

SUSTAINABILITY OF AIR DECCAN

The mission of Air Deccan is "To demystify air travel in India by providing reliable low cost air travel to the common man by constantly driving down air fares as an ongoing mission". It is estimated that about 1.7 lakh people travel by 1st class AC in a day. It is this population that Air Deccan wants to attract. If we take the example of the Delhi-Mumbai route, the 1st, 2nd and 3rd class AC fares are given as follows:

Train Name	Train Number	Class	Fare in Rs.
Paschim Express	2926	Third AC	1129
Punjab Mail	2138	Third AC	1185
Mumbai Rajdhani Express	2952	Third AC	1485
Paschim Express	2926	Second AC	1757
Punjab Mail	2138	Second AC	1847
Mumbai Rajdhani Express	2952	Second AC	2210
Paschim Express	2926	First AC	3338
Punjab Mail	2138	First AC	3513
Mumbai Rajdhani Express	2952	First AC	4135

Source www.indianrail.gov.in

Table 6: **AC Train Fares on Delhi-Mumbai Route**

To ensure availability on the trunk routes one must book the rail tickets, on an average one month in advance. We see that Air Deccan fares are comparable with the first AC and sometimes second AC rail fares (See Table 6). Business class passengers who cannot afford to waste time on long rail journeys now have the option of traveling by LCC at comparable fares.

POTENTIAL OF AIR TRAVEL IN INDIA

A total of 390 to 400 commercial flights operate in a day in India. The US, which has one-fourth of India's population, has 40,000 flights a day. Thus if US were to have India's population nearly 160,000 flights would be needed. If the airlines in India were to tap just 1% of this potential, we would still need 1,600 flights a day and that would mean a jump in the number of commercial flights by four times. Also in India, about 12 million people fly every year. Malaysia also

[1]Source: *Giving wings to 1 billion Indians* by R. Sugant, *Indian Journal of Marketing*

boasts of a similar figure, but on a population of 24 million. If a low cost airline can offer fares at half the price of regular airlines, at least one-fourth of India's middle class population of 200 million will travel.[1]

STRATEGIES FOR THE SUCCESS OF AIR DECCAN

A business model has two components viz. cost of product or service, and number of units of product sold or number of times the service is used. A business model can be successful by adopting one of the following two strategies mentioned:

1. Fixing high price of the product or service and thereby attaining profitability through high profit margins. This would mean attracting lesser number of customers. The model aims to provide additional benefits to the customer besides satisfying the basic needs.
2. Fixing low price of the product or service and attracting many customers. Here the profit margin is very low and various measures of cost-cutting are followed. Thus the model aims at satisfying the basic needs of the customer and attains profit through bulk sales.

Air Deccan follows the second model and attains its profit through volume sales. It also tries to keep its operating costs low by following a host of cost cutting measure as described below:[1]

- Pricing is the key to success of any low cost airline. It has been estimated that the fares of LCA is 43% less than that of a full service airline. Air Deccan's Dyna Fares at the highest end are 30% cheaper than the conventional carriers in the trunk routes and 40 – 50% cheaper on the non-trunk routes.
- Air Deccan not being a part of any GDS (Global Distribution System), uses the Internet extensively for ticket bookings thus saving 15 – 30% of the ticket cost as commission. The travel agents are also provided a commission of 5% instead of the conventional 10%+ as provided by the conventional airlines.
- Air Deccan uses other cost optimization measures such as
  - Since the fares are already low, no further discounts are offered.
  - More trips are made due to low turnaround times of 15 to 20 minutes as compared to the normal 30 minutes by other airlines.
  - Free seating (Uni class) so that passengers sit quickly rather than searching for seats.
  - Air Deccan flights are in skies for an average of 10 hours as compared to 8-9 hours by other carriers.
  - No onboard catering. Food and water to be purchased at cost.
  - No external agency to do housekeeping inside the aircraft. This is taken care by the air hostess. Only one air hostess is deployed in the aircraft.
- Revenue augmentation is done by allowing advertisements to be put up both inside and outside the aircraft.
- Air Deccan has adopted a "lean and mean" approach to staffing and aims at maintaining a

Airlines	Flights	Destinations		Seats	Load in %	Passengers per year (million)
		Domestic	Inter'l			
Jet Airways	250	44	2	28,000	65%	6.8
Indian Airlines	260	64	16	35,000	55%	5.8
Air Sahara	117	22	2	11,000	71%	2
Air Deccan	55	24	—	3,000	NA	0.15

Source: *Turbulent Weathers, Pitch* Case Study, September 2004.

Table 7: **Operational Details of Various Airlines**

low aircraft-to-employee ratio. The organization presently has about 350 employees, out of which about 80% staff is in operations.

CAPACITIES AND LOADS OF AIRLINES

Table 7 shows the number of passengers carried and number of flights taken off by the various airlines. It can be seen that although Jet Airways flies to lesser number of domestic and international destinations as compared to Indian Airlines, it carries maximum load in percentage terms. Air Sahara is far behind Jet and Indian Airlines under all heads as shown. Air Deccan just launched 6 months ago has gained a decent amount of market share in such a short period (See Exhibit 8).

MARKET SHARE OF MAJOR PLAYERS OPERATING IN INDIA

Table 7 shows it can be seen that Jet Airways has the maximum market share in the domestic market. Indian Airlines follows very close to Jet, whereas Air Sahara is far behind in the competition.

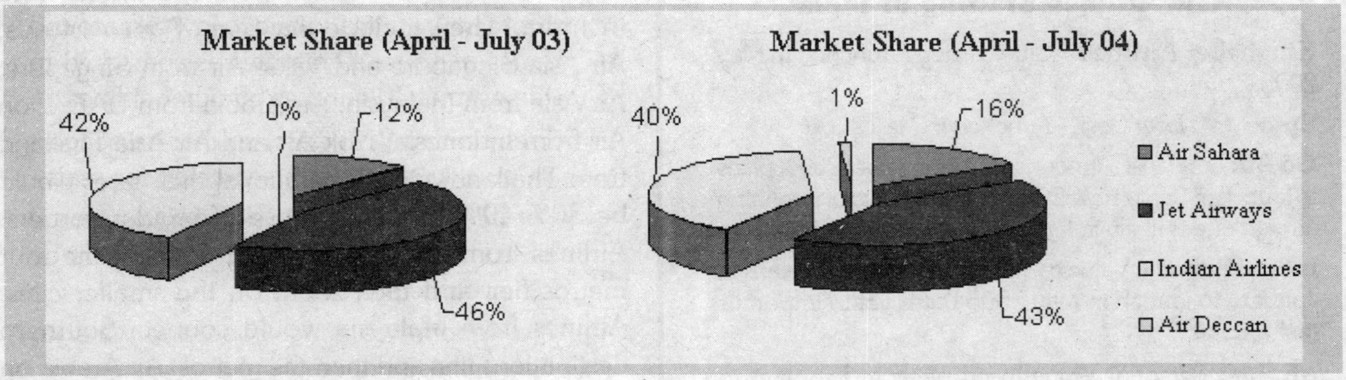

Source: *The Economic Times,* 13th September 2004

Exhibit 8: **Market Share of Various Airlines**

Fleet statistics of the various airline operators in India

Table 9 shows the fleet statistics of the various carriers in India upto the year 2003. It can be seen that Indian Airlines have consistently maintained their fleet strength at around 55 carriers, Jet has increased its fleet strength over the years. A point to be noted is that although Jet Airways has a considerably lesser fleet strength, it still has a higher load factor and carries more passengers per year as compared to Indian Airlines. Sahara Air is still far behind in the competition.

Airlines	Fleet Statistics 2000-01	Fleet Statistics 2001-02	Fleet Statistics 2002-03	Fleet Statistics as on 20th Oct 2005	No. of destinations served as on 20th Oct 2005
Jet airways	30	38	41	50	43
Indian airlines	53*	55*	54*	62	57
Air Sahara	NA	10	12	24	23
Air Deccan	—	—	—	13	34

Source: *http://www.indiastat.com* and the websites of the various airlines * Value indicates total of Indian Airlines and Alliance Air

Table 9: **Fleet Statistics of the Various Airline Operators in India**

NEW ENTRANTS

Every other month a new low-cost or value carrier is taking to the skies.

Among the new entrants as low cost carriers are Vijay Mallya's Kingfisher Airlines and Ajay Singh's SpiceJet. Modiluft's Royal Airlines and Air India's Air India Express are the others which are lined up for launch in the coming months. Air One and Visa to be run by groups of former Indian Airlines pilots are also in the offing.

A detail of the carriers lined up to reach out to Indian skies is given in Exhibit 10.

New Airlines Starting in India

Kingfisher Airlines: Value carrier, Launched in May 2005

Spice Jet: Low Cost, Launched in May 2005

Go Air: Low Cost, Announced in November 2004, plans to launch in September 2005; in the process of importing aircraft and is likely to launch in October-November.

Indus Airways: Value carrier, Had announced plans in January to launch in May 2005 but is yet to import its first aircraft.

AirOne: Regional, Announced plans in February to launch regional services in 2005.

Magicair: No frills domestic Airline, Announced in March plans to launch in second half of 2005 but is yet to get a no objection certificate.

EastWest Airlines: Value Carrier, Had plans to launch in October/November 2005 but now claims that the launch will be by December. Hopes to list on the BSE by July-August.

Interglobe: Low Cost, Has an NoC to start operations but is yet to announce any plans.

Crystal Air: Regional, The Coimbatore-based airline has plans to launch regional services with Embraer 170/175 series.

Visa Air: Low cost, Has an NoC but is in the process of raising funds.

Regional International Low cost operations

Air India Express: Launched in April 2005

Cochin International Airport: Announced plans in March to study launching of low-cost carriers for international regional operations.

(Source: *Businessworld*, June 27, 2005)

Exhibit 10: **New Airlines Starting in India**

For full service airline though, it is a time to worry as the no-frills airlines are certainly making a dent into their markets and profits. To take up the impending challenge the full-service airlines are also harnessing themselves. Air India is set to launch a new subsidiary airline with 25% lower fares to Gulf and Southeast Asian countries in 2005. Air Sahara also plans to restructure and cut its operational costs to offer full service at cheaper tickets to domestic destinations, SAARC and ASEAN countries.

The Indian aviation market grew by 20% last year and since this growth is expected to continue, more low cost carriers from other countries are set to start their operations here in India. They include Jet Star, Tiger Airways, Air Asia Singapore and Value Air from Singapore; Air Asia from Malaysia; Air Arabia from UAE; Lion Air from Indonesia; Nok Air and Air Asia-Thailand from Thailand. Once operational their fares would be 30%-40% less than those of regular carriers. Airlines from Singapore would connect the four metros first and then zoom on the smaller cites. Airlines from Malaysia would connect Southern destinations first and then the metros. Air Arabia on the other hand would connect Kerala first and then the metros.

The Indian carriers are also gearing up to put forth a tough fight against these foreign carriers. This is evident from their expansion plans tabulated in Table 11.

HOW HIGH CAN THEY FLY?[2]

With so many low cost carriers coming up in India, the Indian flier cannot ask for more. Soon we would see even small but important cites also connected by these low cost carriers. But the question to be asked is, how long can these carriers sustain in keeping their fares low as compared to the other traditional carriers?

Taking Air Deccan as an example we see that the airline offers its cabin crew a 10 per cent commission on all beverages and food that they sell passengers on the flight. The airline expects the average passenger to fork out about Rs 75 to pick

Category	Airline	In active	On order	
		No. of aircraft	No. of aircraft	Time frame
Existing traditional carrier	Air India	39	53	2010
	Indian Airlines	52	65	2010
	Jet Airways	50	49	2010
	Air Sahara	26	10	2010
	Air Deccan	16	66	2010
	Kingfisher	3	28	2010
Existing LCCs	Air India Express	3	18	Mar 06
	Alliance Air	15	5	*
Planned start-up carriers	Go Air	0	20	2007-08
	IndiGo	0	100	*
	Magic Airlines	0	10	2007-08
	Spicejet	0	25	2007-08
	Air One	0	25	*
	Paramount Airways	0	5	*
	Eastwest Airlines	0	5	2007-08
	City Air	0	2	*
	Total	**204**	**486**	*

Sources: Air Transport Intelligence; CAPA, Monthly Indian Essentials.
The orders have been announced by the carriers but may still be waiting for government approval. *Data unavailable.
(Taken from *Chartered Financial Analyst*, Dec. 2005)

Table 11: **Aircraft Acquisitions/Expansion Plans**

up a quick meal. On a margin of 30 per cent for the 1 million passengers who have flown Air Deccan over the last 12 months, that means Rs 7.5 crore (Rs 75 million) in extra revenue. That, of course, is not the only way Air Deccan is innovating revenue. It hawks advertisement space on the seats, the cabin interiors, and even on the body of the airplane. To add to this Air Deccan's cost per kilometre per seat is only 4.3 cents whereas its competitors fly at 8-16 cents.

Another point to note is that Air Deccan will have to face intense competition from new airlines like Wadia, Kingfisher Air and Royal Air next year, all of which are looking at low-cost models. Also, the existing carriers will not keep quiet.The three big carriers, for instance, have been quick in responding to the Air Deccan's challenge on metro routes by dropping tariffs on select flights where, unlike an apex fare, you need not book earlier.

Indian Airlines has responded by bringing down tariffs on its flights that coincide with those of Air Deccan. For instance, IA is offering Fly Select fares on three flights from Delhi to Mumbai — at 9 am, 10 am and 6 pm — for Rs 4,200. (Air Deccan flies at 8.55 am and 4.30 pm.) Even Jet (through their Check Fares) and Air Sahara (through Steal a Seat) are using the same model.

The hyped Rs 700 seat is booked within hours, and for many passengers seems more an advertising gimmick than reality. In most cases, the apex fares offered by the three airlines are more or less similar to what you can book on Air Deccan.

On careful analysis we can see that by booking three months in advance, one can get a cheap price, but between the seven-thirty day advance booking period there are many cases where tariffs of full carriers are cheaper.

Air Deccan aircraft have 180 seats — 22 per cent more than what its competitors squeeze in — and it flies for over 12 hours compared to the competitors' eight-nine hours. The sales and distribution costs constitute only 8 per cent of th total cost compared to the full-service airlines that spend as much as 28 per cent. There are also savings in avoiding the printing of tickets, and keeping staff on a tight leash. Air Deccan flies point to point with no onwards or connecting flights, saving on both fuel and time.

But on careful analysis we see that the cost-cutting model might not work here at all. For instance, IA says it also flies its aircraft for 11 hours. Moreover low-cost made sense in Europe and US where labour costs constituted over 45 per cent of total cost; in India it is not more than 15 per cent. Instead, 50 per cent of the cost is fixed. Deccan's ATRs did not have to pay landing fees, and forked out nominal navigation charges (government allows special rates for aircraft with less than 50 seats). But with Airbus, this saving (which is as high as 18 per cent of total cost) will cease to exist.

Considering the points mentioned we see that the success of a low cost model is not just about the price. For every LCA there has been a success and there have been another 10 that have folded up. Market experts predict a big shake-up in the industry and claim that ultimately only 3-4 players will be in the fray once consolidation starts happening. Rather success depends on reading the market right and offering what makes sense for passengers while controlling costs and garnering the adequate revenues. Eventually stability is restored with fewer players, but only after the whole industry has bled massively and the prices land back to the old level. So it is too early in the Indian context to be speculating on such a possibility. But the global experience points to something more nuanced than a simple segmentation between high-cost full service airlines and low cost no-frill ones.

Questions

1. What are the critical success factors and marketing mix offerings of Indian and International low-cost airlines?
2. Which business drivers need strategic attention for the business model of low-cost airlines to be successful in India?

Notes

Easy Charge: Great Potential or a Myth?

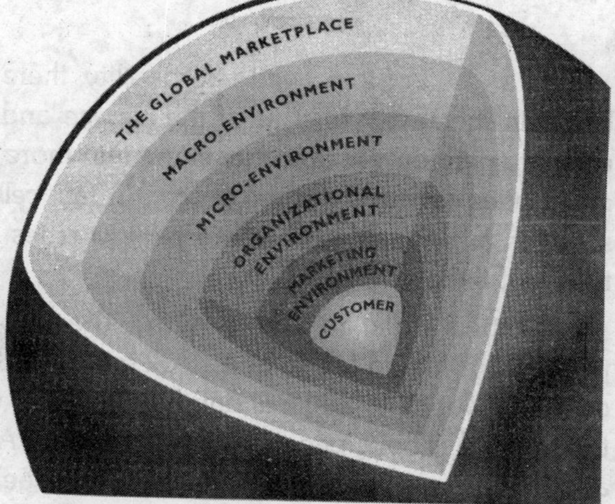

Price Case - 20

Purpose of the Case

The idea is to assimilate the relevant concepts at work and analyse in light of the following issues:

- How do lower tariffs for a service widen and deepen a market especially when it is innovatively coupled with convenience through incorporation of new technology?
- How is m-commerce becoming a reality in India?

"Bharti has "massified" the mobile market with lower tariffs and enhanced product offerings."

Sunil Bharti Mittal *(Chairman and Group Managing Director, Bharti Group)*
Excerpts from tele.net February 2004 issue

MOBILE TELEPHONY IN INDIA: AN INTRODUCTION

The Indian mobile market, according to the COAI (Cellular Operators Association of India), has increased from approximately 1.2 million subscribers as of March 31, 1999 to approximately 29.21 million subscribers as of June 30, 2004.

As per the telecom experts, the demand for mobile services in India will continue to grow rapidly as a result of the following factors:

- Lower tariffs and handset prices over time;
- Falling cost of cellular infrastructure;
- Growth in pre-paid customer category;
- Greater economic growth and continued development of India's economy;
- Higher quality mobile networks and services; and
- Greater variety and usage of value added services.

Indian Telephony industry has been witnessing a stupendous growth since its inception. According to provisional forecasts made by Gartner, the consulting company, cellular connections will reach 56m by the end of 2004, up 96 per cent from 2003, and 130m by 2008. The growth is driven mainly by the reduction in pricing of cellular services, availability of a range of handsets priced at different price points, with several below the Rs. 3,000 mark, and the falling cost of cellular infrastructure.

As a result of improved affordability, there has been an increased take-up of the service and the cellular operators are able to venture into more and more cities & towns of the country. In fact cellular services are available in almost 1400 cities and towns of India.

Despite this rapid growth, the mobile penetration rate in India, at approximately 2.8 per cent as of June 30, 2004, is significantly lower than the average mobile penetration rate in other Asian and international markets. India still lags far behind China and the United States, which have 200 million and 140 million mobile phone users respectively.

MOBILE PENETRATION: INDIA VS COMPARABLE ECONOMIES

India dwarfs all other countries in terms of population and the mobile opportunity. China has 1.7 billion people but already has around 200 million mobile subscribers. According to the World Bank, the gross national income per person in India was $450 in 2001, compared with $890 in China. The Chinese economy may be twice as strong, but there are nearly twenty five times as many mobile users.

Another comparable market like Brazil has 170 million people but around 35 million subscribers. African countries, though suffering from many economic challenges, are very open to the idea of using mobile networks to increase telephone usage.

(*Source:* www.thefeature.com/topic? topicid=37)

The latest developments in mobile market

- The launch of "Push-to-Talk" (PTT) services by Tata Teleservices. This is being touted as the next big thing in cellular circles in India.
- This PTT service has also been launched by Hutch.
- AirTel launched Flexicharge for its mobile service users. The users can now recharge depending on their need for more validity or more value.
- Idea Cellular has launched SMS Bill pay service for its post-paid subscribers in Andhra Pradesh.
- Cellular versus Fixed - The number of Mobile users have far exceeded fixed line subscribers in Delhi, Mumbai, Chandigarh, Vadodara and Shimla. If the trend continues, we would see more mobile subscribers by the end 2004.

GOVERNMENT OF INDIA - REFORM ORIENTED TELECOM POLICY, 2004

In an interview with tele.net correspondent, Mr. Dayanidhi Maran, Minister of Telecom outlined the priorities and the reform oriented policies of the UPA government. The important points outlined in his statement are as follows:

Service Providers	Zones
Aircel Limited	Tamil Nadu except Chennai, & Pondichery
Aircel Digilink India	Haryana, Rajasthan and UP (East) under the brand name "Essar"
Bharti Cellular	Delhi (Metro), Mumbai (Metro), UP (W), Haryana, Maharashtra, Tamil Nadu, Kerala, MP under brand "AirTel"
Bharti Mobile	Andhra Pradesh, Karnataka and Punjab under the brand name "Airtel"
Bharti Mobinet Ltd	Chennai (Metro) as "AirTel"
Bharti Mobitel	Kolkata Metro as "AirTel"
Bharti Telenet	Himachal Pradesh as "AirTel"
BPL Cellular	Kerala,Maharashtra,Tamil Nadu
BPL Mobile	Mumbai (Metro)
Escotel Mobile	Haryana, Kerala, UP (West)
Fascel	Gujarat as "Hutch"
Hexacom India	Rajasthan, North East as "Oasis Cellular"
Hutchison Essar South	AP, Karnataka, Chennai as "Hutch"
Hutchison Essar Telecom	Delhi (Metro) as "Hutch"
Hutchison Max Telecom	Mumbai (Metro) as "Orange"
Hutchison Telecom East	Kolkata (Metro) as "Hutch"
Idea Cellular	Andhra Pradesh as "Idea"
MTNL	Delhi & Mumbai as "Dolphin"
Reliance Telecom	Assam, Bihar, HP, MP, NE, Orissa, West Bengal
RPG Cellular	Chennai (Metro) as "RPG Cellular"
Spice Communications	Karnataka, Punjab as "Spice"

- To usher in convergence technologies, broadband connectivity, incorporating 4G mobile wireless (allowing high quality smooth video transmission) and a national Internet exchange.
- To hasten migration to next generation Internet protocol, IPV6, by 2006 and promote digital signatures in financial sector and R&D to make India a leading outsourcing hub.
- To improve PC penetration and internet subscription in India from less than 1 per cent and 2 million users respectively through development of low cost PC.
- To increase teledensity in India from 7 per cent to 14 per cent by 2007 and thus to bring all round development with special focus to increase rural density to reduce the digital divide.
- To hike foreign investment from 49 per cent to 74 per cent in telecom sector thereby providing the much needed capital.
- Telecom sector to entrust Media Lab Asia to provide connectivity, telemedicine and distance education to rural areas.

(On the basis of Minister of Telecom Mr. Dayanidhi Maran's Interview published in tele.net, Vol No. 5, Issue No 6, June 2004)

GSM SERVICE PROVIDERS IN INDIA

As on July 2004, there are 21 service providers all over India. Some of these are a subsidiary of some major national service providers.

On the basis of service providers all over India, it can be seen that the major players in the mobile telephony sector are only a handful. They are as follows:

- AirTel World
- BPL Mobile
- Hutchison
- Idea Cellular
- RPG Cellular
- Spice Telecom

The following table gives market share of major players in Indian mobile telephony as on April 2004:

Operators	Percent	Rank
Bharti	39.89	1
Hutch	21.86	2
Idea	16.81	3
BPL mobile	12.05	4
Spice	7.44	5
RPG	1.95	6

% Market Share in GSM - April 2004

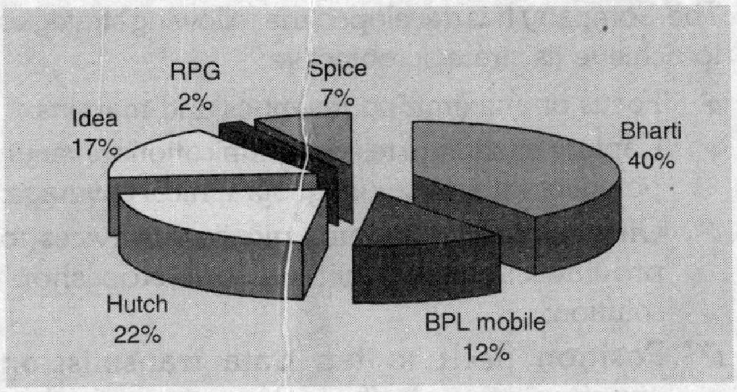

(Source: Cellular Operators Association of India)

BHARTI TELE-VENTURES

Bharti Tele-Ventures Limited was incorporated on July 7, 1995 for promoting investments in telecommunications services. Its subsidiaries operate telecom services across India. Bharti Tele-Ventures is India's leading private sector provider of telecommunications services based on a strong customer base consisting of approximately 8.37 million total customers which constitute, approximately 7.67 million mobile and approximately 704,000 fixed line customers, as of June 30, 2004.

(Source: www.airtelworld.com)

The corporate structure of Bharti Tele-Ventures is shown below:

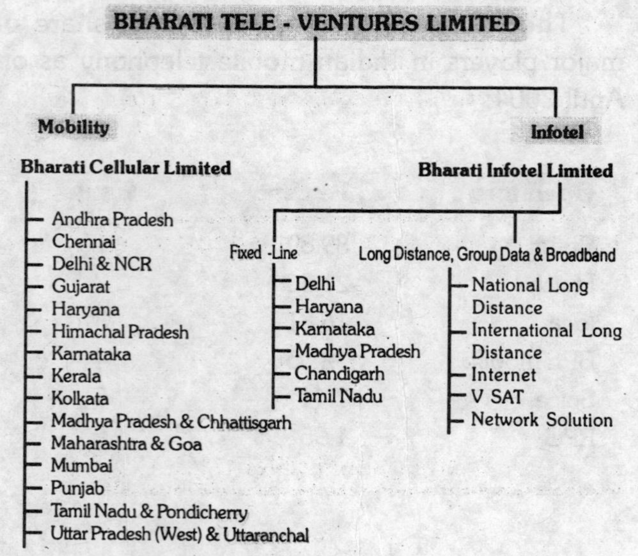

BUSINESS STRATEGY

The Company has developed the following strategies to achieve its strategic objective:

- Focus on maximizing revenues and margins;
- Capture maximum telecommunications revenue potential with minimum geographical coverage;
- Offer multiple telecommunications services to provide customers with a "one-stop shop" solution;
- Position itself to tap data transmission opportunities and offer advanced mobile data services;
- Focus on satisfying and retaining customers by ensuring high level of customer satisfaction;
- Leverage strengths of its strategic and financial partners; and
- Emphasize on human resource development to achieve operational efficiencies.

BUSINESSES

Bharti Tele-Ventures' current businesses include -

- Mobile services under the brand name of "AirTel"
- Fixed-line under the brand name of "TouchTel"
- National and international long distance services under the brand name of "IndiaOne"
- VSAT, Internet services and network solutions as "Bharti InfoTel".

MOBILE DIVISION

Bharti Tele-Ventures' mission is to meet the mobile communication needs of the customer through

1) Error free service
2) Innovative products and services and
3) Cost efficiency.

The Company's strategic objective is to consolidate its leadership position amongst the mobile service providers in India.

Bharti Tele-Ventures, through its subsidiary has the licenses to provide GSM services in all the twenty-two telecom circles in India. It proposes to consolidate all its subsidiaries providing mobile services under Bharti Cellular Limited.

As of June 30, 2004, approximately 92 per cent of India's total mobile subscriber marketresided in the Company's sixteen mobile circles, which collectively covered only 56 per cent of India's land mass.

The sheer dominance of Bharti can be seen from the fact that irrespective of the area considered be it area wise coverage or customers covered, it has share of over 50 per cent in each of the categories.

The areawise presence of players and their respective customer market share also depicts the leadership position AirTel is holding in the Indian market.

MOBILE FOOTPRINT

The map on the next page depicts the location of, and provides certain information for, Bharti Tele-Ventures' existing mobile circles in India.

1) Population estimates are as per National Census, 2001 and are as of March 1, 2001. The population for Uttar Pradesh (West) circle is approximately 37 per cent of the total population for the state of Uttar Pradesh.
2) Mobile subscriber statistics are as of June 30, 2004 and are based on data released by COAI. Mobile market size comprises the total number of mobile subscribers of all the service providers in a circle.

3) Demographics of Maharashtra and Tamil Nadu do not include demographics of state capitals (metros) Mumbai and Chennai respectively.
4) Demographics of Haryana do not include Faridabad & Gurgaon as they are included in Delhi and NCR. Similarly demographics of Uttar Pradesh (West) & Uttaranchal does not include Noida & Ghaziabad as they are included in Delhi NCR.

MOBILE STRATEGY

Bharti has a very clear focus towards the mobile telephony market. These are outlined in the form of their mobile strategy. The mobile strategy of Bharti is as mentioned below.

- Capture maximum telecommunications revenue potential with minimum geographical coverage to maximize its revenues and margins.
- Build high quality mobile networks by deploying state-of-the-art technology to offer superior services.
- Use the experience it has gained from operating its existing mobile networks to develop and operate other mobile networks in India and to share the expertise across all of its existing and new circles.
- Attract and retain high revenue generating customers by providing competitive tariffs, offering high quality customer support, proactive retention programs and roaming packages across all of its mobile circles.
- Provide affordable tariff plans to suit each segment of the market with a view to expand the reach, thereby increasing the mobile customer base rapidly.

EASY CHARGE - A PRODUCT BY AIRTEL

AirTel launched the world's first flexi-recharge pre-paid anytime, any value, any where service in Feb 2004, for its customers in Delhi, Mumbai, & Karnataka. This service offered flexibility to

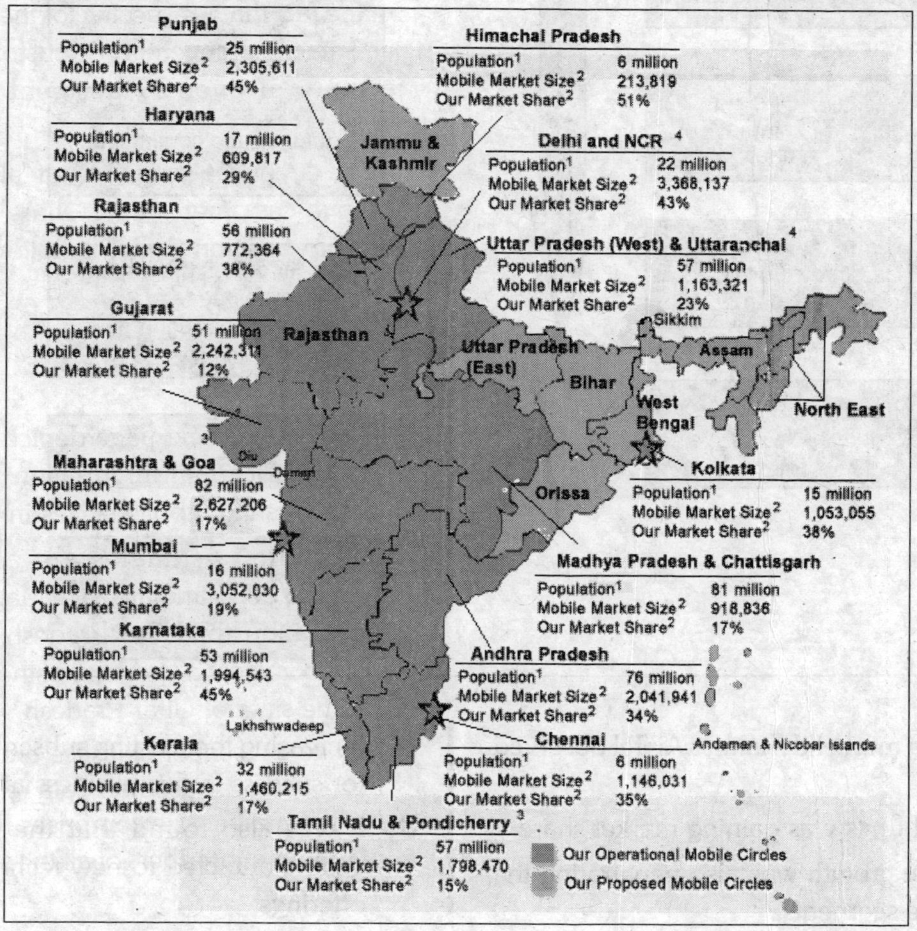

the customer to recharge his mobile at the lowest ever Rs. 54 to the highest ever of Rs. 9999. In between denominations were available at a gap of every rupee, which means a customer could charge his mobile for any amount between Rs 54 and Rs 9999. The product was made available at 50,000 AirTel retail outlets across the country.

This scheme also had the flexibility to recharge from anywhere in India, even on roaming, at no extra cost along with 24x7 availability. The service was named "AirTel Easy Charge".

To avail this service, an AirTel customer had to go to his nearest retailer having a special Easy Charge sim card. The customer had to just give his mobile number to which recharging would be done, and the retailer would confirm the same. In the following stage, the retailer would transfer recharge value from his mobile phone to the customer's. Both retailer and the customer then received a message from AirTel system stating that recharge had been done.

PRODUCT LAUNCH: WHY WAS EASY CHARGE LAUNCHED?

Since there was so much competition in the market,

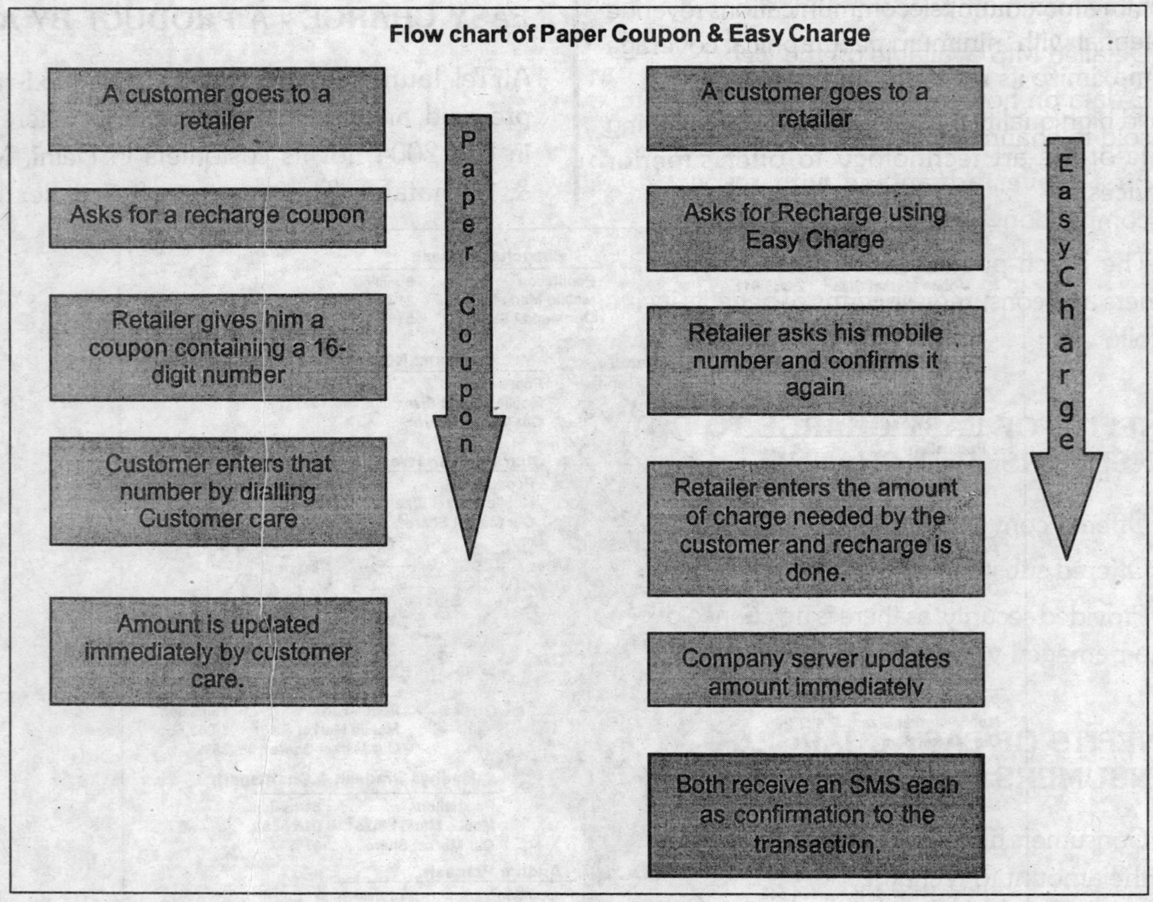

with the changing market dynamics AirTel observed that:

- Sale of small units was gaining market share,
- Rapid market growth was also penetrating the lower income segments,
- Increasing the existing subscriber base is critical for success in this business at this stage, and
- It was also found that the Customers were getting attracted to new technology and better offerings.

On the lines of its commitment to customer delight, AirTel launched Easy Charge in Karnataka, Kerala & Tamil Nadu circles along with Delhi.

There was a very significant advantage to AirTel in terms of control on its distribution channel.

BENEFITS TO AIRTEL

As a company, AirTel had the following major advantages by offering this product.

- Better control on channel in terms of sales volumes,
- Huge savings in terms of cost of printing of recharge coupons,
- Detailed MIS available on the web,
- E-data on how much current stock/ how much sold to channel, and
- First mover advantage with respect to the competition.

The much-publicised information to channel partners and consumers in terms of benefits included the following:

BENEFITS OF EASY CHARGE TO BOTH CONSUMERS AND CHANNEL

- Offered convenience to the customer,
- Offered substantial ease of usage, and
- Provided security, as there is no chance of getting a damaged voucher.

BENEFITS OF EASY CHARGE TO CONSUMERS

- Consumers benefited due to the ease of selecting the amount to recharge,
- Reduced numbers of transactions were required to recharge, and
- Minimum recharge amount was much lesser than the existing.

BENEFITS OF EASY CHARGE TO CHANNEL

Following were the major benefits that AirTel offered to consumers.

- No stock out anywhere in the channel,
- Better utilizations of the channel's working capital,
- Enhanced opportunity to attract cost conscious subscribers who didn't have enough money to reload,
- Helped in winning customers from competitors, and
- It also offered an opportunity to add on new class of dealers into their existing network.

On the basis the above-mentioned advantages Easy Charge was launched.

RESPONSE OF THE MARKET TO EASY CHARGE LAUNCH

When the product was launched first on 26th Jan 2004, the response was overwhelming and is mentioned separately for Retailers and Consumers.

RETAILERS

Retailers grabbed the opportunity as a golden chance to make initial money on the sale from Easy Charge before it became a commodity with its availability at all retail points.

For this purpose, many retailers accepted the Easy Charge sim card for doing business using this new technology.

The Retailers who were well educated accepted the product readily, where as those retailers who were in rural areas declined to do so, since these customers wanted recharge coupons as a physical product in their hand. The consumers were a bit apprehensive and cynical of the product and thus did not believe that such a product could be made available in India at this time.

The upmarket retailers convinced their customers to get their recharge done using Easy Charge. They were earning higher profits out of this new product since this offered an extra margin of 1 per cent than the conventional recharge coupons.

During the course of acceptance of the product, due to some systemic problems in the initial phase, some of the retailers made losses on wrong transactions. This caused market apprehension regarding the product. Even upmarket retailers started going back to paper recharge coupons.

AirTel tried their level best by going on a massive damage-control exercise to prevent negative word-of-mouth publicity.

CONSUMER

The well-educated consumers welcomed the product with open arms. Initially they were a bit apprehensive since it was a completely new concept that they had, not even heard in India.

The other class of customers, especially the non-metro ones, didn't accept the product since they thought that if a company could transfer the charge it could also withdraw that at any time. Thus they saw it as a means of fraud and hence avoided it.

The company here again found that since their retailers themselves were not fully confident of the product, they could not convince the customers.

DRAWBACKS OF THE LAUNCH

Because of the market reactions, AirTel realised that there were some of the problems, which were to be rectified. The problem areas identified were as follows.

- **Lack of training:** AirTel found that it had committed a mistake by neglecting training to its channel partners. These included the retailers, distributors, sales force and even its Territory Managers. This was so because it had launched a completely new technology and this needed effective training to ensure that there were no operational mistakes.
- **Improper Network:** AirTel also found that it had to take care of initial hitches related to Network and working of the system. The technology problem had rendered the entire initial gain ineffective and now the company had to start all over again to achieve a good standing amongst the retailers and consumers by fighting the negative publicity built, building trust all over again.
- **Improper Communication:** It was also found that the communication about the product was improper. This was so because the TV commercial did not reveal much about the product clearly. Through the ads, the customers understood flexibility of payments but could not comprehend the technology part i.e. mobile-to-mobile transfer of recharged value. Rather it gave a completely different picture to the entire product offering. Consumers as well as the retailers both were equally confused about the advertisement and were thus poorly informed of the product.
- **Poor Security of Transaction:** It was found that any transaction that went into the AirTel network due to the network problem was non-recoverable due to lack of responsiveness on part of the AirTel management. None of the transactions which occurred due to some network error, could be recovered. This led to wide spread miscommunication about the product and about the company as a whole.

Shahrukh Khan, a Top Indian film star and a youth icon of 1990s-2005 was roped in by AirTel as a part of AirTel's communication strategy of celebrity endorsement.

RESPONSIVE ACTIONS BY AIRTEL

1. Introducing a new team

To overcome the difficulties of poor training and lack of suitable support at the field, AirTel hired a team of people to move into different parts of the city and talk to retailers about the product. They were mainly meant to train the retailers well so that the awareness on part of retailers could be improved. This team was also to sell this product to small retailers who as of now were not wiling to try this product.

The team members were called Easy Charge Buddies and were assigned the following roles:

- Encourage retailers to transact initially using Easy Charge,
- To help the retailers overcome hesitation,
- To help retailers handle customer queries and objections,
- To solve retailer queries,
- Encourage retailer to increase volume of transaction on Easy Charge,
- To audit the retailers on "Easy Charge Certified Outlet / ECCO Parameters,"
- To identify market reaction to the product, and finally
- To recommend suitable measures to be adopted by AirTel.

2. Well-connected and serviced Network

AirTel at the same time worked on its system and as a result within a week of these buddies going on to the field, the system problems were corrected. Now, the typical response time for a customer and retailer receiving SMS after a transaction reduced to less than 5 seconds. This was phenomenal as far as the service standards in India were concerned.

3. Reworked Communication and Advertisements

Since it was found during the course of market visits by Easy Charge Buddies that the customers did not understand the advertisements and communication with regards to it, AirTel decided to come up with new advertisements on television in this regard. The company also started to focus more aggressively on appropriate supply and availability of POS display material. Now this material was widely and readily available with most of the retailers. The company also started focusing more on the retailers who expected more support from the company and the company started providing more support to them in lieu of higher volume of purchases and corresponding sales.

4. Secure Transactions

Since a major problem area recognised during the initial launch of the product was the lack of ability to get the money refunded, this was taken up as a priority area. Now the company started refunding the money of all those who had lost money in transaction due to the systemic problems. This acted as a major respite to all the retailers who had any fear in this regard in mind.

RENEWED RESPONSE

Because of a team of people in market along with the above-mentioned initiatives, the product sales started growing. The following table highlights the work done by the team of Easy Charge Buddies during the period.

MOBILE COMMERCE IN INDIA: IS IT A POSSIBILITY?

"The customers will be able to use their mobile and pay through their debit card/credit card the way they use Internet banking. The customer will be able to authenticate the transaction and he can make bill payments, mobile top-ups and also online purchases."

Rahul Khosla - Visa International's regional head consumer and commercial marketing (Asia -Pacific region)

(http://www.paymentsnews.com/2003/12/mobile_commerce.html)

FLOWCHART OF MOBILE COMMERCE STAGES

The following flowchart reveals the stages, which are involved in the process of mobile telephony. Stage I explains how the customer would be able to make payments of his regular utility bills using mobile. The next phase would involve even removal of necessity of the carrying your credit cards /debit cards.

M-commerce offers users the possibility accessing the Internet via a rapidly expanding array of mobile devices like smart mobile handsets. As new functions and applications (data, video) are added, mobile communications are radically extending the scope of e-commerce beyond its current boundaries. By the end of 2004-05, mobiles are expected to provide the most common access to high speed Internet, thus enabling transactions and specialized information services on the move for the mass market.

Developments in digital content with particular emphasis on downloadable games, ring-tones and music, video and TV services have also made the telecom industry exciting, literally and metaphorically.

To assess the current status and emerging trends in mobile commerce, it is important for marketers to quantify and forecast the m-commerce market, covering digital content, online shopping, financial transactions, POS retail, proximity payments, marketing and advertising and enterprise segments.

At first sight, the prospects for m-commerce look good. The huge number of mobile phone users offers a potentially vast audience for 3G services. It's predicted that there will be 260 million mobile phones owners in Europe by 2003, while PC ownership lags far behind.

(*Source:* www.datamonitor.com)

Another potentially big advantage for m-commerce is that mobile phones cost very little compared with a PC or interactive television. Even with full WAP capabilities, a mobile phone is still far cheaper than a PC.

But while many people would find it difficult to live without a mobile phone, many IT directors see no sound business reason for investing in services for mobile phones. Even companies that rely on the Internet to push information to users are holding back on investing large amounts in m-commerce.

It's not only the poverty of applications and dire bandwidth of the current technology that is a problem for m-commerce. The demographics are all wrong. The ownership of mobile phones and the usage of text messaging services are largely associated with young people. But the sort of m-commerce services that are being tipped as moneymakers involve offering highly personalised business-critical information - hardly the sort of service younger users will be queuing up for.

But the biggest obstacle of all to the take-up of m-commerce is that users have come to expect that information on the Internet should be free. As a result, many organizations do not feel they can make a success of charging for mobile phone services.

EASY CHARGE: IS IT THE BEGINNING OF MOBILE-COMMERCE IN INDIA?

Easy Charge as a concept in India failed to take off in the initial stage due to it being new and an innovative one. Such was the newness to the concept that even AirTel faltered at it. This was because of the fact that it failed to plan out all the things in advance. Even after that, once it realised and by taking quick and rapid measures it managed to see the product succeeding.

At the very outset this is as what is at the surface. The sound of the major developments can be heard soon. Consider a very simplistic situation. You go to a chemist and ask for a medicine. The chemist gives you the necessary medicine and recharges your cell phone with the remaining change. This is the amount of sophistication that one can have by this product. The day is not far-off when one can start trading for commodity items in lieu of balance in their mobile phones. One can simply transfer money on retailer's mobile number in lieu of products.

M-commerce delivers value in ways that

distinguish it from any other medium. To realize its potential value, companies will need to have a clear view of how the increasingly mobile world drives consumer needs. m-Commerce delivers value to consumers in a unique way in the following manner:

- **Immediacy**-Everything is available anytime, anywhere.
- **Connectivity**-Users sharing common interests can be instantly connected via text messaging and mobile chat capabilities.
- **Localization**-New positioning technologies will enable companies to offer consumers goods and services specific to their location.
- **Personalization**-Users can take their preferences with them wherever they go.
- **Push Capability**-Brief text messages can inform consumers of local offerings that suit their needs.

The key lies in bundling products with related goods and services that meet consumer's evolving needs and lifestyles. Mobile-commerce is going to come in a big way in India. This can be felt from the way even chocolate firms are approaching this technology. Cadbury already has the technology to sell its chocolates through vending machines by SMS and the amount gets deducted from the account.

This is a revolution in the offing and who knows in next five years and there is a high probability that we may see it turning into reality.

Questions

1 How do you think an innovative and revolutionary idea like "Easy Charge" could have been handled by AirTel even more effectively for gaining a higher customer mindshare and profitability?

2 Comment on future business potential and possibilities of mobile -commerce in India.

Notes

Product

Section - Six

CONCEPTUAL FRAMEWORK

To facilitate a better debate on the cases in this section, a quick exploratory review of the promotion function along with areas that need discussion are recapitulated briefly as follows:

- Being a marketing manager you need to communicate to build and maintain relationships by informing and persuading to promote your product. You have to co-ordinate promotion and other marketing efforts through **integrated marketing communications** .
- The **communication process** involves coding of information by source, sending the information through a medium and finally decoding of information by receiver. When the decoded message differs from the encoded one, a condition called noise exists.
- **Promotion** aims,
  - to create awareness of a new product, new brand, or existing product
  - to stimulate primary and selective demand
  - to encourage product trial through the use of free samples, coupons, limited free-use offers, contests and games
  - to identify prospects
  - to retain loyal customers
  - to facilitate reseller support
  - to combat competitive promotional efforts, and
  - to reduce sales fluctuations.
- The promotion mix includes,
  - **Advertising**: Paid by an identified sponsor, non-personal presentation .
  - **Personal selling**: Face-to-face interaction with prospective purchaser
  - **Public relations and publicity**: A series of variety of programs which are paid by sponsor in case of PR and unpaid in case of publicity.
  - **Sales promotion** is an activity or material that acts as a direct inducement, offering added value or incentive for the product, to resellers, salespeople or consumers.
  - **Direct and interactive marketing**: Use of mail, telephone, fax, e-mail or Internet to communicate to customers and prospects.
- A product's **promotion mix** is a function of the organization's promotional resources, objectives, and policies, characteristics of the target market, characteristics of the product, and cost and availability of promotional methods.
- The purpose of **Integrated marketing communications (IMC)** is to manage and co-

ordinate the entire communications process strategically to provide clarity, consistency and maximum impact through the seamless integration of discrete messages.

- **Communications objectives** are to put something into the consumer's mind (cognitive), to change the consumer's attitude (affective), to get the consumer to act (behavioral)
- The **design of message** should be in accordance with content, structure, format and source. **Communication channels** may be personal (advocate, expert and social channels) or non-personal (media, atmospheres and events).
- **Marketing communications mix's effectiveness** is measured by asking members of the target audience whether they recognize or recall the message, how many times they saw it, what points they recall, how they felt about the message, and their previous and current attitudes toward the product and the company.
- Marketers also consider whether to use a push policy or a pull policy:
  - With a **push policy**, the producer promotes the product only to the next institution down the marketing channel. Normally, a push policy stresses personal selling.
  - Firms that use a **pull policy** promote directly to consumers, with the intention of developing strong consumer demand for the products. Once consumers are persuaded to seek the products in retail stores, retailers go to wholesalers or the producer to buy the products.
- Promotional activities may lead to deception rather than making the customer more informed. Although some deceiving or misleading promotions do exist, laws, government regulation and industry self-regulation minimize deceptive promotion.
- Promotional expenses are treated as profit centers and not as cost centers .They lower the overall cost by increasing demand which leads to increased consumption.
- It is debated across the globe that whether it is correct or incorrect to lure customers by promotion for products which they may not need .

Cadbury's Dairy Milk Chocolate

Evolving "Positioning" over Time

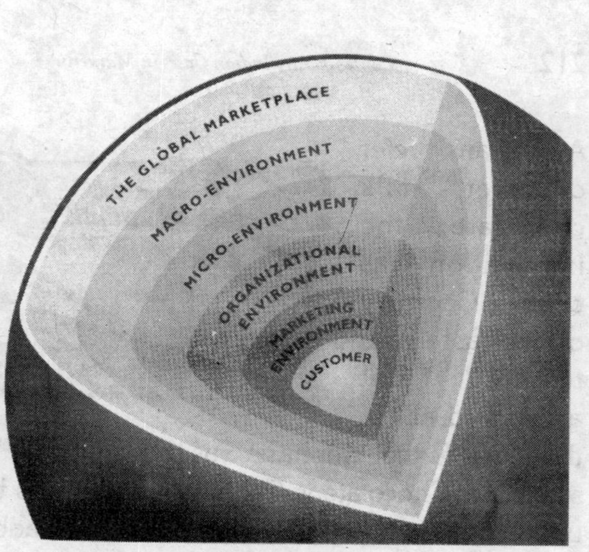

Promotion Case - 21

Purpose of the Case

The idea is to assimilate the relevant concepts at work and analyse in light of the following issues:

- To focus on how a brand is evolved to keep a consumer populace growing across age groups and occasions for consumption
- To appreciate how brand positioning and communication affect the mindset of both potential and existing consumers

Milk chocolate for eating was first made by Cadbury in 1897 by adding milk powder paste to the dark chocolate recipe of cocoa mass, cocoa butter and sugar. By today's standards this chocolate was not particularly good: it was coarse and dry and not sweet or milky enough for public tastes. There was a great deal of competition from continental manufacturers, not only the French with their fancy chocolates but also the Swiss, renowned for their milk chocolate. Led by George Cadbury Junior, the Bourneville experts formulated a recipe incorporating fresh milk, and production processes were developed to produce a milk chocolate 'not merely as good as, but better than the imported milk chocolate. The business changed from a grocery shop and became a manufacturer of drinking chocolate and cocoa, the start of the Cadbury manufacturing business, as it is known today.

Cadbury Ltd. is the confectionery division of Cadbury Schweppes plc, a major force in the international market. By 1913 it had become the company's best-selling line and in the mid-twenties Cadbury's Dairy Milk gained its status as the brand leader, a position it has held ever since.

Enjoyed and recognized by people in over 30 countries around the world, Cadbury's core markets are currently in the UK, Ireland, Australia and New Zealand. The 'glass and a half', corporate purple and flowing script has become synonymous with Cadbury: these design elements have been used to great effect in developing the connotation of goodness that this imagery suggests. In the 1980s another vital attribute - taste - was highlighted. Regardless of national preferences about how chocolate should taste (e.g. dark chocolate is traditionally more popular in Europe whereas

Australians prefer creamier milk chocolate) the implication was clear - Cadbury offers taste and texture that appeals to all. In the 1990s further emphasis was laid on 'taste'. The strap line 'Chocolate is Cadbury', which was built upon previous brand values and allowed Cadbury to stake its claim and taking ownership of the word 'chocolate' and the chocolate eating experience.

The Indian Chocolate market is estimated at around 33,000 tones valued at approx. Rs. 8 billion and is growing at almost 11.5%. Cadbury being the market leader has a market share of 68%, Nestle being a distant follower with 22% market share. Out of the total chocolate market the chocolate bars market is estimated at about Rs. 5.5 to 6 billion which effectively means one-fourth of the total confectionery market. The Indian confectionery market is segmented into sugar-boiled confectionery, chocolates, mints and chewing gums. Cadbury India's market share in cocoa based products is 35% with Dairy Milk alone accounting for 30%. Perk and 5 Star account for another 20%. Cadbury derives 76% of its revenue from chocolates and confectionery sales. The biggest strength of Cadbury is its parent company in U.K, which provides all the technological, and Research & Development help to form new products or launch a product that is already being marketed in other countries.

Chocolate consumption in India is very low, per-capita consumption being 160 gms in the urban areas compared to 8-10 kgs per annum in the developed countries. Chocolates in India are consumed as indulgence and not as a snack food. However, a strong volume growth was witnessed in the early 1990s when Cadbury repositioned chocolates from children to adult consumption. The company had shown great resilience when after the worm controversy Cadbury lost its market share in starting months of 2004 but regained its position soon with due help from great advertising campaigns featuring superstar Amitabh Bachchan.

Major competitors apart from Nestle are the companies in the confectionery industry like Perfetti, Wrigley's, Lotte, etc. and the companies in the food and entertainment industry like Pepsi, Coca-Cola, Haldiram, and Dabur, etc. Nestle India has been deriving its revenue from five product baskets - coffee, milk products, food for infants, chocolate/ confectionery and malted beverages and food products.

Cadbury's Dairy Milk (CDM), which was launched in India in 1948, enjoys a 30% market share of the Indian chocolates market and is available in multiple pack sizes at strategic price points. Further, the plain milk chocolate is now available in several variants – Fruit and Nut, Crackle, Caramello, to name a few. Cadbury, even though a MNC has made CDM a huge brand today but it had to customize its marketing mix to suit the diverse temperature and socio-cultural environments. Cadbury's another big brand *Bournvita* is also the leader in the brown drink (cocoa based) segment.

It would be incomplete to look at Dairy Milk as a brand in isolation. It would be more prudent to look at Dairy Milk as Cadbury's Dairy Milk derives certain brand equity from the name of Cadbury's and remaining from Dairy Milk. In effect, we need to look at Cadbury's as the mother brand while simultaneously looking at Dairy Milk.

Initially, exclusive to Cadbury Dairy Milk as an advertising device, the 'glass and a half' symbol became an integral part of the corporate design for Cadbury in the early 1960s. The icon symbolizes the goodness, quality, freshness and superiority of Cadbury chocolate.

Purple and gold were firmly established as the Cadbury corporate house colors by the early 1920s. The two colors had been introduced within the product range at the beginning of the century. It was in 1920 that the purple and gold colors were used in the pack design for the flagship brand Cadbury Dairy Milk. In the aftermath of the worm controversy, the company came out with a new impenetrable packaging. The new double packaging even for the smallest offering, the 13 gm Rs 5 Cadbury Dairy Milk, had the bar wrapped in aluminum foil and enclosed in a polyflow pack, which is sealed on all sides. The larger Cadbury Dairy Milk packs came in poly-coated aluminum foil, which was heat-sealed and then wrapped in the branded outer package. Both these initiatives are country-specific and Cadbury invested nearly Rs 25 crore (Rs 250 million) this year on new machinery for the improved packaging.

Cadbury's uses its name on all its confectionery products (Dairy Milk, Perk, Fruit & Nut, etc). By doing so, it is using its stature in the form of corporate endorsement. The consumers feel reassured because the endorsing company already has an existing platform of visibility, image and equity. This way the company saves on the investment required to build and promote multiple, independent product brands. In order to obtain cost economies, Cadbury has leveraged the strength of the existing brand, Dairy Milk to launch new variants and product lines. It has been extended to several variants such as fruit & nut, crackles, roasted almond, Caramello, etc.

The sugar confectionery segment in India is largely dominated by the unorganized players. Leading national players in this category include Nutrine, Parry's, Ravalgaon, Candico, Parle's, Joyco India and Perfetti. The MNC's such as Joyco and Perfetti have aggressively expanded their presence in the country in the last few years. Sugar confectionery ventures of Cadbury's have not yielded desired results so far. In the malted food drinks category too, Bournvita market share has remained stagnant at 14-15% in the last few years, despite the company's efforts and investments in repositioning the brand.

Cadbury Script is an element of visual identity unique to the company, which is based on the signature of William A. Cadbury, the son of Richard Cadbury who was Chairman of Cadbury Brothers. The script logo has been modified over the years having been quite fussy initially. The script is exclusive to the word 'Cadbury'. The logo is prominently present on the pack, sign or other material for the chocolates and the promotion.

Table-1 and Table-2 show the pricing of Dairy Milk vis-a-vis the competitors in the milk chocolate segment:

Table 1-Pricing of Plain Chocolates

Company	Brands	Type	Weight	Price (Rs.)	Price/10 gms
Cadbury	Dairy Milk	Plain	13 g	5	3.846
			25 g	10	4.000
			42 g	15	3.571
			105 g	40	3.810
			165 g	60	3.636
Nestle	Premium		15 g	5	3.333
			30 g	10	3.333
Amul	Plain		40 g	10	2.500

Table 2-Pricing of *Dry Fruit based* Chocolates

Company	Brands	Type	Weight	Price (Rs.)	Price/10 g
Cadbury	Dairy Milk	Fruit and Nut	44 g	22	5.000
		Fruit and Nut	80 g	40	5.000
		Chunky	42 g	20	4.762
		Roast Almond	80 g	45	5.625
Nestle	Krunch	Fruit and Nut	40 g	15	3.750
Maestro Vochelle		Almond	200 g	245	12.250
Amul	Fruit and Nuts		40 g	13	3.250

Cadbury follows a dual price strategy i.e. Premium pricing as well as Penetrative Pricing. Cadburys Dairy Milk charges a premium for its milk chocolate in the range of 15-20% higher than similar chocolates from Nestle, and significantly higher than the Amul Chocolates. Such a price premium Dairy Milk is able to charge is reflective of the Brand Equity that this brand possesses. In consonance with its continuing objective of reaching a wider consumer base, Cadbury's Dairy Milk has introduced small pack sizes of Dairy Milk as well as other chocolates at lower price points. Cadbury Dairy Milk currently has three major price points: Rs.5, Rs.10 and Rs.15 per chocolate. While the Rs.5 variant makes it affordable to all consumers including low affordability segment, it has the Rs.40 and Rs. 65 packs for high usage and gift pack segments.

Cadbury's new global marketing strategy called 'Choose Cadbury' perfectly illustrates how a brand can evolve and how different messages can be communicated without losing the core strength and brand values that are already established. The central message of the 'Choose Cadbury' strategy hinges on the established glass and a half symbol. Is the glass half full or half empty? Cadbury suggests that the glass is always half full appealing to our emotions; therefore, in choosing Cadbury, consumers are taking a decision to embrace the positive. In this 'Choose Cadbury' campaign, the product ingredient of milk has been elevated from a practical, rational platform to an emotional one Cadbury promises to deliver on optimism, happiness and a feel-good factor. If a brand can do all this, the decision to purchase this brand over all other chocolate brands seems to be logical and inevitable. The 'Choose Cadbury' strapline is a call to action designed to motivate consumers by giving more reasons to remain brand loyal (Cadbury is Chocolate – feels good i.e. positive, uplifting, mood enhancing, providing enjoyment and happiness). At no stage in the evolution of the Cadbury brand has there been as much reliance on taking ownership of the emotional side of eating chocolate as there is now. Owning the emotional territory for chocolate has helped Cadbury to elevate its product in the mind of the consumer. With the 'Choose Cadbury' campaign consumers are being offered both logical and emotional reasons to buy a Cadbury product as a first option on every occasion.

In India, the challenge that Cadbury's faced was how to align their Indian strategy to their international positioning yet ensuring a significant amount of localization. The challenge has been handled with remarkable effectiveness and innovative thinking, such as active use of Hindi for most of their campaigns. Even while going for celebrity endorsements, category ownerships or such strategies, the cultural aspects have been well taken into account using visual imagery. Before we delve into an analysis of their positioning strategies, it will make sense to look at the key campaigns launched by Cadbury's Dairy Milk.

Since early 1990s, Cadburys ran various advertising campaigns of Cadburys primarily television-led campaigns to re-position Cadbury's Dairy Milk (CDM) depending upon changing marketing requirements. Some of the campaigns of Cadbury's were:

Campaign 1: *Kuch khas hai zindagi mein, kya swaad hai zindagi ka*

This campaign came at a time when Cadbury got stuck in a mindset trap, where it was perceived as something meant for kids, something, which was seen as indulgent product and something, which wasn't meant for the elders. This led to brand stagnation and what was required was to break free of this mould and establish CDM as something that could be enjoyed by people across age barriers.

The jingle stated *'kuch khas hai zindagi mein, kya swaad hai zindagi ka'*. The ad launched Cadbury's Dairy Milk (CDM) as a brand for both the kids and the adults, something that could be savored by people across age barriers. The ad demonstrated the consumption of chocolates in moments of excitement, joy and fun by people including the kids, teenagers and even elders. The message being delivered was- "Dairy Milk is for the joyous moments, and can be enjoyed by people across age groups". Be it the teenager dancing on a winning cricket shot, or a grandfatherly figure kicking a football, the message can be said to have been delivered with perfection.

Campaign 2: *Khaane walon ko khaane ka bahana chahiye*

The previous campaign enforced the idea of chocolate consumption across age groups but the sales again stagnated and then came the *'khaane walon ko khaane ka bahana chahiye'* campaign. The advertisement was communicated to the Indian mindset as simple yet subtle message. The message was "You don't need a special reason to eat a CDM". On the other hand, the visual imagery of a wedding celebration connected the chocolate with such events and this was the first step at moving the brand beyond individual celebrations towards event-level celebrations. This positioning helped in establishing CDM as a popular household name as people started associating with its name, across the big town-small town divide, across age barriers, across income anomalies and across barriers of culture. By including popular MTV bakra fame VJ Cyrus Broacha, the brand continued the association with fun and joy, while projecting the chocolate as a product for all age groups and celebrations.

Campaign 3: *Saath rahe har pal*

This short campaign of 'Saath rahe har pal' had two back-to-back ads enforcing the image of a friend who was there to see you through good and bad times. The idea behind these campaigns was to position CDM as someone you could rely on to be your friend when the chips are down. It was a shift in positioning strategy by not focusing on increasing the category itself but positioning it to be a friend for both good and bad times, a real companion.

Campaign 4: *Kuch Meetha Ho Jaaye*

The new communication from Cadbury's Dairy Milk has extended the core promise of happiness to yet another 'moment of joy' in one's life, with the tag-line *'Kuch meetha ho jaye'*. The communication aimed to turn chocolate consumption into a habit. In spite of a pronounced sweet tooth, chocolates don't figure in our consideration set on an everyday basis. Cadbury wanted to make chocolates and Cadbury's Dairy Milk an intrinsic part of the consumer's life. Such a

strategy makes economic rationale too. Against a Chocolate Market of Rs. 350-400 crores, the Indian sweet market is estimated at Rs. 11,000 crores. By using Amitabh Bachchan in a humorous setting, the message being delivered is to consider Dairy Milk as a 'sweet' and not just a chocolate. The sweets are an important part of the Indian Culture and Dairy Milk wants to be a consideration for the sweets, as a gift or a normal purchase. Once again, the campaign continues to stress the relevance of the product to all age groups as well as the central theme of joy and celebration. Such a category ownership stance that they have taken has the potential to provide big benefits to the company.

The new campaign introduces Cadbury Dairy Milk Desserts with Tiramisu and Kalakand flavored creme centre. The ad focuses on its mouth-watering taste to compliment every meal as the headline and subhead double up to make a good, witty feel to the brand.

In 2005, Cadbury tied up with Mobile2win for their first-ever wireless activity in India. The idea was to create hype and excitement around the re-launch of Cadbury Bytes (a bagged snack with wafers and chocolate, hugely popular as an alternative snack) and felt that the SMS promotion would not only bring in interactivity with the desired TG (kids and teens in Southern India) but also reach out to a large no. of people in the most cost effective manner. It was a pull activity, which was linked to the TVC's broadcast on Cartoon Network & Sun Network in the South. At the end of the TVC there was a 5 sec tag, which said SMS BYTES to 8558, and you could win one of the 2 Sony play stations, T-shirts and 1000 VCDs., in turn receiving an overwhelming response.

Today, India is the second largest market for Cadbury's Dairy Milk in the world. Marketing in Cadbury had been about reshaping consumer habits, about breaking socio-cultural barriers, about emotions. The Indian success saga has been designated as the "Blueprint for success" for all international markets to emulate.

Questions:

1. What does Cadbury India need to do to position their CDM brand and its brand extensions if they want to garner significant volume growth and reduce dependence on a single category – Chocolates - to drive growth?
2. How can the company increase share of chocolates in the total amount spent on an average by a consumer on these impulse products?

Celebrity Endorsement: Is it Worth it?

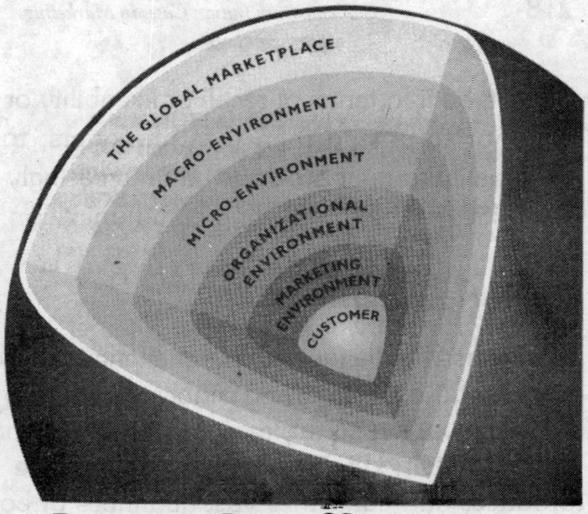

Promotion Case - 22

Purpose of the Case

The idea is to assimilate the relevant concepts at work and analyse in light of the following issues:

- To focus on the need for celebrity endorsement and how to go about operationalising?
- To match the product/service image with that of the endorsing celebrity?
- To list the pitfalls to avoid; and alternative options for small players

Michael Jordan is Nike's "Air" and Pierce Brosnan is Omega's "Sea master." Across the world, celebrities have been used for a variety of brands, big and small, new and old, winners and losers. India has opened its markets only recently and is witnessing an era of competition that its industry never imagined. Many venerable old organizations are now clutching at expensive straws to survive.

Soft drinks, chocolates, biscuits, toiletries, telecom, hi-fi's, hotels, ready-mades, razor blades, paints, cars, tyres, scooters, suitings, footwear, watches, pens, hair oil, *chyawanprash*, insurance packages, diamonds, liquor, photo films ... The list could go on. It appears that, of late, corporate India does not want to sell anything to the consumer without using either a movie star or a sports hero. Across product categories, everyone seems to be roping in a "Brand Ambassador" to sell their products. Vimal, Thums Up, Gwalior and Dinesh are some of the brands that used star-appeal in the early days of mass advertising. And who can forget Kapil 'Palmolive' Dev? With the visual media becoming more popular with the middle class, the use of celebrities in the TV media has increased.

Celebrities create headlines, their activities and movements are being closely watched and imitated. What the heroes and heroines wear in movies becomes fashion; what they endorse sells like hot cakes. The spectator-buyer is meant to envy herself as what she would become, if she bought the product. She is meant to imagine herself transformed by the product into an object of envy for others, envy which will then justify her loving herself. The idea, evidently, is to ride on the immense popularity and goodwill that the celebrities enjoy, and use the positive rub-off of the association to the brand's

This case is intended to be used as a basis for class discussion rather than as an illustration of either effective or ineffective handling of the situation. Authored by Dr. Mukesh Pandey.

benefit, be it in terms of recall or likeability or both. It is not surprising then that marketers, to lend personality to their products, are increasingly using celebrities in their marketing communication.

INDIAN CELEBRITIES

Marketers in India face quite a challenge. If we take a look at the set of brand ambassadors who have been contracted so far, they are all either from the world of film or cricket. This is because India produces and consumes vast quantities of both. In addition, this kind of endorsement or sponsorship marketing is still developing in India and brand managers are just beginning to understand how to associate products and services with the right spokespeople.

Even political parties are awestruck by the charisma of stars; such is the magnetism of celebrities in India that in the 2004 general elections, major political parties fielded a record number of film stars and cricketers to contest from important constituencies around the country.

A *mawali* from Mumbai, a Hyderabadi shopkeeper, a Jat farmer, a Bihari babu, and a Nepali tour guide, Bollywood star Aamir Khan has donned different avatars for the Coca-Cola television ads. Aamir Khan has signed a huge Rs 6 crore deal with Coca-Cola (www.rediff.com) for the *Thanda Matlab Coca-Cola* campaign. *Thanda* means cold, and is a generic term for soft drinks in India. Recent 'Thande ka tadka' campaign also features filmstar Aishwarya Rai. Coke ads have also featured actors Vivek Oberoi, Hrithik Roshan apart from actress Aishwarya Rai, among others. In addition to the high-profile Bachchan, Dabur India has TV hostess Mandira Bedi as the brand ambassador for its Vatika hair care range, while Hindi movie star Karishma Kapoor endorses the Dabur Amla hair oil brand.

Just as movie stars are popular so are cricket stars. Sachin, Mahindra Singh Dhoni, Dravid, Yuvraj, Sehwag, Kapil and Gavaskar are darlings of advertisers. With cricket having a fanatic following in India, it has virtually become a religion, a game of all games in India. Cricket stars are assumed to be energetic, team-players, sincere, dependable, physically fit & healthy, lively, flamboyant and smart in varying degrees and thus represent the aspirations of the crores of younger generation. Players like Kaif, Sehwag and Irfan Pathan have reached the top through sheer competence, hard work and talent and as such are idolized for their achievements by crores of Indians. The cola wars in India were and are fought in cricket stadia; the stars have lent their personality to Pepsi and Coke and a host of other products like health drinks, jams, motorcycles, suiting and shirtings, footwear and even credit cards.

The latest celebrity campaigns use combinations between film stars and cricketers e.g. the ad featuring Sachin Tendulkar, Fardeen Khan and Kareena Kapoor. Sachin also partnered Amitabh Bachchan in a Pepsi campaign aired earlier. Sachin also endorses Colgate Palmolive, ESPN-STAR Sports (the television channel), MRF (tyres), Boost (the health drink), TVS (the Victor scooter), Palio (the car), Visa, Adidas, AirTel and Britannia (biscuits).

Synovate, a leading global market research firm in their survey findings (Source: www.synovate.com) about sport in India and attitudes towards sporting teams, heroes and brand endorsements said that, in India, not surprisingly, the survey findings were dominated by cricket, cricket and more cricket. Sport is a passion; people laugh, cry, cheer and jeer for their teams and this makes it big business as well and there's no bigger sports business in India than cricket. This passion for watching cricket cuts across all ages and genders so the company that can credibly

establish itself as a cricketing partner via sponsorship, advertising or other promotional activities can go a long way towards reaching the bulk of the Indian populace.

Communicating via celebrities - a psychoanalytical framework. In India, it is not difficult to look for the reasons as to why companies are increasingly using celebrities. Indians, forget loving their heroes and heroines, revered their leaders. Unlike their foreign counterparts they always deified them and put a halo around their heads-'they could do no wrong'. The public believed that a movie hero like Shah Rukh Khan, for example, is expected to possess dynamic qualities such as attractiveness, sexiness, likeability, manliness and appeal. Companies vie with each other to use stars, as their spokesperson as these qualities, it is believed, will be transferred to the products they endorse. If Pepsi uses Shah Rukh Khan it becomes Coke's headache to find an equally charismatic character, which they have found in Hrithik Roshan.

Undeniably though some of the attributes associated with the celebrity are passed on to the brand, reflecting either the self-identity or aspirations of the consumer - 'if wearing a brand of clothes can make me appear like I've arrived in life then why go through the trouble of getting there?' The appearance of achievement is easier than the arduous process of attaining it.

ENSURING HIGH RECALL RATES

A consumer is bombarded with hundreds of TV, print, radio, Internet and outdoor ads in a day by marketer of various goods and services. In the midst of the advertisement clutter and mish-mash, the ads that celebrities endorse achieve high recall rates. The theory of 'selective attention' states that people tend to pay more attention to what is important and interesting to their beliefs. Therefore, when people see their favoured reference group members or celebrities in the ads, they pay more attention to the ads. At the same time, the advertiser can be sure that the positive feeling towards the ad has got transferred to the product. When Aishwarya Rai appears in an advertisement appealing (with her beautiful fluttering eyes) to the viewers to donate their eyes she instantly attracts attention, enabling retention of the message and possibly changing people's attitude towards eye donation as well.

To the loyal followers, celebrities represent an idealization of life that most people aspire, dream and would love to live. A movie actress is expected to possess a flawless skin, blemish-free face and, what is more, her fans are curious to know the secret of her beauty. So she becomes a natural endorser for beauty cosmetics, toilet soaps, talcum powder and other related products.

The audience might be attracted to certain reference groups such as movie stars and wish to possess qualities like the members of the groups. Lux, which has distinguished itself as the soap of movie queens, has carved out a unique position for itself in the highly competitive industry (based on the common knowledge that Indian women want to look like movie stars) by getting a host of cinema actresses to endorse its toilet soap.

IMPROVING SOILED IMAGE

When Cadbury India wanted to restore the consumer's confidence in its chocolate brands following the high-pitch worms controversy, the company appointed Amitabh Bachchan for the job. The company tried to live down the 'worm controversy' that tailed its flagship chocolate brand Cadbury Dairy Milk for much of end-2003 (the damaging controversy also caught other Cadbury chocolate brands in its slipstream) and it believed Bachchan was its best bet in the bid to rebuild consumer confidence in the brand. "This is a perfect first between Bachchan and Cadbury chocolates – their timelessness, and the love and trust they both share with people across India, makes this an ideal partnership," Cadbury India's managing director Bharat Puri has been quoted in the media as saying. "Moreover, Bachchan has a universal appeal that extends to everyone from six years to 60, just as our chocolates do." These endorsement deals clearly point that Bachchan seems to be something of a blessing for Indian advertisers when it comes to imparting freshness, vigour and, most importantly, respectability to brands especially to those in need of some sort of image modification or rejuvenation.

Recently, when the even more controversial pesticide issue shook up Coca-Cola and PepsiCo and resulted in much negative press, both soft drink majors put out high-profile damage control ad films featuring their best and most expensive celebrities.

While Aamir Khan led the Coke fightback as an ingenious and fastidious Bengali who finally gets convinced of the product's 'purity,' PepsiCo brought Shah Rukh Khan and Sachin Tendulkar together once again in a television commercial which made references to the 'safety' of the product indirectly.

LEARNING FROM EXAMPLES

Likeability of the endorser- an important factor in selection. People like ads more if they like the endorsers in the ads. When a person likes the endorser in the ad, he or she is more likely to believe what the endorser says about the advertised product and therefore will develop more positive feelings toward the ad and the brand itself. Thus, when Shah Rukh Khan, a popular actor, endorses Clinic Plus-All Clear people get convinced about the ability of the product to clear the head off dandruff. Because they are famous celebrities they are able to attract attention and retain attention by their mere presence in the advertisements.

According to advertising experts, a celebrity does help in increasing brand sales, but only if he/she is selected carefully and used effectively. The personality of the brand and the celebrity have to complement each other and the selection of the celebrity is, therefore, very important. However, a lot depends on how a celebrity is used.

Repositioning/New product launches with celebrities. Celebrities may also help reposition products having sagging sales. Cinthol, when it was introduced as New Cinthol, had Vinod Khanna to endorse it. Boost made use of the combined vigour of Kapil and Sachin to capture the minds of school children.

Post-Bachchan, Parker's sales increased by about 30 per cent encouraging Luxor Writing Instruments Ltd to renew Bachchan's contract and increase its annual ad spend by 30 per cent to touch Rs 10 crore in 2004.

Introduction of a new product can also be done successfully with the help of celebrities. Wagon-R, a newly introduced brand in the already crowded car market, drives home the message it wishes to convey through Shah Rukh Khan. The ad gets attention, recall and what is more, in the crowded car market it gets greater visibility.

Dabur Chyawanprash, although is the clear leader in the chyawanprash market, the category has been a victim of flat growth rates for a while now and needed a makeover, aimed at keeping the brand relevant to consumers. The coming together of brand Amitabh and Dabur Chyawanprash would not only infuse fresh life into the stagnant chyawanprash category and stave off competition from various brands but also the category, which has been witnessing near flat growth rates as per Dabur officials. Amitabh Bachchan, hired for an estimated Rs 8 crore, in fact, is the star brand ambassador for more than one Dabur brand.

Market Research - Achieving more through celebrity endorsements. In order to use a celebrity with greatest effect, marketers need to know which celebrities to choose for a brand's target audience, as well as the demographics this strategy works with. For example, some surveys have found that celebrity endorsement is most likely to work with teenagers and students. It was also skewed towards the West zone of India - perhaps a 'rub-off' effect from the strong Bollywood presence in Mumbai. Also, while cricket is obviously a national obsession in India, market research can still turn up some quirky details and some areas that marketers could target in the future.

What exactly is the celebrity endorsing? Our most celebrated cricket icon, perhaps our most celebrated personality, Sachin Tendulkar endorses everything from radial tires and the Palio car to Pepsi, Visa, Adidas, stock trading portals and music systems. A brand manager is then forced to ask himself a question which every consumer cynically asks viz. Who is the real Tendulkar; can he really be all of these?

It is extremely important to accurately understand the term "endorsement." By definition, we must be endorsing some trait or character of the brand. Theoretically, anybody can endorse anything provided that he or she carries credibility. Celebrities are known for some strong streak they possess. So, Amitabh Bachchan is evergreen, James Bond is dashing, Aishwarya Rai is a perfect beauty, Michael Jordan breaks limits, Rahul Dravid is dependable and Andre Agassi doesn't give up.

THINKING TWICE

Using celebrities has its own disadvantages, foremost being they do not come cheap and may cost the company a fortune. Since, celebrities by themselves do not guarantee success; the risk factor could be high. Companies, which used some cricket stars in their advertisements, have been embarrassed and worried when the latter embroiled in match-fixing scandals and controversies and made headlines for the wrong reasons.

The two cola companies that had a long association with cricket stars have been smart enough to switch over to movie stars as their endorsers and spokespersons. A celebrity may just disappear or lose his importance before the expiry of a contract. Advertisers thus have to study the life cycle of a star's career and ensure that he/she is signed up during his/her growth stage. Saurav Ganguly and Rahul Dravid are ideal choices whose career graphs are still in the growth stage. These two also seem to have emerged untainted by the betting scandal.

The raging controversy over celebrity endorsements has raised another issue: what happens to defunct celebrities? In other words, what happens when sports or film stars signed on by Corporates for lucrative endorsement deals don't perform well professionally? Among the Shah Rukhs, Amitabhs and Sachins, Pepsi India, for example, has had endorsers such as Kajol who has all but retired from active moviedom, Rani Mukherjee whose career graph has been average, Madhavan who failed to make waves in Bollywood, and small-time TV actor Amar Upadhyay who seems to have vanished from the telly.

Fame is a fickle and fleeting companion and can ditch the famous at the slightest provocation. Celebrities, being human, make mistakes but their mistakes get as much attention as their celebrity status and this can adversely affect the brands that they are endorsing. There are a number of examples, both Indian and International, where scandals and scams involving celebrity endorsers have caused embarrassment to the brands they endorse. Companies have to make quick decisions when one of their endorsers comes under fire or their own image could be tarnished. Guilty by association in a consumer's eyes describes it best. Magic Johnson lost his endorsement deals when he announced in 1991 that he's HIV-positive. It's a two-way street: If the brand chooses to distance itself with the tainted celebrity, the huge costs spent on roping in the celebrity and making of the ads may go down the drain and even then the association of the brand with the celebrity might by then be so ingrained that the damage is already done.

Celebrity endorsements, of course, come with risks attached. For example, when Tendulkar went through a prolonged lean patch, the inevitable question that cropped up in corporate circles - is he actually worth it? The 2003 Cricket World Cup also threw up the Shane Warne incident, which caught Pepsi off guard. With the Australian cricketer testing positive for consuming banned substances and his subsequent withdrawal from the event, bang in the middle of the event, PepsiCo - the presenting sponsor of the World Cup 2003 - found itself on an uneasy wicket. Coca-Cola India was caught in a similar situation, when a couple of years ago, one of its star endorsers, Salman Khan was accused in a couple of cases.

Often celebrities-in-the-making are signed by companies before they hit peak stardom because their endorsement deals are cheaper and Corporates want to catch them young. Mostly, ad agencies and marketers work together as a team to arrive at the right choices as far as celebrity endorsement deals are concerned, given that the stakes sometimes run into crores.

Hedging the risk: The first thing to ensure, when zeroing in on a celebrity, is to try and choose someone whose record is impeccable. Having said that, it's best not to depend on one celebrity, for that can backfire. Instead, it's better to use many celebrities who represent the same values. Pepsi does this quite well. Capitalising on the popularity of cricket and films in India, Pepsi uses several cricketers and film stars in their ads. So when Azharuddin and Jadeja got embroiled in the match-mixing controversy, Pepsi's severed its association only with these stars, but its relationship with cricket continued. One should seriously consider the risks of associating with a well-known personality and hedge against a future scandal by not relying on just one celebrity and instead linking the brand's association with a broad theme represented by several celebrities. If the marketer can't afford many celebrities, then he should get his thinking caps on and come up with a better, safer idea to ensure that he's in control of the brand's destiny - not the stars!

RISK OF OVEREXPOSURE

The ever-expanding universe of mega-brand hopefuls is running out of mega celebrities to brandish their products. How many brands does Amitabh Bachchan endorse? What about Tendulkar?.

The marketer must analyse that the law of diminishing marginal celebrity utility is at play no matter how larger-than-life a celebrity may be.

A celebrity may become the spokesperson of many products and runs the risk of getting overexposed. Possible examples are Amitabh Bachchan, Shah Rukh Khan and Sachin Tendulkar, who are spokespersons for about a dozen products or services. When a celebrity is a spokesperson for one product he may have high credibility. When he endorses a variety of products, his or her perceived credibility gets reduced due to overexposure. The economic motivation underlying the celebrities' endorsement effort may also become too apparent to consumers and they may take them for granted. A series of advertisements released by 'Sprite', a soft drink, pokes fun on the above-mentioned two aspects.

In 2003 alone, three big advertisers struck multi-crore endorsement deals with Bachchan viz. Nerolac Paints, Dabur India and Cadbury India. Add to this list previous year's endorsement contract between the star and suiting brand Reid & Taylor and Bachchan's enduring association with ICICI, Pepsi and Parker. Now add to all this those brands that the actor has endorsed at various times in the past – BPL and Maruti Versa – and one gets a fair idea of *l'affaire d'amour* that has blossomed between Bachchan and the advertiser.

Sachin Tendulkar is the hottest property in India's celebrity endorsement market, whose value was estimated at $18-20m over five years. The range of products Tendulkar endorses includes a luxury car, tyres, credit card, motorcycle, television, energy and soft drinks, shoes and biscuits.

The issue of 'overexposure' of celebrities is one that Corporates will need to contend with all the time. There is no gainsaying the fact that with more brand endorsements, exposure gets diluted. These days there is 'commoditization of celebrities', who are willing to endorse anything for big bucks. The celebrities' parade in advertising seems to be just for gaining noticeability, bordering on sham and hypocrisy on part of both the advertisers and celebrities. If advertisers and ad agencies think they can entice and attract consumers through such irrelevant celebrity endorsements, they are insulting their own intelligence (being consumers themselves).

With stars simultaneously endorsing so many brands, another Bachchan endorsement ceases to be a novelty as far as consumers are concerned. It is important to debate if an endorsement deal with the actor worth all that money. However, there is a theory going around that multiple endorsements by your ambassador don't hinder as long as your endorsement is relevant

CYNICISM ABOUT CELEBRITY ENDORSEMENT

Advertisers must realise that celebrity endorsement is not a definitive tool to achieve salience and brand superstardom. The assumed acceptance of celebrity endorsement amongst an audience is the most common advertiser fallacy; depiction of Hema Malini's pleasure at using a brand of detergent is unlikely to convince a housewife that the powder understands her plight. Congruence of the celebrity's image with the category the celebrity is promoting is imperative.

Celebrities are the conduits that convey your advertising message. Far too much depends on the ability to mesh the celebrities' traits with the products' positioning and the consumers' ability to accept it as a reflection of their self-image and aspirations. Sonali Bendre's endorsement of Nirma beauty soap generated lot of cynical reactions as people did not believe that the Bollywood heroine would be using the endorsed soap herself but was rather modeling for Nirma for money and money alone.

Some marketing and advertising experts do not recommend celebrity endorsements because according to them to be really successful, a brand needs to have a strong identity of its own and it should ideally not piggyback on the identity of a celebrity and hope to achieve success.

CELEBRITY SELECTION

The suitability and credibility of an endorser for a product are also important factors for consumers to like the ad. Extensive research must precede the selection of the celebrity and how he/she has to be used. A celebrity like Visvanathan Anand (the Chess legend, who presently endorses Memory Plus) may be found suitable for computers and other products which rate high in cognitive ability. He may however be found unsuitable to endorse soft drinks.

Celebrity endorsement has had its own stereotypes:

- Undergarments (Lux), of course, has traditionally been relegated to the musclemen: actors like Sunil Shetty or Sunny Deol, who it is assumed, might have a large subaltern following, but whose implied stupidity forestalls them from becoming marketing machines for the middle class.
- For banking services? Get an old, respectable, thinking-type man.
- Cars? A young, jaunty hero.
- Cosmetics? Only hysteria-inducing bombshells need apply. And so on, it seems goes the strange tale of advertising, products and endorsement.

It is extremely important that advertisers find a suitable celebrity match for their products. There is so much clutter these days that companies are constantly looking at ways to cut through it. Corporates believe celebrity endorsements are the easy way out, with their mass appeal. However, there are chances of their backfiring if there is a basic mismatch between the star personalities and the brands in question.

Celebrities can definitely prove to be useful

in the cluttered and heavily advertised market where product differentiation is limited. No doubt, celebrities can catalyze brand acceptance and provide the enormous momentum that brands require, however, as the term suggests, *they must endorse something*. It is important that the celebrities' personality is thoroughly studied to match that of the product. Celebrity attractiveness and credibility and the package of meanings and implications that the celebrity could lend to the product should be studied. Celebrities should also be matched with the target audience.

It is important that the brand manager asks the following questions before narrowing down on a particular endorser:

- Does the celebrity appeal to the target audience?
- What is the reference group or aspiring group of the target audience?
- Will the celebrity manage to transfer favourable attributes, traits or values to a particular product or service?
- What is the appropriate media in which the advertisement should appear?

Of course, defining clearly what the marketer hopes the celebrity endorsement to achieve is the key to managing and assessing the return on investment. For example

- Is it merely brand awareness?
- Stronger recall leading to brand consideration?
- More credibility?
- Purchase preference?
- And can these media-made gods achieve these with one deft dialogue in a 30-second spot?

Past experience suggests that not all celebrities succeed as product or service endorsers. Similarly, as pointed out earlier, celebrity advertising is not without its pitfalls. One has to exercise caution and act intelligently to succeed and benefit.

And that something must be intrinsic to the brand. For celebrity endorsements to work, brand managers should work on some fundamental ground rules:

1. Articulate with clarity on the brand promise (What am I?) and the brand personality (Who am I?)
2. Create consensus among the brand team on what the communication objectives for the campaign are.
3. Focus singlemindedly on the characteristics the chosen celebrity should possess, in order to provide synergy with the brand to be advertised.
4. Overtly establish what the celebrity is going to communicate.

Whether celebrity ambassadors are actually a safe bet for brands or the whole effort has become 'overkill' depends on how well or how badly brands use celebrities. It is not that the consumer gets tired or confused about the same star endorsing various products. If an ad film is told well with a differentiated story, it works otherwise, it doesn't; it is as straightforward as that.

Amitabh is one of the rare celebrities who has universal appeal and who still enjoys credibility in people's minds, especially at a time when the lives of celebrities are becoming more and more public. By borrowing from that persona, brands come across as more credible. According to ad agencies, there is great respect for Amitabh among consumers and his endorsement lends dignity to the communication.

Once these criteria are met, endorsements can work as a force multiplier. On the flip side, the greatest danger is that because celebrities already carry a strong brand character, a mismatch could be counterproductive to the brand. It is very tempting to be carried away by the short-term exposure and interest that an endorsement could generate. Finally, given the huge outlay that a celebrity presence demands, shareholders might begin asking fundamental questions on brand investments very soon.

USING SUBTLETY

It is extremely important that brands come across as sincere while leveraging the benefits of celebrity endorsement. The marketer must understand that the new, informed consumer is cynical, as such must know how far he can go. Whatever claim the endorser makes has to be believable. The moment you cross the invisible line, the consumer stops believing in your communication and your endorser. Pulse Polio campaign is an excellent example of clever use of a celebrity endorser. Amitabh Bachchan commands respect, so people listened to him.

One must however note that often, a brand's desperation shows when it tries too hard. In the short-term, Bachchan or a Tendulkar might be able to rescue you if you are down in the dumps, but he cannot be an alternative to a sound strategic or creative idea. If marketers don't have an idea, celebrity endorser will only be parroting a manufacturer's claim, which will ring hollow. Companies must remember that the cornerstone of any good brand is its intrinsic product quality. For a celebrity to add value to a brand, there must be a relevant and recognizable match of values of the celebrity and the brand as perceived by consumers.

PITFALLS TO AVOID

1. Improper positioning: Associating with a star, however big he or she may be, in itself does not guarantee sales. The most it can do is generate interest in the product or create a buzz around it. Take the case of Maruti Versa, which was launched amidst a lot of fanfare in the recent past. In spite of Maruti signing up superstar Amitabh Bachchan and his son Abhishek Bachchan as brand ambassadors for Versa, the brand's sales remained sluggish. To be fair, the Big B magic did work and the ads created significant interest, drawing people into the showroom. But perhaps the positioning itself was faulty as people were expecting a larger-than-life car, just like the brand's ambassador. Last year, we saw Versa being re-positioned as a family car, with the core proposition being, "the joy of travelling together" after which Versa has started doing well and has witnessed an upswing since the new positioning.

2. Brand-celebrity disconnect: If the celebrity used represents values that conflict with the brand values and positioning, the advertising will create a conflict in the minds of the target audience who may reject the proposition. Take for instance Toyota, one of world's leading auto companies. Toyota chose teeny-pop singer Britney Spears for its brand Soluna Vios, a family sedan, which is preferred by married men and women with children. According to Phan, a youth icon like Britney would've been better used by Toyota for a sleek sports vehicle and for Soluna Vios, Toyota should choose someone like a mature man, say Harrison Ford

3. Clutter Flutter: In recent times, there has been such a deluge of celebrity endorsements that it has led to the very clutter that it aimed to break. For instance, Amitabh Bachchan endorses or has endorsed Pepsi, ICICI, BPL, Parker pens, Nerolac, Dabur, Reid & Taylor, Maruti Versa, Cadbury and a few social messages too. Bollywood badshah Shah Rukh Khan endorses Omega, Tag Heuer, Pepsi, Hyundai, Clinic All Clear and Airtel among other brands; has to his credit more television commercials than feature films since 1992. This over-exposure can be bad for the brand. In India, we seem to have just 2 or 3 celebrities in a country of 1 billion people which is a terrible tragedy. Consequently, each celebrity is called upon to push maybe a dozen brands or so which is great for the celebrity but it is pretty bad for the brand because the impact of the celebrity reduces as the number of brands he endorses increases. Unfortunately in India, we have too many brands chasing too few celebrities and the recall value drops by a huge margin when you move from an A Class celebrity to a B Class.

4. Dissatisfaction with product quality/ performance: One cannot sell an ordinary product just by making a celebrity endorse it. In fact, if anything, the product will fail faster because the presence of the celebrity will create a buzz and more people will know about the "ordinariness" of the product. Unfortunately, in India using a celebrity seems to be the easy way out of a parity product situation. Sachin Tendulkar's endorsement of Fiat Palio was quite a success initially but as word about the poor fuel efficiency of Palio spread, its sales took a beating.

5. Confusion/ Skepticism: The use of celebrities can be confusing as some viewers forget the brand that a celebrity is approving; others are so spellbound by the personality of the celebrity that they completely fail to notice the product/brand being advertised. The brand is overshadowed in the overwhelming presence of the star. In some cases, a celebrity can give rise to skepticism because it might be a bit too much for the masses to believe that the celebrities who are rich and can afford the best in the world are actually using a mass product being advertised on television. On the contrary, people might speculate about such things as "how much did the brand pay to rope him/ her in as the brand ambassador?"

VARIABLE COMPENSATION

The days of assured payment for cricketers irrespective of their performance on field have started fading. Sponsors like Airtel and Hero Honda are now insisting on a variable compensation contract where the product or brand endorsement moolah is linked with what they do on the field. Until now, the cricketers used to have their contracts with a fixed component of money. Variable compensation packets, which have now become a byword for human resources across India Inc, adds performance as parameter for salaries. While the variable component is presently low—ranging from 10-25% of the contract sum, sponsors are trying to push this component further up when the existing contracts come up for renewal (Source: *The Economic Times*, 15th Oct, 2004).

SMALL MANUFACTURERS

In the famous cartoon serial Tom & Jerry, Jerry had a perpetual problem. Every time he opened his mouth, Tom shut him up as Tom is bigger, stronger and louder and Jerry has long since accepted this fact. But Jerry hasn't given up and he instead works around the problem and gets noticed by being smarter, either by using Tom's strength against him or using the big props in the battlefield.

An entrepreneur's situation is not terribly different from Jerry's. He is usually fighting big money and clout of a big category with big stakes in it. How does he get himself heard and noticed above the loud growl of the big brothers in the game? In specific terms, he believes that he cannot afford to invest in press and TV time (never mind a branding campaign). He knows that he cannot demand counter space from the retailer. He also knows that he can't afford a fancy PR agency, who will likely charge him a fat retainer.

Let's just examine few different kinds of situations:

- Music Magic is a single store music outlet on Silver Jubilee Park Road in Bangalore. Tucked away in the remote wholesale market area, Music Magic doesn't have the traffic benefits of being on the high street but it has a range of high-quality products and music. The owner, Prakash Aswani, an encyclopedia on music writes a column in the *Economic Times* for hungry audiophiles and invites queries on his e-mail address making his shop a destination store for music freaks.
- When Global Trust Bank, one of the first new generation banks in the country, started business in 1996 its trump card was having one of the most respected bankers in the country, Ramesh Gelli. Global Trust used this property to the hilt. All initial communications to target audiences were either authored by Mr. Gelli or contained his name. This turned out to be ultimately more effective and certainly cheaper than a large and expensive launch campaign.
- It's tempting to say today that Whisper is a large brand from a global multinational. But,

P&G never had a presence in this category before Whisper. Whisper was an unknown brand in India and it was up against the complete monopoly of Johnson & Johnson's Carefree and Stayfree. Yes, some mass media was used to announce the launch. But their most effective communication weapon was a house-to-house demonstration by handpicked women, who were able to make a connection and actually show women the difference in performance. Whisper never looked back.

- Other good examples are the cherubic girl that Amul has been using since years, the moustached maharaja of Air-India and the omnipresent dog in the Hutch campaign.

What these examples demonstrate is that one doesn't always need to compare his resources with the big guys to feel adequate. Every manufacturer's situation may be different, his needs may be different, and therefore, the solution will be different too. In a world where better return on investments also means better advertising, marketers would probably do well to stop asking themselves, 'Does this work?' and start asking themselves, 'What would work better?'

Since, celebrity endorsements are very expensive, therefore their use in an ad should be justified. In other words, the message strategy for a brand should strongly warrant the use a known face in an idea. Sadly, very often the celebrity is hired first and an idea is then woven around his or her presence. The important thing to remember is that putting a celebrity in an ad is not an idea in itself. Unfortunately, this is how most celebrities are being used in Indian advertising, where they just become a prop. Ideally, there should be an idea that makes the celebrity relevant to the product and the consumer.

A celebrity's presence in the ad should be contextual. When Sachin Tendulkar declares, "Boost is the secret of my energy," it doesn't seem out of context. Internationally, Nike's association with Michael Jordan is legendary and also logical.

It can be argued that endorsements work best when the celebrity is not introducing the brand. When the product already has a strong identity and a USP that is well established, then a celebrity can come in and give the brand an added fillip and generate some more interest value. However, what is of paramount importance is to find a complete fit between the values of the brand and the values of the celebrity. One needs to create a unique situation or story that links the celebrity to the product.

Many celebrity endorsements fail because they identify a celebrity they like in an emotive and un-researched manner, and then try to create advertising to force-fit the celebrity into the creative concept. Often, the finished advertising is at best contrived, and often, simply laughable. In the end, the brand suffers from a mismatched concept and celebrity, and millions of dollars are flushed away. If this company is publicly listed, one can imagine the disservice the company has done for its shareholders. It is important to recognize that celebrities can create interest and whether that interest converts into sales depends on various factors such as brand-celebrity disconnect, improper positioning, clutter of celebrities, or even product life-cycle.

Questions

1. Is celebrity endorsement too expensive an idea given the returns it delivers? Discuss.
2. How does it work for a manufacturer's brand?
3. What does it achieve for the marketer in terms of market share?
4. What are the pitfalls to guard against; and alternatives especially for small manufacturers?

Notes

Services Marketing

Section - Thirteen

CONCEPTUAL FRAMEWORK

To facilitate a better debate on the case in this section, a quick exploratory review of services marketing along with areas that need discussion are recapitulated briefly as follows:

- A service is any act or performance that one party can offer to another that is essentially intangible and does not result in the ownership of anything.
- Service industries lagged behind manufacturing firms in adopting and using marketing concepts and tools but this situation has now changed. Services are a growing part of Indian economy.
- Strategy used by a marketer in service marketing is different as it calls not only for **external marketing** but also for **internal marketing** to motivate employees and interactive marketing to emphasise the importance of both 'high-tech' and 'high-touch.'
- A company's offering to the marketplace may be classified under five categories: **Pure tangible good**, **tangible good with accompanying services**, **hybrid**, **major service with accompanying minor goods and services**, and **pure service**.
- When marketers find it harder to differentiate their physical products, they turn to service differentiation. Companies seek to develop a reputation for superior performance in on-time delivery, better and faster answering of inquiries and quicker resolution of complaints.
- Product-based companies provide post-purchase service. To provide the best support, a manufacturer must identify the services that customers value most and their relative importance. The **service mix** includes both presale services (facilitating and value-augmenting services) and post-sale services (customer service departments, repair and maintenance services).
- Services have **six fundamental characteristics**: intangibility, inseparability of production and consumption, perishability, heterogeneity, client-based relationships and customer contact.
- **Intangibility** means that a service cannot be seen, touched, tasted, or smelled. **Inseparability** refers to the fact that production of a service cannot be separated from its consumption by customers. **Perishability** means unused service capacity of one time period cannot be stored for future use. **Heterogeneity** is variation in service quality. **Client-based relationships** are interactions with customers that lead to the repeated use of a service over time. **Customer contact** is the interaction between providers and customers needed to deliver a service.

- Marketers divide services in two parts Core service and Supplementary Service **Core services** are the basic service experiences customers expect; **supplementary services** are those that relate to and support core services.
- Because of the characteristics of services, service marketers face several challenges in developing and managing marketing mixes. To address the problem of intangibility, marketers use cues that help assure customers about the quality of service. The development and management of service products are also influenced by the service characteristics of inseparability and level of customer contact. Some services require that customers come to the service provider's facility; others are delivered with no face-to-face contact.
- **Marketing channels** for services are usually short and direct, but some services do employ intermediaries. Service marketers are less concerned with warehousing and transportation than are goods marketers, but they are very concerned about inventory management and balancing supply and demand for services.
- Intangibility of services poses several promotion-related challenges in front of service marketers. Advertisements with tangible cues that symbolize the service and depict facilities, equipment, and personnel help address these challenges. Service providers are likely to promote price, guarantees, performance documentation, availability, and training, and certification of contact personnel. Through their actions, service personnel can be involved directly or indirectly in the personal selling of services.
- Service marketers have to deal with intangibility, which makes it difficult to experience a service before purchasing it. Heterogeneity and intangibility make word-of-mouth communication an important means of promotion. The prices of services are based on task performance, time required, or demand, perishability creates difficulties in balancing supply and demand because unused capacity cannot be stored. The point in time when a significant number of customers desire a service is called **peak demand**.
- **Demand-based pricing** results in higher prices being charged for services during peak demand. When services are offered in a bundle, marketers must decide whether to offer them at one price, price them separately, or use a combination of the two methods. Because services are intangible, customers may rely on price as a sign of quality. For some services, market conditions may dictate the price, for others state and local government regulations may limit price flexibility.
- **Service quality** is customers' perception of how well a service meets or exceeds their expectations. Although one of the most important aspects of service marketing, service quality is very difficult for customers to evaluate because the nature of services renders benefits impossible to assess before actual purchase and consumption (unlike **search qualities** in case of goods). These benefits include **experience qualities**, such as taste, satisfaction or pleasure, and **credence qualities** which customers may not be able to evaluate even after consumption.
- When competing services are very similar, service quality may be the only way for customers to distinguish among them. Service marketers can increase the quality of their services by following the four-step process of **understanding customer needs**, **setting service specifications**, **ensuring good employee performance**, and **managing customers' service expectations**.
- **Non-profit marketing** is marketing aimed at non-business goals, including social causes. It uses most of the same concepts and approaches that apply to business situations. Whereas the chief beneficiary of a business enterprise is whoever owns or holds stock in it, the beneficiary of a non-profit enterprise should be its clients, its members, or its public at large. The goals of a non-profit organization reflect its unique

philosophy or mission. Some non-profit organizations have very controversial goals but many organizations exist to further generally accepted social causes.

- The marketing objective of non-profit organizations is to obtain a desired response from a target market. Developing a **non-profit marketing strategy** consists of defining and analyzing a target market and creating and maintaining a marketing mix. In non-profit marketing, the product is usually an idea or a service. Distribution is aimed at the communication of ideas and the delivery of services. The result is very short marketing channel.

- **Promotion** is very important to non-profit marketing. Non-profit organizations use advertising, publicity and personal selling to communicate with clients and the public. Direct mail remains the primary means of fundraising for social services. Price is more difficult to define in non-profit marketing because of opportunity costs and the difficulty of quantifying the values exchanged.

Notes

Medical Tourism: 'First World Treatment' at 'Third World Prices'

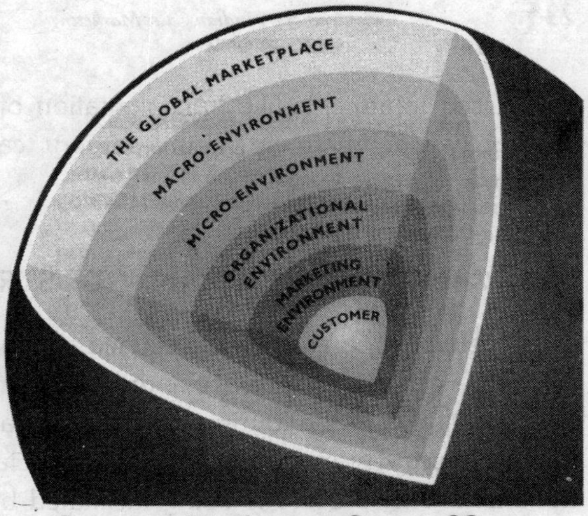

Services Marketing Case - 23

Purpose of the Case

The idea is to assimilate the relevant concepts at work and analyse along the following lines:

- To discuss how India can emerge as a global destination in advanced medical care while cashing in on its numerous places of tourist interest and rich cultural heritage simultaneously
- To focus on the key factors in India's favour vis-a-vis trends and happenings in the field of medical tourism
- To debate how a healthcare service can be marketed effectively (in conformance with the international benchmarks) combining it with the excitement of travel and tourism

Henry Dyson, a Manchester based 52 years old lorry driver is having tough nights. He has to get up about 10 times a night to relieve himself yet the feeling that he has not completely vacated his bladder persists. Diagnostic work-up indicated that he had an enlarged prostate with a suspicious area of malignancy. Biopsy from the region confirmed his most unwanted fear- yes, he has prostate cancer, at an early stage! His check-up regime is eating into his savings, though the government's National Health Service (NHS) has footed most of the bills. A surgery done in the near future will allow Dyson to enjoy his retirement. The only problem-he is way down on the waiting list, which can be as long as two years. It is double jeopardy, if he waits, he will not make it to retirement. If he does make it, the high procedure cost will eliminate most of his savings. In a global world, Dyson looks elsewhere; where the same procedure is done at a fraction of the cost, where a holiday with wife in tow to recuperate is part of the package.

When baby Noor Fatima, a two-and-a-half- year old Pakistani girl, successfully underwent an open-heart surgery in India in early 2004, she opened new vistas reminding the potential of medical tourism. The Ministry of External Affairs took this opportunity to encourage medical diplomacy, by facilitating the visit of cabinet ministers and provincial leaders to India for treatment.

Kerala is in the forefront of this new surge and leads these states, earning revenue by promoting this segment actively. However, Kerala's positions itself more as an ayurvedic and alternate medicinal therapy destination. Ayurveda is more aptly promoted among top executives for distress treatments. The growing need is for high level specialised treatments like transplantation of vital organs, cancer treatment, neuro-surgery, cardiac surgery and many more.

MEDICAL TOURISM AS AN INDUSTRY

Medical tourism can be broadly defined as provision of 'cost effective' private medical care in collaboration with the tourism industry for patients needing surgical and other forms of specialized treatment. This process is being facilitated by the corporate sector involved in medical care as well as the tourism industry - both private and public.

In many developing countries it is being actively promoted by the government's official policy. India's National Health policy 2002, for example, says: "To capitalise on the comparative cost advantage enjoyed by domestic health facilities in the secondary and tertiary sector, the policy will encourage the supply of services to patients of foreign origin on payment. The rendering of such services on payment in foreign exchange will be treated as 'deemed exports' and will be made eligible for all fiscal incentives extended to export earnings". The formulation draws from recommendations that the corporate sector has been making in India and specifically from the "Policy Framework for Reforms in Health Care", drafted by the prime minister's Advisory Council on Trade and Industry, headed by Mukesh Ambani and Kumaramangalam Birla.

INDUSTRY SIZE AND PROJECTED GROWTH RATES

As per the Confederation of Indian Industry (CII)-McKinsey 2002 study on healthcare, 'Medical Tourism' can contribute Rs. 50 to 100 billion additional revenue for up-market tertiary hospitals by 2012. Recent reports show that at present, the size of the medical tourism industry is anything between Rs 1,200 crore and Rs 1,500 crore and it is a sector, which is growing at the rate of 30 per cent annually. Further, postulating the opportunities in health tourism, the report states that the medical tourism market in the country pegged a 30 per cent growth in 2000 and has been growing at the rate of 15 per cent for the past five years. According to this report, by 2012, if medical tourism were to reach 25 per cent of revenues of private up-market players, up to Rs 10,000 crore will be added to the revenues of these players. The medical tourism market would then represent three-five per cent of the total delivery market. The same report highlights tremendous opportunities that exist for India in the area of 'medical tourism' as medical costs skyrocket in the developed world

Karl Wolfgang Menck, the industry analyst commissioned by Messe Berlin feels India can expect to earn US$ one billion in foreign exchange from medical tourism by 2012, when the various industry growth programmes take effect. (Source: www.expresstravelandtourism.com)

The CII-McKinsey Study projects that changing demographic and disease profiles and rising treatment costs will result in doubling over the next 10 years. The study says that private healthcare will be the largest component of this spending in 2012, rising to Rs 1560 billion from the current level of Rs 690 billion. The study indicates that it could rise by an additional 390 billion if health insurance cover is available to the rich and middle class. In addition, public spending could double from Rs 170 billion if the Government reaches its target spending level of 2 per cent of the GDP, up from 0.9 per cent today. And with the expected increase in the pharmaceutical market, the total healthcare market here could rise from Rs. 1030 billion currently (5.2 percent of GDP) to Rs 2320 billion-Rs 3200 billion (6.2-8.5 per cent of GDP) by 2012 (Source: www.indianembassy.org).

EXISTING STATUS OF MEDICAL TOURISM IN INDIA

The CII-McKinsey Study says that the current market for medical tourism in India is small and is mainly limited to patients from the Middle Eastern and South Asian economies. Majority of these patients sought help in the field of cardiac care, joint replacement, cosmetic surgery and lasik eye surgeries.

GENESIS OF MEDICAL TOURISM

Globalisation has promoted a consumerist culture, thereby promoting goods and services that can feed the aspirations arising from this culture. This has had its effect in the health sector too, with the emergence of a private sector that thrives by servicing a small percentage of the population that has the ability to "buy" medical care at the rates at which the "high end" of the private medical sector provides such care. This has changed the character of the medical care sector, with the entry of the corporate sector. Corporate-run institutions are seized with the necessity to maximize profits and expand their coverage. These objectives face a constraint in the form of the relatively small size of the population in developing countries that can afford services offered by such institutions. In this background, corporate interests in the Medical Care sector are looking for opportunities that go beyond the limited domestic "market" for high cost medical care. This is the genesis of the "medical tourism" industry. The following factors indicate how 'Medical tourism' makes sound economic logic and thus a viable business proposition.

1. **Push factor:** This push is created because of two reasons; as such, a clear distinction must be made at this stage itself between the driving factors behind 'Medical tourism' in developed and developing nations. Needless to say, a corporate hospital marketing its services in these two sets of countries with different socio-economic, technological and economic environment would need different set of business strategies.

   (i) Firstly, in the US, the UK, Japan and many European nations, the proportion of the elderly (60 years and above) vis-à-vis the total population is increasingly rapidly. In the US, the baby boomers-the biggest chunk of the population-have either hit retirement age or are heading towards it; also the number of people aged 65 years and above is expected to double in the next 15 years. Even, in the UK, the people aged 60 years and above will form 25% of the population in the next 30 years, up from 16% now. Similar trends are being seen in almost all nations in Western Europe coupled with the steadily rising life expectancy over the years. All these factors have led to a big surge in demand for healthcare. The big problem is that as their health needs increase exponentially, the healthcare systems in these countries are beginning to creak under the pressure. The number of doctors and nurses joining the workforce in both the UK and the US is not keeping pace with all the demands of the aging population. It is estimated that National Health Service, UK alone has over a million patients waiting for treatment; a potential market for India is thus created due to this massive demand-supply imbalance.

   (ii) Secondly, residents of poor developing nations such as Nigeria or Bangladesh travel to their more developed neighbors for medical treatment because there aren't enough good facilities available in their own countries. Hospitals in Kolkata have long queues of patients from Bangladesh, waiting for appointments with Indian medical specialists. The opening of bus service between India and Lahore is expected to bring Pakistani patients as well. Even in a developed nation like Japan, thousands of citizens seeking medical treatment fly abroad because of the prohibitive costs of treatment in their own country.

2. **Pull factor:** Meanwhile, there is a pull factor being created by a handful of developing countries like Thailand and Malaysia that have good doctors and excellent facilities, and which are positioning themselves as medical destinations in order to boost their economies.

Both Thailand and Malaysia see this developing into a multibillion dollars-a-year business. There is also the other factor - like people from the least developed countries who find affordable sophisticated medical care facilities in developing counties like India and Malaysia.

3. **Demand initiation by Indian diaspora:** The demand for medical tourism is most likely to come from among the 20 million strong Indian diaspora. The wealthy first and second-generation expatriate Indians are aware of the rise of India's high quality, low-cost hospitals and there is a potential market of expatriate Indians who would combine regular visits to India and save time and money by undergoing non-emergency procedures such as eye operations, dental work, cosmetic surgery and knee surgery.

4. **'Indian doctors'-an internationally accepted and respected 'brand':** Foreigners have confidence in India's medical system because many Britons and Americans are accustomed to being treated by expatriate Indian doctors. Indian doctors are the backbone of the National Health Services in UK and have won laurels for their competence in other advance countries like USA, Canada, Australia, several Commonwealth and Gulf countries also. In most of these countries, the percentage of Indian doctors far exceeds the percentage of Indian population in those countries. A number of Indian doctors are also serving in the Armed forces of the English-speaking countries.

5. **Rising popularity of preventive heath screening:** With increasingly sedentary lifestyles, rising health awareness, the age old-mantra of 'Prevention, being better than cure' is getting reinforced in the developed nations. However, the differential costs remain high as ever e.g. at one private clinic in London a thorough men's health check-up that includes blood tests, electro-cardiogram tests, chest x-rays, lung tests and abdominal ultrasound costs $574 (£345, €500). By comparison, a comparable check-up at a clinic operated by Delhi-based healthcare company Max Healthcare costs $84 (Source: Ray Marcelo The Financial Times, 2July 2003)

6. **9/11 and its aftermath:** In the Gulf / Middle East and Africa, people preferred to visit India for medical treatment. This demand grew after 9/11 September events in USA, when travel to Europe /USA was a bit difficult for Arab Muslims and India was discovered as the best option. Its proximity and cost effectiveness was an added advantage for India.

KEY DRIVERS

Various factors that are contributing to the rapid growth of 'medical tourism' as an industry are as follows:

1. **Cost Advantage:** India with its rich cultural heritage, world-class health care professionals with proven track records and treatment costs at almost a sixth of that in the US and Europe is an attractive place for healthcare seekers. Dr Naresh Trehan, Chairman, CII National Healthcare Committee has highlighted this cost advantage citing examples of treatments for dental problems or major procedures like bypass surgery or angioplasty; even cardiac surgery in India costs one-tenth compared to the US. Open-heart surgery could cost up to $70,000 in Britain and up to $150,000 in the US; in India's best hospitals it could cost between $3,000 and $10,000. Knee surgery (on both knees) costs 350,000 rupees ($7,700) in India; in Britain this costs £10,000 ($16,950), more than twice as much. As per Ray Marcelo' s report in The Financial Times, 2 July 2003, In April 2003, Madras Medical Mission, a Chennai-based hospital, successfully conducted a complex heart operation on an 87-year-old American patient at a reported cost of $8,000 (€7,000, £4,850) including the cost of his airfare and a month's stay in hospital. The patient claimed that a less complex operation in America had earlier cost him $40,000.

Patients from rich countries in the Middle East don't mind traveling to the US when they need top notch medical care but Americans seeking cosmetic surgery often fly to South Africa for face tucks and breast augmentation because their insurance coverage doesn't pay for those and it is cheaper to get them done in South Africa than back home. Though exact figures for this medical tourism market are not available, a Saudi Arabian report pointed out that in the year 2000, medical travellers from around the world spend in excess of $40 billion, on a conservative basis.

2. **Health Insurance:** India could earn more than $1 billion annually and create 40 million new jobs by sub-contracting work from the British National Health Service (Source: www.acgil.com) Medical treatment in the UK is free under the NHS, but because of the long waiting times some patients opt for expensive private care. Medical tourism, if promoted properly, would reduce pressure on the NHS and offer sub-contracted healthcare at vastly cheaper rates. After this million people, there are thousands of expatriates, not necessarily Indian, but expatriates who may be given the opportunity to come and get themselves operated upon in India. The CII-McKinsey study also says that the health insurance sector is rapidly growing in India also. It is worth noting that as on 2004, less than 10 percent of the Indian population is covered by some form of health insurance, which is however, increasingly rising. The study points out that insurance would be the main driver for raising quality consciousness and increased demand for better standards, hospital accreditation and patient/management information systems. Currently, the voluntary health insurance market is estimated at Rs.4 billion but it is growing fast and the industry expects it to touch Rs.130 billion by 2005.

3. **World class infrastructure and widely acclaimed doctors:** It is important to realize that cost-savings may not be enough to foster a trade in medical tourism as unfairly or not, most foreigners would not think of India as a land of good health especially when they remember the sight of the country's overcrowded public hospitals, open sewers and garbage-littered streets. Private healthcare providers must shelter foreigners from such nastiness to establish that the quality of India's corporate hospitals is world-class. One of the major reasons as to why 'Medical tourism' is the new health business buzzword now is that a number of government as well as private players are keenly assessing the potential and means to tap the same. India has tremendous potential in terms of well-qualified doctors and a recently witnessed boom in state-of-the-art hospitals, which has attracted the patient population from neighbouring countries especially the Middle East and the West.

LEADING HOSPITALS IN INDIA: THEIR STATUS AND FUTURE PLANS

1. Apollo Hospitals:

a) Among private players, Apollo has been a forerunner in health tourism and has been the choicest destination for patients from Southeast Asia, Africa and the Middle East. The group has tied up with hospitals in Mauritius, Tanzania, Bangladesh and Yemen besides running a hospital in Sri Lanka and managing a hospital in Dubai. Thousands of foreign patients who visited the hospital chain or were hospitalized were not only provided treatment but their stay was also taken care of by the hospital itself. The group has at present tied up with hotels in Delhi for this purpose, which can later on be explored as an allied business opportunity.

b) Apollo Hospitals has had meetings in 2003-2004 with UK government health adviser and private healthcare providers from South Africa, Australia, India and the UK to bring their patients for treatment at cheaper rates in India. The hospital already offers the facilities of pick and drop from the airport, arrangement for boarding and lodging at concessional rates and sightseeing after the treatment is over. It is worth noting here that UK has a one million waiting list for all kinds of things, especially orthopaedic surgery and after this million people, there are thousands of expatriates, not necessarily Indian, but expatriates who may be given the opportunity to come and get themselves operated upon in India.

c) Apollo is also negotiating with oil multinational ARAMCO to offer special packages to its employees. Apollo has also tied up with NIIT and Aptech so that attendants of patients who come for treatment for 2-3 months can take short-term IT courses. (Source: www.businessworldindia.com)

d) Apollo is also arranging for ads on Arabic television channels for the people from the Middle-East and plans to create a separate area for foreigners besides providing food according to their specific tastes.

e) Apollo hospital offers the facilities of pick and drop from the airport, arrangement for boarding and lodging at a concessional rates and sight-seeing after the treatment is over.

2. **Indian Spinal Injury Centre (ISIC):** ISIC is another destination for patients from neighbouring countries, Gulf and a few NRIs from the US.

3. **Escorts Hospitals:** Escorts Heart Institute and Research Centre is fast emerging as a favourite destination for patients from neighboring countries, Africa and CIS and treats over 1,000 foreign patients on an annual basis.

4. **Ruby Hospital, Kolkata:** Recently, the Ruby Hospital in Kolkata signed a contract with the British insurance company, BUPA. The management hopes to get British patients from the queue in the National Health Services soon.

5. **Hinduja Hospital, Mumbai:** It has placed advertisements in the NHS Family Choice directory, the yellow pages of world-class health care facilities. Some estimates say that foreigners account for 10 to 12 per cent of all patients in top Mumbai hospitals. (Source: www.expresshealthcaremgmt.com)

6. **Fortis Hospitals:** Mohali based Fortis hospital has already entered into a mutual referrals arrangement with Partners Healthcare System that has hospitals like Brigham Women's Hospital and Massachusetts Hospital, Boston under its umbrella to launch a defined programme for the two-way flow of patients.

7. **Morepen Labs:** Morepen Labs and Apollo Hospitals have taken the initiative of launching a national network of emergency services. While Apollo has provided infrastructure in the form of an emergency center and trained personnel to treat the emergency victims, Morepen has contributed some funds to meet the set-up costs, according to sources from Apollo Hospitals. The ambulance services they offer are free of cost for the patient. This network will be further extended to other hospitals over time, based on their willingness to maintain standards and quality of care.

8. **Manipal Hospital:** Manipal Hospital, Bangalore recently tied-up with EPOS, a German organisation thus benchmarking against the best hospital chains in the world. As medical tourism catches on, these initiatives would help to attract more and more patients from foreign nations.

9. **Aravind Eye Hospital, Madurai:** Eye-care, in fact, is one area where India has a distinct advantage as it has more Lasik centres than some of the developed countries and Aravind Eye Hospital in Madurai conducts the largest number of cataract surgeries in the world. (Source : www.businessworldindia.com)

10. Wockhardt Hospitals has treated US private health insurers Blue Cross and Blue Shield insured patients, which is ample proof of their quality. The British health insurer Bupa also insures the costs of treatment at Wockhardt hospitals. Wockhardt is in talks with Britain's National Health Service about outsourcing the treatment of British patients to India.

Similar actions have also been initiated by L.V.Prasad Eye Hospital-Hyderabad, Breach Kandy Hospital-Mumbai, Rockland Hospital-Delhi, Max HealthCare and Shankar Netralaya-Madras, etc. and other premium hospitals also to tap this burgeoning medical tourism market.

INTERNATIONAL BENCHMARKS IN THE FIELD OF MEDICAL TOURISM

1. Thailand: Even till the late 1990s, Thailand's claim to fame in the medical travel world was cheap and reliable destination for sex change operations. Over the past few years, the Thai government and half a dozen private hospitals have gone into overdrive to change that image. They are now repositioning Thailand as Asia's premier health care hub for everything from cosmetic surgery to hip replacements. The Thai Ministry of Public Health is working closely with the Thai Ministry of Tourism to promote medical tourism in Thailand. They are also exploring possibilities of some sort of joint-promotion with Malaysia to beat competition from other countries but the government initiatives pale before the kind of action that the private hospitals are taking to attract medical travellers.

Bangkok's Bumrungrad Hospital is by far the clear leader in the field boasting of over 500 beds and treatment of over 30 thousand nos. expatriates and foreigners in 2003. In fact, a full 25 per cent of all the patients that the hospital treats today are foreigners. This patient patronage has been achieved not only by superior facilities at competitive prices, which are leading patients in droves to Bangkok but also through inventive marketing practices too. To illustrate, Bumrungrad offers assistance in 13 languages and has got itself accredited from the JCAHO, an international certification recognized by most of the big insurance companies. It has even got a McDonald's and a Starbucks coffee shop in its compound to cater to the tastes of its foreign patients and their companions. To top it all, the hospital has opened offices in Myanmar, Vietnam, Nepal, Sri Lanka, Maldives, Cambodia, the Netherlands and the Middle East. The other private hospitals aren't sitting still either.

The Phyathai hospital is hiring teachers from the British Council to train its staff, including the maids. It has also signed contracts with hospitals in the Netherlands and Bangladesh to bring in patients awaiting heart surgery there. Thailand provides specialized medical clinics, skilled nursing care, long-term care, nursing homes and rehabilitation clinics at costs that are a fraction of what it would cost in the US and Britain. The Japanese still form the biggest chunk of medical travellers coming to Thailand, though the Americans and the British are now coming in significant numbers. After 9/11, it also got a huge share of Arab traffic. (Source: KSec Views Vol-VII, Issue-03, January 16,2004)

2. Singapore: Singapore, with its well-deserved squeaky-clean reputation, is seeking to step up its challenge for the increasingly lucrative market, and the government has set itself the target of attracting up to 1 million overseas patients by 2012. Singapore is focusing on quality assurance like 100 per cent safe blood banks and highest level of training and professionalism among the world.

The private 380-bed Raffles Hospital is hoping to treat up to 300,000 foreign patients a year by 2012 and is offering prices that are competitive and comparable to the Thai hospitals. The hospital is now discounting 10 standard operations and procedures, ranging from having a baby and treating a cataract to undergoing a heart bypass. For example, Raffles is now offering an angiogram, an X-ray picture of blood vessels, for S$1,800 before service tax of 5 percent; the same procedure would cost the equivalent of about S$1,716 in Thailand. The downtown hospital offers comprehensive packages for those going under the knife and for their family members who travel with them like arranging airport transfers, booking relatives into nearby hotels and even helping in local touring.

3. Malaysia: As per an article by Premilla Mohanlall in http://thestar.com on August 21, 2004, Malaysia is well positioned to tap the great business opportunity arising out of 'medical tourism' as it has a well developed and dynamic tourism industry, accustomed to reinventing itself to meet the demands of the day. Over the years, Malaysia has diversified from being a sun-and-sea paradise to embracing eco-tourism, heritage tourism, agro-tourism and has now set its sights on becoming a medical tourist hub. It also has the marketing infrastructure and experience that could be used to develop specialist tour packages and getaways for health travellers. Several hospitals have since teamed up with tour operators to bring patients to their door.

To safeguard its reputation as a medical tourist destination, the Health Ministry recognizes only 35 private hospitals as tourism-friendly and certified to promote health tourism. Of these, 14 have 1SO 9001:2000 certifications and eight have been accredited. Malaysia is promoting two types of healthcare: "Wellness" which includes health screening packages and "disease" packages which include elective diagnostic packages, cardiology, ophthalmology, orthopaedic and plastic surgery. Malaysia also offers more difficult treatments such as hand microsurgery and in-vitro fertilisation.

In a bid to boost Health Tourism in the country, MSCI (Medical Service Coordination International, Malaysia) has signed a Memorandum of Agreement with Gleneagles Intan Medical Centre, Institut Jantung Negara, KPJ healthcare, Pantai Hospitals Sdn Bhd and Country Heights Medical Tourism. MSCI is also providing services like visa arrangements, meet-and-greet services, interpreters and transport arrangements to facilitate and enhance the overall experience of such foreign patients.

In 2002, Malaysia attracted 84,585 patients and raked in RM 35.9mil. The following year, there were more than 100,000 medical tourists contributing RM 58.9mil to the economy. There are rosier days ahead, with revenues forecast to grow to RM 400mil in 2005 and a whopping RM 2.2bil by 2010.

4. Jordan: Jordan is a perfect example of an oasis in the desert, selecting an appropriate business model, given its geographical and economic environment without mindlessly aping another successful model. They have followed a different business model vis-à-vis Thailand's Bumrungrad hospital, which is essentially an innovative marketing of good facilities. In contrast, Jordan has realized that there is also a good potential in trying to target patients from neighbouring countries for hospitals based in the Third world, before scaling up to the top tier as there is a general paucity of fairly priced facilities in the world. Jordan, thus with around 10,000 doctors, 33 private hospitals and 2,000-odd beds, does not threaten to be a competitor to countries like Thailand or India but what matters' is the bottom-line. Jordan attracts a lot of Arab patients from nations like Yemen, Oman and Syria who come in for everything from infertility treatments to organ transplants. So, even though Jordan treated only 126,000 or so foreign patients in 2003, it earned around $500 million i.e. roughly the amount that Thailand earned from 800,000 medical travelers. (Source: KSec Views Vol-VII, Issue-03, January 16,2004). This is a clear reflection of the higher money realization per patient that Jordan is able to achieve vis-à-vis Thailand, a deduction not so difficult to analyze given the fact that two years ago, Jordan set up a special counter at its Queen Alia International Airport to meet Arab patients and offer them a string of free services including transportation to hospitals. A key differential is that when Arab patients come to Jordan for treatment, they typically come with their families. That is why, the entire economy benefits from medical tourists. Jordan has now set a target of $1 billion from medical travel in the next couple of years. Jordan is likely to have competition from its neighbours though as both Saudi Arabia and Bahrain are also seriously looking at the medical travel opportunity.

POTENTIAL COMPETITORS TO INDIA

It is estimated that the healthcare market in the Organization of Economic Cooperation and Development countries alone is worth about $3 trillion, and expected to go up to $4 trillion in 2005. More importantly, it is growing rapidly and turning out to be an immense business opportunity for nations that are positioning themselves correctly. Last year, just five countries in Asia - Thailand, Malaysia, Jordan, Singapore and India - pulled in over 1.3-million medical travelers and earned over $1-billion (in treatment costs alone). But in the past five years or so, the movement has accelerated sharply. For each of these nations, medical travel-spends are growing at 20%-plus year-on-year. Elsewhere around the world, Hong Kong, Lithuania and South Africa are emerging as big medical / healthcare destinations along with a dozen other nations including Croatia and Greece who plan to make themselves attractive healthcare destinations.(Source: KSec Views Vol-VII, Issue-03,January 16,2004)

The following Table gives a snapshot of health tourism, wherein people have traveled abroad for various treatments.

Table: Health Tourism Snapshot

Country	No. Of Foreigners Treated In 2003	From	Earnings	Strengths
Thailand	600,000	US,UK	$470mn	Cosmetic surgery, organ transplant, dental treatment, joint replacement
Jordan	126,000	Middle East	$600mn	Organ transplant, infertility treatment, cardiac care
India	100,000	Middle East, Bangladesh, UK	N.A.	Cardiac care, joint replacement, lasik
Malaysia	85,000	US, Japan	$40mn	Cosmetic surgery
South Africa	50,000	US,UK	N.A.	Cosmetic surgery, lasik, dental treatment.
Cuba	NA	Latin America, US	$25-50mn	Specialist niche treatment, vitiligo, night blindness, cosmetic surgery.

Source: KSec Views Vol-VII, Issue-03,January 16,2004

GREAT SCOPE IN COSMETIC SURGERY

While India can definitely position itself as a specialist in complicated operations, one area, which could fetch good returns, is the area of cosmetic surgery as there are very few countries that have carved out a niche. According to the American Society of Aesthetic Plastic Surgery, in 2002, 6.6mn Americans opted for cosmetic surgery in U.S. itself. They were also the biggest chunk of customers in countries like Thailand, Malaysia and South Africa, which between them treated further 0.1mn patients. Cosmetic surgery is not covered by medical insurance and hence the price differentials are quite high. A full facelift, which costs $8,000-20,000 in US, costs a mere $1,252 in South Africa. (Source: KSec Views Vol-VII, Issue-03, January 16,2004)

CHALLENGES IN PROMOTING INDIA AS A PREFERRED MEDICAL DESTINATION

1. **Poor infrastructure:** While there is a tremendous stock of intellectual capital in healthcare and with state-of-the-art treatment and world-class surgery available in the country but there is a pressing need for qualified

specialist nurses and paramedics and qualified hospital administrators.

2. **Inequitable compensation packages:** Several private hospitals have invested in nursing education, but are concerned about loyalty as trained nurses often leave India, attracted by the higher wages offered in the Gulf countries.

3. **Lack of International certification:** Most corporate hospitals are already in the process of upgradation and accreditation that is required to prove the quality of services. Rating agencies like Crisil and ICRA have graded a few hospitals for setting standards, but certification also needs to come from international agencies like Joint Commission on Accreditation of International Standards (JCAHO), which talks about uniform cosmopolitan standards not only in terms of treatment, but also the infrastructure of the organization and facilities provided. Lack of certification acts as a psychological barrier both to the patient as well as health insurance provider is concerned in choosing India as a health destination.

4. **Visa problems:** The major roadblock in marketing the product is the absence of a visa-on-arrival, which is a must for medical tourists keeping in mind that illness is something one can never 'plan'. But in India, there is no such special medical tourist visa facility available.

5. **Few quality hospitals:** The capabilities of the doctors are not enough to sell the product. To actually market medical tourism, it has to be strongly backed by infrastructure i.e. setting up of specialty hospitals, getting state-of-the-art health and medical equipment and setting up special wards for overseas patients.

6. **Lack of service mindset:** In case of a service industry, people providing the service become an extremely important resource due to intangibility and inseparability factors. For this, we as Indians will have to cultivate the 'service' mindset and establish trust and empathy to build credibility.

7. **Lack of insurance facilities:** Most insurance companies do not cover medical treatment in a foreign country. Further, disciplines including ENT, cosmetic surgery, dentistry and infertility are not covered by health insurance anywhere in the world. It is extremely important that the Indian players should join hands with international insurance companies and tourism agencies to realize the full potential of health tourism.

GOVERNMENT INITIATIVES

Acknowledging the economic importance of the sector, the Indian Government has also undertaken some financial reforms viz.

a) Tourism infrastructure development received a significant shot in the arm with a 44 per cent budget increase, and in just one year, the Inland Air Travel Tax (IATT) and Foreign Travel Tax (FTT) have been abolished and the sales tax on Aviation Turbine Fuel (ATF) reduced.

b) In a significant 'open-skies' announcement, Indian private airlines can now fly to the ASEAN countries and the neighbouring SAARC capitals. The Center has also accepted the industry's demand that all airports, not just a handful, can receive charter flights. In the interim budget, tour operators on the domestic front are now required to pay service tax on only 10 per cent of their earnings.

c) State governments, also beginning to appreciate the true value of the industry, have also started to reduce taxes. In Goa, for instance, the luxury hotels tax was cut from 15 per cent to 8 per cent during the peak season, and down to 4 per cent during the low season, resulting in a 23 per cent increase in Goa's tax revenue.

d) An added boost has come from the Commerce Ministry, which has extended the benefits of zero duty import of liquor and wine against foreign exchange earnings, a concession already granted to three-star hotels and above, to hotels below the three-star category, heritage hotels and stand-alone restaurants.

e) Now, to attract more people, the emphasis is on vacation plus treatment and special packages have been planned for this. On the anvil is another plan to make the patients and their relatives stay in the hospital complex with all the luxuries a hotel provides.

f) The Maharashtra Government in collaboration with FICCI (Western region council) has launched the Medical Tourism Council of Maharashtra to act as a nodal agency responsible for smooth operations in the Medical Tourism sector besides promoting Maharashtra healthcare facilities and tourism attractions in India and abroad. A special website dedicated to this project www.maharashtratour.com was activated recently.

INTEGRATED TOURISM CAMPAIGN

The government has chosen to promote the country through an integrated marketing campaign under the banner of 'Incredible India', encouraging both domestic and international tourists to sample the many unique and incredible experiences that the country offers. The campaign is backed by plans to create 3.6 million jobs a year from tourism and boost foreign arrivals from today's 2.4 million to 5.6 million in the next three years.

With so much going on to promote travel to India, the tourism industry is on a high. Strategic alliances with leading global hotels as well as small, luxury hotels has helped India to move up to world-class accommodation standards, enhancing the country's image in the international market. Leading brands have opened more sales and marketing offices across the US, Europe, Middle East and West Asia to increase awareness and drive up sales. Airlines are joining with hotels and other service providers to provide better value for customers, while newly- introduced Apex fares offer substantial discounts on advanced bookings. One domestic airline is offering a 50 per cent discount to senior citizens with a minimum two-night stay, while another has launched a scheme to compensate people for delayed flights. Still another "no frills" airline offers fares at half those of other airlines, a cabin crew that exists of a single flight attendant who needs a trolley selling cookies, munchies and non-alcoholic drinks. There is first come-first-served seating, neither business class nor frequent flier mileage bonuses are available. The leading THL bodies in India viz. the Federation of Hotels and Restaurants Associations of India (FHRAI), Travel Agents Association of India (TAAI) and Indian Association of Tour Operators (IATO) have agreed to work together to solve industry issues. These include seeking a reduction in sales tax on Aviation Turbine Fuel (ATF) and requesting domestic airlines to abolish the dual airfare system for foreign passport holders. Clearly, much is being done by the Government and the industry to encourage greater numbers of visitors, yet according to the WTTC's recent survey India's star is still not shining brightly enough.

ACQUIRING INTERNATIONAL ACCREDITATION - PRESSING NEED OF THE HOUR

The Indian healthcare industry has failed to impress the British government's National Health Service (NHS) to outsource its patients to India. Sources attribute this to majority of Indian hospitals' lacking accreditation from Joint Commission on Accreditation of Healthcare Organizations (JCAHO), lack of standards in terms of quality and rates for healthcare procedures, absence of gradation system and the far from perfect insurance sector here. JCAHO accreditation is an imperative to win outsourcing contracts. Since most Indian hospitals are not JCAHO accredited, NHS is sending its patients to Spain and Germany. However,

Indraprastha Apollo hospital in Delhi and Wockhardt hospital in Mumbai acquired Joint commission Internaional Acceditation (JCI) in 2005. Now many Corporate hospitals like Escorts-Delhi, Asian Heart Research Institute-Mumbai, Fortis and Max Healthcare are gearing for it.

Acquiring JCAHO accreditation is a costly and continuous process; costing around 50,000 to 200,000 USD. It takes around two years to get accredited by JCAHO. So, if 10 hospitals get together to get accredited, the cost incurred by each hospital will be much less. (Source: www.expresshealthcaremgmt.com)

In stark contrast to the UK healthcare scenario, where hospitals are standardized, audits regularly performed and hospitals graded, the systems are completely absent in Indian hospitals. Top Indian hospitals have high infection and mortality rate, and do not want to share their data regarding these. Indian record-keeping, software and systems are not up to the mark vis-à-vis UK.

The developed countries argue that the administration and services in developing countries do not fulfill the necessary conditions and that the implications could be detrimental to the health insurance schemes responsible for meeting the costs of treatment

In India, less than 0.5 per cent individuals are insured; awareness about healthcare is poor; rules of reimbursement are stringent, performance of third party administrators (TPAs) are not satisfactory; discharge details, disease codings, ICD codings and handling of medical records are not in place, thus making it difficult to get outsourcing contracts from the US.(Source : www.expresshealthcaremgmt.com)

In India, there is no integrated legislation for healthcare providers, hospitals, nursing homes, laboratories, path-labs or for practitioners. Since standardization procedures are not in place, the insurance industry too is facing difficulties.

However, if the NHS would like to benchmark hospitals for outsourcing purposes, then they can engage a rating agency acceptable to them. In the interim, they could do this and on a pilot basis, selective hospitals in major cities could be rated and the NHS could have an MoU with these hospitals.

PITFALLS IN REAPING THE POTENTIAL OFFERED BY 'MEDICAL TOURISM INDUSTRY"

It may not be always possible to take advantage of the niche market offered by medical tourism because of various factors mentioned below:

1. In many developing countries physicians refuse to engage in such commercial activities and Governments are concerned about the limitations to medical services for the local population.
2. The treatment process, often during the patients` holidays, is sometimes of insufficient duration in the case of more protracted illnesses or care. Sick people frequently arrive and undergo the usual exploratory examinations in a relatively short period of time, and sometimes the results of earlier examinations are ignored. The medical treatment is carried out and after a usually brief period of recuperation the patient, having recovered, travels home. This may be acceptable for cosmetic surgery or basic dental treatment but not in the case of illnesses where recovery is dependent upon long term medical attention and extensive after-care. In many cases it is advisable for the after-care to be in the hands of doctors and nurses who have been well acquainted with the patient's history for some considerable time.
3. Another prerequisite is that the costs should be shared between the health insurance scheme in the home country and by other comparable institutions. This is not always the case, because the health schemes only give their approval if they can be sure that

the services provided are of an equivalent standard. Furthermore the physicians and hospitals have to meet the same liability and accounting conditions as those that apply in the industrialized nations.

4. Another requirement is that invoices must be clear and in accordance with the health insurance organizations' rules, and capable of withstanding close scrutiny.
5. As the contractual partners of professional medical organizations and hospital associations, the health insurance schemes in the patient's home country sometimes find themselves under considerable pressure. In order to safeguard doctors' incomes and hospital occupancy, their ability to use cheaper services abroad is subject to strict limitations.

MANTRAS FOR A TERTIARY HOSPITAL TO SUCCEED

Tertiary hospitals must ensure the following to make a name for themselves:

1. High quality talent: Hospitals would need to hire well-reputed doctors, either high profile Indian educated surgeons / specialists or NRI doctors that have returned to India. Besides the doctors, the nurses and support staff should be well trained and have adequate experience.
2. Cost Management: Hospitals are capital-intensive projects, and it is important to understand how the costs and revenues work in this business. While the financials for each hospital will vary depending on the size, specialties and location, there are some basic components that can be assumed on an average for the industry. The hospital should manage costs effectively to be able to keep operating margins above 25 per cent. Hospitals need to ensure adequate economies of scale and consolidation of materials procurement costs for materials.
3. Financial Management: Given the huge capital costs required to set-up the hospitals, it is essential to price services to be able to recover these initial investments. While raising funds for building and equipment, it is important to ensure that a low debt-equity ratio is maintained, as higher debt equity ratios make it hard to raise funding.
4. Customer Relationships: The most critical success factor of any tertiary hospital is the ability to develop customer relationships. The hospital must have a large enough paying patient population to recover the investment costs. A strong referral network with General Practitioners, linkages with secondary care facilities and links with corporate health plans will help to drive revenue growth. Since the richest 15 per cent will account for over 50 per cent of private healthcare spending over the next few years, it is necessary to orient the facilities towards this patient group. One of the ways to mitigate the risk of developing and maintaining a loyal patient pool would be to have feeder networks, otherwise known as the "hub and spoke model".

JOINT VENTURES- POINTING THE WAY FORWARD

One way of overcoming such problems would be in the form of joint ventures involving physicians and hospitals in various countries, in order to facilitate the coordination between health insurers, medical needs and the possibilities offered by medical tourism. In this way some of the current objections could be eliminated. This proposal has already been put into practice, and agreement on such joint efforts has been reached by Indian and American hospitals. There has been sharp rise in the number of companies in the United Kingdom that organise travel to Turkey, Costa Rica and India and are working in close consultation with hospitals in those countries. This is not just another form of north-south tourism but a defined program for the two-way flow of patients.

Such bilateral collaboration can enable the provision of long-term medical care in accordance with the same performance standards, provided that this is preceded by an accurate exchange of data. Independent monitoring of performance and success eliminates the risk of disputes about the cost of treatment and the settlement of liability issues. Joint ventures between companies not only provide for an accurate division of labour and reduced costs but such long-term forms of collaboration also enable suppliers in developing countries to unlock commercial possibilities in the industrialized nations.

TRAVEL AND TOURISM FACILITIES AS 'VALUE ADDITIONS'

Various tour operators are also seeing 'Medical tourism' as a lucrative business. They not only take care of all the travel and stay-related aspects of the patient and his family/ attendant, but also arrange for the hospital and appointment with doctors. Kerala-based Air Travel Enterprises group of companies owns Kerala Institute of Medical Sciences, a multi-specialty hospital under the Great India Healthcare Management Limited. They offer leisure packages along with medical treatment to patients who mostly come from the Gulf countries, Canada, and Maldives.

But if we study the bigger picture, travel agents and tour operators are yet to seriously consider this niche segment. Further, there are hardly any packages for medical tourists. They can tie up with hospitals to offer complete healthcare packages that would include recuperating in a resort in some scenic area. For instance, Great India Tours has come up with a complete package that includes consultations with doctors, hospital admission, accommodation for escorts and visit to some resort post-treatment. Cross-border travel for healthcare reasons is still a highly disorganized movement, but nations are slowly waking up to its potential. In some places the governments have taken a lead. In others, like South Africa and Lithuania, travel agents specializing in medical tourism are driving the trend. In India, private hospitals like Apollo and Escorts Heart Institute and Research Centre are trying to attract patients on their own.

Keeping in mind the potential of healthcare tourism, which is gearing up to be the next `big boom' business in the country, Sita Inbound Division has launched `Sitacare', a business unit that will focus exclusively on healthcare-based tourism. Under this venture, Sita, a leading name in travel and tourism, has tied up with VedicIndia, a medical NRI health management tourism company, which has compiled the healthcare tourism project after three years of intensive research and study. While VedicIndia will do the front-line promotion and contracts with the hospitals, Sitacare will plan the back-end handling and co-ordination through its vast network of offices in the country. Sita will also help promote the product through its Web site, overseas offices and database on foreign travel partners. Additionally, it will also seek the assistance of the Department of Tourism in promoting the health service. The key-operating base of Sitacare in India will be in Mumbai with support offices in Delhi, Chennai, Kolkata, Hyderabad and Bangalore. (Source:www.blonnet.com/2003/08/23/ index.htm)

Special flights targeted at international travelers, improving the flight connectivity of Mumbai and Delhi (where most international flights land) with Hyderabad or Chennai, where there are many private hospitals, could help in harnessing the potential of this sector too. Building dedicated medical clusters outside, say, Mumbai, or Goa, and aggressively promoting them could be another major step. Finally, the opportunity needn't be limited to conventional medical treatment. The study by SSDS,

Inc. for WHO pointed out that retirement homes for the aged could be a big opportunity, especially if they were targeted at the clientele in the expensive, developed countries.

Understanding patients and 'knowing them' requires that the marketer of services remains in touch with their deeper emotions, understand their cultural, social, personal and psychological characteristics to satisfy their needs and wants. The heath service providers will have to design competitive intelligence systems, study their competitors' strategies and then design sustainable business strategies. Hospitals may like to specialize in a particular field or serve a particular segment of customers and position their differentiated offer accordingly. A hospital, which is able to occupy a distinct niche in the customers' mind through proper combination of product, price, promotion and distribution offerings, will be a winner in the long run.

Question

1. Assume a leading Rs 1000-crore Indian industrial house, which has no prior experience of the services sector, has hired you as their CEO. They have studied about the 'medical tourism' sector and want you to plan, strategize and implement the owners' vision of a dream hospital, which will cater primarily to International patients. The target is to achieve 50 per cent foreign patients within 7 years of commencement of hospital services. Present your complete business model to achieve this vision of the owners.

Notes

International Marketing

Section - Fourteen

CONCEPTUAL FRAMEWORK

To facilitate a better debate on the cases in this section, a quick exploratory review of international marketing along with areas that need discussion are recapitulated briefly as follows:

- **International marketing** involves developing and performing marketing activities across national boundaries.
- Companies cannot simply stay domestic and expect to maintain their markets. Companies selling in global industries need to internationalize their operations.
- With faster communication, transportation and financial flows, the world is rapidly shrinking. Products developed in one country are finding enthusiastic acceptance in others. International markets can provide tremendous opportunities for growth. Advances in technology have greatly facilitated international marketing.
- In deciding to go abroad, a marketing manager needs to define its company's international marketing objectives and policies. It must determine whether to market in a few countries or many countries. It must decide which countries to consider. In general, the prospective countries should be rated on three criteria: **market attractiveness**, **risk** and **competitive advantage**.
- Marketers are required to do a detailed analysis of the environment before their company enters a foreign market. Environmental aspects of special importance include **cultural, social, ethical, economic, political, legal** and **technological forces**. And as marketing activities are primarily social in purpose, they are influenced by **beliefs and values** regarding family, religion, education, health, and recreation.
- A good marketer should understand that **cultural differences** might affect marketing negotiations, decision-making behavior, and product adoption and use. A nation's economic stability and trade barriers can affect marketing efforts.
- Significant **trade barriers** include import tariffs, quotas, embargoes, and exchange controls (government restrictions on the amount of a particular currency that can be bought or sold). Gross domestic product (GDP) and GDP per capita are common measures of a nation's economic standing. Political and legal forces include a national political system, laws, regulatory bodies, special-interest groups, and courts.
- Various regional trade alliances and specific markets create both opportunities and constraints for companies engaged in international marketing. These include the South Asian Association for Regional Cooperation (SAARC), the North

American Free Trade Agreement (NAFTA), the European Union (EU) and the World Trade Organization (WTO) among others.

- There are several ways to get involved in international marketing:
  - **Importing** - the purchase of products from a foreign source
  - **Exporting** - the sale of products to foreign markets. Importing and exporting are the easiest and most flexible methods.
  - Markets may employ a **trading company** which links buyers and sellers in different countries but is not involved in manufacturing and does not own assets related to manufacturing.
  - **Licensing and franchising** are arrangements whereby one firm pays fees to another for the use of its name, expertise, and supplies.
  - **Contract manufacturing** occurs when a company hires a foreign firm to produce designated volume of the firm's product to specification and the final product carries the domestic firm's name.
  - **Joint ventures** are partnerships between a domestic firm and a foreign firm or a government; **strategic alliances** are partnerships formed to create competitive advantage on a worldwide basis.
  - Finally, a firm can build its own marketing or production facilities overseas. When companies have direct ownership of facilities in many countries, they may be considered **multinational enterprises**.
- Depending on the level of international involvement, companies manage their international marketing activity in three ways: through export departments, international divisions or a global organization.
- Although most firms adjust their marketing mixes for differences in target markets, some firms standardize their marketing efforts worldwide. Traditional full-scale international marketing involvement is based on products customized according to cultural, regional, and national differences.
- At the product level, firms can pursue a strategy of straight extension (introducing a product in the foreign market without any change), product adaptation or product invention. At the promotion level, firms may choose communication adaptation or dual adaptation (both product and communication). At the price level, firms may encounter price escalation and gray markets. At the distribution level, firms need to take a whole-channel view of the challenge of distributing products to the final users.
- International marketing strategies fall along a continuum from customization to globalization.
- **Globalization**, however, involves developing marketing strategies as if the entire world (or regions of it) were a single entity, a globalized firm markets standardized products in the same way everywhere. International marketing demands some strategic planning if a firm is to incorporate foreign sales into its overall marketing strategy.

Ranbaxy Laboratories Limited: A True Indian MNC

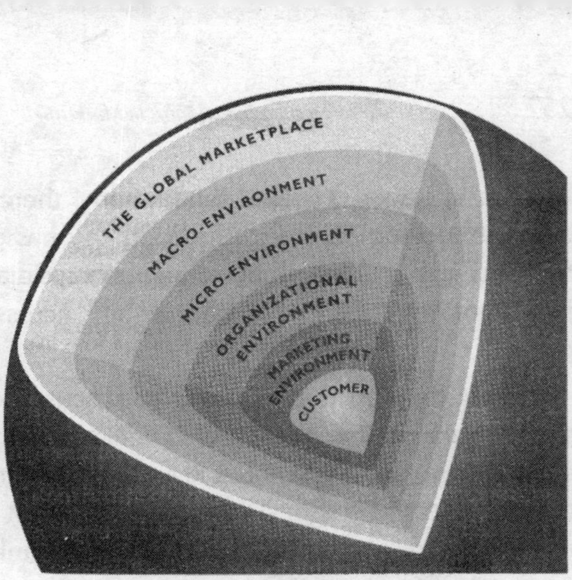

International Marketing Case - 24

Purpose of the Case

The idea is to assimilate the relevant concepts at work and analyse along the following lines:

- To discuss how India's largest pharmaceutical company, Ranbaxy is currently operating on a global scale and how truly global Ranbaxy is.
- To focus on different strategies adopted by the company to expand its global reach across national precincts and staying on as one of India's top 10 most valuable companies in terms of market capitalisation

"Ranbaxy aims to be a Research based International Pharmaceutical Company."

Late Dr. Parvinder Singh, Chairman of Ranbaxy Laboratories.

HISTORY

Ranbaxy Labs Limited traces its history back to 1961 when it was a small company based in the Northern state of Punjab. It was a small partnership firm incorporated to import capsules from abroad to India. The company derives its name from its original promoters i.e. Ranveer Singh and Gurbax Singh. It was then acquired by a businessman, Mr. Bhai Mohan Singh who identified the potential of pharmaceuticals at that time. After a few years, Bhai Mohan Singh's son, Dr. Parvinder Singh joined the business to take the charge. In 1973, the company went public to raise money to set up its own manufacturing facility at Mohali near Chandigarh in Punjab. The company is today managed by the Late Dr. Parvinder Singh's core team which is based in the capital city of New Delhi. The management team consists of CEO with a group of VPs who manage separate functions.

THE BIRTH OF THE CONCEPT OF BEING "GLOBAL"

Ranbaxy's global vision took birth long back even when Indian companies were shy enough not to showcase their products in the global market. In 1977, India was marked by the traditional corporate such as Tata, Birlas etc, Ranbaxy formed a joint

This case is intended to be used as a basis for class discussion rather than as an illustration of either effective or ineffective handling of the situation. Authored by Dr. Mukesh Pandey along with Rahul Gupta, Director, Biztantra.

venture in Lagos, Nigeria. Since then , there has been no looking back and the company has gone from strength to strength by setting up subsidiaries, joint ventures, alliances & partnerships across the globe.

From then on the company has focused on a step by step multipronged strategy of identification, experimentation, invest, expand and compete in the market place. In the past few years, one can also add the word "acquire" as well. In 2003, Ranbaxy acquired RPG Aventis, France (the French arm of Aventis) for over $80 million in a landmark deal which is the highest amount paid by any Indian pharmaceutical company.

The Global Footprint:- Businesses across 4 continents

Ranbaxy's global operations have been divided into seven divisions:

1. India
2. Middle East
3. North America
4. Europe, CIS & Africa
5. Asia Pacific & Latin America
6. Global API (Active Pharmaceutical Ingredients)
7. Global Consumer Healthcare

India:- Ranbaxy is India's largest pharmaceutical company with a leadership in generics segment. It has a domestic market share of 4.83%(July 2003 MAT).The company has a strong brand in the market with its products i.e.Cifran & Sporidex amongst the top 10 brands in the industry. Its revenue through India is close to $300 million. The company has over 5,000 people workforce in India. Ranbaxy's global headquarters are in New Delhi itself. In addition to this, the company has a large R&D Facility in Gurgaon (outskirts of Delhi) spread over 17 acres with a world class research team.

Ranbaxy operates in India through its seven marketing arms i.e. Croslands, Stancare, Pharma, Rexcel, Solus, Rexstar,Blue R, Ranbaxy CV(CV for Cardio vascular) and Super Speciality. The company's manufacturing operations are in Western and Northern India which meet world standards for quality.

In India, Ranbaxy has also diversified into different sectors such as Healthcare services. The company operates super speciality hospitals in Mohali,Punjab and Delhi through its subsidiary "Fortis Healthcare". It also has SRL Ranbaxy which is a health services chain with showrooms all over India.

The company has also invested significantly in internet related services and community building activities for doctors,etc. Ranbaxyfordoctors.com is one such venture in which thousands of Indian medical professionals get information on new ailments at no cost. This is in fact a direct marketing tool for the company through which they reach out to people in every nook and corner of India as the services are accessible to people free of cost.

Middle East:- Ranbaxy has a reasonably strong presence in the Middle East with revenues in excess of $10 million with a healthy growth of 32% in 2003. The company operates in the entire region with it being the largest generics player in UAE itself. This region also includes Sri Lanka which is a small but growing market. Here, the company has three brands which produce revenue of over $1 million each. In Oman as well, Ranbaxy continues to be the leader fourth year in a row. The company also added three more countries such as Kuwait, Lebanon, Saudi Arabia to this operation. It is India's first company to address these countries in the pharma industry.

Europe , CIS & Africa:- Europe alone is the second largest market for Ranbaxy with operations in UK,Germany,France, Poland,Russia & Spain. Ranbaxy UK is the largest here with revenues of over $50 million in 2003. Europe is primarily a success story coupled with strategies of acquisition & brand development backed by sound financial investments. In 2000, Ranbaxy acquired the generics business of world giant Bayer which is now known as Basics GmbH. This is a wholly owned subsidiary of Ranbaxy. The sales in Germany touched a figure of $14 million. This represented a growth rate of over

56%. In Poland, the company operates through a joint marketing alliance with Glaxo SmithKline and UCB to market Ranbaxy's products. The company has already captured a sizeable share of the hospital market with sales of approx. $8 million. France saw probably the biggest investment of the company till date. In Jan. 2004, the company went to the generic pharma business of Aventis to mark its entry into the world's fourth largest pharmaceutical market. Ranbaxy paid over $80 million for this purchase representing the biggest overseas buyout by any Indian pharma company. Here the company has been positioned as a high quality generics player. The company employs a strong field force , business development and regulatory team. Russia too was a success in 2003, Ranbaxy Russia sales touched $18.3 million showing a growth of over 55%. The products are known for their reasonable prices and high quality.

In CIS, Lithuania is where Ranbaxy markets and is doing well. But Ukraine is a sure success story. In 2002, the company posted a turnover of $ 12.8 million and a position amongst the top 20 companies. This region also covers Romania & other countries in the Ukraine belt.

Africa is another key area for Ranbaxy. It is this continent in which the company formed its first ever overseas alliance in 1977 in Lagos, Nigeria.

Ranbaxy 's subsidiary RXSA in South Africa has sales of over $10 million which is a growth of over 100% over the last year. This makes the company as the fastest growing pharma company in the region. Ranbaxy has also formed a JV with Adcock Ingram (the largest pharma company in SA) to market ARV medicines called 'Thembalami'.

RNXL is Ranbaxy's subsidiary in Nigeria which is the oldest operation of the company in the world. The company here operates with a manufacturing facility which is state of the art and boasts of a production of 500,000 packs a month. This facility is approved by NAFDAC. The company also has a team of over 20 sales personnel. Turnover in 2003 was close to $ 13 million with a growth rate of 12%. Here again ARV medicines do well.

Ranbaxy Egypt also witnessed a growth of 37% with products designed to suit the patients in the region.

The company's operation in Ivory Coast is also encouraging. Ranbaxy in Ivory Coast does a turnover of $1.5 million in a market estimated at $12 million annually.

Ranbaxy Zimbabwe has been a victim of political upheaval and the downfall of the Zim currency. Market has shrunk to the size of $50 million. The company has managed to post a revenue of half a million dollars.

Ranbaxy operates in Zambia and Mauritius through joint marketing alliances.

Latin America & Asia Pacific :- Ranbaxy is operating in the Asia Pacific region by covering China,Malaysia,Thailand,Vietnam,Mynamar.The Latin America operations cover Brazil. Ranbaxy has been operating in China for almost over a decade. The company was intelligent enough to recognize the potential of the country much earlier than other companies.It first entered the country in 1990 and by 1993 formed a joint venture company. It started its manufacturing operations in China in 1995. Today Ranbaxy is a well-known company with over $13 million in sales and Cifran is the leading brand in the segment with a market share of over 39.4%. Manufacturing in China is done in a state of the art facility. The subsidiary is named as Ranbaxy Guangzhou.

Ranbaxy Malaysia is a joint venture company with Malaysian shareholders. It started operations in 1984 as Ranbaxy Malaysia Sdn Bhd. It has a manufacturing facility in Kedah to cater to the Malaysian and Singapore markets. Now it also exports to Brunei as well. In 2003 Ranbaxy Malaysia recorded turnover of $11 million and was ranked 13th in the Malaysian market.

Ranbaxy Thailand is a smaller operation than Malaysia with a turnover of $ 5.5 million. This subsidiary sources its products from India as well. It is now recognized amongst the top 40 companies in the pharma industry in Thailand.

Vietnam business is also done by sourcing most of its requirements from India. The company is opening up a manufacturing facility in Vietnam to cater to the needs of the region in a more efficient manner.

In Brazil, the company entered the scene in 2000 by setting up a joint venture called Ranbaxy SP Medicamentos Ltd. The company is now ranked as the 5th largest generics company in Brazil. The company has also set up a quality testing laboratory for expansion as well.

This region also caters to Australia and New Zealand.

North America:- This is Ranbaxy's biggest operation in the world. The company had entered the market in 1995 with its two subsidiaries Ranbaxy Pharma Inc. and Ohm Labs. It's the company's largest market and also the centre for its biggest investment. Ranbaxy's USA operations recorded a mammoth sales of $423 million in 2003 accounting for almost 50% of the company's worldwide revenue. It operates in USA with a large team of 400 people employed in three locations i.e. New Jersey,New York and New Brunswick. The company has been ranked amongst the top 10 pharma companies in the generics market in the United States. This remarkable progress has taken place in just a few years. This market is a great platform for Ranbaxy to grow on a global scale. A lot of new products developed by the company are introduced here. Notably , products launched here include Sotret which gained a market share of 8% within a short span of time. Ranbaxy USA was recently ranked as the fastest growing pharmaceutical company in the United States in a poll conducted by a leading magazine.

THE STRATEGY OF GLOBAL BUSINESSES AT RANBAXY

At the heart of the core strategy at Ranbaxy lies the concept of test, create and compete with a focus on core competencies. Most of the activities of global expansion have been in tune with one goal ie." To create an international Research based pharmaceutical company". In 1993, Ranbaxy started taking steps in putting up the building blocks of a global pharma company. Dr. Singh envisaged a vision to create a $1 billion revenues company by 2003. Each and every step was taken from there on to follow that vision. Most of Ranbaxy's overseas subsidiaries were set up in 1993 in order to expand the reach and increase sales.

At that time in 1993, India hardly had any global

companies. Ranbaxy has never entered into a market unless and until it wants a big piece of it. Traditionally, Indian companies set up overseas offices and call themselves global. On the other hand, the company has invested colossal sums of money in building infrastructure, manufacturing bases, teams and competing with the local leaders.

This strategy has been underlined with the core competency of Ranbaxy which is generics drugs. In almost every financial activity done by the company in overseas markets, the point is to acquire, create and invest in primarily the generics segment.

The company positions itself as a market leader in generics worldwide ranking amongst the top 10 in the world. In fact , in all its acquisitions , Bayer, Aventis (Ranbaxy paid over $100 million for these), generics was the area where the company has relentlessly invested all its resources. Even in the US, when the company was importing cephlaxine generics from Eli Lilly, and the company was incurring losses of $2.5 million, D.S.Brar (former CEO) took a tough decision of increasing the stocks of generics which was quite contradictory as it was incurring losses. The gamble paid off well; he is sharp focus on cephlaxine generics alone resulted in a business of over $25 million with a net profit of 5% in the US itself.

It is imperative to realize that along with the business being global, Ranbaxy had envisioned to set up systems to tackle the various socio-political-climatic conditions of each country it entered. There

1-The Ranbaxy Plant in China 2-The plant in the US
3-The Malaysian Facility; 4-The Ranbaxy team in Nigerea
5-The Vietnam Plant; 6-The Ireland facility that feeds Ranbaxy's European market

are various regulations and policies which might come in the way of expansion. The fact that Ranbaxy operates in the healthcare sector, it becomes all the more important to take quick and effective measures. All drugs produced at Ranbaxy in India are approved by all the leading regulatory agencies worldwide. They include MCA of UK, MCC-South Africa, FDA-USA and TGA- Australia. All of them have approved the company's manufacturing facilities for the compliance with international Good Manufacturing Practices and have registered its products for safety as well as quality. At all the locations abroad, all leading agencies of that region have approved Ranbaxy's production facilities and products. The benefit of alliances and acquisitions comes into picture when Ranbaxy wants to speed up its work. Local expertise and experience of investors, partners and employees come in handy saving the company capital as well as time.

STRATEGY AS PER GEOGRAPHY

Ranbaxy's global marketing strategy is largely defined geography,demography,political conditions, consumer behavior of the region it is planning to enter. The company has been flexible enough to alter its strategy. If one looks at it, it's a combination of acquisition, experimenting, joint ventures, distribution and marketing alliances,infrastructure and brand building. This broadly explains the range of marketing strategies as the company operates out of 44 countries. Ranbaxy has been investing large

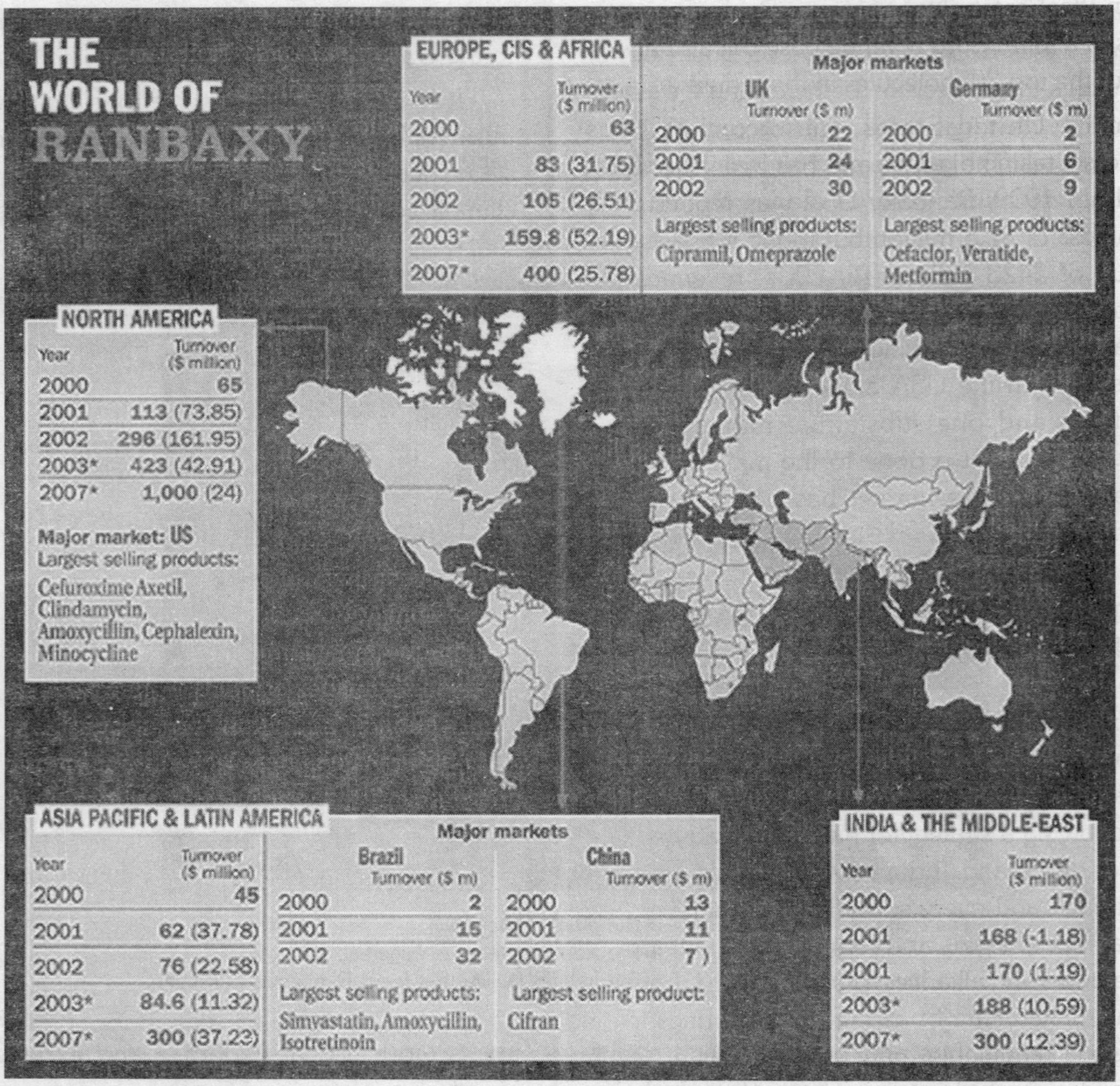

amounts in key markets primarily. But it has been patient enough to maintain a sizeable presence in small and growing markets. Even in a small country like Ivory Coast, the company has gone and created a subsidiary. The company has done brisk business by capturing a substantial share in the generics market.The market size there is around $12 million only. These kind of strategies have been embraced by world leaders as they give a very positive message to the investor as well as employees worldwide.

The Nigerian operation which is almost 18 years old is a case in point. Ranbaxy's first overseas venture was initially a small one but today it boasts of a revenue of $12 million and with a wide acceptability of the Ranbaxy brand name. The manufacturing facility has been approved by leading regulatory agencies. The management team comprises of leading professionals both from India and Nigeria.

In high growth areas such as USA and Europe, the company has invested considerably large sums of money. Europe houses one of the largest generics markets such as France and Germany. It also is home to leading pharma giants such as Bayer etc. The company had been looking at France for a long time and was also doing some business through its alliances. As the company's clear strategy has been to have a sharp focus on generics, RPG Aventis (Aventis' generics business, fifth largest in France) was an ideal catch. Not only was Ranbaxy getting access to a 44 m Euro revenue base but also access to 18 of the top 20 molecules in the industry.

In the United States, Ranbaxy has been relentlessly taking big risks and has been successful as well. In 1999, Ranbaxy USA was reporting an annual loss of $2.5 million but today it boasts of a revenue of $423 million. By 2007, revenues are expected to touch $1 billion in this country alone.The company has been working with a team of over 350 professionals in the USA alone across three large operations and one substantial manufacturing facility. Investment is done to the maximum after the potential of the market has been evaluated properly.

HR STRATEGY ON A GLOBAL BASIS TO ACHIEVE ROBUST GROWTH

Ranbaxy's global presence has been managed by a team of dedicated and committed professionals. In order to operate in a better way, the company has been following a strategy of having a heady mix of local residents and Indian professionals as well. Almost each and every subsidiary of Ranbaxy has an ideal mix of locals and foreigners. By means of joint ventures and alliances, most of the HR problem is usually taken care of as the partner brings local expertise. This flexible entry strategy has enabled Ranbaxy to enter new markets swiftly and managing the local environment better than its competitors.

THE RESEARCH AND DEVELOPMENT IMPERATIVE

Research is at the heart of any organization engaged in pharmaceuticals. In order to tackle new and unknown diseases, the company has to relentlessly invest in this area. The R&D strategy is under the logic of create, introduce, experiment and launch. Every new molecule found is a possible hope to a number of patients. Because of Ranbaxy's global footprint, the company gets feedback on its drugs from a global basis. This is truly genuine for any pharma company which aims to compete internationally with its own brands. It is because of this, Ranbaxy's R&D budget is the highest in the Indian pharmaceutical industry at close to $75 million. It is this investment from which the company derives its core strength i.e. belief and commitment in building a global brand. The company's R&D headquarter is at Gurgaon, Haryana where a number of scientists and professionals from India's leading research bodies have been recruited. Dr. Parvinder Singh's qualification as a PhD from University of Michigan laid this very foundation as well. The costs of development in India being much lower than the other countries adds another feather in the cap. With acquisitions now being done on a global basis, Ranbaxy is exposed to state of the art manufacturing and research in all parts of the world which helps in setting own benchmarks in line with the world's standards as well. All drugs manufactured are now approved by leading health agencies worldwide.

Questions ~~for Discussion~~

1. What do you think were the primary reasons for Ranbaxy's success on a global scale?
2. Does the focus on generics drugs help Ranbaxy? Should they also aggressively market their other product lines?
3. How can Ranbaxy's leverage its global image to consolidate further in the Indian market?
4. What can other pharmaceutical companies do to emulate the Ranbaxy model?
5. Which other areas can Ranbaxy diversify into given its current size and scale?
6. How should Ranbaxy expand its reach in USA and China further?

Notes

Growth Strategies of Nokia in China

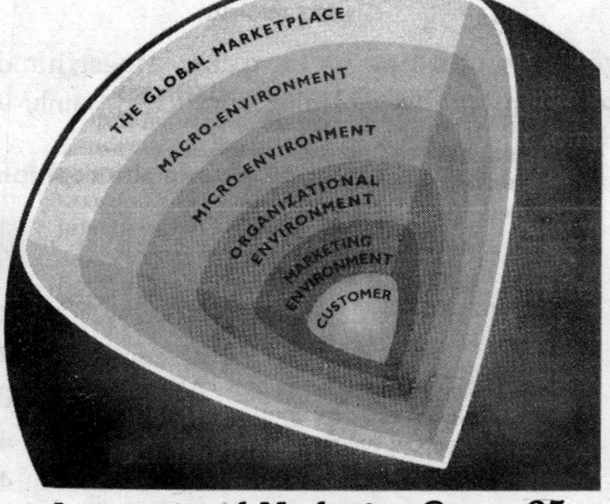

International Marketing Case - 25

Purpose of the Case

The idea is to assimilate the relevant concepts at work and analyse in light of the following issues:

- How to foray into the market of a developing economy after micro- and macro-level analysis of current market opportunities?
- How to formulate global marketing strategies to bring about a steady growth of the enterprise?
- What are the pitfalls to watch out for while venturing into global arena?

FACTS ABOUT NOKIA

- Nokia is the world leader in mobile communications dedicated to enhancing people's lives and productivity by providing easy-to-use and secure products like mobile phones, and solutions for imaging, games, media, mobile network operators and businesses.
- Nokia has established manufacture bases in 9 countries, R&D centers in 11 countries. Its products have been delivered and sold to 130 countries all over the world.
- Nokia is a broadly held company with listings on five major exchanges. Nokia has ranked among top 10 most valuable brands in the world for 4 consecutive years.
- In 2003, Nokia's global sales reached Euro 30 billion

CORPORATE INFORMATION

Nokia is a major supplier of mobile communications systems and the largest handset vendor in China. It sold the first analog cell phone system in China in 1986 and GSM in 1994. China is Nokia's largest market in the world; revenue for 2003 was 2 billion Euros ($2.4 billion), export $1.7 billion Euros, 35% of total handset exports by China. Nokia has invested more than 2.3 billion Euros ($2.9 billion) in China; it operates 22 local offices, five R&D centers and four production plants in China with 4,500 employees. In 2004, Nokia made China a separate region in Asia and consolidated four joint ventures into one to form the largest handset company in China. Nokia competes mainly with Motorola and Chinese companies in GSM/GPRS handsets.

Mobile phone shipments and market shares for 2004

Rank	Vendor	2004 Shipments	2004 Market Share
1.	Nokia	207,600,000	31.2%
2.	Motorola	104,500,000	15.7%
3.	Samsung	86,500,000	13.0%
4.	Siemens	49,400,000	7.4%
5.	LG Electronics	44,400,000	6.7%
	Other	172,000,000	25.9%
	Total	664,500,000	100.0%

Source: IDC

NOKIA'S PRODUCTS AND SERVICES

Nokia makes a wide range of GSM/GPRS handsets, from mono LCD to color, from bare-bones with basic features to advance models designed for business customers. Nokia sells its handsets by an extensive reselier network with more than 1000 outlets in China and has begun to work with regional distributors such as electronics store chains. Nokia launched 14 GSM models in China in 2003 and claims it sold more GSM handsets than anyone for the year. Most of Nokia products enjoy strong customer recognition in China, including 5510i, 3350, 3610, 2100, 3108, 2300. Other popular models include 7250i (built-in camera), 3300 (MP3 player), 6108 (clam shell with handwriting support). Many high-end models support advanced data functionality such as stock trading, GPS, streaming video, and e-mail. Nokia is a major contractor for GSM/GPRS networks in China. In 2003, Nokia debuted first CDMA handsets in China aimed at low-end and mid-range segments.

Nokia also sells trunked radio (TETRA) to subway companies, governments and police. Other products include DSL and software solutions for operators. Nokia participated in MII 3G compatibility tests for WCDMA equipment.

NOKIA'S CURRENT MARKETS

Nokia's main business is the development and manufacture of mobile phones and wireless data products, complying with all major analog and digital standards. There are three divisions of Nokia, which are:

- Nokia Networks,
- Nokia Mobile Phones, and
- Nokia Communications Products.

Nokia Networks supply the mobile information society with data, video and voice network solutions, used by Internet service providers.

Nokia Mobile Phones produce phones for all major user and consumer areas worldwide. The mobile phones also conform to all relevant standards.

Nokia Communications Products was set up to research and develop digital multimedia terminals for digital TV, as well as interactive services through satellite, cable and standard networks.

At the end of 2003, Nokia had sales to over 140 countries, research and development in 14 countries, production in 10 countries and a global network of distribution, sales, customer services and other operational units1.

NOKIA EYEING THE FUTURE MARKETS

The telecommunications business is currently undergoing great change as many different mediums and technologies merge together. The basic driving forces behind them are the following:

- The rapid expansion of the Internet and interactive services.
- A huge growth, especially in WAP technology, has led to a need for increased network capacity, speed, and reliability.
- With emergence of new communications companies to compete successfully, they must devise new and innovative solutions.
- Need for existing operators to improve their own services and networks, which increase the demand for high performance telecommunications equipment.

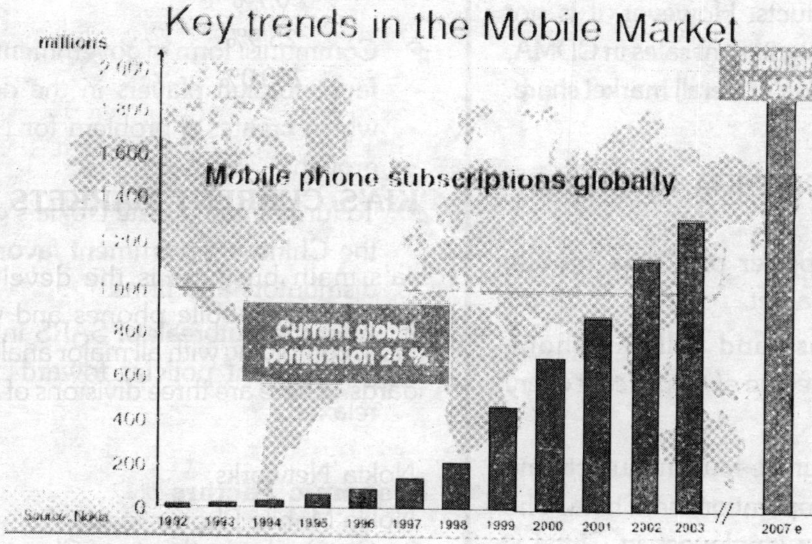

TRUCTURING OF CHINESE OPERATIONS

As growth in China is stabilized and competition intensified, Nokia restructured its China operations to four divisions: handsets, multimedia, network and enterprise solutions. While rivals like Motorola are trying to expand business to other areas such as home electronics, Nokia wants to be more focused on handsets by keeping introducing new models with features appealing to different users, especially moving away from voice to image, games, music and business applications. In January 2005, Nokia completed consolidation of four joint ventures under the new name "Nokia Capitel Communications," the

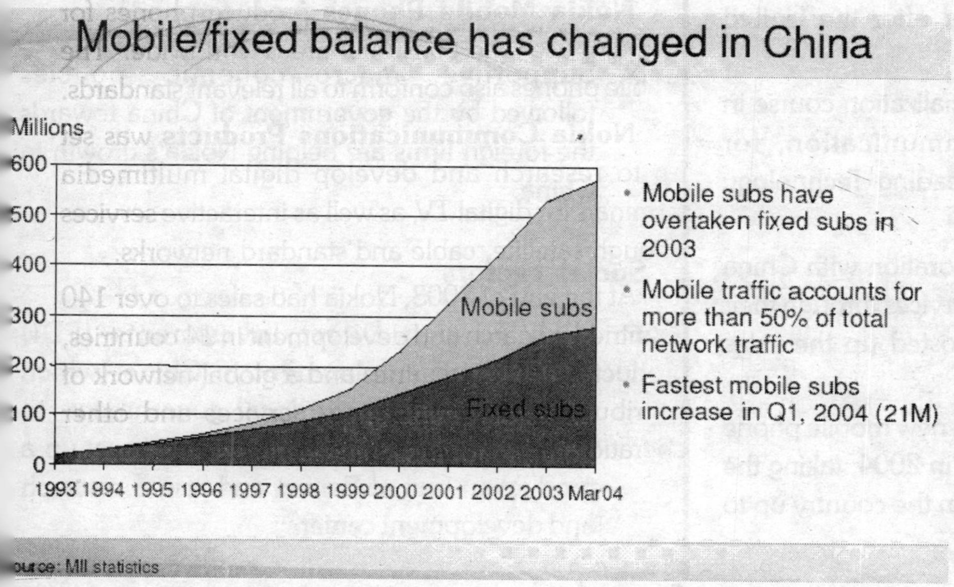

largest communications manufacturer and exporter in China.

Nokia is facing strong competition in the handset market, mainly from Chinese companies in low to mid-range segments. Nokia's market share in China is in steady decline from 30 per cent three years ago to 20 per cent in 2004 due partly to insipid flat designs that are less attractive to the Chinese consumers. The company began selling CDMA handsets in 2004 and opened an R&D center dedicated to CDMA products. However, it is not expected Nokia will make significant sales in CDMA, nor will it help improve Nokia's overall market share.

MORE FACTS ABOUT NOKIA IN CHINA

- Nokia is leading supplier of China mobile telecommunication market.
- The Chinese wireless and cellular phone market is growing at the rate of 40 per cent every year
- Nokia has five R&D units, four manufacturing sites and widespread operations in China. The total number of Nokia employees in China is over 4,300.
- Nokia's sales in China in the year 2003 hit US$3.01 billion and exports grew by 50 per cent to US$2.22 billion. China is Nokia's second largest market in the world after the United States.
- Nokia has sponsored a specialization course in Electronics and Telecommunication, for meritorious students in a leading Technology School in Beijing.
- In Beijing Nokia, has collaboration with China Unicom to provide mobile services through their cell phones, which has boosted up the sales manifold.
- China contributed 60 million new mobile phone users to the world economy in 2004, taking the total number of subscribers in the country up to 145 million.

PEST Analysis of Nokia in China

PEST is an acronym for Political, Economic, Social, and Technical factors of the environment. We can use this tool to examine a company's environment in the PEST analysis model. It can help us to define which environmental factors are affecting Nokia in China, and which of these are the most important, both now, and in the future.

Political Factors

- Communist form of government, which does not favor foreign players in the domestic market, which creates a problem for Nokia for further growth.
- To further complicate Nokia's growth in China, the Chinese government favors local vendors, distributors and firms.
- After the outbreak of SARS in early 2003, the government policies towards FDI have been relaxed.

Economic Factors

- Constant growth rate of Chinese GDP since the year 2000. (7-8 per cent).
- Since the disposable income of the Chinese people is increasing, the propensity to consume has increased, which propels the growth of Nokia in the Chinese market.
- Supportive macro-economic policies followed by the government of China towards the foreign firms are helping Nokia's growth in China.

Social Factors

- High Foreign Direct Investments (FDI) is providing employment in China, which is encouraged by the local government, to exploit this benefit; Nokia has already set up a production unit at Beijing and also a research and development center.

- High migration rate of rural workers to the cities and urban population of more than 350 million creates a potential target segment of people who will be the first time buyers of mobile phones.
- Chinese consumers are quiet finicky and get angry over defective products; Nokia needs to have a firm control over its product quality to avoid any customer dissatisfaction.

Technological Factors

- Due to the global IT boom, Nokia's investment for growth in developing Chinese economy was quiet obvious.
- With the innovation of CDMA technology and third generation mobile phones Nokia's growth prospects in the Chinese market is quiet high.

SWOT ANALYSIS OF NOKIA IN CHINA

Strengths

- Nokia is a global company.
- Availability of local talent and resources in Chinese market.
- Products - very new, dynamic & fashionable.
- Three diversified operational wings (i.e. Nokia Networks, Nokia Mobile Phones and Nokia Communications Products) increase the overall company's chance of survival.
- Market leader across the world and a well-known name, for quality products.

Weaknesses

- Nokia has a weak supply chain in Chinese market.
- Nokia needs to have a thorough check on the product quality, as some of its phones are not of the same quality, as the consumers perceive them to be.

Opportunities

- Robust Market Growth as per industry reports.
- Availability of local talent and resources.
- As the standards of living continue to increase along with individual's disposable income, and there is a high need of managing time and keeping in touch with the world.
- WTO breaks down trade barriers.

Threats

- Health warnings due to the radiation caused by mobile phones have the potential to knock customer confidence.
- Competitors in the Chinese market both local and multi-national companies.
- Stringent Govt. policies and favoritism towards local firms in the Chinese market.

GROWTH STRATEGY OF NOKIA IN CHINA

In this case, Ansoff matrix has been used to determine the strategic growth alternatives, since it is a well-known tool to determine the growth strategy of a company in domestic, as well as in international market.

	Existing Products	New Products
Existing Market	Market Penetration	Product Development
New Markets	Market development	Diversification

Through the Ansoff product-market expansion grid, we try to determine, the appropriate window of the matrix, through which, Nokia can possibly grow in the Chinese market.

After our analysis of the Chinese market we can suggest that Nokia can gain better market share by using *market penetration* and *product development strategy.*

Market Penetration

As we can see that the Chinese market is expanding, Nokia can grow with nominal outlays of marketing expenditure by getting more first-time users to buy the mobile phones or to increase the usage of existing buyers.

Nokia can gain and capture better market share with the help of advertising, promotion and price reduction.

Nokia is also collaborating with mobile service providers like China Unicom, which is increasing its sales and profit margin.

Market penetration of the Nokia mobile phones can be increased by weaning the customers from competitors and converting the non-users.

Product Development

The introduction of new products can have a positive impact on sales growth. A business organization develops new products for one of the two reasons:

1 To replace or supplement its existing offerings in their present markets.

2 To serve new markets in terms of customer benefits or geography.

In this case, Nokia can make profits by supplementing new product offerings in the present markets. Initially, their profitability may not increase, since there may be substantial expenditure on R & D and launching cost. But in the long run they are bound to make profits or return on their investments, because of the large size of the attractive Chinese market.

NOKIA MARKET SEGMENTATION WITH RESPECT TO CHINESE CITIES

1st &2nd Tier Cities

Population in these cities consists of higher income areas of China with the market penetration greater than 20 per cent and Replacement Rate of two years and looking for the best mobile phone in terms of technology and fashion. The segment prefers Branded Goods-International better. Nokia is strengthening its image through targeted advertising, and is being sold through targeted channels

3rd & 4th Tier Cities

Population in these cities consists of lower income areas of China with market penetration less than 10 per cent and replacement rate of greater than three years, this segment is the first time buyer of the phone and is very price-sensitive. Over here Nokia faces firm competition with competitively priced local brands which are well-positioned in this market. To succeed and gain a higher market share Nokia needs deep distribution along with strong retail management

Nokia is 'localised' in Chinese market – Analysis for Nokia 3610

Nokia's mobile phone offerings include a completely "China-localised" product.

The Nokia - 3610 was conceived in Nokia's Product Creation Centre in Beijing, manufactured in the Beijing Capitel Nokia Mobile Telecommunications (BNMT) factory and customized for the Chinese market in terms of price, form factor, design and software.

Targeted predominantly at the youth market, it was launched at the Ele/Expo Comm Shanghai in the year 2002.

Nokia established itself in China in 1985 and now has more than 50 offices and two R&D centers there, employing about 4,700 people.

Features that will appeal to the Chinese-speaking market include:

- A Chinese Lunar calendar with Chinese festival dates,
- An improved Chinese phonebook sorting, and
- Pinyin predictive text input.
- Nokia has also included local language support for other Asian markets.

The attraction of a Nokia, still remains as of its being an "international brand" and the high quality of products and service associated with it.

Nokia takes a step further in Chinese market

In 2003, Nokia took a further step into China's marketplace when it got the license from the country's government to manufacture and sell the mobile terminals using the Code Division Multiple Access (CDMA) technology there.

'The manufacturing license is not only a statutory requirement for manufacturing and selling CDMA based products in China. It also demonstrates that Nokia's CDMA technology meets the high level of expectations and contains the advanced features required by the Chinese consumers,' said Urpo Karjalainen, president of Nokia (China) Investment, in a statement. Nokia also plans to build an equally strong presence in CDMA in China as it has in the GSM.

Questions

1. List the key success factors for Nokia's notable performance in the Chinese market and order them according to significance of each success factor.
2. Discuss market penetration strategy vis-à-vis product development strategy. How can Nokia gain better market share from these two strategies?
3. How does localization help in succeeding in a foreign market? Apart from Nokia, can you cite two more examples where a product incorporated local preferences to lower the consumer's resistance level?

Notes

Advertising and Communication

Section - Fifteen

CONCEPTUAL FRAMEWORK

To facilitate a better debate on the cases in this section, a quick exploratory review of the advertising and communication function along with areas that need discussion are recapitulated briefly as follows:

- **Advertising** is a paid form of non-personal communication transmitted to consumers through mass media such as television, radio, the Internet, newspapers, magazines, direct mail, outdoor displays and signs on mass transit vehicles.
- When organizational images, ideas and political issues are prompted it is known as **Institutional advertising** (for example - any campaign by the company before carrying out an IPO).
- When a company promotes its position on a public issue like taxation, institutional advertising is referred to as **advocacy advertising**.(for example - the campaign of VAT by the union of accountancy software firms)
- **Product advertising** promotes uses, features, and benefits of products. The two types of product advertising are **pioneer advertising**, which focuses on stimulating demand for a product category rather than a specific brand (for example - the condom awareness campaigns), and **competitive advertising**, which attempts to stimulate demand for a specific brand by indicating the brand's features, uses and advantages (for example - the advertisement of condom brand Kamasutra).
- To make direct product comparisons, marketers use **comparative advertising**, in which two or more brands are compared.(for example - the newspaper advertisements of the supermarkets like The Big Bazaar or the travel agencies like Thomas Cook) . Two other forms of competitive advertising are **reminder advertising**, which tells customers that an established brand is still around, and **reinforcement advertising**, which assures current users they have made the right brand choice.
- A marketers should follow a general pattern while developing an advertisement.
  - First, they must identify and analyze the target audience,
  - Second, they should establish what they want the campaign to accomplish by defining advertising objectives.
  - Third, marketers must create the advertising platform, which contains basic issues to be presented in the campaign.
  - Fourth, advertisers must decide how much money to spend on the campaign; they arrive at this decision through the objective-and-task approach, percent-of-sales approach,

competition-matching approach, or arbitrary approach.

- Advertisers must then develop a **media plan** by selecting and scheduling media to use in the campaign. Some of the factors affecting the media plan are location and demographic characteristics of the target audience, content of the message and cost of various media.
- The basic content and form of the advertising message should be in accordance with the product features, uses and benefits, characteristics of the people in the target audience, the campaign's objectives and platform, and the choice of media.
- Finally, advertisers must devise one or more methods for evaluating advertisement effectiveness. Evaluations performed before the campaign begins are called **pretests**, those conducted after the campaign are called **posttests**. Two types of posttests are a **recognition test** in which respondents are shown the actual advertisement and asked whether they recognize it, and a **recall test**. In aided recall tests, respondents are shown a list of products, brands, company names or trademarks to jog their memories. In unaided tests, no clues are given.
- Advertising campaigns can be developed by personnel within the firm or in conjunction with advertising agencies. When a campaign is created by the firm's personnel, it may be developed by one or more individuals or by an advertising department within the firm. Use of an advertising agency may be advantageous because an agency provides highly skilled, objective specialists with broad experience in advertising at low to moderate costs to the firm.
- **Public Relations (PR) managers** communicate to create and maintain favorable relationships between an organization and its stakeholders.
- **Marketing Public Relations (MPR)** which was earlier known as **publicity** is communication in newsstory form about an organization, its products, or both, transmitted through a mass medium at no charge. Problems that organizations confront in using publicity-based public relations include reluctance of media personnel to print or air releases and lack of control over timing and content of messages.(The positive publicity –The Mittal Steel's proposed takeover of the Arcelor steel. The negative publicity- The Ambani brothers' feud for ownership issues of the Reliance corporation).
- Environmental monitoring, public relations audits, and counting the number of media exposures are all means of evaluating **public relations effectiveness.**

Asian Paints

Going Where the Consumer is

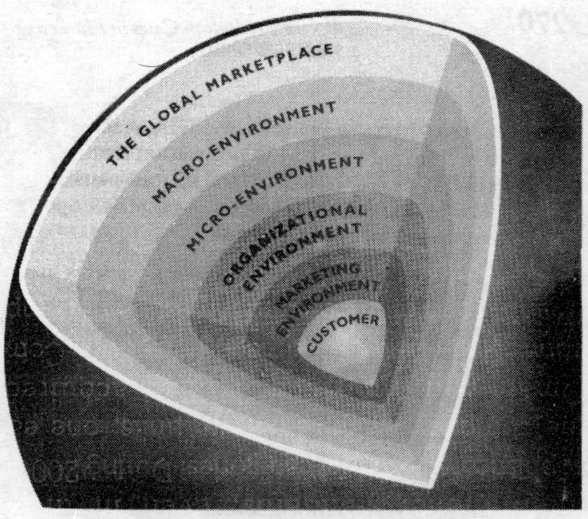

Advertising & Communication Case - 26

Purpose of the Case

The idea is to assimilate the relevant concepts at work and analyse along the following lines:

- *To discuss how Asian Paints has kept its advertising in tune with evolving customer preferpences.*
- *To focus on the key points, in favor of Asian Paints, being projected as an umbrella brand under which different variants are advertised*
- *To debate how a company with a range of products in domestic and industrial categories should structure its advertising budget*

> **Vision Statement of Asian Paints**
>
> *"Asian Paints aims to become one of the top five decorative coatings companies world-wide by leveraging its expertise in the higher growth emerging markets. Simultaneously, the company intends to build long term value in the industrial coating business through alliances with established global partners." (www.asianpaints.com)*

The Indian paints industry in 2005 (according to industry estimates) is around Rs. 85 billion. The organized sector consists of 65% whereas the unorganized sector still controls a large portion of 35%. The paint industry is bifurcated into two segments viz. Decorative Paints and Industrial Paints (Exhibit 1). Around 70-75% of the domestic paints industry revenues come from the decorative segment, whereas the industrial segment constitutes around 25-30%. The major portion of demand for decorative paints is from fresh coats in existing and new wall finishes. Three main segments of the industrial sector include automotive coatings, powder coatings and protective coatings. User industries for industrial paints include automobiles engineering and consumer durables. The industrial paints segment is far more technology intensive than the decorative segment. Automotive coatings constitute nearly 50% of the industrial paints market, high performance coatings, which have about 15% market share, are used in facilities for fertilizers, petrochemicals and offshore oil installations where anti-corrosive protection is essential. Powder coatings for white goods have a 10% market share, while marine paints account for another 10%. In 2005, the manufacturing sector has shown good activity with new projects in roads, ports and industrial segments. (Source: Capitaline Corporate Database)

This case is intended to be used as a basis for class discussion rather than as an illustration of either effective or ineffective handling of the situation. Authored by Dr. Mukesh Pandey.

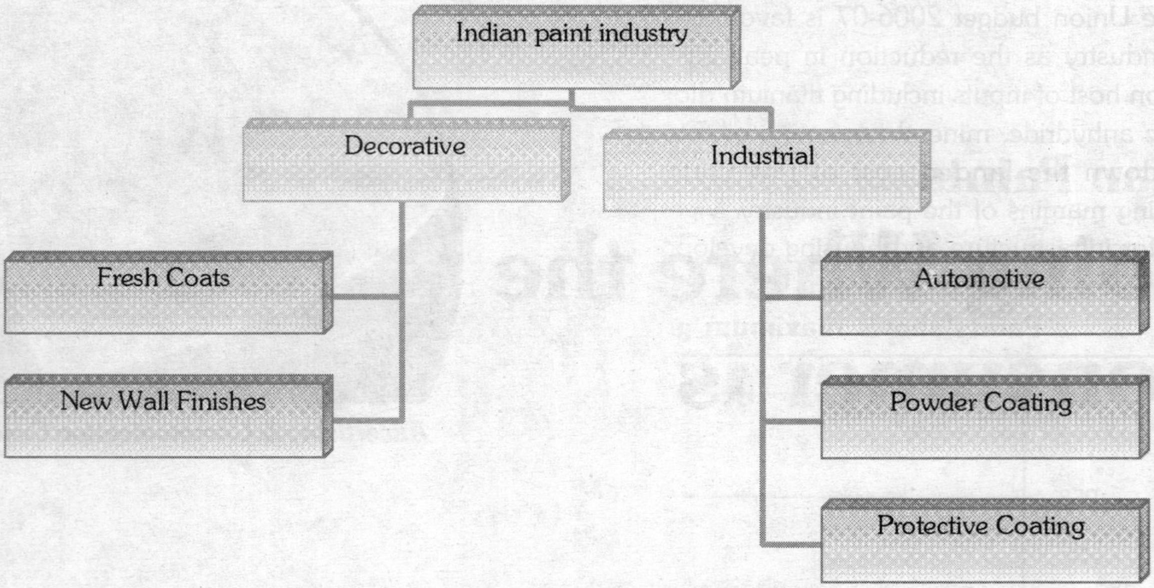

Exhibit 1: ***Various Segments of Indian Paint Industry***

The market share of the organized players in the paints market is as shown in Exhibit 2. In the decorative paint segment, Asian Paints is the leader, while Goodlass Nerolac dominates the industrial paint segment. In the enamel category, Jenson Nicholson dominates the market while Berger Paints and ICI have sizeable presence in emulsion category. Snowcem India dominates the exterior paint category, which accounts for nearly 21% of the decorative paint segment.

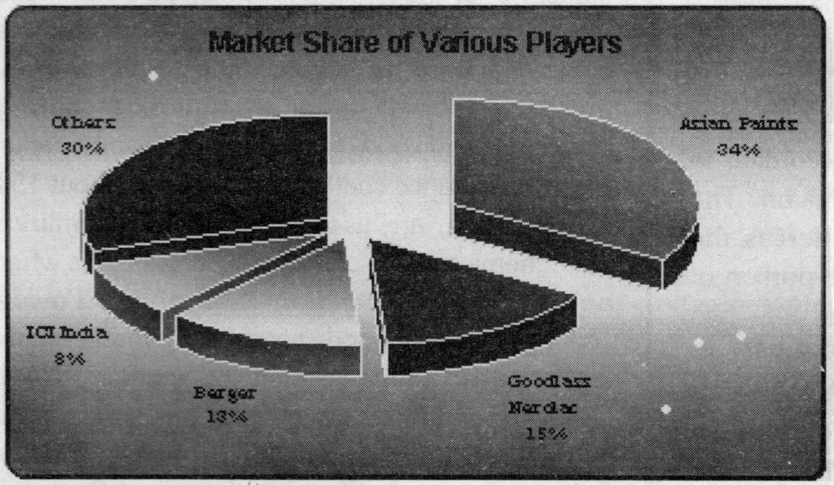

(Source: APIL Annual Report, 2004-05)

Exhibit 2: **Market Share of Various Players**

The Indian paint industry has a huge potential, as the per capita consumption of paint in India is only 800-900 grams compared to 15-25 kg in the developed countries. Further, the middle class population of India estimated at 150 to 300 million will have good purchasing power with the advent of financial schemes for purchase of house and consumer durables.

Decorative paint segment has always been lucrative in India. Large players like Goodlass Nerolac, ICI are now focusing on decorative paints segment by carrying out huge branding and awareness exercise. The demand for decorative segment can be directly linked to the boom in housing and construction sector, and at the same time, repainting demand from existing households is also on a rise due to rising disposable income of the people. From the point of view of new construction activity, a healthy trend in housing loan disbursement is a good indicator on how the homes market is likely to be in the near future. Industry believes that the decorative paints segment will continue to achieve the expected growth rate of 10-12%.

The Union budget 2006-07 is favourable for paint industry as the reduction in peak customs duties on host of inputs including titanium dioxide, phthalic anhydride, mineral turpentine oil, etc will bring down the landed cost of raw material, improving margins of the paint industry. Vigorous layout for infrastructure and housing development via Bharat Nirman Programme is likely to increase the demand for paints for decorative as well as industrial.

Paint advertising in India is too festival-driven in India as people usually get their houses repainted around Diwali which is also the start of Indian marriage season (Exhibit 3).

Paints shows maximum growth before the festival season on TV

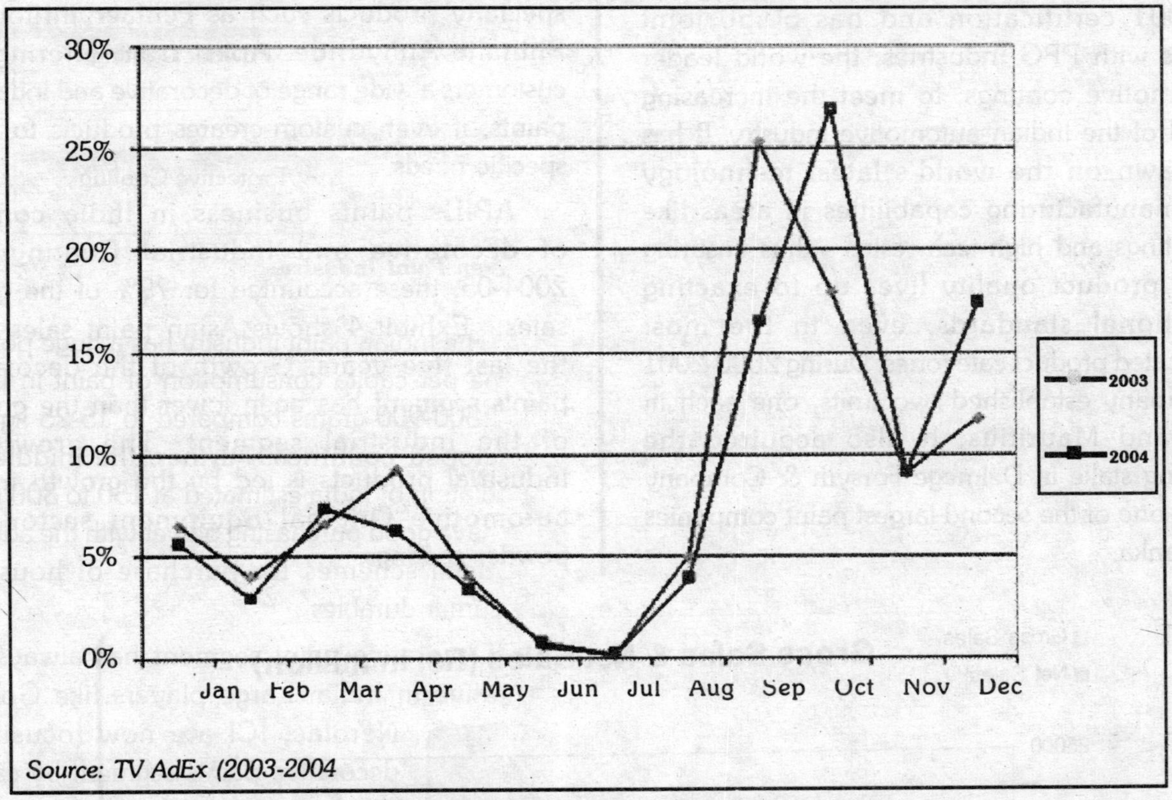

Exhibit 3: **Advertising Clutter-Month wise**

Asian Paints India Ltd. (APIL) is India's largest paint company and ranks among the top ten decorative coatings companies in the world today, with a turnover of Rs.25.6 billion (around USD 585 million). APIL, promoted in 1942, now has an enviable reputation in the corporate world for professionalism, fast track growth, and building shareholder equity. Asian Paints operates in 22 countries and has 29 paint manufacturing facilities in the world servicing consumers in over 65 countries. Besides Asian Paints, the group operates around the world through its subsidiaries Berger International Limited, Apco Coatings and SCIB Chemicals.

APIL was started by four entrepreneurs, Champaklal Choksey, Chimanlal Choksi, Suryakant Dani and Arvind Vakil, as a partnership firm for manufacturing paints, in a garage rented for Rs 75 a month. In 1945, the partnership firm was turned into a private limited company named Asian Oil & Paint Co. Pvt. Ltd. And in the same year, its turnover touched Rs 0.35 million. In the 1940s, it was largely multinational companies such as British Paints and Jenson & Nicholson that dominated the Indian paints market. Asian Paints, however, slowly but surely made a mark for itself through proper managerial planning.

APIL has state-of-the-art manufacturing plants at Bhandup in the State of Maharashtra; at Ankleshwar in the State of Gujarat; at Patancheru in the State of Andhra Pradesh; and at Kasna in the state of Uttar Pradesh. The company has been awarded the ISO 9001 certification and has 50:50 joint ventures with PPG Industries, the world leader in automotive coatings, to meet the increasing demand of the Indian automotive industry. It has also drawn on the world's latest technology for its manufacturing capabilities in areas like coil coatings and high-tech resins - thus ensuring that its product quality lives up to exacting international standards, even in the most sophisticated product categories. During 2000-2001 the company established two units, one each in Oman and Mauritius. It also acquired the controlling stake in Delmege Forsyth & Company (Paints), one of the second largest paint companies of Sri Lanka.

APIL's brands, Royal in the premium segment, Apcolite in the middle segment, Gattu, Tractor, Utsav, 3-Mango, etc, in the lower segment, are all well-established brands in their respective segments. Its one-stop colour shop has software to choose and select more than 1,500 combinations of various colours. APIL's product range includes Wall paints, Metal paints, Wood Finishes, Primers and others. Vertical integration has seen it diversify into specialty products such as Pentaerythritol and Phthalic Anhydride. Apart from offering the customers a wide range of decorative and industrial paints, it even custom-creates products to meet specific needs.

APIL's paints business in India consists of decorative and industrial Coatings. In 2004-05, these accounted for 78% of the group sales. Exhibit 4 shows Asian paint sales over the last five years. Growth of the decorative paints segment has been lower than the growth of the Industrial segment. The growth in Industrial products is led by the growth in the automotive Original Equipment sector and powder coatings.

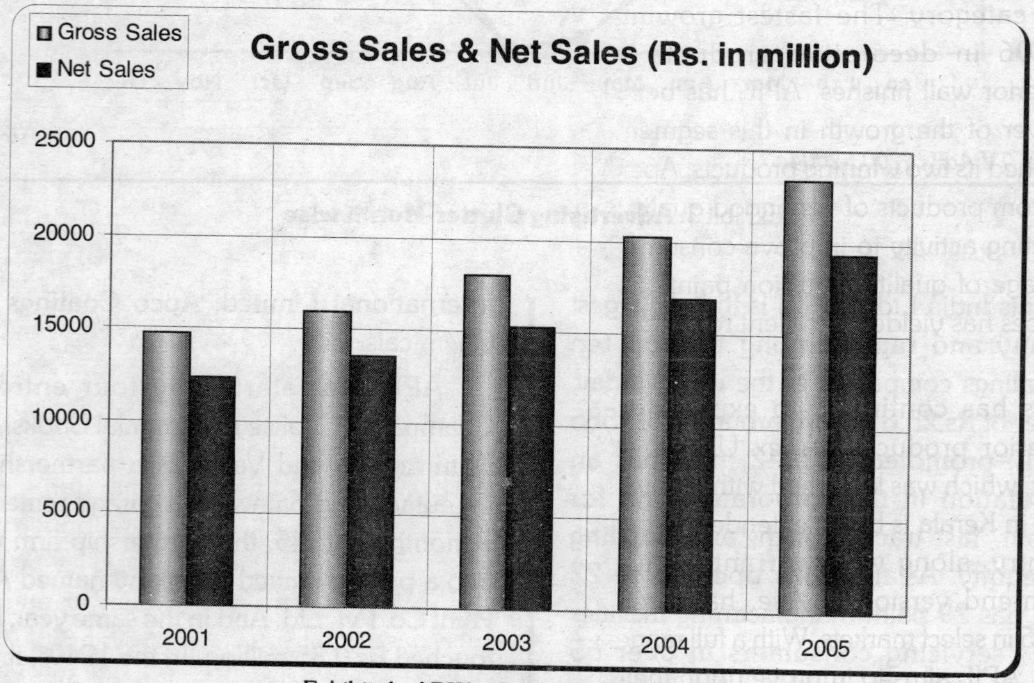

Exhibit 4: **APIL's Sales Performance**

Decorative paints accounts for around 70-75% of the overall paint market in India. In this segment, APIL has been a leader for almost four decades. Decorative paints include interior and exterior wall finishes, enamels, wood finishes and ancillary products such as primers, putty etc. Decorative paint sale in India accounts for about 70% of the APIL's sales in 2004-05. Industry estimates place the overall decorative paints market growth including the small and medium scale segment in India at about 11-12% in volume and marginally higher in value.

Asian Paints is the leader in interior wall finishes and has an entire range of products for this segment. In 2005, APIL extended Utsav Acrylic distemper throughout the country as the economy distemper; it also aggressively pushed Tractor emulsion to upgrade the market, introduced extremely attractive dark shades in the high-priced emulsion product range and stepped up marketing activities. As a result, APIL had a robust growth in the distemper segment and the emulsion category despite continued competition from lower priced products from large companies and from a large number of regional players in the distemper category. The fastest growing segment in 2006 in decorative products is undoubtedly exterior wall finishes. APIL has been the principal driver of the growth in this segment ever since it launched its two winning products, Apex and Ace. Apart from products of very good quality, aggressive marketing activity to improve consumer awareness for usage of quality emulsion paints on the exterior surfaces has yielded excellent results for the company.

Asian Paints has continued to expand its portfolio of exterior products. Apex Ultima, a premium product, which was launched with a novel warranty scheme in Kerala is being extended to the rest of the country, along with warranty. Ace Supreme, a high-end version of Ace, has been introduced in 2005 in select markets. With a full range of these products, APIL aims to improve upon their already strong position in the market.

The enamel segment is by far the largest segment, which has been growing slower than decorative paints as a whole for some years now. This is because it is being replaced by other materials on hoardings, signboards and the like. Aggressive marketing and pricing policies coupled with extension of Utsav Enamel, an economy product, enabled APIL to grow well in the category.

Industrial Coating is classified into automotive and non-automotive industrial paints. This market is catered to by three entities: the parent company Asian Paints (India) Limited (APIL), its subsidiary company Asian Paints Industrial Coatings Limited (APICL) and the joint venture Asian PPG Industries Ltd. Together, these three contributed to around 8% of the group's sales in 2005. While Asian PPG Industries Ltd. caters to the automotive coating segments, the wholly owned subsidiary APICL services the powder coating segment. APIL services the remaining non-auto industrial coating segments viz., protective coating, road marking, floor coating and general industrial liquid paints. With the automobile industry continuing on its growth trajectory, white goods manufacturers registering good growth and Government's focus on enhancing the road network in the country, the company's overall performance in industrial coating has been commendable. The group's total sales of industrial coating in India are growing at 35% approx.

Asian Paints is the second largest player in protective coatings in the country; they have also emerged as the second largest player in road marking paint in just a few years of entering this segment. APICL, the Company's wholly owned subsidiary which services the requirements of powder coating customers in the country registered an impressive net sales growth of 23% in 2005. APICL has technology collaboration with Canada based Protech Chemicals Ltd., one of the top ten powder coating companies in the world. The process of technology absorption is well underway and several products based on Protech technology have been developed at APICL. Trials for commercialization of these products have also commenced.

Simultaneously, in-house R&D efforts at APICL have continued and efforts to enter into specific large OE accounts have borne fruit. The combination of inputs from Protech and in-house R&D efforts will enable APICL to provide customers with state-of-the-art technology products for existing and new applications.

The communication strategy has evolved scientifically over the decades. In late '40s, Asian Paints hit on the innovative marketing strategy of "going where the consumer is", reaching out to the remotest corners of the country to give consumers products the way they wanted them, i.e, in conveniently-sized packs.

In order to increase revenue, AP concentrated on the smaller towns ignored by multinationals. In 1954, Asian Paints asked the famous cartoonist R.K. Laxman to create a mascot for the company, and from his pen was born – Gattu – which emerged as one of India's most memorable mascots (Exhibit 5). APIL's market research found out that in rural India, farmers who wished to paint the horns of their bullocks preferred to buy paint in small packs. Soon APIL came out with 50-ml packs, which became very popular. Simultaneously the company embarked on an ambitious marketing campaign, forming close bonds with thousands of dealers in small towns all over India. By 1968, the company surprised its big-name multinational competitors by emerging as India's No. 1 paint company. Ever since 1968, the company has been a leader in this industry.

Exhibit 5: **Asian Paints mascot – "Gattu"**

From its inception, APIL focused on marketing to create greater brand awareness and to increase its market share. It realized that in products like paints, consumers were very marginally involved in purchase decisions, as they generally fixed the budget with the contractor, who bought the paints. The company realized that consumers were not brand -conscious, and it was price that influenced the buying decision. In order to keep its prices low, APIL had to keep its production costs low so it undertook backward integration to reduce production costs.

The earlier ad campaigns of APIL stressed on the functional benefits such as durability, availability of wide range of color shades, etc. They showed paint chipping of walls when painted with inferior brands with an implied aim at establishing the superiority of Asian Paints over other brands; consequently emphasizing on the freedom from hassles of getting the house painted every year. Functional benefits such as long lasting beauty of the walls, durability, etc. were the mantras behind earlier ad campaigns.

In 1990, APIL actively promoted the Apcolite brand which offered 151 shades, in contrast to the general practice of offering just 30–40 shades. It also gave consumers an Apcolite shadecard to help them select the shades they wanted. According to reports, many consumers insisted on referring to the Apcolite shadecard, even if they bought another brand or kind of paint.

In 2002, APIL dropped its famous mascot - 'Gattu'- from its logo despite it being one of the most recognizable mascots in India. Gattu was first dreamed up when the company was still small and struggling against large British companies like Imperial Chemicals. The mascot, created by cartoonist R.K.Laxman, was mischievous, aggressive, Indian urchin and made a lot of sense then, attacking the large foreign players. Gattu, which Asian Paints phased out from its logo and corporate image, in a comprehensive brand overhaul was like the 'common man', so it served well for Asian Paints till it wanted a mass-market appeal. Realising that in the world of marketing, the common man is no more relevant; Asian Paints got a brand new logo designed by Enterprise IG Singapore (a branding consultancy that's part of WPP, the communication company that owns O&M, Asian Paints' long-time agency). However, Gattu is retained as a small graphic element on the packs for re-assurance. Asian Paints is now being touched up with the proverbial brush and is being given an upmarket, modern, urban, more dapper image.

The present campaigns have moved on to emphasizing on the emotional as well as social benefits that the customer derives from the brand. Few of the recent ad campaigns are as follows:

1. ***Badiya Hai Campaign:*** In this ad, a neighbour meets Sunilbabu and appreciates him for new house, new car and new wife. A few years later he again meets that person and sees his house is still new whereas his car has become old and wife had put on weight over the years. This campaign depicts how the brand helps the customers achieve social appreciation for one's house. The customer is appreciated by his neighbors and passer-bys who admire the longevity of the paint quality of their house painted with Asian Paints. (Exhibit 6)

Exhibit 6: **Asian Paints Badiya Hai Campaign**

2. ***Har Ghar Kuch Kehta Hai* Campaign***:* The ad encourages people to use more colors in their house apart from the regular colors in more innovative and imaginative ways. It aims at bringing the brand close to Home Décor. The tag line "Har Ghar Kuch Kehta Hai Ki Andar Usme Kaun Rehta Hai", encourages the customers to express themselves through their homes with the use of different colors of Asian Paints. Asian Paints wants to be a company which is about people who invest emotional energy in creating their homes. It is about homes which reflect the taste and love of their residents. The purpose of this communication was to shift the brand to a higher moral ground so as to ensure connect with the customer at the emotional level. (Exhibit 7)

Exhibit 7: **Har Ghar Kuch Kehta Hai Campaign**

3. **Somethings in life need a Royale wall** (Asian Paints Royale)*:* In this ad Saif Ali Khan finds a gift lying at his doorstep. The identity of the sender is revealed as he reads the cards," Happy birthday son". Looking at the gift, the son smiles and is immediately transported back in time. When he was walking down a street, he suddenly stops on seeing a beautiful chain and pendant at shop window. When he looks at the high price, he wonders for a moment and then looks at his guitar. He decides to sell his guitar so that he can manage to get the money and returns to buy his necklace. After buying the pretty pendant and chain, he adds a small note to it, saying "Happy birthday mom". Coming back into the present, Saif takes up a paint brush and dips into an Asian Paints bucket. After

painting a wall with blue paint he hangs the gift from his mother on it i.e. his old guitar." Somethings in life need a Royale wall". (Exhibit 8).

Exhibit 8: **Asian Paints Royale ("Somethings in life need a Royale Wall")**

The idea is to convey that Asian Paints as the brand with the largest range of colours and one that will satisfy the consumer and is able to give him precisely what he wants. The advertising through the campaign is single-minded and focused in its proposition, communication and target audience. Other print campaigns of Asian Paints are as per Exhibit 9.

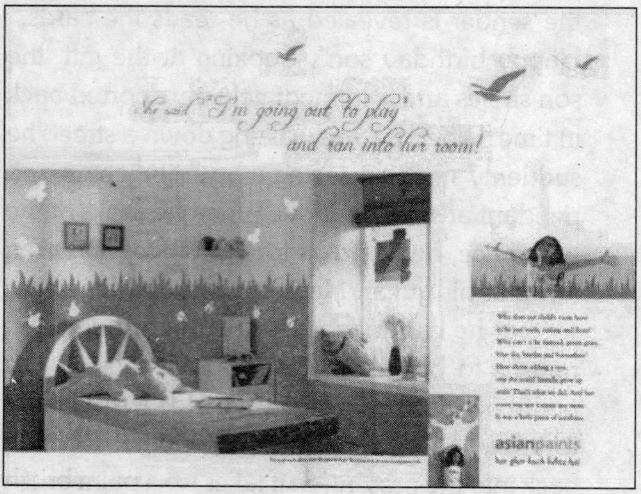

Exhibit 9

By 2004, Asian Paints had 13 brands with over 1,100 shades, targeting different niches. They were beginning to realise that though some brands like Apex emulsions, Royale interior emulsion, Apcolite and Touch Wood had high recall; none except Tractor distemper were almost generic. Therefore, they decided to promote the corporate image and the various brands under their umbrella brand 'Asian Paints' through their communication, pushing the generic Asian Paints brand instead of pumping in investment on individual brands. The idea was to leverage on the advantage that Asian Paints was one company in this low-involvement segment where people actually asked for the paint by brand, breaking away from the earlier tradition where consumers were not known to be very brand-conscious in this low-involvement segment and, more often than not, relied on what the painter bought for them within the budget allocated, being more specific about the colour than its source.

Discontinuing the promotion of individual brands in favour of corporate branding was also a logical step to take, given that media costs have increased — along with the high degree of media-fragmentation. Brand portfolio rationalisation has become something of a marketing fad, with companies realising the benefits of focusing media spends and creative inputs on a few, strong brands. So Asian Paints, which launched a new brand with almost every product, a la the FMCG marketers is cutting back as well. The fact is APIL tried to create around 20 brands but only one got created i.e. Tractor, which of course has a high recall and equity amongst the company's brands. The only other brand APIL wants to retain and promote outside the company umbrella brand is Utsav but Utsav is a brand with a rather different function as it is aimed at upgrading users of chuna, cement paint, etc.

APIL realised the new generation consumer has changed and festivals have become less important in the overall scheme of things. Also, too much clutter around the festival platform reduced the uniqueness of the proposition. Painting itself had become less seasonal. There is an increased consciousness about home décor. Urban home makers are getting more and more involved in homemaking. The trend is catching up in smaller towns too and it is obvious that Asian Paints wants to be a part of this high voltage emotion of home décor creation. This would also serve in increasing the role of painting in the creation of home décor.

A very important objective of APIL in 2002 onwards was to give the brand image an upgrade, give it a facelift, with new packaging, a contemporary logo and corporate colours. So all the new packaging feature the new look (Asian Paints is the logo, in yellow and red, with the vertical of the 'p' converted into a brushstroke), giving all the company's products a uniform look. Previously, if one went into a retail store that sold almost 70 per cent Asian Paints, he wouldn't know it because each pack was designed when each new product and brand name was introduced; there was no family feeling for them. Now, each of the packs uses the mnemonic of the "drip" — the sheet of paint flowing down the tin, in blue for all products — and has the new logo, a sub-brand if necessary, and a graphic that indicates its usage. It's all very much more contemporary and more urban, upmarket, modern. And that's the reason for Gattu's exit. APIL thought for a long time if they could fit Gattu in with the new visual identity, but the two don't seem to go together so he's removed, except as an inch-high mnemonic on the back and lids of the paint tins, that too for reassuring customers. (Exhibit 10)

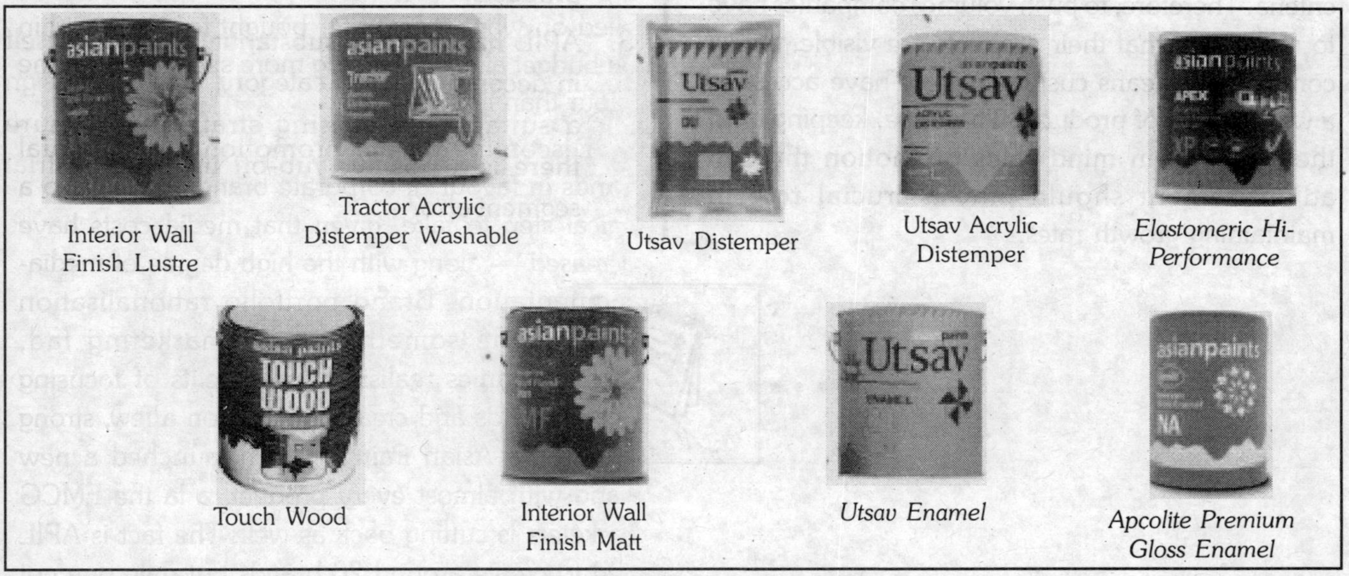

Exhibit 10: **Asian Paints – New Packaging**

Today, Asian Paints is realising that consumers have become harder to reach, they are busier; more distracted and lead more complicated and less predictable lives. The traditional patterns of family life are also getting sharply eroded with the rise of dual income families. It is common to see husband and wife spending a lot of time outside home. Communicating with them and building a community of brand loyalists have become much more difficult. Another challenge Asian Paints is facing is that in many cases customers pay a premium not because of its functionality but because it represents a way of life. So when launching or repositioning a brand, companies have to understand the emotional needs as well as the functional ones.

The potential for decorative paints does look bright, considering the new housing policy. Moreover, the potential that lies in exterior segment has opened a new avenue for paint companies to exploit. The wood finish segment is another area, which is growing rapidly. The growth of the industrial segment will be directly related to industry growth.

Indian industry is bound to do well and this will have a rub-off on the industrial paint segment also. There is an increase in consumer preference for branded goods leading to a shrinking unorganized sector. The share of the unorganized sector in the paint market has been shrinking, primarily due to increasing awareness and increasing consumer literacy.

Asian Paints has always been involved in product innovation that has helped create new segments and expanded the market. APIL ensured constant touch with their consumers to feel the pulse of the market and understand the needs of the consumers, in turn providing them value-for-money products. Paints have taken on some of the traits of FMCG products in terms of being pull-driven, extensive reach, and packaging becoming defining criteria. Therefore, to push volumes companies have to make sure that their products are visible. Rising competition means customers now have access to a wider range of products. Therefore, keeping both these factors in mind sales promotion through advertisement should play a crucial role in maintaining growth rates.

Questions

1. The customer today is much more involved with the process of painting and is looking at the whole experience of interior decoration as well as painting as an expression of their personalities. They're buying into a product that's promising self-expression, sophistication, technology and even services. How should APIL's advertising evolve itself to remain continuously relevant to these customers?
2. How should APIL, as a market leader in decorative paint category, upgrade its customers to value-added/ superior-quality/ high-margin products?
3. APIL has made a substantial mark for itself in decorative paints category. Can you design a suitable advertising strategy to ensure there is a positive rub-off in the industrial segment also?

Launching a Cigarette under Banned Promotional Environment

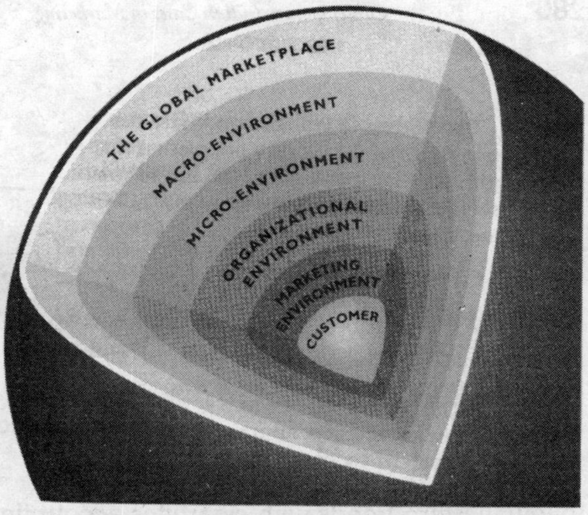

Advertising & Communication Case - 27

Purpose of the Case

The idea is to assimilate the relevant concepts at work and analyse in light of the following issues:

- How to go ahead with advertising and promotion activities under banned promotional environment?
- How to build on pre-launch market research for formulating an effective launch strategy for Tipper Cigarette?

INDIAN TOBACCO INDUSTRY

The tobacco industry holds tremendous potential for India. For the government, it means excise duties and export revenues, and for the country in general, it translates into huge employment opportunities with 35 million people being directly or indirectly engaged in producing and selling of tobacco and tobacco products.

India, the second largest producer of tobacco in the world after China, produced 572 million kgs of tobacco in 2002-2003. India, however, holds a meager 0.7 per cent share of the US$ 30 billion global import-export trade in tobacco with cigarettes accounting for 85% of the total tobacco exports. Despite being the second largest producer, India is only the ninth largest exporter of tobacco and tobacco products in the world as out of the total tobacco produced in India, only one-third is flue-cured tobacco suitable for cigarette manufacturing and having an export demand. Most of the tobacco produce is suitable for the manufacture of chewing tobacco, bidis and other cheap tobacco products, which have no demand outside the country.

Tobacco production is integral to the economies of Andhra Pradesh, Karnataka, Gujarat, Uttar Pradesh, Andhra Pradesh and Karnataka, where it is grown. Tobacco cultivation is a lucrative agribusiness proposition owing to its short growing season and the profitability in relation to other cash crops.

TOBACCO CONSUMPTION

Indian consumption pattern of tobacco does not

This case is intended to be used as a basis for class discussion rather than as an illustration of either effective or ineffective handling of the situation. Authored by Dr. Mukesh Pandey.

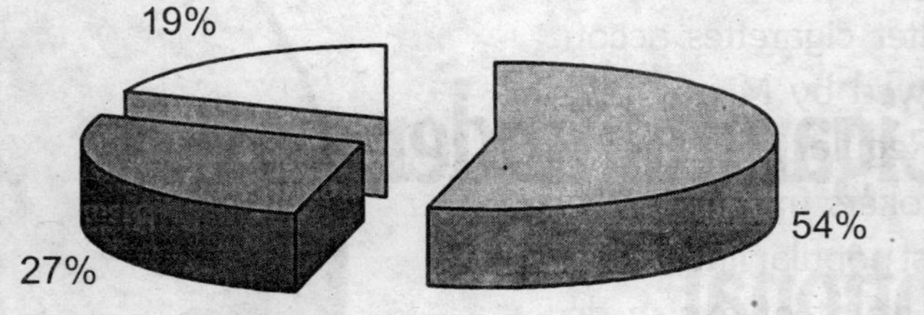

Tobacco Consumption in India

follow western trends with cigarettes accounting for only 19% of the tobacco consumed in the country as against 85% internationally. In fact, the per capita consumption of cigarettes in India is merely 1/10th of the world average. The figure for consumption of bidis in India is as high as 54%. Pan Masala, Snuff, Chewing Tobacco (gutka, khaini and zarda) and such other products account for the rest 27%.

This unique tobacco consumption pattern is a combination of tradition and more importantly the discriminatory tax imposed on cigarettes over the last 2 decades. Cigarette smokers pay almost 85% (Rs 5,181 crore) of the total tax revenues generated from tobacco, which is justified by authorities on the grounds that it is a "luxury" tax.

The non-smoking tobacco includes chewing tobacco, which has grown at a rapid rate from almost zero a decade ago to its current position. The market is divided between chewing tobacco, snuff and hookah. Chewing tobacco and hookah occupy about 25% of the total tobacco grown in India and are consumed internally in the form of chewing, hookah, paste, quiwam, candy and gutka purposes. There are some 400-500 products of pan masala available in the market such as scented supari, aromatic powder, khaini, mishri, mawa, snuff, zarda, cheroot, etc. The non-smoking tobacco industry is also very regional in character with only two brands having a national presence viz. Pan Parag and Manikchand.

BAN ON TOBACCO ADVERTISEMENT - THE DARK ENVIRONMENT

On 1st May 2004, the Indian Government imposed a ban on cigarette and tobacco advertising and smoking in public places. As a result the tobacco industry, which contributes Rs 70 billion to the government by way of excise, had to cut down Rs 2,500 million of their advertising budgets with the ban. As a result of this ban, companies had to heavily depend on local micro marketing, POS marketing and subtle promotional activities focusing on in-shop advertising. Farsighted tobacco companies who saw the ban coming, however, successfully ventured into trademark diversification or brand extensions and surrogate advertising like Wills lifestyle stores, Red & White bravery awards etc.

INDIAN CIGARETTE INDUSTRY

The cigarette industry in India is one of the oldest and an important agro-based industry. It is highly labour intensive and provides livelihood to about five million people directly and indirectly. At present, there are 19 units in the organized sector engaged in manufacturing cigarettes with a total installed capacity of about 147.377 billion sticks per annum.

MARKET SIZE

The market for cigarettes in India is estimated at 100 billion sticks per annum and valued at Rs. 90

billion. The cigarette market in India is characterized by low penetration (as compared with bidis) and high excise duty. Regular filter cigarettes account for 47% of the market followed by Micros (19%) and Plains (almost 19%). Regular cigarettes are entry-point cigarettes for smokers upgrading from plain cigarettes. Being the most popular line, regulars have historically faced the brunt of excise duty increases. The micros segment witnessed strong growth after the cut in excise duty in FY1995 but the growth has stagnated in recent years. Four important trends are affecting the cigarette market in India.

1. The Government has disallowed foreign owned companies in the segment thus limiting competition in the market.
2. Smuggling of cigarettes, especially king-size ones, is on the increase, which is affecting sales of Indian cigarette companies.
3. In line with the international trena, anti-smoking pressure is increasing.
4. Last, the litigation risk for cigarette companies is increasing.

The cigarette market is classified into the high-priced filter and low-priced non-filter segments. Under these two broad segments, cigarettes can be further classified on the basis of length as follows:

Segment	Length
Non-Filter	
Micros	*Up to 60 mm*
Plain	*Longer than 60 mm & up to 70 mm*
Filter	
Regular	*Up to 70 mm*
Long	*Longer than 70 mm & up to 75 mm*
King-size	*Longer than 75 mm & up to 85 mm*

EXCISE DUTY

Central Excise Duty (CED) on tobacco was introduced in 1943-44. Until 1986-87, the rates of the excise charged by the government varied with the various cost slabs declared by the cigarette manufacturers. The minimum slab of cost per thousand cigarettes was Rs 10-Rs 35. In November 1982, the effective rate of excise duty was made a uniform 440%. In February 1983, the government introduced rates on the printed price on the cigarette packs. In September 1985, the government revised the structure by narrowing down the slabs to 5. But, on 28th February 1987 the government decided to charge duty on the basis of the length of the cigarette. The tax collection from cigarettes is the highest with duty per kg for cigarettes being as high as Rs. 722 per kg, while combined duty per kg for other tobacco products like bidis and chewing tobacco is only Rs. 21 per kg. The excise duty structure for cigarettes , as on May 2004, is as follows:

Segment	Length (mm)	Excise Duty (Rs. per'000)
Filter		
King Size	81-85	1450
Mini King Size	71-75	1090
Regular Filters	Up to 70	670
Non-Filter		
Regular Plains	61-70	450
Mini Plain	Up to 60	135

Three companies dominate the Indian cigarette market: the two BAT affiliates-ITC and VST (Vazir Sultan Tobacco) and Godfrey Philips India Limited (GPI). Together, these three companies account for 99% of the market for cigarettes with ITC being the market leader. These players have benefited from the booming domestic tobacco crop and declining tobacco prices.

Cigarette companies in India & their Market share

Major Players	Volume market share (%)	Value market share (%)
ITC	67%	74%
GPIL	12.40%	11.40%
VST	12.50%	7.40%

ITC, the market leader, has leading brands in all the segments and holds a large chunk of the market at the premium end. VST is particularly strong in the low and medium ends of the market. GPI has a strong presence in the medium (regular) segment while GPI is relatively stronger in the North and West, ITC and VST have a stronghold of the South.

Major players and their brands in India

Company	Non-filter micros	Filter Plain	Regular	Long	Kingsize	Premium
ITC	Scissors Std.	Scissors	Bristol Filter	Wills Filter	Gold Flake	India Kings
	Capstan Std.	Gold Flake	Gold Flake Filter		FTK	Classic
VST	Charminar Std	Charminar	Charms filter			
	Vijay Delux		Charms Mini Kings			
GPI	Cavendar	Red & White	Four Square Special		Four Square	
	Magna	Cavanders	Red & White Filter		FTK	Jaisalmer
	Tipper	Gold leaf				
	Gold					
	Tipped					
	Four Square					
	Super					

GODFREY PHILLIPS INDIA LIMITED - A LEADING TOBACCO COMPANY IN INDIA

Godfrey Phillips India limited (GPIL), is an affiliate of Philip Morris International, the largest privately owned cigarette producer in the world. In 1979, Philip Morris joined hands with the K.K. Modi Group in India. Presently, GPI is a joint venture between K.K.Modi (36.67%) and Philip Morris of US (35.93%). Godfrey Phillips is today the second largest player in the Indian cigarette industry with an annual turnover of over US$ 265 million. Today, Philip Morris is the largest US based international cigarette company having a strong presence in three large industries viz. Cigarettes, Beer and Food. GPIL today owns some of the most popular cigarette brands viz.

Cigarette Brands of GPIL

International	Indian
Marlboro, Philips Morris, Bond street, Rothmans, Chesterfield, Virginia Slims, Parliament, Merit	Jaisalmer Four Square FTK, Four Square Special, Red & White Filter, Cavanders Commando, Originals, Tipper and Prince

GPI also manufactures Marlboro, Philip Morris's leading international brand, which is marketed by Philip Morris India through GPI's distribution network. The company also markets international brands like Rothmans and Chesterfield. GPIL operations span the entire northern and western part of the country, with two manufacturing facilities located in Ghaziabad (near Delhi) and in Andheri (Mumbai), a state of the art R&D centre in Mumbai and a tobacco-buying unit in Guntur (Andhra Pradesh). Headquartered in Delhi, the Company has its sales offices across the country at Ahmedabad, Mumbai, Delhi, Chandigarh and Hyderabad. In India, Cavanders has strong franchise in the rural market, Four Square and Red & White are strong in the urban market whereas Four Square has a strong market in the North and West. Large chunks (about 70%) of GPIL's cigarette sales consist of 70 mm filter cigarettes.

LAUNCH OF TIPPER BY GPIL

GPIL launched its new non-filter cigarette named 'TIPPER - GOLD TIPPED' in January 2002 in Orissa and then later in Jammu, Saharanpur, Cuttack and Telengana and in Kanpur. The implied mission to launch Tipper was to continuously upgrade lifestyle of those consumers who are not cigarette smokers (but bidi smokers or gutka consumers) by offering new generation cigarettes in all formats with the aim of making it a destination brand for non-filter segment smokers. As such, it was important to know the perception of the smokers about the newly launched Tipper cigarette. Retailers' study was conducted in order to know the retailer's satisfaction and to maintain good relationship with them.

CLASSIFICATION OF OUTLETS

The different types of outlets from where GPIL's cigarettes are sold in the country include pan/ cigarette outlets, grocery stores, tea shops and street-vendors. Cigarette outlets are classified depending upon the volume of cigarette purchases at that outlet as follows:

Class of Outlet	Daily Purchases of all cigarette brands
A	Rs 1,000 or more per day
B	Between Rs 500 to Rs 999 per day
C	Between Rs 200 to Rs 499 per day
D	Below Rs 200 per day

MARKET RESEARCH REPORTS

Market researches on cigarette smoking in India conducted by GPIL revealed that people were dissatisfied with their current brand due to the following reasons:

1. **Non filter smoker's dissatisfaction:**
   - Tobacco falling into the mouth was a regular complaint from smokers of non-filter cigarettes like, Capstan Standard, Panama Regular and Charminar etc.
   - Smokers of Capstan Standard, Panama Regular, Charminar, etc. complained that the smoking end got soggy and spoilt.
   - Lack of image and style as people associated smoking of cigarette with image building and stylish looks.
2. **Dual smoker's dissatisfaction:** Dual smokers i.e. those smokers who switched frequently between non-filter and filter cigarettes preferred filter cigarettes over non-filter cigarette as it helped in filtering the smoke and prevented tobacco from falling into the mouth while smoking. They also wanted the taste of a filter cigarette at the price of a non-filter cigarette. Dual smokers usually smoke for style and image; since non-filter cigarettes do not have stylish looks, they avoid smoking them.
3. **Bidi smoker's dissatisfaction with Bidis:** This was due to inconsistent quality of tobacco, packing, number/ Broken sticks in a packet, lack of image and style and erratic extinguishing of bidis.

CONCEPT DEVELOPMENT, DESIGN AND TESTING

Concept Development: Based on the above findings of the research study, GPIL developed the concept of a new cigarette to provide the following benefits:

- Compact tip: The tip of the cigarette was made compact to block tobacco from entering the mouth while smoking, to prevent smoking end from getting soggy, as a results not letting the tobacco get spoilt; also the stick does not get squeezed from the smoking end.
- It looks like a filter cigarette and has similar benefits: The ciga-rette was developed keeping in mind the style and image fac-tor of the smokers. It has a gold paper at the tip, giving the ciga-rette

a look of a filter ciga-rette and similar benefits.

- Good clean smoke: The compact end blocks the tobacco from entering the mouth; the smoke gets filtered and cleaned, thus enhances the taste of the cigarette.

Brand	Company	MRP	Price to Retailers	Price per Stick	Selling Price	Income to Retailers	Profit to Retailers
Capstan Standard	ITC	4	3.7	0.4	0.5	5	1.3
Capstan Star	ITC	5	4.54	0.5	0.5	5	0.46
Charminar	VST	4	3.7	0.4	0.5	5	1.3
ACE	VST	4	3.7	0.4	0.5	5	1.3
Panama Regular	GTC	4	3.7	0.4	0.5	5	1.3
Tipper Gold Tipped	GPI	5	4.5	0.5	0.5	5	0.5

MARKETING STRATEGY

Conscious, meticulous efforts were made by GPIL in identifying the right marketing mix so that marketing objectives could be realized.

- **Product:** Following features were incorporated to ensure superiority of Tipper over its competitors:
- Compact tobacco tip, generated by using Double Density Technology wherein one part of the cigarette is hard and the other soft.
- **Superior packaging:** to provide premium image to the brand.
- **Insert:** High quality inserts for value addition, knowledge and image around the brand by educating the smoker about the technology used in developing the brand.
- **Pricing:** Tipper was launched in the price bracket of Rs 5.00 per pack. Loose cigarettes were sold at 50 paise per stick. The retailer price was kept at Rs. 4.5/ packet and MRP at Rs. 5/packet. The excise duty charged on 59mm cigarettes is Rs. 135 per '000 nos. i.e. Rs. 1.35 per pack of cigarette. Since the industry trend shows that the prices increase every 2 years, therefore it was decided to hold these prices at this very level for at least two years. Prices of the various other brands in the same segment are as follows:

Distribution strategy: The distribution channel used by Godfrey Phillips India Limited is as follows:

GPIL initially placed their brand Tipper for the first time for about 10 days wherein all the outlets of local Kanpur area were covered to start with. The dealers were supplied only on demand without any inventory pressures. A and B class outlets were given 10 packets of cigarette whereas C & D class outlets were handed over 5 packets or less of cigarettes.

Promotion Strategy: GPIL used a combination of in-shop and on -shop merchandising displays to stand out in a cluttered cigarette shops. Post ad-ban, GPI had to cover or remove all the posters from the market.

Surrender to the Ad-ban on Tobacco

GPIL could not put dealer boards, glow signs and hoardings due to ban on tobacco advertising from 1st May 2004 and had to comply with the new law, which restricted any company to advertise anything related to tobacco. So the following measures were taken:

- Tearing - off the art cards/posters from the retail outlets
- Covering all the thematic displays
- Covering all the lighters and clock dispensers
- Painting of all the dealer boards/glow signs.

Putting' up of Warning boards at retail outlets.

They also had to make the following modifications in their outdoor advertising:

Market Testing: Tipper, the new micro-segment cigarette was already test marketed in Jammu, Saharanpur, Cuttack and Telengana. The product came upto the expectations of the company and was declared successful. The decision to launch in Kanpur was taken post a successful launch in Eastern Uttar Pradesh & Uttranchal, large numbers of floating smokers from Eastern Uttar Pradesh and excellent market potential of micro-cigarettes in Kanpur where already brands like Capstan Filter, Capstan Star, Capstan Standard, Ace, Panama Regular, etc are well established.

Target-market prospects: Initially, the retailers especially those selling micro-cigarettes were targeted as they were likely to be early adopters and could become heavy users.

Introductory market strategy: The retailers were approached with a box of sweets and then introduced to the company in a positive manner. The retailers were then educated about the benefits of the newly launched micro-cigarette Tipper. The retailer was convinced to keep the brand for the first time and let Tipper be sold through his/her shop. As an introductory offer, the retailers were given an extra pack of cigarette, free of cost, as a trial pack called Bonus so that he could further educate the smokers coming to his/her shop by providing them with a free stick.

LAUNCH OF TIPPER IN KANPUR

Invitation to retailers

GPIL organized three retailer meets in Kanpur city in March 2004 to announce the launch of their new non-filter (micro-segment) cigarette Tipper. Approx. 5000 retailers were invited through the strong sales force of the company.

Changes done in display items by GPIL post ad-ban

Item	Pre ad-ban situation	Post ad-ban situation
Display racks	Consisted of a bracket for 16 and 20 packs of cigarettes with a poster. Poster described the features of the cigarette. Pasted on top and lights on the border.	Poster on top was covered with plain white/green sticker and 5 packs of cigarettes were pasted on that sheet.
Gravity	Consisted of a column wherein 5 packs of cigarettes could be inserted.	No modification was needed as it did not contain any kind of poster.
Bunting:	Consisted of 3 hanging posters surrounded by lights.	The 3 hanging posters were removed and the lights were then handed over to the retailers for their in-shop beautification.
Sampling	Free trial samples were given to people . as well as retailers	Sampling was avoided as per the rules of the ban.
Art Cards	Art cards of different sizes were put on display.	All art cards were removed to avoid penalties.
Big lighters	Lighters having poster of the brand were given to retailers	The poster over the lighter was covered with white/green sheet 1 pack of cigarette was pasted over it.

Retailer Meet

Invitation to retailers in the city was followed by the retailer meet, which was held in three different places stretching over a period of two days. These retailer meets were organized to introduce the new non-filter (micro-segment) cigarette Tipper to the retailers and acted as a relationship building exercise with them. Press conference was also organized to ensure extensive coverage in newspapers.

During the meet GPIL decided to distribute water-cooling bottles to the retailers and organized an orchestra party along with refreshments. Alongside all this fun and frolic, camaraderie was built up wherein they were asked to feel & test the product, which was followed by a contest for retailers to answer the questions asked in context to the product and the company to get their valuable feedback.

Initial Placement

The launch started with a puja, which was performed at Wholesale Distributor's office to generate a sense of belongingness and pride. The following methodology was used for promoting Tipper:

In-shop promotion: The following Point of Sale (POS) material was strategically used during the launch to grab the consumer's attention and to ensure brand awareness and to increase trials through impulse purchase:

- **Thematic posters/ Art-cards** were pasted strategically at shop fronts and at eye level at every outlet so as to make the brand visible right at outlet entry.

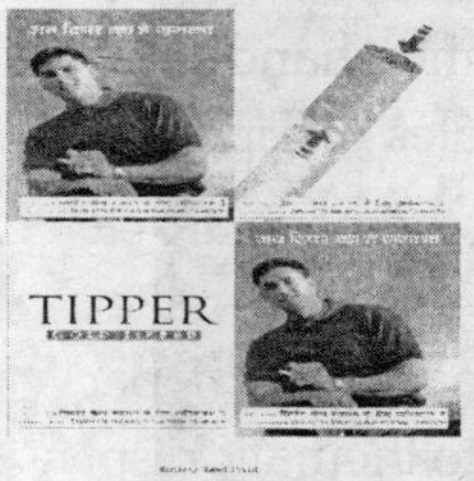

- **Backing sheet** comprised of four equal perforated pieces with one of the parts clearly showing the compact tip, the USP of the brand.

- **Lit racks** with a capacity of 16 cigarette packets were given to selective retail outlets. These racks were strategically positioned in the shop as to make it properly visible to the smokers.

- **Lit buntings** were distributed to several retailers which displays the features of the brand and adds to the visibility in the outlet

SWOT Analysis for Tipper cigarette

Strengths

- *Compact tip due to Double Density Technology.*
- *Enhanced taste due to hardened tobacco Filter*
- *Unspoilt tip of the cigarette, not soggy.*
- *Strong sales and distribution network of GPIL*

Weaknesses

- *Low margins as compared to its competitors like Capstan Star, Capstan Standard, etc.*
- *Low brand awareness, launched just 17 days before the ad-ban*

Opportunities

- *Kanpur -a high potential micro-cigarette market with high growth rates*
- *ITC's brand Capstan Star is slowly phasing out of the market due to low quality*

Threats

- *Major competitor ITC-aggressive and proactive in responding to the market changes*
- *Launch of Tipper may cause cannibalization of Cavanders Magna, cigarette of the same segment, which is strong in Kanpur territory.*
- *Effect of ad-ban esp. on a new brand*

Later Tipper was launched in rural parts of Kanpur (known as outstation sales) in the company accompanied by the same above-mentioned activities. The Initial Placement process continued for the entire month of April 2004 simultaneously with repeat sale and more than 4,000 retail outlets were covered by GPIL where Tipper was successfully placed. GPIL took an extensive merchandising blitz and sales promotion to repeat sales of Tipper:

In-shop promotion: More thematic art-cards, lit buntings and lit racks were used to make the product visible. The lit racks (16-packet & 20- packet capacity) were now converted into thematic displays in which the retailer would get Rs 100 for 45 days only if he maintains the stock of 15 packets of Tipper till the given time period. Other promotional material was also used.

- **Dispensers with Clock** were distributed to the retailers. These dispensers had the capacity of holding five packets of cigarette at a time

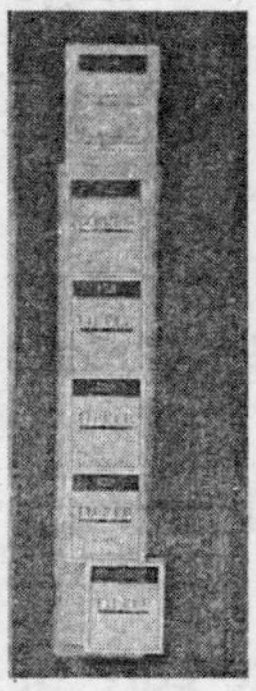

- **Gravity:** These dispensers were very useful in creating the visibility of the brand at outlets, which does not have proper space to place the brand in the shop and are not properly lit. The dispenser had the capacity of holding five packets of cigarette

- **Lit rack** (20 cigarette packets capacity) were given to selective outlets with the understanding that the retailer will have to keep 20 live packets of cigarette along with the strategically placed rack to ensure higher visiblity.

- **Lighter with POP** were distributed as another promotional activity. They used to run on electricity and were available at retailer outlets for the convenience of smokers.

PROMOTIONAL SCHEMES

1. Redemption offer: This scheme provided the retailers to redeem 10 empty packets with a free cigarette packet of Tipper.

2. Plus minus scheme: This scheme offered the retailers 1 matchbox free with every purchase of Tipper and 1 matchbox free on returning 1 empty pack of the cigarette.

COMPETITORS' REACTION TO TIPPER GOLD LAUNCH

1. There was a swift reaction from the major competitor ITC who quickly introduced three schemes on its Capstan Star and Capstan Standard brand of cigarettes. ITC introduced the plus minus scheme on its brand Capstan Star wherein the retailer was offered 2 free packs of the cigarette on purchase of 9 packs. He was also given 1 free pack of the cigarette on returning 10 empty packs. This scheme played a big role in reducing the sale of Tipper and it marked the first attempt by the competitor to save its share in the market. Simultaneously, ITC also introduced a purchase scheme on its brand Capstan Standard wherein the retailer was being given 1 free pack of the cigarette on a purchase of 20 packs. ITC also modified the existing scheme on Capstan Standard to a plus minus scheme from a purchase scheme. The scheme offered the retailer I matchbox on the purchase of every pack of the cigarette. It also offered 2 matchboxes on return of empty packs of the cigarette. This scheme proved to be very beneficial for the retailers and the sale of Tipper was badly affected ITC even increased the retailer's margin, since they were aware of the problem of margin with Tipper.

2. Seeing the launch of Tipper in the Kanpur market, the major competitor, ITC increased the number of its displays in the market and offered display incentive of Rs 60 for 30 days which affected sales of Tipper.

3. With the launch of Tipper, another competitor VST introduced a plus minus scheme on its brand

ACE wherein the retailer would get 1 pack of cigarette free with every purchase and 1 matchbox free on returning 1 empty pack of the cigarette.

Keeping in mind the margin problem of the retailers, a redemption scheme was started wherein the retailer was being offered one pack of Tipper free on returning back 10 empty packs. He could also avail this offer on loose cigarettes. With the introduction of this scheme the margin rose to Re 1 from 50p per pack, due to which the sales also increased.

SALES ANALYSIS POST-LAUNCH

1. In many areas, it was noticed that the sale of Tipper is adversely affecting the sale of GPI's own brand Cavanders Magna. This was due to the fact that the retailers were pushing the brand to all the micro-segment smokers, which included Magna smokers also.

2. In order to tackle the margin problem in Tipper, a scheme of redemption was introduced. But the retailers complained of keeping the empty packs with as a problem. Therefore, a plus minus scheme was introduced wherein matchboxes would be given on purchase as well as redemption.

3. Most of the retailers were not happy with the margin offered before the redemption scheme but were satisfied later on.

4. Since, smokers had their own brand of cigarette in mind while making a purchase due to habit formation, most smokers smoke Capstan Filter followed by Bidi. It was found that a 2 month's old Tipper is not far behind and is quickly catching up to be in the third place.

5. Highest brand switching was found to take place from Capstan Filter cigarette.

6. Most smokers in Kanpur are not aware of Tipper, therefore proper and timely action must be taken in order to increase sales of Tipper. The main source of awareness for people is retailers, that is to say, that most people came to know about the brand through retailers. Awareness spread through the POS material is low in case of Tipper. This means that the effort of putting up the POS Material before the ad-ban was not of much help.

7. Most smokers felt that the pricing of Tipper is right. Usually, Bidi smokers wanted the prices to be less whereas people, who smoke just for style and image, felt that the price should be higher.

8. Most smokers liked the taste of Tipper and quality of tobacco used in Tipper; even the retailers have rated Tipper as a good cigarette.

Questions

1. Assess the success potential of Tipper as launched by GPIL. What makes a cigarette brand endure in the marketplace?
2. What else can GPIL do to establish Tipper as a successful cigarette brand?
3. What are the parallel factors to take care of during the launch of FMCGs.

Notes

Notes

B2B Marketing

Section - Sixteen

CONCEPTUAL FRAMEWORK

To facilitate a better debate on the case in this section, a quick exploratory review of the B2B marketing function along with areas that need discussion are recapitulated briefly as follows:

- Many business-to-business (B2B) marketing executives feel traditional marketing concepts and principles have to be adapted while offering products and services to an organization.
- Business marketers need to be aware of the role of professional purchasers and their influencers, the need for multiple sales calls, and the importance of direct purchasing, reciprocity, and leasing.
- **B2B transactions** tend to be larger, and negotiations occur less frequently, though they are often lengthy. They often involve more than one person or department in the purchasing organization. They may also involve reciprocity, an arrangement in which two organizations agree to buy from each other. Business customers are usually better informed than ultimate consumers and more likely to seek information about a product's features and technical specifications
- The **business markets** consists of all the organizations that acquire goods and services used in the production of other products and services that are sold, rented or supplied to others. **Institutional markets** (schools, hospitals, nursing homes, prisons, etc.) provide goods and services to people in their care. Catering to **Government markets** requires a great deal of paperwork.
- When purchasing products, business customers are particularly concerned about quality, service, and price. Quality is important because it directly affects the quality of products the buyer's firm produces. To achieve an exact level of quality, organizations often buy products on the basis of a set of expressed characteristics, called **specifications** (or specs.).
- As services have such a direct influence on a firm's costs, sales and profits, such matters as market information, on-time delivery, and availability of parts are crucial to business buyer. **Price** is of prime concern because it directly influences profitability.
- Business buyers use several **purchasing methods**, including description, inspection, sampling, and negotiation.
- Most organizational purchasers are new-task, straight rebuy, or modified rebuy. In a **new-task purchase**, an organization makes an initial purchase of items to be used to perform new jobs or to solve new problems. In a **modified rebuy**

purchase, a new-task purchase is changed the second or third time it is ordered or requirements associated with a straight rebuy are modified. A **straight rebuy purchase** occurs when a buyer purchases the same products routinely under approximately the same terms of sale.

- **Industrial demand** can fluctuate widely as it derives from demand for consumer products. At the industry level, industrial demand is relatively inelastic. Some industrial products are subject to joint demand, which occurs when two or more items are used in combinations to make a product.
- Business, or organizational, **buying behavior** refers to the purchase behavior of producers, resellers, government units, and institutions.
- Business purchase decisions are made through a buying center or a group of people involved in making such purchase decisions. **Users** are those in the organization who actually use the product. **Influencers** help develop specifications and evaluate alternative products for possible use. **Buyers** select suppliers and negotiate purchase terms. **Deciders** choose the product. **Gatekeepers** control the flow of information to and among individuals occupying other roles in the buying centre.
- The stages of the **business buying decision process** are as follows:
  - Problem recognition
  - Development of product specifications to solve problems
  - Search for and evaluation of products and suppliers
  - Selection and ordering of the most appropriate product
  - Evaluation of the product's and supplier's performance.
- Four categories of factors influence business buying decisions:
  - **Environmental factors** include political forces, laws and regulations, socio-cultural factors, economic conditions, competitive forces, and technological changes.
  - **Organizational factors** include the company's objectives, purchasing policies, and resources, as well as the size and composition of its buying center.
  - **Interpersonal factors** are the relationships among people in the buying center.
  - **Individual factors** are personal characteristics of members of the buying center, such as age, education, personality, tenure, and position in the organization.

Centaur India - Better Business through Better Customer Satisfaction

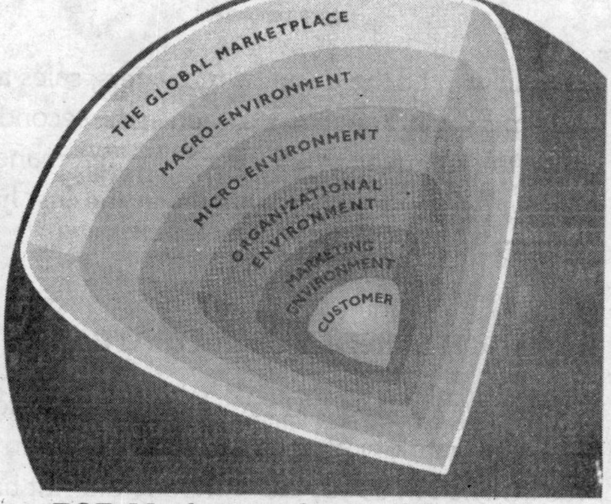

B2B Marketing Case - 28

Purpose of the Case

The idea is to assimilate the relevant concepts at work and analyse along the following lines:

- To discuss how Centaur India can rise above the current dampeners in the customer satisfaction area
- To focus on key strengths in favour of Centaur that a well-orchestrated B2B Marketing effort can derive advantages from

Shriram Jairath has just taken over as the President of the Centaur Elevator Company India Limited (CECIL). With a working experience of around 25 years in the elevator industry he has successfully managed important positions like Director-Sales, Director-Marketing, Head Operations – Delhi, etc. It was a cold January day, circa 2005 and Shriram wore a deep frown on his face. Lying on his table was a recently compiled "Customer Satisfaction Result" for the Quarter 4 (Oct.-Dec.), 2005. Together with the quarterly sales figure, this made for a very poor reading.

The major customers were highly dissatisfied especially on account of logistics, installation, methodology, product reliability and stability specific to Indian conditions. Maintenance services were also a minor contributor. The sales people invariably maintained that in India, elevator consumers were sensitive to price only and hence this product was treated as a commodity. However, surveys indicated that service was also a key factor in the buying decision, along with the supplier's financial terms. At the core of the problem was the human factor, especially in the sales, logistics and service functions. Shriram decided to think deeply about the whole issue since there was an ongoing boom and growth in the construction industry and Centaur could capitalize heavily on it.

He called up his Secretary Ms. Mary and instructed her to fix up a two-day program with all the top brasses and the sales team on January 14, 2006 and January 15, 2006 and to book the conference room at Hotel Park Royal. Ms. Mary booked the conference room and circulated the schedule to all concerned. The meeting was scheduled for 9:00 am on January 14, 2006, for the

This case is intended to be used as a basis for class discussion rather than as an illustration of either effective or ineffective handling of the situation. Authored by Dr. Mukesh Pandey.

first half with all the business managers, sales teams and other department heads, then in the second half, a one-to-one meeting with the Sales Team and day after with the business managers in the first half of January 15, 2006.

CENTAUR'S INDIA EXPLORATIONS

Centaur had a long and rather disjointed history in the Indian market. Although its first elevator in India was installed in 1945, the company did not have a local market presence until it appointed a local distributor to set the ball rolling. Almost 50 years later, Centaur decided it was time to take an even bolder step and enter the market through a wholly owned subsidiary.

THE INDIAN ENTRY PROJECT

In 1996, the company decided to engage Boston Consulting Group (BCG) to identify and evaluate alternative local partners with whom Centaur might build a more significant business in India. However, they found that there was no ideal partner. When it was determined that it was now legally and practically feasible to start up a 100% wholly owned company in India. By year 2000, Centaur India had established itself as a provider of trailblazing solutions in the filed of vertical transportations. Centaur India offered customers the latest models of their world renowned range of products - technologically superior to those currently on offer in the Indian market - at affordable prices and in accordance with customer requirements. In addition to new installations, Centaur also provided full modernization and maintenance services to transform and protect existing vertical transportation, as well as safeguarding owners' investment. With a comprehensive range of services as theirs, they ensured the smooth functioning of these installations throughout their service life of around 30 years.

Note: The names have been changed to protect identity of companies

THE ELEVATOR INDUSTRY

Five companies dominated the worldwide elevator industry in the early 1990s: Polar India, Centaur, Halo, Noisette and Climber. The elevator industry business was traditionally split into two sectors: new equipment and service that accounted for approximately $9 billion and $13 billion in global sales. The traditional separation of product and service had generated interesting competitive dynamics in the elevator industry. Competition for new elevator installations was fierce leading to new elevator equipment often being sold at or below cost by the large competitors. Competition for elevator service contracts, on the other hand, was traditionally more orderly. Equipment suppliers usually had an advantage in winning contracts to service their installed bases. By tacit agreement, elevator companies maintained high margins on annual service contracts that were roughly equal to 5% of the purchase price of an elevator.

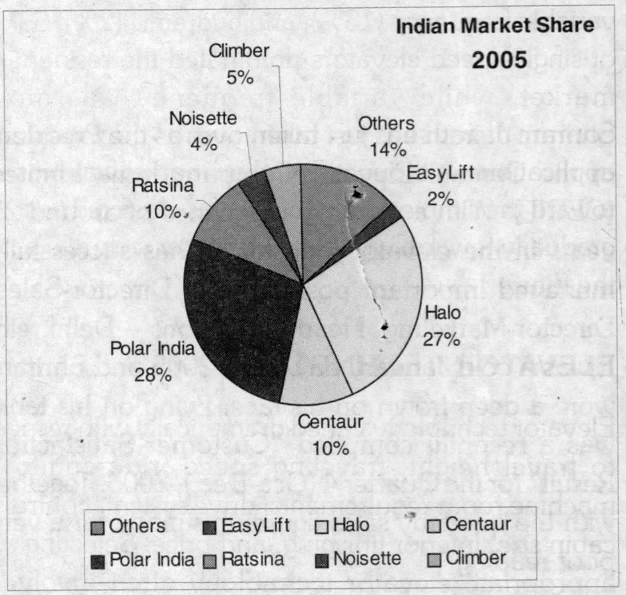

Exhibit - I

Low entry barriers due to the relatively simple electro-mechanical technology, steady demand and high margins in the service market had recently attracted many new competitors. (See Exhibit I for details on Indian Market Share.) These include small, local service-only providers that often enjoy an advantage over the big manufacturers in terms of price, proximity and speed to service, important factors in the award of service contracts. Despite this trend, the large equipment suppliers had continued to do well given that approximately 80% of service contracts still flowed automatically from new equipment sales. However, there was some doubt that this situation would last for very long given the current economic environment.

The demand for elevators and escalators depend upon growth of the construction industry in general and high-rise buildings in particular. The Indian elevator market size is estimated at Rs. 4bn., with an installed base of 45,000 elevators. The current demand is around 15,000 units p.a., which is low even by developing country standards. China has an annual demand of 30,000 units p.a., while South Korea has 15,000. Volume growth in India has however been to the tune of 15% p.a.

In India, most sales were of single-speed elevators (65%), followed by two-speed (20%), variable frequency (13%), and hydraulic (2%). Sales of single-speed elevators dominated the residential market, while variable frequency was most commonly used in higher-end commercial applications. Although the Indian market was biased toward the simplest products, it was expected to shift gradually toward two-speed or higher technology in the future.

ELEVATOR TECHNOLOGY

Elevator technology varied dramatically with respect to travel height, traveling speed, ride comfort, machine room requirements, drive system, controls, cabin size, interior finishing, and price. Selecting an appropriate elevator technology often involved making multiple trade-offs that were all related to the type of drive system used to lift the elevator cabin. Based on their performance characteristics and cost/benefit analysis, hydraulic elevators were suitable only for low-rise applications, gearless elevators for high-rise. Geared traction elevators had the widest application, primarily in mid- and low-rise, but occasionally in high-rise, buildings.

ELEVATOR LIFE CYCLE

The elevator life cycle had seven distinct phases: engineering, production, installation, service, repair, modernization, and replacement. Over the 30-year life cycle of an elevator, the first three stages accounted for about one-third of the labor content but only 20% of the profits. In contrast, the latter four accounted for two-thirds of labor content but 80% of profits. As a result, annual maintenance contracts covering routine maintenance and breakdown service were vital. High-margin spare parts were billed separately. Service response time varied across segments. Most five-star hotels with multiple installations had a technician on call or on-site; for important commercial buildings and hospitals, the response time was usually within two hours, but many residential and some commercial customers reported an average response time of between six to eight hours.

THE ELEVATOR PURCHASING DECISION

The complexity of elevator purchase decisions varies with building type and design. Generally, the taller, costlier and more complex a building, and thus the elevator system, the larger the number of people

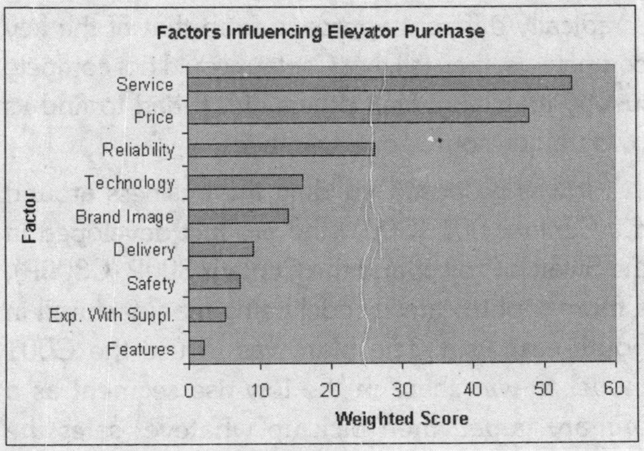

Exhibit - 2

involved in the decision and factors to be considered. Selection of a high-rise commercial building elevator system, for example, might involve the property developer, building owner, construction contractor, architect, elevator consultant, and major tenants.

The factors that influence the purchase of elevators are highlighted in Exhibit 2.

Prioritization of features and properties varied among individual participants, even within a class. Owners' decisions, for example, reflected their post-construction purpose. Owner/developers who intended to sell a building upon completion, tended to be most concerned about up-front costs. Owner / landlords were likely to care more about life-time costs, but, unless they could command a premium from their tenants, they cared little about riding comfort and aesthetics. Owner/ tenants, being involved throughout an elevator's life cycle, usually considered most factors.

A low-rise residential elevator purchase decision might involve from one to as many as five parties in decision making, the latter typically being property owner, construction company manager, architect, construction company purchasing agent, and building service manager.

THE STANDARD PRODUCT STRATEGY

Analysis of the Indian environment concluded that the most effective way for Centaur to enter Indian market would be to focus on a narrow product line of simple, standardized elevators. Although this was a radically different approach from that of the key competitors, they felt that Centaur could not compete just by matching what others did. It had to find its own unique source of advantage.

It was proposed building the business around the Centaur 001 (C001)-the product developed in the Swatch Project-and the Centaur 300P (C300P), a more sophisticated model being manufactured in South-east Asia. The plan was to use the C001 model to win share in the low-rise segment as a primary target, then pick up whatever sales the company could in the mid-rise and high-rise segments with the C300P.

Both products could be adapted to meet Indian requirements with only minor modifications (e.g., adding a ventilator, a fire rescue controller function, a stop button, and different guide rails). Equally important, both products could be priced appropriately, for the local market as long as the company stuck to the principle of no customization. The plan called for Centaur India to sell 50 units in the first year and to win a 20% share of the target segments in five years. It aimed to break even after four years and eventually to generate double-digit margins.

When this strategy was communicated the Management was pleased about the innovative approach of selling the standard line. If the product was standardized, they argued, the sales and service should be differentiated.

THE OUTSOURCING STRATEGY

India's high import duties had forced most foreign elevator companies to manufacture locally. But again, Management chose a different approach. To keep overheads low, the business plan proposed a radical sourcing concept for the C001 that was expected to account for 75% of sales: Centaur India would have no in-house manufacturing, no centralized assembly, no logistics infrastructure. Instead, the production of most components for the dominant C001 model was outsourced to approved local suppliers. As on 2006, the C300P model is planned to be wholly imported from South-east Asia. Centaur would manufacture only safety-related components (the safety gear and speed governor, together representing 10% of the value), which would be imported from Europe. In addition, the entire logistics function was outsourced to an internationally reputed logistics service provider. Some basic installation work-part of the on-site assembly of the drive, controller, car, doors, rails, and counterweight was also outsourced. However, maintenance contracts resulting from new sales would stay with Centaur.

As scheduled, the meeting started on January 14, 2006, 9:00 am at conference room no. 1, with all the members of the organization. President started the meeting with a welcome note and started highlighting the recently received disappointing customer survey results.

Mr. Shriram Jairath – President: Friends I am not at all happy with the customer survey report for this quarter - Q4, 2005. As per the report, there is a sharp decline observed in the customer satisfaction level. And if you look at the new installations curve for the satisfaction level, it is constantly declining. Customers are highly dissatisfied in terms of deliveries, installation time frame and coordination activities. Similarly, higher dissatisfaction level has been observed in the maintenance activities.

After the declaration of survey results, all had lunch together in a very grim mood and proceeded towards the conference rooms for one-to-one discussions with Sales managers who were handling different territories across the country.

Rakesh Kumar – Sales Manager: Sir, we had picked up an order for lifts at Manocha Builders and committed to carry out installation in 90 days. However, our installation team ended with a cycle time of 120 days due to which we lost the client, its next upcoming order as well as the goodwill. We had tried to make amends for the damage but it's been quite an uphill task.

President: Pramod, why did it take you so long to complete the installation?

Pramod Kumar – Manager Installations: Sir, we received the information about the project, when 30 days were left, at the time of arrival of material at site. Also, there was a delay from the customer's end in providing the power supply. I also requested Rakesh to intervene. In fact, because of this my guys were without work for at least a week.

President: Rakesh, you have to seriously look into the matter, we cannot afford to lose customers like Manocha Builders. They have given us good business last year and they are very committed towards the growth of Centaur. Rakesh, fix up a meeting with Mr. Manocha, next week, with Mr Ranganathan. Rangathan, please see him personally and try to convince them.

Deepak Sharma–Sales Manager: Sir, Mr. Praveen Soni of M/s. Ragnik Exports wanted to install 2 elevators at his new office building in Gurgaon. He was very well aware of Centaur and its product quality. He was looking at Centaur as the most preferred supplier. Everything had been finalized even advance cheques were signed and suddenly he started insisting on center opening doors, I tried to convince him with the advantages of Telescopic Doors but he was adamant and we lost the order to Polar India because of this small feature. This is not the only case where we have lost the order because of telescopic doors. Now the trend is changing especially in the commercial buildings. Clients nowadays are asking for center opening doors because they are earning money by putting advertisements on it.

President: We are in the process of testing new products at our test tower. The kind of model with the center opening will take another 3-4 years for its launch, till that time you guys have to bear with the circumstances.

Ankush Jain – Sales Manager: Sir, we had picked up a bulk order of 50 lifts from a building society in Dwarka. The lifts were delivered on time and installed on time. The LOP buttons are constantly giving problems. Also, the cost of maintenance was so high that the society was not in the position to afford it. The client is planning to award the contract to some local contractor at a lower price. They are coming up with new society in Gurgaon, if we do not take any action now, we will end up losing order for those 100 lifts also.

President: Prabhakar, can you check and revert with the actual causes? If we keep losing business like this, very soon we will have to wind up.

Prabhakar – Manager Maintenance: Sir, I am aware of this issue and we are working on it. Actually, the problem is of the awareness of usage. The LOP buttons installed are the imported button with the plastic top and in India we keep on pressing the button till the time lift comes to the floor. Our Engineering department is working on the possibilities to change the plastic buttons with the steel buttons that we use in C001. We have planned to replace the current ones with the steel buttons free of cost.

President: What about the high maintenance cost? Why the hell is our maintenance cost higher than others. Have you done any comparison with the maintenance costs of other companies?

Prabhakar: Sir, we are actually charging the maintenance cost at 4% instead of the current 6% which is a good price according to that area. Actually, the society is facing some funds problem and is looking for a cheaper source of maintenance.

President: Ankush Jain, try to fix up the maintenance price for first few years in consultation with the Maintenance team for the new project. I want that order.

Sachin Shukla–Sales Manager: Sir, Centaur picked up an order for high-speed elevators in stainless steel from Everest Transmission Pvt. Ltd. To match the low purchase price, we ordered the elevators from China. When the material arrived at site the client found it not to be of the quality, which he had seen and approved. We underwent a lot of troubles to get our payment released. The same company came up with another mall in the vicinity, with a requirement of 20 escalators, and did not invite us to participate in the tender.

President: But, I don't see any difference in a Chinese and Swiss product. The quality control department is there at both the places and they are maintaining the standards. Take the help of Engineering department and get the client convinced that our product is of superior quality, and again take them into confidence.

Vineet Nair – Sales Manager: Sir, let us take the case of Krishi Bhawan. Tenders were lost to M/s. Thyssen elevators as our price was Rs. 14.50 lacs, and their price was Rs. 11 lacs only. The elevators were of the same specification and quality. Price is the main reason why we lost. M/s. Thyssen managed to get the order because it mostly operates in Govt. Departments. They initially charge less for the elevators but gain the margins with high Annual Maintenance Charges, as no other company can maintain another company's equipment.

President: You are aware of our code of conduct. We have to abide by them. We want to do business, but a fair business. Try to convince the customer on the basis of our superior quality, services and safety features of our products.

Subodh Sharma – Sales Manager: Sir, at Centre Stage Mall in Noida, firstly, the delivery was late, then the installation got delayed, as we were not geared to handle such a big project with 14 escalators and 20 elevators. Breakdowns were high because of the involvement of local solutions for short shipments. Annual Maintenance Charges agreed as per the contract was Rs. 60 lacs for 10 years. Now, since there was no mention of Comprehensive / Standard / Oil and Grease, we manipulated the situation, and offered only Oil and Grease at that amount, the client being left with no option than to shell out extra money. As such, we lost the order to A. B. Movies, Lucknow (14 Escalators 26 elevators) and also for Centre Stage Mall's other new upcoming projects in Ludhiana and Chandigarh.

President: I see from the report in my hand that there are still Rs 32 lacs due with them, which they are not clearing. Try to extract those dues. If they are not ready to clear the dues by this month end send them the notice through company lawyer. We cannot afford such a huge loss on that small project. I am aware about the delays and also aware that we worked in double shifts to complete the project and managed to complete the installations before the inauguration of mall.

Manit Ahuja - Sales Manager: At Delhi Metro Rail Corporation, some company or the other always offered a price lower than ours, as we always quoted the rates of offers from Switzerland and the competitors quoted for material from China. Although we tried to convince DMRC to the best extent possible that the Chinese factory cannot meet the specifications of DMRC and neither can they match the quality standards of Switzerland but the end result was a loss of order worth Rs. 250 crore till date, and it seems it will continue till such time we do not come up with a solution.

President: As I said earlier also, we are in the process of testing the new equipments at our test tower and it is sure to come up with the products suitable to the specifications of DMRC.

Mayank Shukla – Sales Manager: The case of AFNHB is in reference to the deliberate assault on our engineers, at site on August 6, 2003. A dog, owned by a resident of the complex, residing in M block, was deliberately set upon our service personnel who were replacing the parts of the lift doors damaged by the users in M Block. One of service technician people jumped into the lift pit and managed to close the door. The other person ran to another building and the dog chased him. In another incident, one person threatened our technician by placing a gun on his head and made him climb up and down the building. This has all happened because of poor and unduly maintenance services.

President: Please write a letter to the President of the society, with a copy to the local police commissioner office and file an FIR against those people. Stop the services with immediate effect till the time no positive response came from the society. I cannot take risk with the life of my people.

Finally The President showed on a LCD projector his accumulated findings. Exhibit 3 shows the findings put forth by him of various factors contributing to the loss of Centaur India's market share. It clearly shows that how poor quality of maintenance and inefficient delivery system has resulted in loss of major market share and business worth crores of rupees.

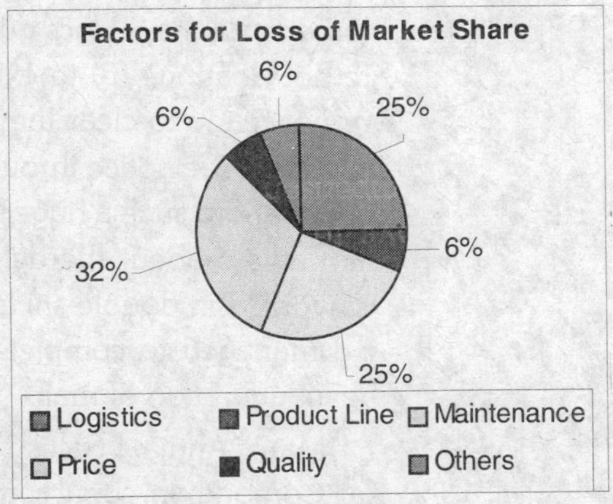

Exhibit - 3

After the meeting was over , Jairath was very upset. Having looked at the disappointing survey reports and subsequent discussions with the sales, installation and maintenance teams, it seemed that he had lots to chew on. He knew if he had to keep pace with the present dynamic environment, he had to ensure his people inculcated a service attitude, he was worried how should they nurture relationships with their esteemed clients as well as ensure timely delivery of equipment and availability of spares. The market was growing at the pace of 20% plus every year and he was worried that Centaur may miss the bus despite having a well-manufactured quality product.

Question

1. How do you think Centaur India Pvt. Ltd. can not only prevent loss of business to competitors and in fact, can become the *numero-uno* player in the Indian elevator industry?

Notes

Internet Marketing

Section - Seventeen

CONCEPTUAL FRAMEWORK

To facilitate a better debate on the case in this section, a quick exploratory review of the internet marketing function along with areas that need discussion are recapitulated briefly as follows::

- The internet technology has changed the dimensions of marketing and hence it has given rise to more dynamic regime of marketing.
- Brand recognition is likely to become increasingly important in the marketing of services online.
- Due to its **interactive** nature, the Internet can be used to inform, entertain, and persuade target markets to accept an organization's products. The accessibility of the Internet gives marketers an opportunity to expand and complement their traditional media promotional efforts.
- The Internet gives consumers **access to more information** about the costs and prices of products than has ever been available before. Marketers can use the Internet to facilitate both price and non-price competition.
- Electronic commerce (**e-commerce**) refers to sharing business information, maintaining business relationships and conducting business transactions by means of telecommunications networks.
- **Internet marketing** (**e-marketing**) is the strategic process of creating, distributing, promoting, and pricing products for targeted customers in the virtual environment of the Internet.
- The Internet has changed the way marketers communicate and develop relationships with their customers, employees, and suppliers. Telecommunications technology offers marketers potential advantages such as
  - rapid response
  - expanded customer service capability
  - reduced operating costs, and
  - reduced geographic barriers.
- Despite these benefits, many Internet companies have failed because they did not realize Internet markets are more similar to traditional markets than they are different and thus require the same marketing principles.
- **Addressability** is a marketer's ability to identify customers before they make a purchase. One way websites achieve addressability is through cookies, identifying strings of text placed on a visitor's computer.
- **Interactivity** allows customers to express their needs and wants directly to the firm in response to the firm's marketing communications. It also enables marketers to capitalize on the concept of

community to help customers derive value from the use of firm's products and websites.

- **Memory** refers to a firm's ability to access databases or data warehouses containing individual customer profiles and past purchase histories and to use these data in real-time to customize their marketing offer to specific customers.
- **Control** refers to customer's ability to regulate the information they view as well as the rate and sequence of their exposure to that information. Control is possible largely because of hypertext, which allows users to jump from one point in a website to another or to other websites.
- **Accessibility** refers to customers' ability to obtain information available on the Internet. This is enhanced by the recognition value of a firm's Uniform Resource Locator (URL), or website address.
- **Digitalization** is the representation of a product, or at least some of its benefits, as digital bits or information.
- The addressability, interactivity, and memory characteristics of e-marketing enable a marketer to identify specific customers, establish interactive dialogs with them to learn their needs, and combine this information with their purchase histories to customize products to meet their needs. Thus e-marketers can focus on building customer loyalty and retaining customers.
- E-marketing involves **business-to-business (B2B)**, **business-to-customers (B2C)**, and **consumer-to-consumer (C2C)** dimensions.
- The ability to process orders electronically and to increase the speed of communications via the Internet reduces inefficiencies, costs, and redundancies throughout the marketing channel. It also speeds up delivery time and improves customer service.
- More firms are exploiting advances in information technology to synchronize the relationships between their manufacturing or product assembly and their customer-contact operations. This increase in information sharing among various operations of the firm facilitates **product customization**.
- The use of **extranets** has facilitated co-ordination of physical distribution of products, order processing, and inventory management activities. The Internet is increasingly becoming a retail venue.
- The characteristics of e-marketing make promotional efforts on the Internet significantly different than those using more traditional media. Advertising and publicity are probably the most visible promotion mix elements on the World Wide Web.
- Advertising most often occurs in the form of banner ads, keyword ads, button ads, pop-up and pop-under ads and sponsorship ads. Companies are also using the Internet to facilitate personal selling and sales promotion activities.
- The Internet has evolved so rapidly that numerous new legal and ethical concerns have emerged. One of the most controversial issues is personal privacy, specially the personal information companies collect from website visitors.
- More issues are likely to emerge as the Internet and e-marketing continue to evolve.

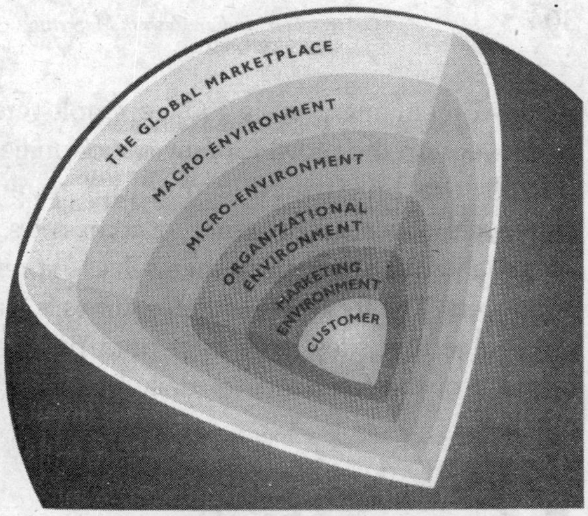

Naukri.com

Challenges and Opportunities

Internet Marketing Case - 29

Purpose of the Case

The idea is to assimilate the relevant concepts at work and analyse along the following lines:

- To discuss how naukri.com created a successful business model based on thorough understanding of needs of job seekers & recruiters.
- To focus on the most-sought-after features necessary in an e-commerce site for its successful marketing
- To debate whether naukri.com will be able to retain its leadership position over a long term

Till the end of last century, job hunters used to wait the whole week for the weekly supplements with various newspapers or sundry employment journals and gazettes to learn about the vacancies and job openings in their respective industries. Recruitment industry in India went by the maxim that "If it's Friday, it must be Employment News or If it's Saturday, it must be UPSC." Friday was the day the government's weekly magazine of job advertisements, *Rozgaar Samachar* in Hindi as well as avatars in various other languages including English hit the newsstands nationwide. One could witness long queues of job seekers lined up early at one's neighbourhood kiosk; in a small town one went to the railway station and picked up a copy from the platform bookstall as soon as the parcel office delivered the copies. And for those whose job search extended to the private sector, there were special days when different dailies came out with their `opportunities' pages. Those who went through their job-hunting phase in the decades 1970s to 1990s, will need no further explanation. Well guys, then came the Internet and threatened to push the days of white envelopes into oblivion.

A job portal is essentially a medium, which helps bring employers and job seekers together. In this respect, the success of any job portal is measured by how effectively it is able to accomplish the task of matchmaking and the satisfaction that it is able to provide its customers. The other measures of effectiveness can be the number of people recruited through the portal, cost –benefit while recruiting at various levels, the number of resumes in the database and the number of page views.

For job-portals, the value-proposition is to provide 24x7 access to jobs for a job seeker and the reduced recruitment cycle for the employers. For employees on the prowl for new opportunities, job portals are an attractive medium to enable employers to locate them, while for companies, these sites enable them to position themselves as preferred employers. The freshness of the resumes is a major advantage that sites have over print publications because of the frequency of daily uploads that is possible.

naukri.com
India's No.1 Job Site

It is a natural transition from traditional recruitment to technology-enabled solutions that simplify the recruitment process since employees have been increasingly frequenting job search sites for newer employment avenues. Today websites offer users exhaustive job search options as well as through SMSs on mobiles at the same time organizing regular job fairs to ensure an ideal mix of online and offline options for job-seekers. Though their core offering is still online, the job portals do conduct offline promotions like having strategic tie-up with newspapers, conduct and participate in job fairs

The trend to outsource technology jobs to India is creating a more tech-savvy populace and has propelled many laborers into jobs with higher education requirements and greater skills. Since innovation is driving things, the low-end worker will continue to be contracted out. Though outsourcing represents just the beginning for India's tech market studies reveal that more service and product companies will follow it.

Recent increase in the number of job sites could well be a sign of India rapidly moving to the next level of maturity. Fuelled by a rising internet penetration and 5.06 mn users i.e around 4.5 % of the population of India, (see Exhibit 1) e-recruitment is gaining ground as a preferred medium of seeking jobs and hiring in India.

Year	Users	Population	% Pen.	Usage Source
1998	1,400,000	1,094,870,677	0.1 %	ITU
1999	2,800,000	1,094,870,677	0.3 %	ITU
2000	5,500,000	1,094,870,677	0.5 %	ITU
2001	7,000,000	1,094,870,677	0.7 %	ITU
2002	16,500,000	1,094,870,677	1.6 %	ITU
2003	22,500,000	1,094,870,677	2.1 %	ITU
2004	39,200,000	1,094,870,677	3.6 %	C.I. Almanac
2005	50,600,000	1,112,225,812	4.5 %	C.I. Almanac

Source: www.internetworldstats.com

Exhibit 1: **Internet Usage and Population Statistics in India**

According to a recent survey by Juxt Consultant, an online research and advisory organization, job search is the 7th most popular reason for Indians to be online (see Exhibit 2). Other triggers of the surge in the number of users include the falling cost of broadband, a rising demand for e-commerce, a record growth in internet adoptions and the availability of computers at sub-Rs 10,000 levels. It is important to note that online recruitment is dependent on computer literacy and Internet penetration and as of now these portals are known amongst those having email accounts.

Early adopters of online recruitment continue to reap benefits of a medium that is 60-80% cheaper than traditional methods; other sectors are also waking up to the advantages of easy availability of a dwelling skill-set. Even placement agencies are relying heavily on this medium to meet their demand.

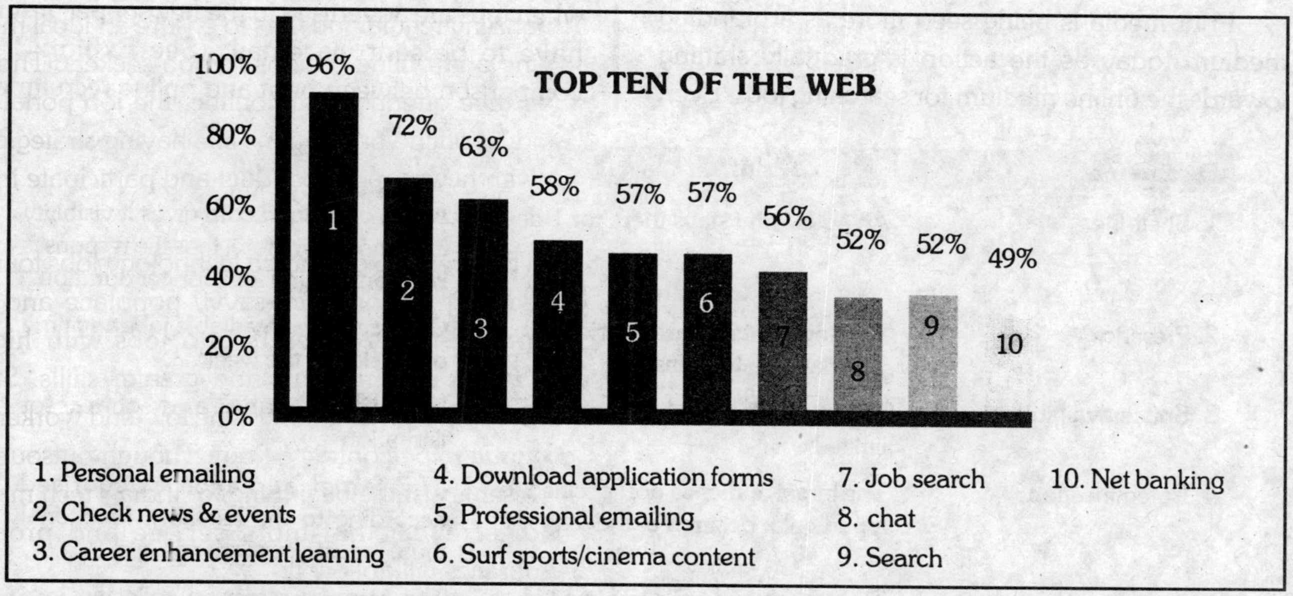

Source: juxt consult, online research and advisory
http://www.juxtconsult.com/press_room/press_release/indians_net.asp

Exhibit 2: **Reasons why Indians log on to the internet**

Not long ago, job portals received the bulk of their business from the IT sector. In recent times, however, the dependence of e-recruitment companies on the IT sector is falling. With increasing employee attrition, now companies in the fast moving consumer goods (FMCG) sector, telecom, pharma, automotive companies, banking and financial services have begun to move on to e-recruitments to widen the base of respondents and simultaneously save on costs. Lots of manufacturing companies like Flex Industries, LG Electronics, Goldstar Enterprises, Havell's, Ashok Leyland and others have been following suit. Lots of leading job portals, as such, expect financial services and insurance sector, retail, airlines and manufacturing to be the largest employers apart from the IT and ITeS sectors in the post-2006 era.

The overall recruitment market In India including the cost of paper advertisements, consultant fees and others is estimated to be around Rs1, 300 crore. The online recruitment industry is around Rs150 crore and is growing by at least 50 per cent and industry estimates that the growth rate will remain the same for the next five years. (Source: Job sites in overdrive, www.domain-b.com, 31 March 2006 report)

Online recruitment is now witnessing some spillover with the demand for top-level executives as well. Till three years ago, this medium was looked at only for and by junior-level employees, freshers and middle-level management. But now, even company Vice-Presidents are being hired through this route though, the numbers are rather small. Also, replacement hiring is giving way to fresh hiring using this medium.

Now, in the internet era, platforms are made for direct people-to-people interaction. Both job seekers and human resource hunters have taken with enthusiasm to the new online resources for matching with the right person with the right kind of a vocation and vacancy. In India the major online jobsites claim to display between 40,000 and 60,000 jobs at any given time and report anywhere between 20 million to 60 million page views in a month. More than 10 lakh job seekers have registered with various job sites. Most job sites offer a complete service, formulating the job requirement, posting it online, collating the results. These sites have also started making it easier to shortlist the aspirants for an interview.

Print media is being seen more as a branding medium today as the action is gradually shifting towards the online medium for searching jobs. Even when jobs are advertised in the newspaper, resumes have to be sent via email. (See Exhibit 3, for comparison between print and online recruitment)

Parameter	Print	Naukri.com
1. Shelf-life	An ad in print stays there for 1 day	An ad on Naukri.com gives it visibility for 1 month or more, thus the responses keep on coming for a longer duration.
2. Presence	Employment ads are restricted to a Tuesday or a Wednesday	Can access the available jobs any time of the day or the week
3. Space available	Space available for the posting is limited	Unlimited space and character limitation
4. Categorisation	The target audience not specified for a particular position or industry	The target audience categorised according to the location, functional area, industry, experience, etc.
5. Response management	The responses come in e mail id or physical address, thus making it a hard work for the HR person to sort through the large number of the applications against different positions.	The responses can be collected in a software called eApps, that sorts the responses against the different positions. Search functions and filters are also present to avoid the junk.
6. Branding	You can speak as much about the company that the character limitation or the space allocated allows	According to the solutions subscribed to, Naukri.com can give branding at various levels starting from the logo on the job and a descriptive company profile to designing an entire microsite for the company that can be linked to the website of the company.
7. Price	1 Day presence in the newspaper can be a costly affair	At the same price, Naukri.com can offer a longer duration and a higher branding product
8. Reach	It has regional reach	The site has national reach thus giving the company also an access to the quality talent in remote areas at no additional cost
9. Lead time	It is a week long activity prior to the release of an ad in the print, thus wasting that much time in fulfilling the urgent requirements	It takes 45 minutes for the responses to start trickling in, once a position has been opened.

Source: naukri.com office

Exhibit 3: **Comparison - Print vs Online recruitment**

Sanjeev Bikhchandani, co-founder and CEO, InfoEdge India, better known by his web site naukri.com, encashed on this idea of job hunting on internet and has today created business worth Rs 45 crore with 600 employees and 35 offices all over the country. The idea for naukri.com came to Bikhchandani while he was working with GlaxoSmithkline and also part time as Consulting editor of "Avenues" - the careers supplement of *The Pioneer* after obtaining his graduate degree in Economics from St Stephens's and PGDM from IIM-Ahmedabad. While with GlaxoSmithKline (then called HMM), Sanjeev noticed that marketing executives, who used to sit in an open hall, would take the copy of *Business India* and read the 'appointments' section first. This observation stayed with him and he figured that even if one is not looking for a job, he will still look at a job. Jobs, he realised, are extremely high interest information category for almost everybody.

It was on his visit to IT Asia Expo in Pragati Maidan in Delhi in October 1996 that he became aware of the World Wide Web. The naukri.com site was set up in March 1997 as a division of InfoEdge. What was interesting was that he could not get any of the domain names he wanted (all such names which had the word job were already registered) and had to settle down with the Hindi term "naukri", which actually makes it sound different leading to high recall vis-a-vis other jobsites. During the first half of the day, Bikhchandani used to work for his website naukri.com, at *The Pioneer* during the day and then get back to naukri.com in the evening.

Since then a lot has changed. As we all are aware that naukri.com is India's number 1 and largest job site till date, its statistics/figures speak of its success — serving 2,000 clients, with 84,000 job listings and 5.5 million registered users. Naukri.com is a forerunner in ushering the change in the way we look at job hunting today. Today, it is regarded as one of the most resourceful destinations for job hunters – be it a seasoned professional or a fresher who has just got his/her bachelor's degree.

Today naukri.com offices exist all over the country viz. Noida (Head Office), Ahmedabad, Aurangabad, Bangalore, Baroda, Bhopal, Bhubaneswar, Chennai, Chandigarh, Coimbatore, Delhi/NCR, Connaught Place Delhi/NCR, Pitampura Delhi/NCR, Gurgaon, Hyderabad, Hosur, Indore, Jaipur, Jamshedpur, Kochi, Kolkata, Lucknow, Ludhiana, Mumbai, Mumbai, (Vashi), Nagpur, Pune, Surat, Trivandrum and Visakhapatnam, Naukri.com also has an international presence with its offices in Africa, USA, Dubai, Middle East and South East Asia.

Naukri.com as a job portal has a 48% market share making it the number one job site in India. *(see Exhibit 4)*, it is well ahead its nearest competitor

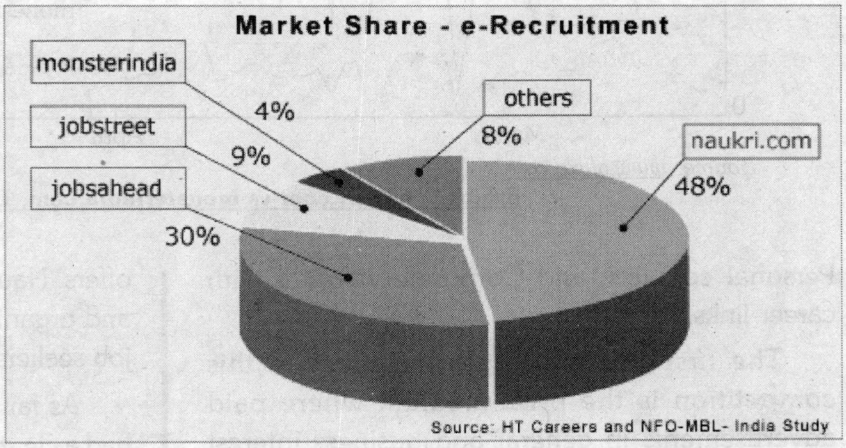

Exhibit 4: **Market share-naukri.com vs other job sites**

monsterindia.com *(see Exhibit 5)*. Giving competition to job websites are India's major IT companies like Infosys, Genpact, Wipro, TCS. Industries from other sectors like Reliance, HLL, etc. have a link to careers in their organizations which does the needful for their respective companies.

Naukri.com, India's number 1 job site had a direct competition from other job sites, as well as an in direct competition from alternate ways of recruitment like Print Media (TOI, HT, and *Employment News*), Placement and HR consultants,

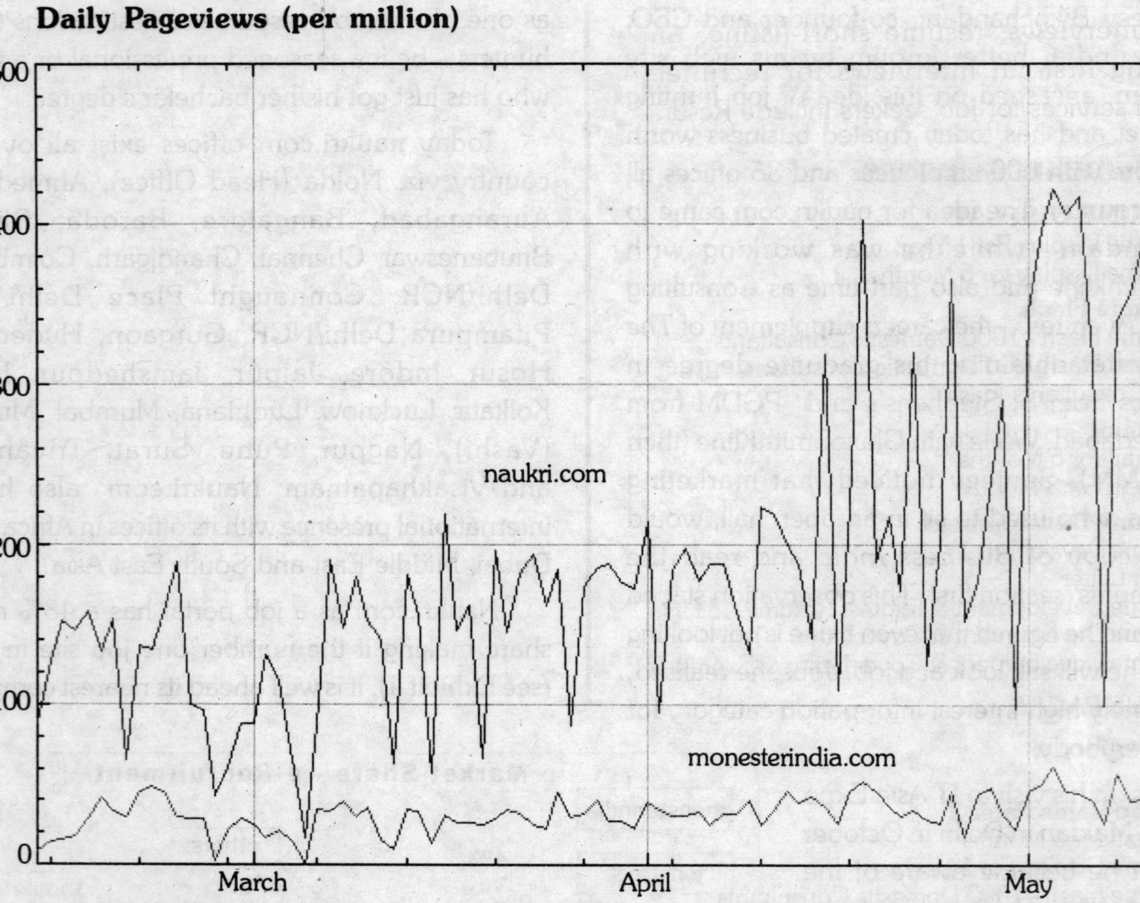

Source: www.alexa.com

Exhibit 5: **naukri.com vs monsterindia.com, Daily Page views**

Personal contacts, and Corporate websites with career links.

The first and the largest category in this competition is the print medium where paid advertisements in general and business interest newspapers and magazines dominate. Newspapers such as *The Times of India* and *Hindustan Times* have an employment supplement on the weekdays. At the low end and for government-related jobs are outlets like *Employment News* and local language newspapers. Also in this category are trade magazines like *Data Quest*, *Business India* that carry sector- specific advertisements.

Naukri.com offers end-to-end recruitment services. Bringing together job seekers and recruiters at a single platform, it allows job seekers to post their resumes for free at the same time taking a subscription fee from recruiters to post their job offers. Naukri.com thus creates value for customers and organizations by connecting people to people, job seekers to job recruiters.

As far as pricing is concerned, naukri.com has had a clear revenue model since its inception. While it has selected few services that are free to both job seekers and job providers, recruiters pay for the majority of its services. The company has three paid services – *Job Posting Services, Response Management Software* (e-application through which recruiters can manage response collected through advertised vacancies and reduce the time spent on handling applications by over 80 per cent), and *Resume Database Product or RESDEX* through which it grants access to its registered CVs to Corporate clients and Placement agencies (see Annexure I on Offerings from naukri.com). The company also offers services such as organizing walk-in interviews, resume short-listing, and conducting first-cut interviews for recruiters. Additional services for job seekers include Resume Development, Resume Splash and Job Alert, etc. Pricing structures for these services are given in Exhibits 6 and 7.

INDIVIDUALS SERVICES	**US $**	**Rate in Rs.**
RESUME DISPLAY		
Resume Display For 1 Year.	35.00	800.00
Resume Display for 6 Months	30.00	700.00
Resume Flash		
Resume Flash - 1000 Domestic Consultants	40.00	900.00
Resume Flash- 800 Domestic Consultants	35.00	800.00
Gulf Consultants-Flash	35.00	550.00
Job mail		
Jobmail for 6 Months	35.00	800.00
Jobmail For 3 Months	25.00	600.00
Resume Development		
Resume Development	50.00	1400.00
Cover Letter	15.00	325.00
Resume Development & Express Resume-48 Hrs.	60.00	1650.00
Resume Development & Cover letter	60.00	1650.00
Resume Development & Cover Letter & Express Resume	70.00	1900.00

VALUE PACKS

Services	**Actual Price**	**Value Pack Price**	**Saving Price**	**Price in US $**
Jumbo Value Pack-2	3900	2850.00	1050	95.00
Jobmail for 6 Months				
Resume Display For 1 Year.				
Resume Flash - 1000 Domestic Consultants				
Resume Development				
Jumbo Value Pack-1 with Resume Display Service	3100	2200.00	900	75.00
Resume Display For 1 Year.				
Resume Flash - 1000 Domestic Consultants				
Resume Development				
Jumbo Value Pack-1 with 6 Month Jobmail Service	3100	2200.00	900	75.00
Jobmail for 6 Months				
Resume Flash - 1000 Domestic Consultants				
Resume Development				
Jumbo Value Pack-3	4400	3350.00	1050	110.00
Jobmail for 6 Months				
Resume Display For 1 Year.				
Resume Flash - 1000 Domestic Consultants				
Resume Development & Cover Letter & Express Resume				
Mini Economic Pack -1	1700	1400.00	300	55.00
Resume Display For 1 Year.				
Resume Flash - 1000 Domestic Consultants				
Mini Economic Pack-2	2400	1800.00	600	65.00
Jobmail for 6 Months				
Resume Display For 1 Year.				
Resume Flash- 800 Domestic Consultants				
Value Pack	2900	2000.00	900	65.00
Resume Display for 6 Months				
Resume Flash- 800 Domestic Consultants				
Resume Development				

Exhibit 6: **Pricing structure for job seekers**

Product	Rate in Rs.	Rate in US $
Vacancy Listings - Hot Vacancies and Classified		
Classified Single Listing	620.00	35.00
Classified Annual Subscription (Upto 1000 Job Postings)	14,030.00	450.00
Hot Vacancies Single Listing	1,685.00	50.00
Pack of 5 Hot Vacancies	8,420.00	200.00
Pack of 10 Hot Vacancies	15,715.00	370.00
Pack of 15 Hot Vacancies	23,630.00	550.00
Hot Vacancies - 3 month subscription (Upto 1250 Job Postings)	28,060.00	650.00
Hot Vacancies - 6 month subscription (Upto 2500 Job Postings)	50,510.00	1,150.00
Hot Vacancies - 1 year subscription (Upto 5000 Job Postings)	84,180.00	1,850.00
Resume Database Access (RESDEX)		
1 Month RESDEX Subscription	22,450.00	500.00
3 months RESDEX Subscription	50,510.00	1,125.00
6 months RESDEX Subscription	89,795.00	2,000.00
1 year RESDEX Subscription	168,360.00	3,750.00
High visibility vacancy listing - Job Gallery (Hot Vacancies + Microsite)		
Vacancy Listings - Job Gallery-1 Month Subscription (Upto 500 Job)	28,060.00	650.00
Vacancy Listings - Job Gallery-3 Month Subscription (Upto 1250 Job Postings)	78,570.00	1,700.00
Vacancy Listings - Job Gallery-6 Month Subscription (Upto 2500 Job Postings)	145,915.00	3,200.00
Vacancy Listings - Job Gallery-1 Year Subscription (Upto 5000 Job Postings)	280,600.00	6,000.00
Premium Vacancy Listings - Best Places to Work		
Vacancy Listings - Best Places to Work-1 month subscription (500 Job Postings)	67,345.00	1,500.00
Vacancy Listings - Best Places to Work-3 month subscription (1250 Job Postings)	168,360.00	3,750.00
Vacancy Listings - Best Places to Work-6 month subscription (2500 Job Postings)	308,660.00	6,700.00
Vacancy Listings - Best Places to Work-1 year subscription (5000 Job Postings)	589,260.00	13,000.00
Response Management Solutions - Hot Vacancy with eApps Pro		
Hot Vacancy with eApps Pro - 1 listing	4,490.00	100.00
Hot Vacancies with eApps Pro-Quarterly Subscription (Upto 1250 Job Postings)	42,655.00	950.00
Hot Vacancies with eApps Pro-Half Yearly Subscription (Upto 2500 Job Postings)	78,570.00	1,800.00
Pack of 5 Hot Vacancies with eApps Pro	16,840.00	400.00
Pack of 10 Hot Vacancies with eApps Pro	28,060.00	650.00
Pack of 15 Hot Vacancies with eApps Pro	39,285.00	900.00
Hot Vacancies with eApps Pro-Annual Subscription (Upto 5000 Job Postings)	145,915.00	3,250.00
Hot Vacancy Postings with eApps Basic		
Hot Vacancies with eApps Basic-Half Yearly Subscription (2500 Job Postings)	61,735.00	1,400.00
Hot Vacancies with eApps Basic-Annual Subscription (Upto 5000 Job Postings)	106,630.00	2,375.00
Featured Companies		
Featured Company - 1 week visibility	16,840.00	370.00
Featured Company - 2 weeks visibility	28,060.00	620.00
Featured Company - 1 month visibility	39,285.00	870.00
Featured Company - 3 months visibility	95,405.00	2,200.00
Featured Company - 6 months visibility	168,360.00	3,700.00
Featured Company - 1 Year visibility	308,660.00	6,800.00

Exhibit 7: **Pricing structure for recruiters**

Naukri.com calls its advertising and promotional strategy "a low-cost guerrilla brand building" plan. The company has never had huge advertising budgets that many other online ventures had. Instead, it used PR, viral marketing, events, and to some extent press and TV to build its brand. Alliances with media partners like HT Careers, Headstart, *Deccan Chronicle*, *Business Today* and *The Tribune* have also given it a lot of visibility in the past. Currently, the company has alliances with *The Telegraph*, *Linux for You*, *The Himalayan Times* (Nepal) and *New Indian Express*. Naukri.com in association with CNBC TV18 also launched India's first ever Job Show, live on TV which was watched by billions of people around the world. Interestingly, of all job portals, today only naukri.com spends money on television commercials while others advertise online and in the print media.

Naukri.com will always have the first mover advantage, but to sustain and increase its clients it needs to shift more and more job recruiters from print media to an online media, and even when they do so, it has to ensure that they come to naukri.com and not to other job sites. However, it is important to note that switching over to online recruitment is not like surfing the net as online recruitment requires dealing with large volumes of applications, choices are many and so it is critical to have necessary tools to identify the right kind of candidates. Also, a better understanding of what the candidate intends to communicate is needed.

Also the success of any portal depends upon the number of visitors. As of now naukri.com is number one, but how does it maintain its position when the world leader in job portals like monster.com has started off with aggressive advertising campaigns needs to be seen.

For online recruitment to be effective, it is important that the top management should be committed to this method of recruitment and ensures dedicated resource to use this medium. Similarly, it should devote enough time and energy to design the advertisement for the advertised positions. In order to derive the full benefit companies should put all its positions online and decide to be committed to long term. How does naukri.com convince print media job advertisers to this will be an important factor in determining the profitability of the portal.

There is quite a possibility of leading job consultants starting their online portals soon. As such, job sites do consider recruitment consultants entering this space as a threat. Despite the fact that whereas the portal business is transaction-based, a consultancy is more relationship-based and as such both require different skill sets. The prospect of newspaper groups launching job sites that is in fact an even bigger a threat, since online sites eat into the ad revenues of newspapers. Except for *The Times of India* group, no other news organisation has launched a job site. It is important for naukri.com to remember that this business is essentially a media business, and therefore it is best done by a media company. In fact, reach is a constraint for most players in the business. The site leverages The Times group's resources like the print, Internet, television, and the radio. Consequently, within just two years of its launch, Timesjobs.com has emerged as one of the leading jobs portal in the country.

With phenomenal growth potential, foreign portals like Monster.com are coming to India. Lots of industry watchers predict a shake-up in the industry and believe only serious players will survive the onslaught. The other interesting possibility is the emergence of regional language job portals; for example, in Malaysia, even drivers are recruited online.

Naukri has also started a new online venture for the Gulf , Naukri Gulf. The site will assist recruiters and jobseekers in the Middle East region targetting jobs in Bahrain, Kuwait, Oman, Qatar, Saudi Arabia, UAE and other countries in the region. Present in all major Indian cities now, even Timesjobs is starting operations in the Gulf and the Middle East. On its part, ClickJobs, which is present in Chennai, Delhi, Mumbai, Hyderabad and Bangalore plans to expand to Trivandrum, Pune and Kolkata. Incidentally the country's first ISO 9000 certified site is fine-tuning its features in line with the demands of the market

There is also this problem of over-crowding as job portals today are inundated with far too many advertisers vying for the same space. The portals depict hundreds of logos and look cluttered. The corporates and the agencies are all addressing the same job seeker pool. As a result of this, the brand recall value is getting limited.

Also, *lack of specialization* amongst portals means advertisers from a spectrum of industries tend to advertise, thus diminishing the desired focus approach for specific skills.

A high volume of candidate traffic is not commensurate with high quality and recruiters are engaged in long drawn processes to shortlist/funnel suitable candidates. Moreover, the recruiters today are pitched against hundreds of agencies that are all trying to access the same candidate database. It is becoming too common to see the candidates being represented by one or the other agency. In this situation, the recruiters are increasingly finding it difficult to establish a clear ROI on the e-recruiting expenditure.

It is interesting to note that corporates as well as numerous agencies who claim to represent them are all advertising the same jobs on the portal. The candidates who visit the job portals are left in a confusion of whether to apply to one or apply to all. Also, job portals in their enthusiasm to generate revenues sell resume database access to agencies further. As a result, the database, which was created with the sole purpose of servicing the job seekers and job providers, seem to be hijacked. Recruiters today have to really ponder over all these issues before embarking on huge spends on e-recruiting.

Questions

1. What should Sanjeev Bikhchandani do to motivate recruiters to move from Print to Online recruitment?
2. How should naukri.com ensure that it remains the most preferred portal both with job seekers as well as job recruiters?

ANNEXTURE - 1

Offering from naukri.com

RESDEX (Resume Database Access)

RESDEX makes recruitment exercise simple, easy and targeted. Resume Database Access of naukri.com brings the most comprehensive methodologies that give recruiters its search options.

Naukri INSTA hire

- ***Insta Recruit*:** Here recruiters can send instant customised messages from Resdex to candidates over the mobile as SMS.
- ***Insta Contact*:** Through this recruiters can run SMS Campaigns and send instant messages to the candidates.
- ***Insta Job*:** This service gives recruiters responses to their job posting instantly.

eApps Pro (Resume Management Software)

A resume management tool that helps recruiters to organize resumes, job requisitions and other recruiting information. It pools data from a wide variety of sources including resumes from print, email, hardcopies and company website to create a central data bank of candidates that can be accessed from anywhere across the world. Some major benefits of eApps Pro are many. This software can even accommodate resumes sent in on paper or via email, collect additional information from the candidate i.e. customize the resume form and also store comments on resumes for future reference. Also, one can forward/download/share resumes with/to colleagues in other branches at the click of a mouse.

Recruiters receive and manage response from all sources–newspaper ads, job postings on naukri.com or their own web site, contact multiple candidates across job vacancies to schedule/confirm/conduct interviews together.

Resume Display for job seekers

Resume Display is somewhat like a Situation Wanted advertisement. Job seeker's resume is searchable by HR Managers/Recruiters/Consultants who visit naukri.com daily.

Resume Development for job seekers

This process involves winning resumes by developing and organizing the content of the resume as per prevalent industry norms, making it easy for a hiring manager to quickly peruse the resume. Naukri's resume writing team comprises of highly skilled and qualified professionals who have vast experience in this field. Regular interaction with HR managers from diverse functional areas ensures a better insight into the current market trends. The service involves high levels of interaction between the client and the developer ensuring effective and satisfying end results.

Resume Flash for job seekers

This is a facility through which the CVs of the job-seekers are sent across to various search firms or placement agencies. The database comprises of the consultants who are based in all the major cities of India. It is one of the most effective tools in the present employment scenario which helps in tapping the vacancies filled only through Search firms.

Job Mail for job seekers

The Jobmail service is designed to select relevant vacancies from over 50,000 live jobs that are displayed on the site and e-mail them to the seekers twice a week. A unique user-friendly system helps job seekers monitor a log of all the JobMails sent to the job seeker. With this service the seeker receives emails of jobs that matches his/her profile.

Resume Posting

Free service by naukri.com, giving job seekers an opportunity to post their resumes free of charge and search for the job of their interest.

Notes

Supply Chain Management

Section - Eighteen

CONCEPTUAL FRAMEWORK

To facilitate a better debate on the case in this section, a quick exploratory review of the supply chain management function along with areas that need discussion are recapitulated briefly as follows:

- Marketing manager has to manage a **supply chain** after developing a proper distribution channel to create a competitive advantage. The management of a supply chain includes building of a long-term partnership with channels members for working together to reduce inefficiencies, costs, and redundancies and to develop innovative approaches to satisfy customers.
- Whereas marketing channels (also called channels of distribution or distribution channels) connect the marketer to the target buyer, the supply chain describes a longer channel stretching from raw materials to components to final products that are carried to the final buyers.
- Supply chain management facilitates distribution for the benefit of all channel members, especially customers
- The supply chain represents a **value delivery system**. Each company captures only a certain percentage of the total value generated by the supply chain..
- The key tasks in supply chain management comprise
  - **Planning** - Organizational and systemwide coordination of marketing channel partnerships to meet customers' product needs
  - **Sourcing** - Purchasing of necessary resources, goods, and services from suppliers to support all supply chain members
  - **Facilitating delivery** - All activities designed to move the product through the marketing channel to the end user
  - **Relationship building** - All marketing activities related to selling, service, and the development of long-term customer relationships
- Supply chains start with the customer and require the cooperation of channel members to satisfy customer requirements. When the buyer, the seller, marketing intermediaries, and facilitating agencies work together, the cooperative relationship results in compromise and adjustments that meet customers' needs regarding delivery, scheduling, packaging, or other requirements.
- Often companies need to increase the quality of good or service, which results in such goals as reducing the time from production to customer purchase, reducing transportation costs, or

lowering information management or administrative costs.

- Achieving these goals to attain a more competitive position often requires that channel members cooperate and share information as well as accommodate one another's needs.
- Technology has dramatically improved the capability of supply chain management on a global basis. The **information technology revolution**, in particular, has created a virtually seamless distribution process for matching inventory needs to customers' requirements.
- With **integrated information sharing** among channel members, costs can be reduced, service can be improved, and value provided to the customer enhanced.
- Tools like electronic billing, purchase order verification, bar code technology, and image processing integrate needed data into the supply chain and improve overall performance.
- Intensely competitive industries, such as the telecommunications, computer, apparel and retail industries, operate the most sophisticated system of supply chain management.
- Several companies provide **supply chain management software** to assist customers in managing sales orders, procurement, warehousing, transportation, and customer service.
- Supply chain management is **not just a buzzword**. Reducing inventory and transportation costs, speeding order cycle times, cutting administrative and handling costs, and improving customer service are all improvements that provide rewards for *all* channel members. The rewards will come as companies determine their positions in the supply chain, identify their partners and their roles, and establish partnerships that focus on customer relationships.

McDonald's & Domino's: Supply Chain to Enhance Customer Value

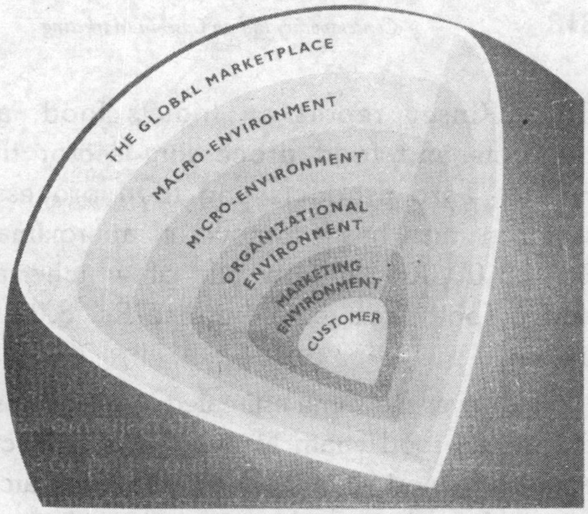

Supply Chain Management Case - 30

Purpose of the Case

The idea is to assimilate the relevant concepts at work and analyse along the following lines:

- To focus on how supply chain can provide a strategic competitive advantage in terms of streamlining operations and passing on the benefits of low costs achieved to the customer
- To study two real-life examples of fast food chains and find out what is behind providing the customer with a location-independent assurance of quality and ensuring fast deliveries without compromising on the quality

SWEEPING CHANGES HAPPENING IN INDIAN FOOD INDUSTRY

The Indian food processing industry is witnessing a lot of activity in the ready to cook, ready to eat and snack foods as well as beverages and nutraceutical foods. With changing food habits and market dynamics, the scope of processed food has graduated from bakery, milk products and confectionery to ready-to-eat products like cooking pastes and packed agro products. Growing urbanization coupled with improvement in overall education levels and infrastructure is providing a strong impetus to the Indian food processing industry With food processors like Britannia, Godrej, GCMMF (Amul), Parle, Tasty Bite eatables, MTR Foods, Nestle, Dabur, Cadbury's, ITC Foods, Satnam Overseas, Enkay Texofood, Mother Dairy, ADF Foods and many other dishing out newer and newer products to meet the demand of Indian palate, the ready-to-eat foods business is reported to have reached a turnover of around Rs. 70 crore (Year 2003). Ready-to-eat foods have now become a strong option in Home-meal-replacement segment along with conventional fast food joints and take-away/ carry-home outlets.

India, which an agrarian economy, is considered major granary of the world and has developed self-reliance in cereals, grains, and vegetables and fruits. This self sufficiency over a period of time turned out to have its own drawbacks like agricultural surpluses, wastages, reduction of rural jobs, lower pricing for growers etc. This clearly indicates that there is immense potential to fight out the evils associated with an excessive food scenario and its alleged drawbacks. As per

CII-McKinsey report on India's food, agro products and food processing sector titled FAIDA, agro products and food processing sector in India has a turnover of approximately Rs. 25,00,000 million out of which value added food products comprise Rs. 8,00,000 million.

However the same estimated 'wastage' loss in the Indian food chain at over Rs 50,000 crore annually, almost all of it attributable to the archaic intermediary chain food has to go through to reach the end customer. This wastage in India is because of lack of proper infrastructure for storage and transportation under controlled conditions, which ranges from physical damage and vermin infestation to improper temperature, humidity and airflow. It's a double whammy, so that while the customer ends up paying more, the original producer, in many cases the Indian farmer, gets paid much less than what he would have got in a modern retail environment.

LOGISTICS MANAGEMENT PRACTICES

The integration of the economies of the world has forced the companies to look for the minimum cost locations as a means of satisfying increased demand. Studies reveal that total logistics cost constitute nearly 10 per cent of India's GDP, of which nearly 40 per cent is due to transportation alone. In today's competitive environment, companies all over the world are shifting their attention towards understanding and implementing extended supply chain management that integrates product, process and information flows within and across organizational boundaries. Rapid developments in information technology are forcing companies to look for and implement continuous improvements in their supply chain models. Infrastructure in India is considered to be very poor compared to other developed and developing countries.

Agricultural raw materials sourcing is a key factor for controlling production costs as well as for ensuring quality of food products, the social, sensorial or food safety aspects. Thus, it is important that reliable sources of raw materials are ensured at the qualities and quantities needed and at competitive conditions. A link with farming and farmers therefore is needed but the form of this link depends on overall business conditions, the availability of the raw materials, their characteristics and the company's needs (qualities and quantities). Thus, food-marketing companies buy raw materials through the trade as primary processed materials or directly from farmers, in the process securing long-term business objectives by building long-term collaboration with suppliers, the farmers, traders and primary processors. Keeping this in mind we decided to analyse the logistics management practices of Domino's and McDonald's.

Domino's entered India in 1996 through a franchise agreement with Delhi based industrial Vam Bhartiya Corp. In late 1999, Indocean Chase, the private equity fund bought a 25 per cent stake in Domino's operations from the Bhartia's, who held Domino's franchise in India. Indocean Chase then advised Domino's to go beyond its 16 outlets in Delhi to exploit the potential in the pizza delivery business. By 2002, Domino's had around 150 outlets covering over 20 major cities in India.

DOMINO'S USP OF HOME DELIVERY IN 30 MINUTES

When Domino's entered Indian market, the concept of home delivery was still in its nascent stages . It existed only in some major cities and was restricted to delivery by the friendly neighborhood fast food outlets. Eating out at "branded" restaurants was more common . To penetrate the Indian market, Domino's introduced an integrated home delivery system from a network of company outlets within 30 minutes of the order . This home delivery proposition worked its way into the Indian mindsets as it offered compensation of Rs 30 on the price tag if there was a delay in delivery , thus for the first four years Domino's concentrated on "Delivery Strategy".

INITIAL SUPPLY CHAIN MODEL OF DOMINO'S

Initially, Domino's had a simple mode comprising of three self-contained commissaries in New Delhi, Mumbai, Bangalore which bought their own wheat, tomatoes and other ingredients, processed them and then delivered them in refrigerated trucks to each outlet.

However, with increasing volumes due to rapid expansion across India of Domino's, the existing Supply Chain model of Domino's had to be revamped. It was necessary for Domino's to rethink its supply chain operation, as it was the biggest area of costs. However, there was one favourable business situation and that was that almost 75 per cent of Domino's customer's ordered either from office or home; as a result, it did not have to lease large plots of land in prime locations to attract traffic.

DOMINO'S REVAMPED LOGISTICS MODEL-2000

Domino's felt the need to revamp its supply chain operations primarily because it wanted to open a large number of new outlets to increase the volume of its operations. Another reason was the company's realization that an efficient and improved supply chain would help it significantly to reduce costs. Further cost effective supply chain offered many opportunities for flexible pricing making the product affordable to large number of customers. In early 2000, Domino's came out with its own unique logistics model revamping it's entire supply chain operations, from sourcing raw materials to shipping them from processing at central location to delivering it to the customer's plate. This model had the following features:

1. **Cost effective procurement:** It began at the point Domino's purchased wheat for making the pizza dough. Domino's first decided the procurement for its key raw materials: wheat, baby corn, tomatoes and spices. However, regular ingredients like onions were sourced and processed locally by the commissaries. For instance, wheat was procured from Jalandhar (Punjab) wholesale markets as it offered an excellent quality-value proposition. Based on the agricultural map of India, Domino's looked at the best product at the lowest cost. Thus, tomatoes would come from Bhubaneshwar, spices from the South, baby corn from Nepal (where it is 40 per cent cheaper than in India) and vegetables from Sri-Lanka. Domino's refrigerated trucks got the wheat commissary in Delhi. Commissary processed the wheat and prepared the pizza dough. The pizza dough and other item prepared in the Commissary's were then sent to the retail outlets by refrigerated trucks. The temperature was fixed based on the distance between the retail outlets and the commissaries.

   This new model offered opportunities for achieving not only the cheapest procurement rate but also provided substantial economies of scale vis-à-vis the old model wherein each commissary purchased its own raw materials within its area of operation and thus was not getting the benefits of cheapest rates available. Earlier Domino's used to sell its products only from its in house outlets but in the new model it started supplying the products to outlets to co-operate offices, railway stations, cinema halls etc. This move increased the company's reach and improved its profits. The benefits derived from the Domino's revamped supply chain were easily seen; in April 2000 Domino's announced a cut in Pizza prices to Rs. 49. This was a clear cut progress towards price flexibility in the market.

2. **Converting logistics problems into business opportunities:** This can be best understood through this real life example. To get to Jalandhar, the trucks had to pass Chandigarh, which because of its cosmopolitan population, was a potential market; therefore Domino's opened a

outlet there as the cost of entry was low because there was no additional cost incurred on transportation of products.

3. **Excellent fleet management for optimum resource utilization:** Domino's opened an outlet in every potential market, which fell in route between the commissary in Delhi and Jalandhar, its prime-sourcing base. The same logic was extendable to large market (especially in the tourist season) Shimla that is just a three-hour drive from Chandigarh. On their way back to Delhi, the trucks could pick up cheese from Karnal, a small town on the Chandigarh - Delhi highway and transport it to its commissaries across the country. Similarly, Domino's India planned to extend its operations in Nepal, Sri-Lanka and Dhaka. The company plans to commissary in Sri-Lanka. Earlier if Domino's had to open a new outlet, the commissary in Delhi would have to process the raw material and send it to the outlet and the truck would return empty. With the revamped supply chain Domino's was able to leverage its fleet much better. The logistics model adopted by Domino's offered some obvious benefits including lower transportation cost, cheaper procurement and economies of scale. Domino's has already cut out the duplication in procurement and processing of raw materials across each of the three commissaries.

4. **Understanding Agro-climatic zones-crop specialization practices:** Domino's identified specialty crops in each region and then entrusted the commissary in that region to process that specialty crop. For instance, the commissary for the Eastern region in Kolkata was responsible for buying tomatoes, processing them and then sending them to all commissaries. Similarly the Northern commissaries had to deliver Pizza bases.

5. **Developing the cold-chain logistics:** Once the new model was formalized, Domino's used 25 Refrigerated trucks to transport its raw material. Refrigerated trucks were also used to transport product for other companies in the same route. For instance, if an operator in Kochi (Kerala) needed to transport specialty cheese, he could use Domino's fleet to transport his product. The reason for this is simple: not too many people have refrigerated trucks in the country. And Domino's can offer them quality service because it will give them the same standards what they use for themselves. Company sources said that in queries from clients for such working for Domino's were confident that the logistic profit center has the potential to bring in Rs. 10 billion by 2006. However they said that profit center would not be allowed to impede the growth of Pizza business, Domino's core operation. Only those deliveries that do not delay or de-route the truck would be considered.

Domino's: Outsourcing the ingredients

Ingredient	*Source from*
Wheat	*Jalandhar (Punjab)*
Cheese	*Karnal, Haryana*
Tomatoes	*Bhubaneshwar, Orissa*
Spice	*South India*
Baby corn	*Nepal*
Exotic Vegetables	*Sri-Lanka*
Pepperoni	*Australia*
Jalapeno	*Spain*

Source: Business World June 2000

MCDONALD'S SUPPLY CHAIN

For a common man, who may not know the complexities of a supply chain model, it is difficult to fathom how a burger gets served in McDonald's so fast and in the most hygienic packing with consistency in quality and at such cheap prices (just Rs. 40/- for two burgers.). This all has become possible as the traditional three golden mantras of retailing success i.e. location, location, location has been augmented by three more ingredients i.e. supply chain, supply chain, supply chain by McDonald's. McDonald's, through its unique cold chain, has been able to both cut down on its operational wastage, as well as maintain the freshness and nutritional value of raw and processed food products. This has involved procurement, warehousing, transportation and retailing of perishable food products, all under controlled temperatures. An in-depth analysis shows that a super efficient supply chain is what lies behind this global food chain's ability to deliver high customer value at purse friendly prices.

MCDONALD'S-STARTING EARLY TO ENSURE PRODUCT COMPLIANCE

From farm to factory to fast food in a customer's tray, the well-oiled supply chain of McDonald's has taken several years to build. Although McDonald's made it's entry around the same time as fellow American food giant Kentucky Fried Chicken but eight years later, Kentucky is still a non-starter in India whereas McDonald's has gone places. For McDonald's, foray in India goes back quite a time as it's supply chain work began almost four years before it started its operations in India in 1996. McDonald's not only identifying farmers for each of its ingredients but also hand-held them to churn out products as per company's specifications. For example iceberg lettuce, peas etc. need to be of certain weight and dimension lest they protrude through the patty and get burnt.

McDonald's has one of the best logistics model in India, which follows an extremely systematic procedure outlined as follows:

1. **Quality Assurance:** To maintain consistency and quality of it's products, McDonald's ships all the raw materials viz. Lettuce, patties, et al to a cold storage close to the main market.
2. **Demand based delivery:** Based on a daily demand schedule that is prepared a day in advance, the required amount of raw material is transported to individual outlets.
3. **Centralized warehousing:** In India, McDonald's selected Mumbai based Radhakrishna Food Land Pvt. Ltd (RFPL) as a distribution agent, which acts as a hub for all its vendors. The iceberg lettuce from Ooty, the mutton patties from Hyderabad or the sesame seed buns from Punjab are all brought to RFPL's distribution center (cold storage) in its refrigerated vans. RFPL then stores the products in controlled conditions in Mumbai and New Delhi, and supplies it to McDonald's outlet on a daily basis.
4. **Cold chain maintenance:** The semi-finished raw material is then transported at a particular temperature to ensure freshness and adequate moisture content in the food. This temperature is maintained inside the chamber of specially made trucks throughout the journey and drivers are instructed specifically not to switch off the chilling system to save electricity even in the case of the traffic jam.

VITAL LINKS IN MCDONALD'S COLD CHAIN

In India, all suppliers have to adhere to Indian government regulations on food, health and hygiene. Over and above the McDonald's suppliers have to continuously maintain company recognized standards. As the ingredients move from farms to processing plants to restaurant, McDonald's quality inspection programme (QIP) carries out quality checks at over twenty different points in the cold chain system thus enabling the company to cut down on operational wastage.

Focus on prevention than detection through HACCP: McDonald's systematic approach to food safety through Hazard-Analysis-Critical-Control-Point (HACCP) emphasizes prevention at supplier's facility and restaurants rather than detection through inspection of illness or presence of microbiological data. Based on HACCP guidelines, control points and critical control points for all McDonald's major food processing plants and restaurants in India are identified and limits are established for those followed by monitoring, recording and correcting any deviations. HACCP verification is done twice in a year and certified.

RELATIONSHIP BETWEEN MCDONALD'S AND ITS SUPPLIERS

To ensure that its relationship with its chain of Indian suppliers is mutually beneficial McDonald's gave its suppliers the opportunity to expand their business and have access to the latest food technology, exposure to advance agricultural practices and ability to grow or to export. There are many cases of local suppliers operating out of the small town who have benefited from their association with McDonald's India.

Some of the suppliers who have benefited immensely due to their relationship with McDonald's India are:

1. Trikaya agriculture-Supplier of iceberg lettuce

Exposure to better agricultural management practices and sharing of advanced agricultural technology by McDonald's has made Trikaya Agriculture extremely conscious of delivering its products with utmost care and quality. Initially lettuce could only be grown during the winter months but with McDonald's expertise in the area of agriculture, Trikaya Farms in Talegaon, Maharashtra, is now able to grow this crop all the year round. McDonald's has provided assistance in the selection of high quality seeds, exposed the farms to advanced drip-irrigation technology, and helped develop a refrigerated transportation system allowing a small agri-business in Maharashtra to provide fresh, high-quality lettuce to McDonald's urban restaurant locations thousands of kilometers away. Trikaya has implemented advance agricultural practices to successfully grow specialty crops like iceberg lettuce, special herbs and many oriental vegetables. Their farm infrastructure features:

- A specialized nursery with a team of agricultural experts.
- Drip and sprinkler irrigation in raised farm beds with fertilizer mixing plant.
- Post harvest facilities at Trikaya include a cold chain consisting of a pre-cooling room to remove field heat, a large cold room and a refrigerated van for transportation where the temperature and the relative humidity of the crop is maintained between 1° C and 4° C and 95 per cent respectively. Vegetables are moved into the pre-cooling room within half an hour of harvesting. The pre-cooling room ensures rapid vacuum cooling to 2° C within 90 minutes. The pack house, pre-cooling and cold room are located at the farms itself, ensuring no delay between harvesting, pre-cooling, packaging and cold storage.
- Refrigerated trucks for transportation.

With this cold chain infrastructure in place, Trikaya Agriculture plans to export this high value product to other international markets, especially to McDonald's Middle East and Asia Pacific operations. McDonald's expertise in packaging, handling and long-distance transportation has helped Trikaya to do trial shipments to the Gulf successfully. In addition to export, McDonald's assistance has enabled Trikaya Agriculture to supply this crop to a number of star-rated hotels, clubs, flight kitchens and offshore catering companies all over India.

2. Vista Processed Foods Private Limited-Supplier of chicken and vegetable range of products

Having struck a joint venture with OSI Industries Inc, USA and McDonald's India Private Limited the organisation called Vista Processed Foods Private Limited produces a range of frozen chicken and vegetable foods. Their world class infrastructure at their plant at Taloja in Maharashtra has:

- Separate processing lines for chicken and vegetable foods.

- Capability to produce frozen foods at temperature as low as -35 degree Celsius to retain total freshness.
- International standards, procedure and support services.

With continued assistance from its international partners, Vista has installed hi-tech equipment for both the chicken and vegetable processing lines, which reflect the latest food processing technology (de-boning, blending, forming, coating, frying and freezing). For the vegetable range, the latest vegetable mixers and blenders are in operation. Also, keeping cultural sensitivities in mind, both processing lines are absolutely segregated and utmost care is taken to ensure that the vegetable products do not mix with the non-vegetarian products.

Now, at Vista, a very wide range of frozen and nutritious chicken and vegetable products is available. Ongoing R&D, both locally and in the parent companies, work towards innovation in taste, nutritional value and convenience. These products, besides being supplied to McDonald's, are also offered to institutions like star-rated hotels, hospitals, project sites, caterers, corporate canteens, schools and colleges, restaurants, food service establishments and coffee shops.

3. Dynamix Dairy-Supplier of cheese

Dynamix Dairy, which is situated in Baramati district of Maharashtra, has brought immense benefits to farmers by setting up a network of milk collection centers equipped with bulk coolers. This easy accessibility has enabled farmers to augment their income by finding a new market for surplus milk. Dynamix Dairy has also made efforts to see that the bulk cooling centres are located in a way that farmers do not have to travel more than an hour from their farms to reach the collection centre thus drastically reducing the time from milking to refrigeration, which is critical, especially since the lack of proper refrigeration can greatly impact the quality of milk. On receipt, the milk is immediately stored in the bulk coolers at the collection centres, to prevent growth of bacteria in the milk and preserve its freshness - thus, maintaining the 'cold chain'. The factory has:

- Fully automatic international standard processing facility.
- Capability to convert milk into cheese, butter/ghee, skimmed milk powder, lactose, casein and humanized baby food.
- Stringent quality control and continuous R&D.

4. Amrit Food-Supplier of long life UHT Milk and milk products for frozen desserts

Amrit Food, an ISO-9000 Company, which manufactures widely popular brands-Gagan milk and Nandan ghee at its factory in Ghaziabad, Uttar Pradesh has:

McDonald's-Outsourcing Base

Ingredient	*Supplier*
Cheese	*Dynamix Dairy Industries, Pune*
Dehydrated onions	*Jain Foods, Jalgaon*
Iceberg Lettuce	*Trikaya Agriculture, Pune*
	Mina Agritech, New Delhi
	Ooty Farms and Orchids, Ooty
Chicken Patty	*Vista Foods, Taloja*
Vegetable Patty, Veg Nuggets, Pineapple Pie, Apple Pie	*Kirten Foods, Taloja*
Chicken Dress	*River Dale, Talegaon*
Buns	*Cremica Industries, Phillaur*
Egg less Mayonnaise	*Quaker Cremica Pvt. Ltd., Phillaur,Punjab*
Sesame Seeds	*Ghaziabad*
Fish Fillet Patties	*Amalgam Foods Ltd., Kochi*
Vegetable For Patties	*Finns Frozen Foods, Nasik*
	Jain Foods, Jalgaon
Mutton and Mutton Patties	*Al-Kabeer,Hyderabad*

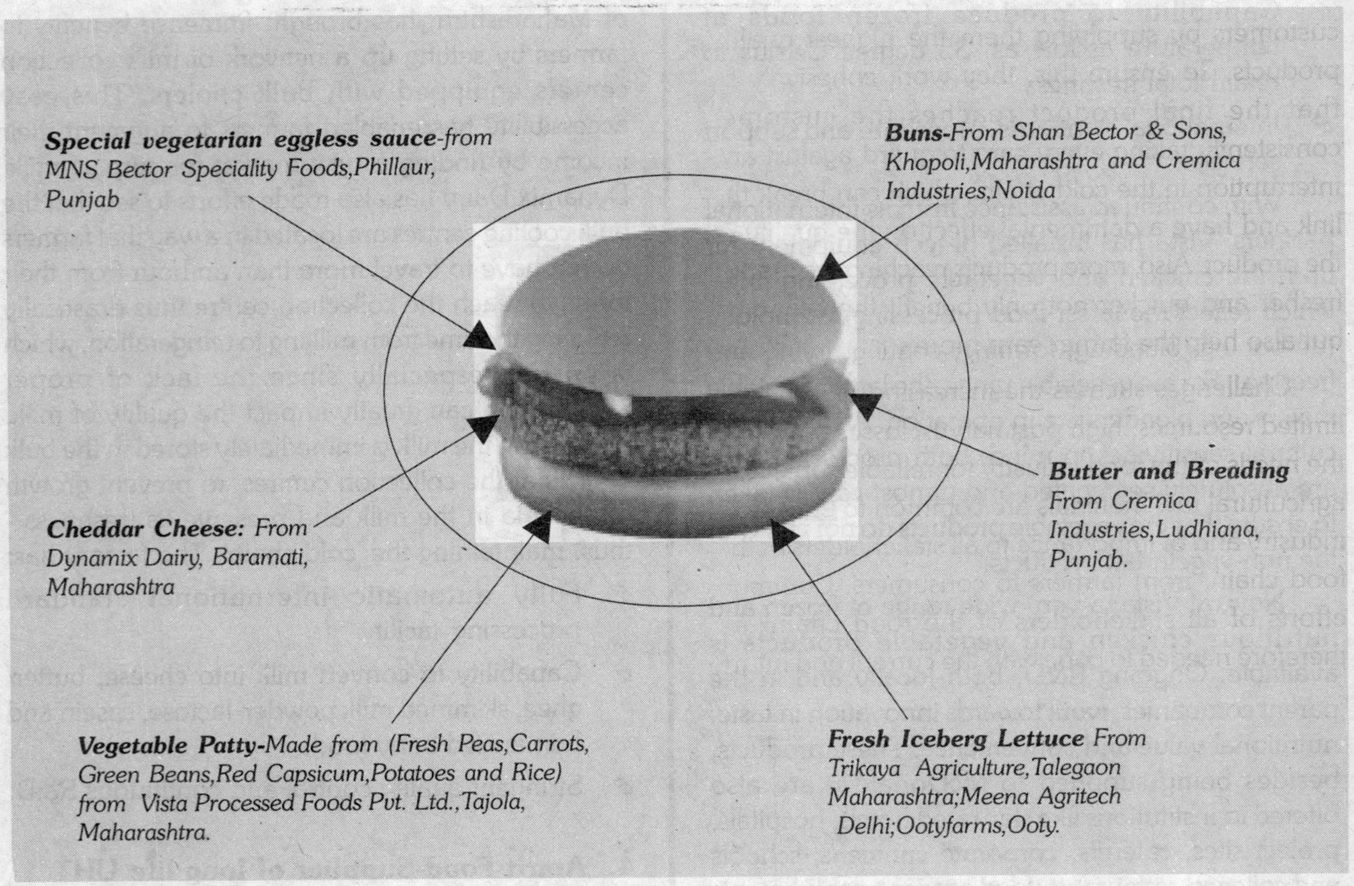

- State of the art fully automatic machinery requiring no human contact with product, for total hygiene.
- Installed capacity of 6000 liters/hr for producing homogenized UHT (ultra high temperature) processed milk and milk products.
- Strict quality control supported by a fully equipped quality control laboratory.

5. Radhakrishna Foodland-Distribution centers for Delhi and Mumbai

An integral part of the Radhakrishna Group, Foodland specializes in handling large volumes, providing the entire range of services including procurement, quality inspection, storage, inventory management, deliveries, data collection, recording and reporting. McDonald's local supply networks through Radhakrishna Foodland, which operates distribution centres (DCs) for McDonald's restaurants in Mumbai and Delhi. The DCs have focused all their resources to meet McDonald's expectation of 'Cold, Clean, and On-Time Delivery' and plays a very vital role in maintaining the integrity of the products throughout the entire 'cold chain'. Ranging from liquid products coming from Punjab to lettuce from Pune, the DC receives items from different parts of the country. These items are stored in rooms with different temperature zones and are finally dispatched to the McDonald's restaurants on the basis of their requirements. Its salient strengths are:

- A one-stop shop for all distribution management services.
- Dry and cold storage facility to store and transport perishable products at temperature up to -22 degree Celsius.
- Effective process control for minimum distribution cost.

All the suppliers of McDonald's share the company's commitment and education to satisfying customers by supplying them the highest quality products. To ensure this, they work cohesively so that the final product reaches the customer consistently taking every care to guard against any interruption in the cold chain, which can break the link and have a detrimental effect on the quality of the product. Also, more products reaching the market fresher and quicker not only benefit the economy but also help the farmer earn more.

Challenges such as the increasing food needs, limited resources, high post harvest losses as well as the needs of the food industry for reliable sources of agricultural raw materials are common to the whole industry and of importance to all stakeholders of the food chain, from farmers to consumers. Common efforts of all stakeholders of the food chain are therefore needed to cope with the current and future challenges to cover the increasing food needs. The role of the food industry in preserving food quality, in reducing food losses, in bringing food to the places of need is increasing in significance.

Questions

1. What are the key changes which have made supply chain management a critical function to succeed in present day business world?
2. How does an efficient supply chain lead to strategic competitive advantage? Answer this question keeping the case of McDonald's in mind.
3. Write a short note on how Domino's revamped its supply chain model in the wake of its extended spread in Indian cities.

Notes

Rural Marketing

Section - Nineteen

CONCEPTUAL FRAMEWORK

To facilitate a better debate on the cases in this section, a quick exploratory review of the rural marketing function in India along with areas that need discussion are recapitulated briefly as follows:

- The **villages and small towns** of India, which were once inconsequential dots on maps, are now **getting the attention** of global marketing giants and media planners.
- The **main reasons/drivers** of growing importance of rural markets are rising literacy levels, media explosion especially increasing reach of cable television, globalization, economic liberalization, IT revolution, Indian diaspora, female power, and improving infrastructure.
- Today, middle class rural India has **more disposable income** than urban India which attracts all the marketers to rural Indian markets.
- In the Indian context, approximately **three-fourth of the population** is rural and nearly **one-third of the National income** is generated by rural areas. As such, it becomes increasingly necessary to understand the rural marketing environment, needs and aspirations of the rural population, the various institutions – financial and social - operating in rural areas before recommending marketing strategies for the rural markets. Only then rural markets will become **real growth engines** for corporate business houses.
- There has always been a vast difference between the urban and rural markets for a long time now. The **difference** is **not only between urban and rural but also within the rural areas** — between regions, states and districts, let's say between villages of Punjab and villages of Orissa. There is a difference in the media reach, the education levels, the attitude, the culture and the type of products that the two markets are exposed to.
- Many products like economy soaps, tape recorders have achieved near maturity in the urban market but in upcountry are still in the growth phase. In fact, whereas urban market has become congested with too many competitors, rural markets offer an **extremely lucrative potential** for consumption of a variety of products and services.
- Rural areas have their intrinsic problems as majority of the people are poor, have small agricultural landholdings and are tradition-bound. India's **627,000 villages** are **spread over 3.2 million sq km**; they don't have all-weather roads, which affects distribution, and power supply is still highly irregular. Other **infrastructure** facilities like roads, warehouses,

communication system and financial facilities too are inadequate in rural India.

- In India, even though the number of recognised languages is only 16, the **dialects** are estimated to be around **850**, which make the task of media very difficult and costly affecting reach and effectiveness. A **low level of literacy** also leads to problems of communication for promotional purposes.
- Rural marketers have understood the media habits of the rural customers and are using **traditional media** like "Nautanki" , 'Ramleela' , **rural sports** like kho-kho, kabaddi, **rural fairs and haats** etc. to generate great interest amongst rural customers.
- Lots of companies manufacturing biscuits, shampoos, candies, etc have launched **small unit packing**: to ensure easy affordability and trials. Products are now designed **keeping the rural lifestyles in mind** and at the same time ensuring that the product literature is simple and easily understandable.
- Lots of organisations are using **innovative distribution strategies** like petrol pumps located across the length and breadth of the country, tying up with Non-governmental organisations etc. Mobile distribution through a fleet of delivery vans is also explored as a possible solution as it can take the products to the customers in every nook and corner of the market. It also enables the company to have direct contact with its consumers, understand them better and design suitable sales promotion strategies.
- Companies also appoint **opinion leaders** as they have found by experience that rural consumers do not decide on the basis of information provided by companies or their advertisements alone; they prefer to consult others who actually possess the various brands of the products. For example: purchase decision for tractors. The farmer seeks information on trouble-free operation, fuel economy, after-sales service facility, spare parts availability, sources of credit, resale value, maintenance costs, etc.
- Companies are also changing the profile of their **marketing managers** and sending their urban-bred MBAs, fed on a staple diet of western marketing principles, to rural India so that they **can assimilate cultural dynamics** before designing marketing programs.
- According to rural marketing experts, 4A's that means ***"Affordability, Availability, Acceptance, Awareness"*** will be the mantras to succeed in rural India.

CavinKare Ltd.

Challenges in Rural India

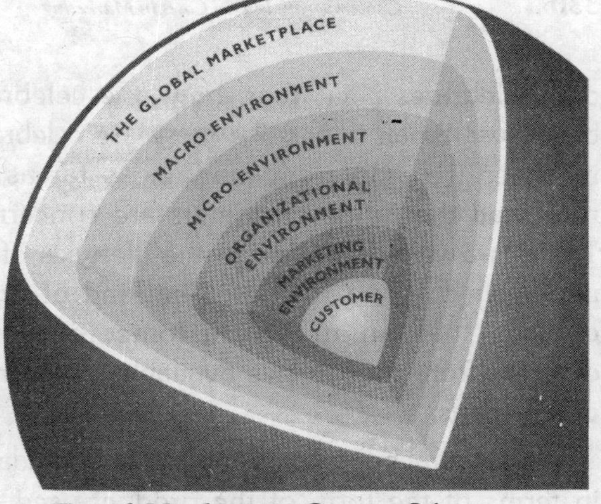

Rural Marketing Case - 31

Purpose of the Case

The idea is to assimilate the relevant concepts at work and analyse along the following lines:

- To discuss how rural markets are getting receptive to new personal hygiene and lifestyle products as the winds of change blow
- To focus on key factors which made CavinKare score over the MNCs in rural markets
- To debate whether CavinKare will be able to hold on to its leadership position in shampoo in parts of rural India, and what it should do to build on the success

Has rural India become fashionable? Is there a dramatic change in progress? Are rural markets the new growth engines? Villagers who used to crack open peanut candies, eat the nut and throw away the shell are now demanding chocolate candies that will melt in their mouths, not in their hands. Charcoal-cleaned teeth are a rare sight; so is the case with twigs of neem and babul tree. Today, the ultra bright shine of Colgate or some other international brand of toothpaste holds more appeal than the traditional methods of cleaning teeth. Even the native expressions of cleaning teeth, such as *daatun karnaa* and *musaag lagaana* are endangered to being replaced by new expressions such as paste *karnaa* ('to brush teeth with paste'). Even a simple query such as 'Where are you from?' is not free from the overtones of marketization and globalization in rural discourse. Consumerism and globalization are invading parts of India where, as some would venture to say, time seems to have stood still for centuries.

In the Indian context, approximately three-fourth of the population is rural and nearly one-third of the National income is generated by rural areas. Thanks to globalization, economic liberalization, IT revolution, Indian diaspora, female power, and improving infrastructure, middle class rural India today has more disposable income than urban India. The advent of commercial and market–oriented farming, use of manufactured inputs like fertilizers, pesticides, high-yielding varieties of seeds, etc has given a general feel-good factor.

There has always been a vast difference between the urban and rural markets for a long time now. The difference is even in routine things like - how one celebrates New Year, how one celebrates birthdays? Small things like these are celebrated in an entirely different manner as far as the rural and the urban customers are concerned. There is a vast difference in the lifestyles of the people in the two regions. The kind of brand choices that an urban customer enjoys is different from the choices available to the rural counterparts.

In the rural households, there is an upgradation in terms of the form of the product used. For example, households are upgrading from traditional mosquito repellents such as gobar (cow-dung) to coils to mats. There is also an upgradation from local or unbranded products to national brands and from low-priced brands to premium brands. This is primarily due to the influence of the youth in the households. The rural youth are more open to fresh concepts as against their elderly family members. They are better educated and have aspirations similar to those of the youth in urban India. With increasing literacy levels and the media explosion brand consciousness is on an upswing. With the spread of cable network all across the country, awareness of the branded products like Surf, Cinthol, Rin, Clinic Plus and Old Spice has gone up.

At a time when most FMCG (fast moving consumer goods) categories are inching along, personal products are being seen as the harbinger of prosperity and haircare products are the fastest-growing category within personal products. Between 1994 and 1998, the market size of products such as skincare and toothbrushes doubled in value. But the size of the shampoo market expanded two-and-a-half times over the same period. Not surprisingly, shampoo is a high priority area for major players such as Hindustan Lever. The size of the shampoo market, according to ORG-MARG (for the year 2001), is Rs 850 crore — equivalent to 30,000 tonnes in volume terms. (Source: FMCG Market Washed by Shampoo & Soap Together, Mayur Jain, *The Financial Express*, 20 July 2002).

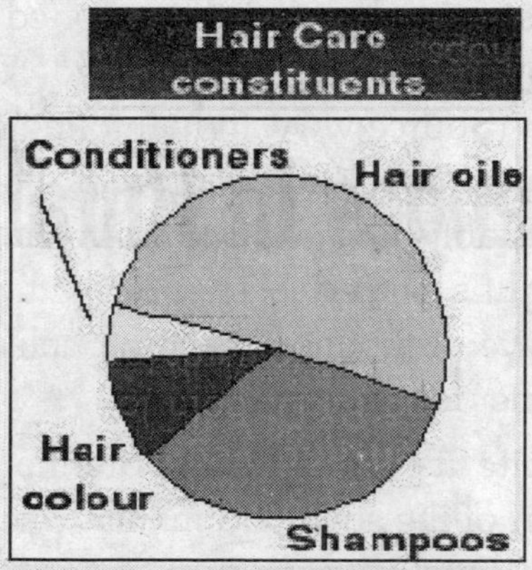

Hair oil	*Rs.1300 cr*
Shampoos	*Rs.850 cr*
Hair colour	*Rs.250 cr*
Conditioners	*Rs.130 cr*

(Source: The Hindu Business Line, 22 Sept. 2003).

Exhibit 1

Unlike other FMCG categories such as soaps and detergents, which boast of a penetration level of more than 90 per cent (as in 2001), shampoos remain a low penetration category .Industry sources estimate that the urban market penetration of shampoos is a modest 36 per cent. Shampoo usage in the rural markets is even more infrequent, with a penetration level of 12 per cent. Thus, even for the largest player in this industry, there is considerable scope for volume expansion by converting non-users. (Source: Shampoo & Soap Make a Go at FMCGs, Mayur Jain, *The Financial Express*, 20 July 2002).

For a market with high potential, the shampoo market in India is dominated by just a few players. From scores of brands five years ago, the shampoo market has been whittled down to a handful in 2004. Hindustan Lever (HLL), with a 65 per cent volume share (68 per cent share by value), dominates the market with brands such as Sunsilk, Clinic Plus and Clinic All Clear. CavinKare Limited, a company from Chennai, with brands such as Chik and Nyle follows with a 19.8 per cent volume share (Source:www.indiainfoline.com). Procter & Gamble (P&G) is the only other large player in this category with brands such as Pantene Pro-V and Head & Shoulders. P&G discontinued its shampoo manufacturing operations in India in 2000. Most of its brands are today directly imported from other Asian countries such as Thailand, Taiwan and Vietnam. (Source:www.indiainfoline.com). New entrants are probably discouraged by the formidable task of establishing a distribution network from scratch. HLL's long established ties with retailers and its extensive distribution reach probably acts as an entry barrier for new entrants.

Despite its undisputed potential, the rapid expansion of the shampoo market was interrupted in 1999. Overall growth rates in the market slowed to 1.7 per cent in 1999, from 16 per cent the previous year. In 2000, however, the market appears to have recovered some, and the shampoo category has grown by around 10 per cent (www.indiainfoline.com). Lack of innovation is the probable reason for slowdown. To counter this HLL has identified three major barriers to shampoo use in India — the perception that shampoos contain harsh chemicals that could damage hair, high price and the view that the shampoo is more of a glamour product rather than a hygiene product. Therefore, the strategies of the major players have revolved around attacking these barriers to usage.

The players obviously believe that the key obstacle to recruiting new users lies in the high price of shampoos as a product. Unlike other FMCG categories, where marketers are experimenting with low unit packs, as a concept, the low unit shampoo packs have been around for over a decade since 1990s. Therefore, marketers have been working at scaling down prices further with the belief that it could help pep up volume growth rates for major players but they have also had the effect of lowering the per ml cost of the major brands retailed through sachets. Till the time the players upgrade users to the larger pack sizes, the sachet revolution could restrict margin expansion for the players.

Players have also tried other routes to expand the shampoo market. Fighting the perception that shampoos are essentially glamour products, marketers have tried to add a utility value to shampoos by offering functional benefits. Anti-dandruff shampoos represent this attempt. Clinic Plus, one of the first anti-dandruff brands, is the largest shampoo brand with a market share of 31 per cent: (Source:www.indiainfoline.com). Clinic All Clear, an anti-dandruff extension targeted at the youth has also managed to garner a 13 per cent share. Due to its low pricing (Rs 71 for a 160 ml bottle against Rs 68 for a 100 ml bottle of Head & Shoulders anti-dandruff shampoo), the brand also has a significant rural market share of 44 per cent. (Source:www.indiainfoline.com)

HLL has also experimented with different versions of Sunsilk for dry, normal and oily hair. Procter & Gamble's Head & Shoulders Menthol and Pantene Lively Clean also offer functional benefits to users. Since these add-ons enable brands to command a price premium over the plain shampoos, this strategy could aid both volume and margin expansion. One of the key barriers to shampoo usage lies in the reluctance to use a synthetic product on hair. Worldwide, therefore, herbal shampoos or botanicals, are a fast growing category. Ayur from RDM Traders Private Limited and Nyle Herbal, a herbal shampoo launched by CavinKare, have been some of the early entrants in the Indian herbal shampoos market. These products claim to use traditional Indian herbs such as shikakai, soap nuts and amla as ingredients and have been a success.

Nyle Herbal is among the top five shampoo brands in the country and herbal shampoos today account for 10 per cent of the market size.

However, high price could be a key barrier when it comes to herbal shampoos. The key challenge in manufacturing herbals lies in efficacy. Users typically require larger quantities or higher concentrations of herbal shampoos to replicate the results of synthetic shampoos. Bringing down prices can therefore be quite difficult in this case. This is probably why 90 per cent of the herbal shampoos still sell only in the urban markets.

The value-added shampoo segment is getting quite crowded, with a range of pharmaceutical and cosmetics companies launching specialised products. While Dabur has leveraged Vatika's brand equity to launch Vatika Herbal shampoo, Godrej Soaps has leveraged its dominance of the hair colour market to launch Godrej Colourgloss shampoo, for users with coloured hair. This apart, several pharma companies (including Johnson & Johnson) have launched medicated anti-dandruff shampoos (which will probably carry higher credibility with buyers), while cosmetic companies such as Biotique and Lotus Herbals also have herbal shampoos on the shelves.

The Rs 400-crore Chennai-based CavinKare Ltd. has often been the David in market dominated by giant multinational companies. In many of the categories the company has carved out its market share with innovations in packaging, which forced the competition to follow suit. It is primarily into two categories - hair care and skin care and fragrances. In the hair care, there is Chik shampoo, Nyle shampoo, Meera shampoo and powder, Meera - a value added coconut oil, Karthika which is very much a Chennai brand and Indica - a hair dye which comprise its hair care business, which in turn contributes to approximately 70 per cent of the total personal care business. (Source:www.cavinkare.com). In skin care and fragrances, there is a Regular Fairever and Fairever Mantra, Spinz talcum powder deodorant and a small pack perfume, which is called a 'dab-on'. There is also Chik, extended into the talcum powder category, and Raaga Cool, hair oil.

CavinKare Limited, which has managed to garner a significant share of the shampoo market despite the handicap of competing with established big MNCs with deep distribution penetration, has focussed on scaled-down versions of its brands and herbal shampoos — two segments where the market leader did not have a presence. CavinKare's shampoo business has grown faster than the overall market, at 20 per cent in 1998, 4 per cent in 1999 and 34 per cent in 2000 (Source: *The Economic Times*, 12 Aug. 2001)

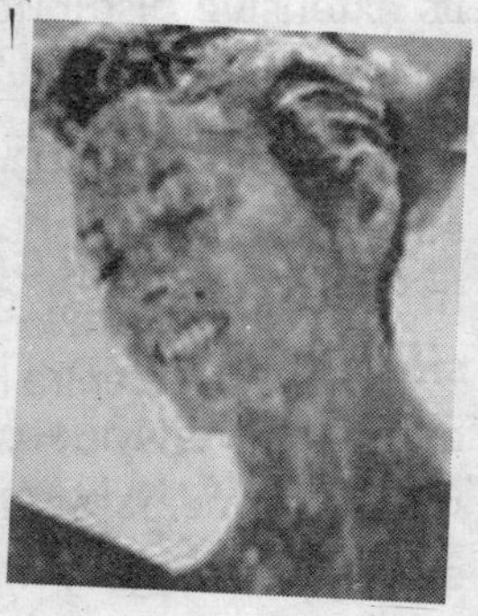

CavinKare Limited has stood against giants by finding unique niches for itself. They have positioned themselves as a strong value-for-money brand. They find these particular niches (for each brand). In the case of Chik, instead of going into urban areas the product was developed as a rural product. Since there is a vast rural area, which needs categories like this, the product was conceptualised for the rural market.

As it competes with big companies, the key strategy is value pricing, product performance and brand building. Pricing is important, but pricing is not the only component of the value equation we provide. It goes along with product performance and brand building. There are three legs to their strategy - strong research and development, investment into advertising processes and outstanding efficiencies in manufacturing and sourcing for good pricing options.

CavinKare realized early on that major multinational players with localised offerings

Personal products	Food division	Home care
HAIR CARE		
Chik Shampoo	Chinni	Everglow
Karthika Shikakai Powder	Ruchi	
Meera Badam Shampoo		
Meera Herbal Powder		
Nyle Herbal Shampoo		
PERSONAL CARE		
Chik Talc		
Electrix Perfume		
Indica Hair Dye		
Raaga Cool		
Spinz Deodorants		
SKIN CARE		
Fairever		
Mantra Fairness Cream		
Nyle Herbal Cold Cream		
Nyle Moisturising Lotion		

Table1: **Product Profile of CavinKare**

dominated the industry. The strategy adopted by the young company was to move in as a regional player, offering unique products, establishing its brand identity and gaining critical mass. The primary business model has remained unchanged till date. In the hair care category the company has 25 per cent of the volume market, in fairness creams it has 9 per cent, in the hair wash powder category it is 72 per cent and for talcum it is 4 per cent. (Source:www.cavinkare.com)

CavinKare has perhaps the best new brand success ratio in the FMCG industry today. That's one reason why its turnover rose to Rs 264 crore in '02-03 from Rs 85 crore in 1998-99. CavinKare has been growing at a CAGR of 31% over the past 10 years. Its growth has been funded through internal cash flows and sound working capital management

By virtue of brands owned like Chik (shampoo, hair dye, talc), Meera (herbal powder, liquid hair wash, soap), Nyle (herbal shampoo, moisturising lotion, cold cream), Fairever (fairness cream), Spinz (perfumes, deos and talc), Indica (hair dye), Raaga Cool (cooling hair oil) and Karthika (hair wash powder), CavinKare has identified gaps in the market and moved in quickly to plug them. The backbone of this strategy is to gain critical mass by side-stepping competition. They have essentially worked around competition till a direct confrontation with a competitor's brand became inevitable.

The flagship brand of CavinKare Limited is Chik shampoo which offered floral fragrances for the first time in shampoos. This was based on the consumer insight in Southern markets where women keep flowers in the hair for fragrance. the concept was a hit and sales jumped three times. (Source: Praxis, *Business Line*, July 2004). Instead of going into urban areas the product was developed as a rural product. There is a vast

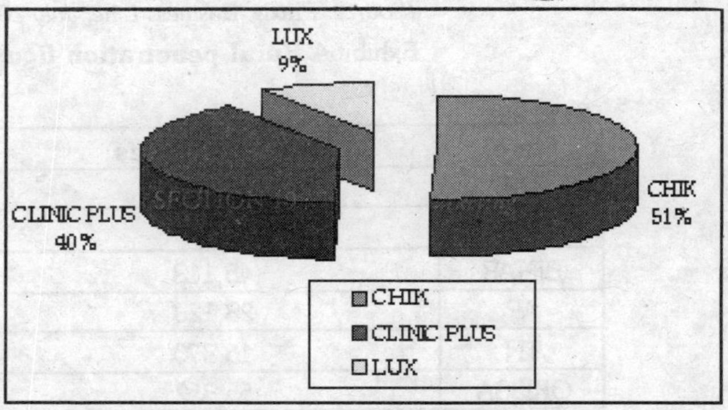

(Source: Praxis, Business Line, July 2004)

Exhibit 2: **Rural Market Share of Chik as in April 2003**

rural area, which needs categories like this. The product was primarily targeted at the rural market

CavinKare introduced a smaller 50 paise sachet of Chik, when most other sachets retailed at Rs 2. The effort appears to have been an

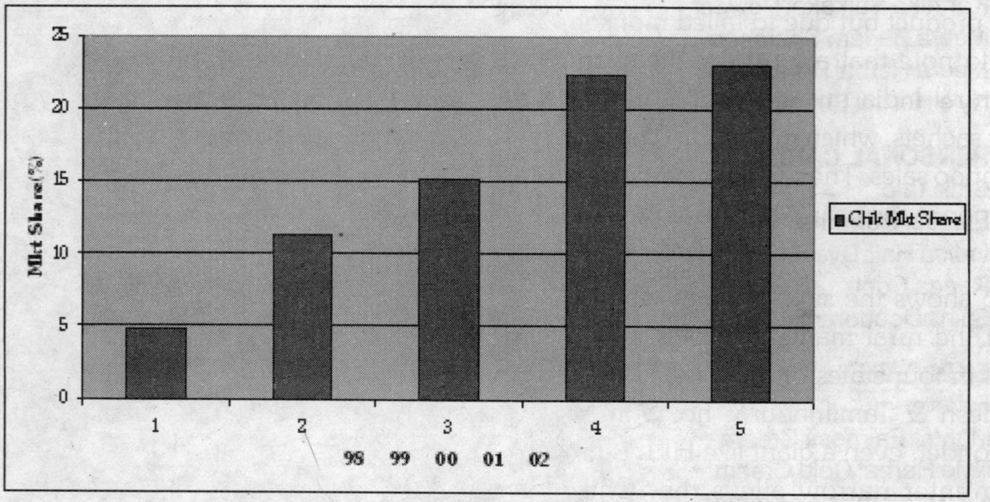

(Source: Praxis, Business Line, July 2004)

Exhibit 3: **Growing Market Share of Chik shampoo**

unqualified success, with the Chik brand expanding by 40 per cent after the launch. A new 50 ml bottle of Chik priced at Rs 6 (when most other brands were available in 100 ml bottles and above) has also helped expanding the brand. (Source:www.indiainfoline.com)

From Exhibit 2, it is evident that strategy of rural concentration has really paid off for Chik shampoo and it has consistently beaten the overall market leader Clinic Plus in the rural markets by its exclusive price and distribution tactics.

Exhibit 3, shows the overall market share of Chik Shampoo. Thus, we find that it is on a rapid growth spree courtesy its focus on rural markets.

Population Size	No. of Villages	Percentage of Total
Less than 1000	459465	69.6
1000 to 1500	58029	8.8
More than 1500	143248	21.6

(Source: Praxis, Business Line, July 2004)

Exhibit 4 **Rural penetration figures of Chik shampoo in the year 2002**

States	No. of Villages	Market Share (Volume in %)	Position
UP	1,07,440	66.86	1
MP	55,392	21.96	2
BIHAR	45,113	31.82	1
AP	28,123	39.01	1
TN	16,870	45.77	1
ORISSA	55,352	18.42	2

(Source: Praxis, Business Line, July 2004)

Exhibit 5 **Rural hold of Chik**

CavinKare has an all-India reach with over 10 lakh outlets, which are serviced by 1,700 stockists. However, there was a slowdown in growth rate in the year 2002 but it was not due to decreasing popularity of product but due to failed monsoon. It is important to note that a fourth of the shampoo market is in rural India but the rural market is the key driver for sachets, which make up 70 per cent of the total shampoo sales. The rural penetration figures of Chik shampoo in the year 2002 are as per Exhibits 4 & 5.

Exhibit 5 shows the strength with which Chik has captured the rural market. It holds a *numero uno* position in four states of India i.e. U.P., Bihar, Andhra Pradesh & Tamilnadu & no. 2 in MP & Orissa. No wonder, even a giant like HLL is finding it difficult to enter narrow alleys that Chik has managed to enter.

The key strategy for promotion of Chik shampoo has been through demonstration route. CavinKare's team traveled extensively in rural pockets, caught hold of school boys to demonstrate how to lather and wash, comb hair and show the difference. This exercise had significant impact in breaking the ice and made people comfortable with the concept. Another method used to encourage trials was through a consumer scheme, where anyone could take empty shampoo sachets to a retailer and take home a Chik Sachet for free. Once this scheme too paid off CavinKare Ltd imbibed the low-price sales promotion scheme as the permanent feature in its business model.

Question

1. Although the marketing strategy of Chik Shampoo, based entirely on rural focus, aggressive pricing and innovative promotions has emerged successful so far, do you envisage a problem when rising competition in rural markets will force CavinKare to increase branding and promotional costs and getting out of aggressive low pricing will pose its own challenges? Comment.

Notes

Notes

Retailing

Section - Twenty

CONCEPTUAL FRAMEWORK

To facilitate a better debate on the cases in this section, a quick exploratory review of the retailing function along with areas that need discussion are recapitulated briefly as follows:

- **Retailing** is selling goods or services directly to final consumers for personal, family or household use. Retailers operate through store retailing, non-store retailing and retail organizations.
- Retailers are important links in the marketing channel because they are both marketers for producers who directly interact with the end customers and customers for wholesalers and producers. Retailers provide services to add value and influence product selections.
- Organized retailing is a growing trend worldwide which stresses on experience of convenience in shopping and focuses on ease, economy and elegance rather than just the availability of goods
- **General-merchandise retailers** type of retail stores include convenience stores, department stores, discount stores, supermarkets, superstores, hypermarkets, warehouse clubs, and warehouse and catalog showrooms.
  - One can purchase a limited line of high-turnover convenience products at slightly higher prices at **convenience stores** which are relatively small stores located near residential areas and remain open for long hours, seven days a week
  - **Department stores** are large retail organizations employing at least 25 people and characterized by wide product mixes in considerable depth for most product lines. Their products are organized into separate departments that function like self-contained business.
  - **Discount stores** are self-service, low-price, general merchandise outlets.
  - **Supermarkets** are large, self-service food stores that also carry some non-food products.
  - **Superstores** are giant retail outlets carrying all the products found in supermarkets and most consumer products purchased on a routine basis.
  - **Hypermarkets** offer supermarket and discount store shopping at one location.
  - **Warehouse clubs** are large-scale members-only discount operations.
  - **Warehouse** and **Catalog showrooms** are low-cost operations characterized by warehouse methods of materials handling and display, large inventories, and minimal services.

- **Specialty retailers** offer a very few types of products but provide a very great depth in a particular product line., One can get seconds and production overruns of branded goods at deep discounts at **off-price retailers. Category killers** are large specialty stores that concentrate on a major product category and compete on the basis of low prices and enormous product availability.
- **Non-store retailing** is the selling of goods or services outside the confines of a retail facility. The three major types are indicated below:
  - **Direct selling** is the marketing of products to ultimate consumers through face- to-face sales presentations at home or in the workplace. Amway's products are sold through direct selling.
  - **Direct marketing** is the use of telephone and non-personal media to communicate products and organizational information to consumers who then can purchase products by mail or telephone. Forms of direct marketing include catalog marketing, direct-response marketing, telemarketing, television home shopping, and online retailing. For example, Dell computers.
  - **Automatic vending** is the use of machines to dispense products. The cola majors are well known for using vending machines.
- Retail organizations achieve many economies of scale such as greater purchasing power, wider brand recognition and better-trained employees. The major types of organized retailing are **corporate chain stores**, **voluntary chains**, **retailer cooperatives**, **franchise organizations** and **merchandising conglomerates**.
- **Franchising** is an arrangement whereby a supplier grants a dealer the right to sell products in exchange for some type of consideration.. Retail franchises are of three general types:
  - A manufacturer may authorize a number of retail stores to sell a certain brand name item. Exclusive outlets of Ray ban glasses or Nokia showrooms fall in this category.
  - A producer may license distributors to sell a given products to retailers.
  - A franchiser may supply brand names, techniques, or other services instead of a complete product. This type includes coffee chains like The Barista.
- A retailer must prepare **marketing plan** considering target markets, product assortment and procurement, services and store atmosphere, price, promotion and place.
- When evaluating potential **location**, retailers take into account a variety of factors, including the location of the firm's target market within the trading area, kinds of products sold, availability of public transportation, customer characteristics, and competitors' locations. Retailers can choose among several types of locations, including free-standing structures, traditional business districts, traditional shopping centers, or non-traditional shopping centers.
- **Retail positioning** involves identifying underserved market segment and serving it through a strategy that distinguishes the retailer from others in those customers' minds.
- The location, products offered, customer services, prices, promotion, and the store's overall reputation creates **store image**. **Atmospherics** refers to the physical elements of a store's design that can be adjusted to appeal to consumers' emotions and thus induce them to buy. **Scrambled merchandising** adds unrelated product lines to an existing product mix and is being used by a growing number of stores to generate sales.
- The retail business undergoes a cycle wherein new retail institutions start as low-status, low-margin, and low-price operations. As they develop, they increase service and prices and eventually become vulnerable to newer institutions, which enter the market and repeat the cycle. This is better known as **wheel-of-retailing hypothesis.**

Large Format Rural Retail Stores: *Mera Gaon, Mera Desh*

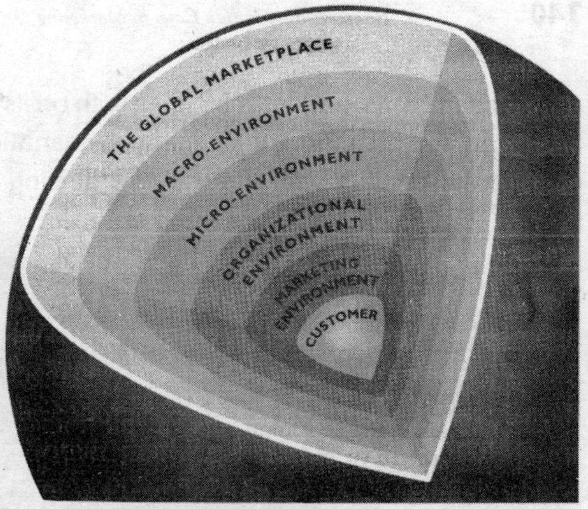

Retailing Case - 32

Purpose of the Case

The idea is to assimilate the relevant concepts at work and analyse in light of the following issues:

- To discuss how an innovation in retailing, Chaupal Sagar, a rural hypermarket can be a typical urban mall selling at cheaper rates as compared to traditional stores elsewhere, and cater to the needs of rural customer
- To review the operation of Chaupal Sagar to glean how this novel concept in rural retailing aims to sustain footfalls from farmers and their families throughout the year

"Retailing is the pivotal part of delivering value to the consumers. Moment of Truth is spelt at the end of every retailing business."

Y.C.Deveshwar, Chairman, ITC Ltd, Kolkata at Retail India 2004 meet organized by CII.

"Ordinary people are buying what the rich can afford,"

Kishore Biyani, CEO-Pantaloon and Food Bazaar in a panel moderated by Harvard Business School professor Ananth Raman as reported by Julia Hanna, Associate editor of the Harvard Business School Bulletin, April 19, 2004.

"The urban-rural divide gap is melting."

Rajesh Jejurikar, Executive V.P.-Marketing at Mahindra & Mahindra

As a country of enormous economic and social contrasts, India offers a complex marketing arena and demands high specificity in the assessment of its market opportunities for various classes of goods. India's complexity goes beyond sheer numbers: its one-billion people inhabit four climatic zones-from the temperate north to the tropical south, from the parched west to the inundated east; speak one or more of at least 15 official languages, follow several religious and personal beliefs, differ enormously in their food habits and social customs, and live *together* under varying states of human development, from the highly affluent to the utterly destitute. Besides internal contrasts, India is culturally different from several other markets including Asian markets for historical and social reasons. Consumer goods marketers find India a very unique market that may defy replication of strategies used successfully in other emerging markets, and must be dealt with on its own terms. In the experience of many transnational companies, dealing with India is like dealing with several small markets, at the same time...

YOUNG INDIA

Compared with several advanced countries, where the overall population is aging, India is a very young nation, with more than 70 per cent of its population below the age of 40, and more than 47 per cent below the age of 20. This age distribution is of significance to various consumer product marketers, and explains the boom in all Indian cities in consumption of impulse products and leisure-related expenditure in general, since the onset of liberalization. The projected increase in the economically active population of young Indians holds the key to India's prosperity and its economic potential over the next twenty years, and is expected to unlock a new wave of consumer demand provided the current trend of economic liberalization continues and generates continued investment and trade opportunities in the economy.

GEOGRAPHICAL DISPERSION OF MARKET POTENTIAL

There is considerable variance in economic prosperity levels among various Indian states, linked to the overall wealth creation from agriculture, trade and industrial development. Accordingly, there are affluent and poor districts in most states, classified according to their market potential. At a national level, India has 500 active districts (excluding Jammu and Kashmir), of which the top 150 districts (Class A) account for 78 per cent, while the next 150 (Class B) account for 15 per cent of the national market potential for a wide category of goods. The remaining 200 districts (Class C), which have 40 per cent of the geographical share, are backward and account for only 7 per cent of India's market potential. The spread of affluent and non-affluent districts is uniform in all the four regions. However, the Eastern, Northeastern and Central regions of India have the largest share of backward districts.

These villages and small towns of India, which were once inconsequential dots on maps, are now getting the attention of global marketing giants and media planners. Thanks to globalization, economic liberalization, IT revolution, Indian diaspora, improving infrastructure, advent of commercial and market–oriented farming, use of modern agricultural technology, manufactured inputs like fertilizers, pesticides, high yielding varieties of seeds, middle class rural India is emerging as a growth engine for Indian economy.

NCAER RURAL SURVEY

According to the NCAER, there are five classes of consumer households, ranging from the destitute to the highly affluent, which differ considerably in their consumption behaviour and ownership patterns across various categories of goods. These classes exist in urban as well as rural households both, and consumption trends may differ significantly between similar income households in urban and rural areas.

India's rural areas also have a high incidence of weekly floating and assembly markets besides seasonal markets linked to special occasions, festivals, and harvest seasons, etc. Given the lower quality of infrastructure (all weather roads, telecommunications density, organised banking and finance and credit systems) in rural markets, cost-effective marketing and distribution of goods in rural areas is a continuing challenge in India. The growth of the rural market is considered very important to the overall growth in all essential and basic consumer goods.

Age distribution of Indian population (Millions)

Year	Kids	Children	Adolescents	Young Adults	Mid Aged	Aged	Total
	0-4 years	5-14 years	15-19 years	20-34 years	35-54 years	55 & above	
1996	119.5	233.2	90.7	224	178.1	88.7	934.2
2001	108.5	239.1	109.0	246.8	207.3	101.7	1012.4
2006	113.5	221.2	122.4	279.1	239.2	118.7	1094.1

REASONS FOR RURAL-URBAN DISPARITY IN RETAILING

The main reasons why rural India is not getting the kind of retailing urban India gets are lack of economic power and connectivity among the rural producers, markets and consumers. Since 72 per cent of India lives in villages and agriculture being the main source of income, and due to various uncertainties rural people save more and invest less thus caught in a vicious circle.

An idea, according to Mr. Y.C.Deveshwar, Chairman, ITC Ltd to overcome this could be:

- Building retail services to increase productivity and income of the rural population and also providing them with risk and insurance claim facilities.
- On reaching surplus productivity, helping individual farmers with the alternate uses of land.
- To cluster number of goods and services, lay infrastructure and make return on it.
- Bringing extension services to the farmers.

INDIA-THE BRIGHTER SIDE OF LIFE

The Indian economy, which registered growth of 8.2 per cent in FY2003 as a result of nearly 15 years of reforms, is now one of the world's fastest growing economies. This high growth is likely to be sustained over the next three years, unless there are major shocks.

The gold rush in retailing seems to be shifting to the villages. More big-ticket companies, including tobacco-to-hospitality major ITC, petroleum marketers BPCL and HPCL, and the DCM Shriram group, are making a beeline to set up elaborate shopping plazas in the villages to tap the purchasing power of the rural folk.

The creation of infrastructure like rural roads, IT initiatives and corporate India's rural focus have started throwing up jobs in non-urban areas and thus got a huge potential for temporary or contract staffing in secondary locations mainly in sectors like FMCG, banking and insurance and telecom. Companies involved in agri-inputs and fertilizers need temporary employees, as the nature of business is very seasonal. There is lots of action in rural areas with NGOs, educational bodies and hard-core Corporates doing their bit to create infrastructure, both tangible and intangible. There are efforts at providing urban infrastructure in rural areas. Projects like IIT-developed SARI, which aim to provide internet access via 1,000 connections in 350 villages in Madurai, go a long way in creating rural IT infrastructure. IT infrastructure in rural areas will bring low-end, data entry kind of outsourcing jobs in the future to the village level.

On the corporate side, Hindustan Lever's Project Shakti has 540 exclusive sales promoters in four states and the self help group-driven model is proposed to be extended to other areas. According to industry sources, other FMCG majors like Dabur and P&G are also upping their ante on rural penetration. ITC plans to cover one lakh villages through its e-choupal network by 2010. ITC e-choupal, an online initiative, gives information of crops to farmers,and is present in over 4,000 village clusters as on Oct, 2004 (*J.Padampriya, http://economictimes.indiatimes.com of 8th Oct 2004)*

RURAL RETAILING VENTURES IN INDIA

- ITC has already taken the lead by soft-launching its first rural hypermarket 'Choupal Sagar,' at Sehore in Madhya Pradesh.
- DCM Shriram Consolidated Ltd (DSCL) is planning to tap the opportunity, with plans to open up 30 stores in rural areas of north India over the next two years.
- Not to be left behind, the local sugar cooperatives in rural Maharashtra have opened comparatively smaller supermarkets on their own. These markets stock goods at cheaper prices than those available in the local kirana shops.
- HPCL's venture, called 'Apna Pump', consists of de-scaled petrol pumps situated away from the highways and run by rural entrepreneurs.
- Petroleum major BPCL has also kicked off its rural retail foray with its "Hariyali Kissan Bazaar" store at Shahjehanpur in Uttar Pradesh. BPCL plans to extend the Bazaar, which stocks a host of items ranging from pesticides to farm equipment currently, to include large format retail stores stocking grocery and other everyday items. (*Source: Anil Sasi ,www.thehindubusinessline.com, New Delhi , Sept. 24, 2004)*

CHAUPAL SAGAR- ITC'S RURAL RETAILING INITIATIVE

Shopping malls are unlikely to remain a purely urban phenomenon for long. ITC soft-launched its first rural hypermarket called Chaupal Sagar, spread on 8 acres of land with a shopping area of 7,000 square feet at Rafiqganj village of Sehore in Madhya Pradesh in late rainy season of 2004 recording an initial response of about 700-800 footfalls on weekdays and soaring to 1,000 on weekends with conversion levels of 35 per cent. ITC now plans to open about 50 such stores, spread across rural Madhya Pradesh and Uttar Pradesh by end 2005 investing in the range of Rs 2-4 crore for each such store; ultimately taking the figure to 1000 malls based on successful results and acquired experience.

Let us attempt a simple concept explanation of Chaupal Sagar's business model:

- ITC has derived this concept from the traditional *haat* system only difference being the permanent nature of Chaupal Sagar.
- Assumption: Farmers who will come to ITC godowns to sell their produce and with cash in hand would visit the mall nearby.
- By setting up the mall next to the warehouse, it is possible to monetize the footfalls from farmers. The mall will store things of daily needs from soaps/oil/grocery/clothes/pumps/agri-inputs etc and appear like a urban Delhi mall but without the razzmatazz and will sell at cheaper rates compared to traditional stores elsewhere.

CHAUPAL SAGAR: 'SECOND LAYER' OF ITC'S E-CHOUPAL AGRI-BUSINESS MODEL

- ITC management calls the initiative as 'second layer' of its agri-business model viz. e-Choupal.
- While the first layer provided the farmers necessary information about weather and prices, the hypermarket initiative is aimed at providing them another platform to sell their

produce and purchase necessary farm and household goods under the same roof.

- Chaupal Sagar is the logical culmination of the e-Choupal scheme launched by ITC. Prosperity in Bhopal region has been rising for the past ten years - ever since farmers began switching to soya bean cultivation. Thanks to the information revolution catalysed by the choupals, farmers are beginning to hold their stocks, knowing that there is an advantage in selling later. It helps that most of them grow soya, which is very inexpensive to store. In that sense, what ITC is doing with this warehouse is similar to what it did with its kiosks. In the first phase, having wired up the hinterland, it began using the network to enable a two-way flow of products and services to the rural economy. Working through the sanchalaks, ITC first pushed its own products, like salt, into the hinterland, and then invited others like Parachute and Philips to ride on this distribution chain.

CATCHING THE FARMER WHEN HE HAS THE MONEY AND THE MOOD

- What had started four years ago as an experiment to use IT tools to enable farmers find the best price for their produce has now metamorphosed into this shopping idea.
- The scenario ITC foresees is something like this: Post-harvest, the farmer, with his family, drives into Chaupal Sagar in a tractor trolley laden with the grain he proposes to sell. He parks the tractor on the digital weighing bridge close to the entry point. His grain weighed, he drives on to the godown where the produce is unloaded and he gets his money.
- Meanwhile, his kids can enjoy the swings and video games and his wife may be going around the shopping mall mentally drawing up a shopping list.
- Cash in hand, the farmer family can then make its purchases and drive back by evening, with the tractor laden with the goodies. If they like, they can have a bite in the cafeteria. And the farmer may even carry fertilizers and pesticides for the next crop and get his tractor fuelled at the diesel pump.
- ITC realised the importance of capitalizing on the farmers' good mood, who having got money would spend it anyway and who also have an empty vehicle with which they can lug the stuff back.

FEATURES AND FACILITIES AT ITC MALLS

Creating a one-stop destination for farmers, the very sharply thought-out ITC rural store has opted for self service, stocking its merchandise on shelves lining the neat aisles. It stocks and sells everything that a rural consumer may ask for-sarees to kurta-pyjamas to shirts (in the range of Rs 99-500), footwear, cigarettes, soaps, biscuits, namkeens, watches, detergent, toothpaste, oil, spices, other groceries, electronic durable from fans, TVs, microwaves, refrigerators, washing machines, DVD players, pressure cookers, room heaters, watches, sewing machines, grinders, educational supplies, plastic household items, cosmetics and other accessories, farm consumption products like seeds, fertilizers, other agri-inputs, pumps, generators and even tractors, motorcycles and scooters. ITC has launched its own rural range of clothing and shoes too—trousers at Rs 166 a pair tailored for the village folk. According to ITC, fast moving consumer goods and white goods manufacturers are keen to tap the fast prospering rural markets.

Other proposed facilities include:

- A fuel pump for which ITC has tied-up with BPCL
- A cafeteria
- A primary healthcare facility to be serviced by a private healthcare service provider. Here, farmers can consult a doctor who will be available on the premises.

- Veterinary doctors and artificial insemination banks
- Display of large agricultural machinery like threshers and implements.
- Banking facilities and Automated teller machines. ITC is in talks with various financial sector entities in this regard.
- Soil-testing laboratory
- Entertainment area with video games and swings
- An insurance company office
- A training centre for farmers on improved, modern farm techniques.
- Restaurants, public facilities and parking space.

ITC will charge a fee for the services and items sold at the mall limiting its role to creation of infrastructure such as space, computers, building, etc. By offering a slew of other goodies and the above mentioned value add-on facilities, the company is also trying to ensure that farmers keep coming to Chaupal Sagar even at times other than harvest thus hoping to capture the rural folks' out-of-village shopping desire.

TRADING OPERATIONS AT CHAUPAL SAGAR

- ITC is planning to set up 40 rural shopping centres in those states where it has a presence through its e-choupals and IT hubs.
- The trading operations will be on the lines of e-choupals.
- E-choupal is an internet knowledge provider to the farmers started by ITC. Each choupal is made up of 5 villages; 25-30 choupals make way for one Choupal Sagar. The first Choupal Sagar was set up in Madhya Pradesh. The sanchalak of the Choupal Sagar provides services, knowledge to the farmers and sells his produce on behalf of them. This further induces in converting village population into economic organization. Thus, it provides disintegrated, customized and appropriate information to the farmers enabling them to increase productivity leading to increased income and spending capacity. E-choupal also aims at giving the farmers a larger share of consumer spend by giving them multiple choices both on the market and supply side.
- The supermarkets are coming up at ITC's 'hubs', where farmers can come to sell their produce. The hubs are a part of ITC's e-choupal project, wherein farmers can come and log on to the Internet and check the pricing and sell their commodities. During the peak season, a hub sees traffic of about 200 tractors per day on an average, as farmers come to sell their crops at the hubs.
- Samyojaks, who are basically traders, will operate the shopping malls and ITC will place all household items, commodities there and will create facility for providing online information on commodity rates and weather.
- ITC is offering a very compelling proposition to the companies whose brands it sells, most of whom are national players like Marico, LG, Philips, Eveready, ITC's apparels, TVS bikes and Eicher tractors.
- To solve age-old problem of reach and setting up viable distribution channels in rural India, Eicher Tractors evolved a rental model and gave about 50 tractors to the sanchalaks, who in turn leased them out to farmers, thus generating awareness; Now, lots of companies like Philips, TVS and Eicher plan to use the mall to showcase their entire range. On its part, ITC is accepting stocks on a consignment basis.
- To attract footfalls during the lean season, ITC plans to organise various activities and events including melas. Also, the hubs are strategically located to attract suburban crowds as well.

ITC: SOLVING ONE OF THE BIGGEST BUGBEARS FACING INDIAN RURAL MARKETERS

Companies like Philips Lighting, riding on its own distribution network, have reached all Indian villages with a population of 20,000, but could not go any deeper. Trouble is that if a marketer has to go deeper into the country, beyond the 20,000-population villages, he would have to hire a van that would blow a hole in his economics, a conundrum that all rural marketers are familiar with.

Philips can now tie-up with ITC, which is anyway looking for other companies to ride on its chain. Today, Philips dealers in the 20,000-population villages' supply to ITC, which in turn sends a van to all its sanchalaks once every 15 days, dropping off their orders. This has enabled Philips to cover 50-60 per cent in these areas, which was only 20 per cent two years ago. On their part, the sanchalaks either sell the goods directly, or, more often, sell them to the village's shopkeepers.

Philips only distributes its 60W and 100W bulbs through the sanchalaks; it is hard to get the more costly products like energy-saving bulbs, placed in the village shops as they are too costly and block up too much of the village kiranas' working capital. However, Philips plans to use the mall to showcase its entire range. At the same time, the basic products will continue to go to the village as bulbs are bought only when the previous one fails, and thus, need to be sold through the village.

CONSUMER'S REACTION: AN ENIGMA TO DECODE

The rural malls will throw up a lot of valuable, real-life data about the rural consumer, thus allowing the rural customer to test a lot of assumptions and myths, like:

- How hard is it, to change villagers' buying habits? For the first six months Choupal Sagar began offering tractors on rent, there was no offtake. Slowly, some people used them, word of mouth got generated, and rentals picked up gradually.
- It is important to gauge the rural consumer's buying patterns. Is it true what people say about the rural consumer i.e. the men do all the shopping and that the women aren't allowed to go out? How does one then explain groups of village women who descend on the store and spread out across the shop examining the soaps, hair oil, face creams, tooth powder, cooking utensils, refrigerators, plastic-ware and so on.
- The proof of success of these farmer-run centres of ITC will be in the volume of sales. In the metros many malls are doing slack business with more window-shoppers than buyers. It will be interesting to study whether the rural populace be any different?

It is important that marketers don't try to copy any Western model blindly rather adopt a flexible model that captures the value chain and allows the organization to evolve with the customer. It's possible to adapt successful U.S. strategies but India would need a sustainable competitive advantage to survive.

Questions

1. Discuss how can the concept of ITC's Chaupal Sagar be replicated in other parts of India. What are the key success factors?
2. What are the distinguishing characteristics of organized rural retailing in India as brought to light by Chaupal Sagar?
3. Chaupal Sagar represents just a tip of the iceberg for rural marketing in India. Comment.
4. What could be the issues in having the right manpower in running a rural mall?

Notes